THE HERZL YEAR BOOK

Essays in American Zionism
1917-1948

edited by
Melvin I. Urofsky

THE HERZL YEAR BOOK
Volume 8

HERZL PRESS • NEW YORK • 1978

Contents

Introduction

When American Zionists learned of the Balfour Declaration in late 1917, they received the news first with dazed incredulity, and then with open joyousness. Herzl's great dream of an international charter leading to the reestablishment of a Jewish homeland in Palestine seemed on the verge of fulfillment. Moreover, a partnership between the Crown, European Zionists led by Chaim Weizmann, and American Zionists led by Justice Louis D. Brandeis, gave every indication of coming into being and providing the moral, political and financial support necessary to rebuilding Eretz Yisrael.

Unfortunately, it would be more than three decades before an autonomous Jewish state would be created in Palestine. In those years, the British Government consistently reneged on Lord Balfour's promise; the Americans, pursuing their vision of the Zionist dream, split with their European colleagues, and the schism nearly crippled the movement; the American government, which through President Wilson had welcomed a Jewish return to Palestine, became more and more pre-occupied with geopolitical considerations and the appeasement of British and Arab interests; and, most tragic of all, a madman came to power in Germany, and butchered six out of every seven European Jews.

Yet for all these problems, American Zionism pressed forward in the development of a unique synthesis between the ideals of Zionism and American progressive reform. This synthesis, originally developed by Louis Brandeis and Horace Kallen, allowed the American Jew to work for the redemption of Zion within the framework of a particularly American set of premises. The old bugaboo of "dual loyalty," for all practical purposes, died in the interwar years, its moribund corpus occasionally twitching in the hands of extremist — and repudiated — groups such as the American Council for Judaism.

In fact, the story of American Zionism between Balfour and the States takes a number of parallel tracks. One of which is the growing harmony between the Zionists and the so-called "non-Zionists," those who accepted the spiritual and cultural goals of the movement, but who for many years felt uncomfortable with the idea of a Jewish political state. The Holocaust confirmed in their minds the validity of the Zionists' claim that only an independent Jewish homeland could be counted upon to protect and take in persecuted Jews. Another theme is the growing sophistication of American Zionists in recognizing and dealing with their opponents in the government, especially the careerists in the United States Department of State, men who by background and training were unsympathetic or outrightly hostile to the dream of Jewish redemption. A third part of the story is the internecine strife that seemingly plagued American Zionism, but which was inevitable in any movement comprising so diverse a group of constituents. Except for the Brandeis-Weizmann battle in 1921, the resolution of these family quarrels in the end strengthened the movement.

The historical study of American Zionism was for too many years a neglected field, too often relegated to footnotes by scholars trained in Europe or Israel, and influenced by the ideological premises of those areas. In the last decade, however, we have witnessed an enormous growth in interest in American Zionism, and the publication of several scholarly works dealing with the movement as a whole or with related aspects. The essays in this current volume of the *Herzl Year Book* reflect the diversity of this new historical growth. Our contributors range from established scholars in the field to graduate students first venturing into the, at times, murky and dangerous waters of Zionist historiography. These essays do not cover all the aspects of American Zionism in this period, but they give some indication of the wide range of Zionist-related topics now being explored.

*   *   *

With this volume, the *Herzl Year Book* resumes publication after a hiatus of several years. I am grateful to Kalman Sultanik, Marie Syrkin and Sam Bloch who agreed that the *Year Book* was too valuable an instrument to lie dormant. In future years other volumes will hopefully emerge, dealing with specialized areas of Zionist history, and the *Year Book* will again fulfill its unique function of being an indispensable resource for all those, laymen and scholars alike, who wish to explore the many facets of Zionist history.

— Melvin I. Urofsky

Ideology and Practice in American Zionism: An Overview

by Howard L. Adelson

By 1914 American Jewry has been estimated to have numbered three million, but it was sadly divided over the question of redemption in Palestine. In addition to the German Jewish opponents of Zionism who espoused the supposedly universalist ideals of Reform Jewry, there were the extreme Orthodox groups who felt that Zionism was a clear case of human intervention in divine matters. They in turn were joined in opposition to Zionism by the orthodox socialists who were committed to the Bundist idea that nationalism detracted from the Jewish involvement in the class struggle. Among the supporters of the new ideas of Herzl were the secular Zionists who adhered to the Zionist program because they felt that it was the only solution to the Jewish dilemma of survival in a hostile environment. They were joined by growing numbers of religious Jews of various degrees of observance. The Orthodox of the Mizrachi were committed Zionists who recognized love of Zion as a divine injuction. There were also Jews of the growing Conservative movement centered at the Jewish Theological Seminary, where Solomon Schechter, the Seminary president, and many of his colleagues were committed Zionists. Finally there was the socialist wing of the Poale Zion who expected to create a socialist utopia in Zion. Under the circumstances it is somewhat surprising that the number of registered Zionists in the United States was still a very tiny fragment of American Jewry. Most of the Eastern European immigrants were undoubtedly sympathetic toward Zionism, but there was a vast gap between sympathy and identification. American Zionism, morever, was sadly governed before the First World War. It could not produce the funds necessary for its own work, let alone the task of sending money to Europe for the World Zionist Organization, and

1

lacked a centralized authority which could wield influence in a meaningful way. Herzl had even gone to the extreme of sending his own
personal representative to this country in 1900. The arrival of that
emissary, Jacob deHaas, however, had had very little effect for the
moment except to infuriate several American Zionist leaders.

The true change in American Zionism came with the First World
War and the appearance of Louis D. Brandeis on the Zionist stage.
Jacob deHaas for a number of years had been slowly nurturing the
distinguished Boston attorney's interest. When the outbreak of the
First World War cut off the settlements in the Holy Land from the
normal supplies of money from the European belligerent countries and
brought about a rupture in the contacts between various Zionist leaders, it became necessary for American Zionists to step into the breach
with both money and leadership. At a meeting in August 1914, Brandeis was elected to the chairmanship of the group that would be known
as the Provisional Executive Committee for General Zionist Affairs.

Brandeis performed two absolutely necessary functions for American Zionism. By his mere presence within the movement and his ability
to identify Zionism with the American dream, as well as his bringing
order and efficiency to Zionist ranks, Brandeis changed the history of
American Zionism. Perhaps the most important part of his work lay in
formulating the position that Zionism was a form of Americanism, a
fulfillment of American ideals. He proclaimed that "To be good Americans, we must be better Jews, we must become Zionists." That simple
credo was sufficient to answer much of the carping criticism that came
from the Reform movement. Zionism, for Brandeis, was Americanism
in action, and together with Felix Frankfurter, Horace Kallen, Judge
Julian Mack and others, he instilled a new vigor into American
Zionism. Brandeis' appointment to the Supreme Court in 1916, the
first such appointment of a Jew, seemed to confirm his views about the
identification of Zionism with Americanism, that the establishment of a
Jewish state in the Holy Land with complete democracy and social
justice would be a fulfillment of Americanism.

We must compare the adherence of Brandeis to Zionism with the
position taken by Jews of similar background such as Judge Joseph
Proskauer. Judge Proskauer for most of his public career castigated and
attacked Zionism because it suggested that Jewry was a nation and not a
religious brotherhood. As president of the American Jewish Committee he was perhaps the foremost opponent of American Zionism until

the overwhelming evidence of the Holocaust showed him exactly how tenuous Jewish existence really was, and even then he attempted to exclude American Jewry from the essence of Zionist activity, forming a state and supporting immigration to the Holy Land. Proskauer, in contrast to Brandeis, could never bridge the gap which existed in his own mind when confronted with the needs of Jewry as a people or a nation. Brandeis spanned it easily, and he gave the answer to large number of Jews and non-Jews. He made Zionism a part of the Americanization of numbers of recent immigrants.

Brandeis was, in addition, a magnificent organizer. Under him men like Rabbi Stephen S. Wise were brought back into the Zionist movement. He gathered around him distinguished members of the Jewish community such as Julian Mack. A fact often ignored is the activity of Felix Frankfurter, a Brandeis disciple, on behalf of Zionism during the crucial years of Brandeis' leadership. Jacob deHaas, who had brought Brandeis to Zionism, became Brandeis' instrument for building the Zionist movement, serving as executive secretary and doing much of the actual work.

For the future develpment of Zionism in the United States, however, the most important step in the years just before the First World War was taken when Henrietta Szold founded Hadassah in 1912. She had long been interested in Zionism and had been a member of the Federation of American Zionists. A visit to the Holy Land in 1909, however, stimulated her to work in the field of health services. By 1913 Hadassah under her inspiration had dispatched its first two nurses to Jerusalem, and the marvelous work to be carried out by Hadassah had begun. It was practical work which could be seen and understood by all, and it has continued to the present day.

Under Brandeis' leadership American Zionist ranks swelled. An effective recruiting campaign was instituted and money raised for the improverished struggling colonies, more money than ever before, and it was done in the shortest possible time without resorting to the wealthiest class of American Jews. At the same time the Zionist movement under Brandeis began a relief campaign for Europe which allowed Jews and non-Jews to transmit money to their struggling relatives abroad. This was done in such a businesslike fashion that the Zionist movement achieved great popularity with all classes of American society and even served as a conduit for the American government in such relief work.

It was the struggle to democratize American Jewish life, however, which endeared Brandeis to the masses of Jewry in this country. The American Jewish Committee, a highly undemocratic organization controlled by the wealthy elements of German-American Jewry, held the dominant position in dealing with officials about Jewish matters. Shortly before the outbreak of the First World War, however, it became apparent even to the leaders of the American Jewish Committee that it could not claim to represent the masses of American Jewry. It therefore suggested a system for enlarging its members by drawing in other Jewish organizations, but it intended to keep strict control of all power. Such a proposal for control of the majority by a minority ran directly counter to all that Brandeis and the Zionists believed. In addition, since the American Jewish Committee included many of the leading anti-Zionists and non-Zionists in the country, it constituted a threat to Zionism itself. Louis Marshall was certainly the most tolerant of the leaders of the American Jewish Committee in terms of willingness to understand the Jewish masses and their sense of Jewish national identification. Most of the leaders of the American Jewish Committee, however, conceived of their role as that of providing a reputable leadership for the voiceless Jewish masses in order to protect the interests of Jewish toleration and Americanization as *they* understood it. They hoped to do this without calling undue attention to the presence of masses of Jewry in the country and without stimulating a sense of Jewish identity. Under the circumstances they were bound to oppose the formation of an umbrella American Jewish Congress in which the voice of the majority would be predominant. When faced with the reality that they could not really speak for the masses, however, they chose to work out some sort of conference which would be under their control and would allow them to make the claim that they spoke for American Jewry. Brandeis, however, demanded real democracy in Jewish life. The struggle actually lasted through 1916; it was carried on with unrestrained bitterness and resulted in Brandeis resigning from most of the posts that he held within the Jewish community. Nevertheless the cause of democracy in Jewish life was vindicated, and by the end of December 1916, as a result of a compromise worked out by Justice Brandeis, even the American Jewish Committee participated in the first stages of the work to found a truly representative American Jewish Congress. But American entry into the war brought all of this work to naught for the moment, and the

Congress itself never became the effective voice of American Jewry that its founders had envisioned.

The disruption of Zionist activity in Europe was already three years old when America entered the war on the side of the Allies. During that period most American Zionists tried to be truly neutral in deed, if not always in thought. The vast majority of those who had come from the Russian Empire eagerly desired a German victory over Russia because of the suffering of Russian Jewry. Three events, however, brought about a sharp change in the views of American Jewry. The Russian Revolution of February 1917, American entry into the war in April 1917, and the Balfour Declaration of November 2, 1917 brought most American Jews into the Allied camp. American Zionists, particularly Brandeis, Frankfurter and Wise, were of great help in getting Wilson to endorse the Balfour Declaration to the British even though they had to be very cautious in dealing with the matter.

American Jewry, for the most part, greeted the issuance of the Balfour Declaration with tumultuous expressions of joy though many in the Reformed Jewish community continued to regard it as catastrophe. Nevertheless even in the ranks of the older German-American Jews the Balfour Declaration was not attacked too violently. Rather it was interpreted as meaning little more than an endorsement for a "center" for the Jewish religion in the Holy Land. Within the State Department opposition to Zionism was evident even before the Balfour Declaration and continued unabated.

By the end of the war, the strongest Jewish community in the world existed in the United States. The fact that it was not totally united even among those who were declared Zionists (the Mizrachi and the socialist Poale Zion were not aligned with the Provisional Committee) did not conceal the fact that American Jewry would now be the primary source of financial support for world Zionism. Indeed the fact that the world Zionist leadership under Chaim Weizmann contined to regard American Jewry primarily as a financial resource which would be ignored in determining policy was a source of great difficulty and friction. This was true despite the fact that almost 200,000 Jews were declared Zionists in America at the end of the war. Even men like Jacob Schiff and Louis Marshall, who were non-Zionists, cooperated in Zionist work. Louis Marshall, in fact, headed the American Jewish Congress delegation to the Paris Peace Conference where he fully supported the Balfour Declaration as he understood it and fought for the protection of

Jewish national rights in the Diaspora. The American Jewish delegation played a crucial role in maintaining the support of the official
government delegation from the United States for Zionism.

American Zionism at the end of the war seemed secure. It had never
been as strong as at that moment, but it was in fact a loosely constructed
organization with poorly defined purposes. Although Brandeis had a
characteristically American position favoring efficiency and clearly
defined goals, American Zionism, however, was not efficient, and
many of its grass root supporters objected to the emphasis on practical
organization rather than on the ideological foundations of Zionism in
Jewish thought. In 1918, at the Pittsburgh Convention of the Zionist
Organization of America, a total reorganization of Zionism in this
country was urged. Local leaders, however, feared the concentration
of power at the national level, while the national leadership felt the
need for greater discipline. The 1918 Pittsburgh Convention endorsed
greater centralization, and Brandeis produced a platform which reflected his liberal ideas favoring freedom for the individual, social
justice, and cooperative enterprise for the aims of Zionism which
would lead to practical Zionist endeavour rather than ideological bic-
kering. European Zionism, with its earthy, nationalistic, ideological
fervor failed to awaken a response in the American leadership, and
Chaim Weizmann, who was the soul of European Zionism, was soon in
conflict with Brandeis, Julian Mack, Jacob deHaas, and Stephen S.
Wise, the leaders of the American movement.

The Americans were shocked at the administrative chaos of the
World Zionist Organization and at a plan suggested by Weizmann for
placing all power in the hands of the executive establishment, a plan
they believed to be both undemocratic and inefficient. American
Zionists argued that only an efficient organization could conquer the
physical difficulties such as malarial swamps in the Holy Land to make
large scale immigration feasible. The European Zionists tended to
minimize the physical difficulties in favor of such matters as the rein-
troduction of Hebrew as the national language. In addition the European Zionists wanted to work in the Diaspora communities to awaken
the Jewish national sentiment by the spread of Hebrew as a spoken
language and Jewish culture. Brandeis and most Americans dreaded
such activity outside of the Holy Land, and regarded it as particularly
dangerous in the United States because of the attitude of the non-
Zionists. They wanted to have the non-Zionists assist in the practical

work of preparing the Holy Land for mass Jewish immigration. As a result of this difference of opinion the American diverted whatever funds they raised into specific practical projects such as Hadassah medical work.

In 1920, a *Jahreskonferenz* was summoned by the World Zionist Organization to deal with these differences. It came at a particularly bad time for the American Zionists, for the membership had dropped to one-seventh of what it had been in the summer of 1919 as a result of a variety of factors. Brandeis was the only American with sufficient stature to offer a challenge to Weizmann, but that would have involved resigning from the Supreme Court, and that Brandeis refused to do. Various plans for reform were submitted by the Americans and the Europeans, but the net result of the *Jahreskonferenz* was to widen the breach between them. Brandeis refused to accept the personal responsibility for leading world Zionism, and asked that other Americans follow his example. Weizmann was equally unprepared to yield such responsibility; he considered stimulating Jewish nationalism in the Diaspora as the essence of Jewishness, and regarded Brandeis as lacking precisely this sense of Jewishness. The *Jahreskonferenz* highlighted the American commitment to practical Zionism; the Europeans wanted to continue the ideological and political struggle in the Diaspora, while the Americans felt that the Balfour Declaration had solved the political issue, and what remained was practical work in building up Palestine.

Brandeis had failed to capture the World Zionist Organization for his views because he would not accept the position of leader of Zionism. Men like Louis Lipsky, who had been deeply involved in American Zionism from the first decade of the century, and Emanuel Neumann, a young leader of enormous promise, as well as many others, now turned against Brandeis. The Yiddish press, which had often received rather high-handed treatment by the followers of Brandeis, now came out in open opposition. Weizmann thus succeeded in cutting the ground from under Brandeis and his loyal supporters even in the United States, and now moved to the attack. At the Cleveland Convention of the Zionist Organization of America in 1921 the final break came, resulting in a victory for Weizmann and his followers in the United States, notably Louis Lipsky. But the most distinguished leaders of American Zionism, including men like Brandeis, Rabbi Stephen S. Wise, Harry Friedenwald, Nathan Strauss, Jacob deHaas, Felix

Frankfurter, Judge Julian Mack, Robert Szold, Abba Hillel Silver, and
Benjamin Cohen, all resigned from their posts.

   Louis Lipsky thus became President of the Zionist Organization
of American in troubled times. Antisemitism was on the rise in
Europe and America. In Palestine the first Arab riots took place, and
the British showed a pro-Arab bias in dealing with the problem. Zionist
membership continued to decline, and within a year the Zionist Organization of America was heavily in debt. Even the struggle with the
European Zionist leadership was not eased by the change that had
taken place in America. In addition to all of these difficulties the
ineffectiveness of Zionist leadership in dealing with the American
government was easily visible. Rebuffed by the State Department,
they turned to Congress and barely succeeded in getting a joint resolution passed in support of a Jewish homeland in Palestine. In like
manner their attempts to raise money were extremely disappointing.
Keren Hayesod failed in America to realize the sums that were needed.
Weizmann had to turn to the wealthy non-Zionist Jews just as Brandeis
had proposed, and he was forced to make compromises to get their
support. To do this he proposed enlarging the Jewish Agency, which
had been recognized in the mandate as the representative of Jewry, to
include non-Zionists, and Louis Marshall was prevailed upon to take
the lead in gaining the assistance of the non-Zionists. To get that
support, Weizmann led the non-Zionists to believe that statehood was
not the goal of Zionism while he told the Zionists that he was avoiding
ideological confrontation. Weizmann, moreover, now suggested giving the non-Zionists a much greater voice in deciding policy than
Brandeis had ever proposed, because he recognized that their wealth
and social position could contribute greatly to the work of practical
Zionism which he now espoused. Unfortunately Weizmann's plan was
not well timed. It coincided with the famines in Russia that threatened
the lives of millions of Jews, and came into conflict with the non-Zionist
Joint Distribution Committee which sponsored the creation of Jewish
agricultural settlements in the Crimea. Even attempts at joint fund-
raising for both Keren Hayesod and the Joint Distribution Committee
collapsed with the result that the United Palestine Appeal was founded
in 1925 to funnel money into the Holy Land.

   In 1929, after five years of hard work, a pact between the Zionists
and the non-Zionists was ratified. Of the 220 members of the enlarged

Agency half were to be non-Zionists, and the influence of American Zionism would thus be markedly reduced. All of the Zionist parties with the exception of the Revisionists accepted the new enlarged Agency as a necessity to get on with the work of building the *Yishuv*. The Revisionists remained firmly committed to sole Zionist control and ideological purity no matter what the cost. Their fears were somewhat unfounded because control of the enlarged Jewish Agency effectively remained in Zionist hands, and the Great Depression had the effect of reducing the funds available no matter what form the Jewish Agency took. Brandeis' earlier proposals, without their safeguards, were now the official Zionist policy.

Peace for the Zionists was not possible even though both sides were now fully committed to practical economic work. Louis Lipsky's attempt to marshal Hadassah in the ranks of the Keren Hayesod to give the appearance of improved collections would have deprived Hadassah of the guarantee that all Hadassah funds would go for medical work, and brought about a schism between Lipsky and the women. By the time of the Great Depression, Hadassah was substantially larger than the ZOA, and the women's group demanded efficiency and devotion to practical work in a measure that the faltering Lipsky group could not give. Brandeis and his ousted followers, of course, provided a magnet around which the opposition could coalesce. Even those leaders such as Emanuel Neumann, who had been ardent supporters of Lipsky as Weizmann's voice in America, were by 1927 totally disillusioned. The emphasis on work in Palestine marked the complete acceptance of Brandeis' vision of Zionism in America. Even the ideological framework produced by Mordecai Kaplan for his followers in the Conservative Movement involved merely a Palestine-centered spiritual Zionism broad enough to encompass virtually all Americans other than those committed to a strong anti-Zionist position. Still Zionism did not flourish under Lipsky despite such broad definitions. With enormous help from Weizmann, who dreaded a return of Brandeis to control of American Zionism, Lipsky weathered the storm in 1928 to remain in control. Perhaps Lipsky became overconfident as a result of his momentary success. His attempt to influence the Hadassah elections in 1928 failed completely and actually yielded greater independence for Hadassah from the Zionist Organization of America.

The Arab riots of 1929 and the subsequent British White Paper in

1930, combined with the ineffective administration of Chaim Weizmann on the world Zionist stage as well as Lipsky's inability to wield
the American Zionists as an effective force on the local scene, led to an
alliance of the non-Zionist fund-raisers and the Brandeis-Mack group
within the American Zionist movement. According to the terms of the
compromise worked out in 1930, a new eighteen-man Administrative
Committee was created to govern American Zionism, twelve of whose
members were nominated by the Brandeis group and six by the Lipsky
faction. Lipsky was only able to retain some influence because Brandeis was constrained by his position as Associate Justice from assuming
an offical role. Robert Szold, a Brandeis adherent, served as chairman
of the committee, and Abba Hillel Silver, another believer in the
Brandeis philosophy, was vice-chairman.

The growth of Nazism in Germany in the aftermath of the Great
Depression created a threat to Jewish existence which was recognized
if only in feelings of abhorrence at this early stage. The apathy of the
democratic powers in the face of this challenge to modern western
civilization, if not expressed as actual hostility toward Zionism, as in
the case of Great Britain which proposed to stem the tide of Jewish
immigration to the Holy Land at precisely the time of greatest need,
was seen as a distinct threat. Jewish interests were being sacrificed on
all fronts, antisemitism was on the rise throughout the world, and the
Great Depression severely limited the fund-raising capacity of Jewry.
Membership in both the ZOA and Hadassah fell disastrously as masses
of American Jewry were impoverished.

Lipsky, who still had a semblance of some power within the American movement even after the reorganization of 1930, felt that he alone
could carry the banner of ideological Zionism in the threatening circumstances. He promptly seized upon the lack of success of the Administrative Committee in its efforts to revive the Zionist Organization of
America and moved to the attack while Weizmann was still in office.
This rear guard action by Lipsky, however, coincided with a massive
Zionist attack on the new British policy, the Passfield White Paper,
which would have spelled ruin for Zionist visions. A mass meeting of
protest was held in Madison Square Garden in New York, but it is now
clear that a great deal of quiet diplomacy by Brandeis working through
Harold J. Laski finally yielded success and resulted in a reinterpreta-
tion of the White Paper that excised its most anti-Zionist provisions.
Nevertheless the Passfield White Paper revealed British policy in its

true colors and showed Weizmann to be unable to lead the fight against the mandatory power. Weizmann had lost his faith in the creation of a Jewish state in the face of British opposition. His presentation to the non-Zionists when trying to form the expanded Jewish Agency now became his real policy.

Under the circumstances Emanuel Neumann, who had been a strong Weizmann supporter, and Stephen S. Wise, who had been in the Brandeis-Mack group, led the Americans into the anti-Weizmann camp, and in 1931 Weizmann was forced to step down from the presidency of the World Zionist Organization. Lipsky, who was so closely identified with Weizmann, was unable to do anything to support him or to weaken the hold of the Brandeis group on the Zionist Organization. The election of Morris Rothenberg to the Presidency of the organization in 1931 to replace the Administrative Committee did not mean a revival of Lipsky's power even though the new president had been identified with the Weizmann supporters. The governing council of the organization was still firmly controlled by the Brandeis faction. By this point, however, the older struggle of ideology versus practical Zionism was at an end. American Zionism was firmly committed to practical Zionism and to work in Palestine to create favorable conditions for renewed waves of immigration.

The tragic situation in Germany after the rise of Hitler to power was the primary motive force in Zionist life after 1932. It was apparent from 1935 or 1936 on that the Nazi menace would not collapse of its own weight. The introduction of the Nuremberg Laws and the *Kristallnacht* of 1938 demonstrated that the only hope for German Jewry lay in emigration, and in a world which was closing its doors to Jewish refugees only the Zionist dream offered any hope. After a very slow beginning American Jews began to realize that fact, and the steady growth of Zionist membership initiated in 1935 gained momentum. It was impossible to move the British to open the doors in the name of suffering humanity, but the Youth Aliyah movement to save the German-Jewish children which began shortly after the Nazi rise to power became a primary function of Hadassah after 1935. The success of Youth Aliyah work cannot be exaggerated. It has continued to the present day, and well over 135,000 children have literally been saved by the efforts of Hadassah.

Stephen S. Wise took the leading role in bringing the Nazi menace to public attention in the United States, even though his efforts to warn American Jewry brought him enmity and slander from the American Jewish Committee and its supporters, including the N.Y. *Times*. Wise became the President of the Zionist Organization in 1935, and it was in that role that he helped to forge the chain that bound American Jewry to President Roosevelt and the Democratic party. In the Holy Land the renewed Arab rioting brought another Royal Commission which recommended partition, a plan acceptable to neither Jew nor Arab. The British government, after a short delay brought about by the intervention of President Roosevelt, began to implement a policy which restricted Jewish immigration. In 1935 Weizmann regained the presidency of the World Zionist Organization, and was now prepared to accept partition with a very truncated Jewish state. Zionists were torn between the necessity for saving German Jewry and the fight for a truly viable Jewish homeland. The British appointed still another commission and then decided on a policy of sharply restricted Jewish access to the Holy Land as a means of preserving Arab predominance. Under the circumstances the charade of a conference about German-Jewish refugees was carried out without anyone believing in it. The White Paper of 1939 was the final act of perfidy in British policy. It not only restricted Jewish immigration but even limited the area within which Jews could purchase land in Palestine. Although Zionists had taken the lead in the struggle for German Jewry, they had been frustrated by the machinations of American policy-makers and the determination of the British to appease the Arabs. When the war came in 1939 European Jewry was therefore virtually helpless.

American Jewry was the last source of strength available to the *Yishuv* during the Second World War, and the only body of Jewry outside of the Holy Land which could play a significant role in Jewish destiny. If anything the Second World War accentuated the dominance of American Jewry which had first become evident in 1914. Realization of this fact was widespread in the community, but at the same time there was full knowledge of the risks that American Jewry might incur if it pushed too hard for America to enter the war. Fear of anti-Semitism which could menace the last stronghold of Jewry outside of the Holy Land was never far from the minds of Jewish leaders as they cautiously probed their way in influencing the American people and the American government. Nevertheless, as the war brought the Depression to an end, Jews increasingly joined the Zionist movement and gave ever larger sums for the work of rescue. Even the non-Zionists joined in excoriating the White Paper policy which was dooming European Jewry to excruciating torment and death. In the period from 1940 to 1942 increasing militancy against the White Paper became evident. Under the leadership of Emanuel Neumann, a brilliant tactician with a fine sense for public relations, the Zionists began to reach out to the gentile community and to stimulate sympathy through the agency of the American Palestine Committee. An Emergency Committee for Zionist Affairs was established in 1939, and it became a vehicle for uniting all Zionist groups. Under its auspices in May 1942 at a special meeting at the Biltmore Hotel in New York which has assumed virtually mythical dimensions in Zionist thought, the American Zionist movement committed itself not merely to free Jewish immigration into the Holy Land, but also to the creation of a Jewish commonwealth. The old Zionist demand was now seen as the only solution to the helplessness of Jewry.

The official demands of Zionism were now those which had been advocated by Ze'ev Jabotinsky, the Revisionist leader, but Jabotinsky's followers had moved on to newer ground. The demand for a Jewish state immediately and a Jewish army became the core of a new struggle in the United States led by Peter Bergson (Hillel Kook) on behalf of the Revisionists in Palestine. With little money and a tiny staff, but with the support of Ben Hecht, a popular author, the Revisionists mounted a propaganda campaign for a Jewish army and for effective steps to save the remnant of European Jewry. Since they were applying pressure to Roosevelt, a man with whom Stephen S. Wise felt that he had reached agreement, and since they were drawing resources from Zionist sources and creating schism in the Zionist world, they became the object of a campaign to discredit them. Despite the virulent opposition of the established Jewish leadership in the United States the Revisionists managed to convince a number of American legislators of the righteousness of their cause, and they certainly aided in bringing American public opinion to a recognition of Jewish claims. The efforts of Emanuel Neumann were probably more important in the final analysis in stimulating pro-Zionist attitudes throughout the United States, but the Revisionists provided a more militant position which gave an air of moderation to the accepted Zionist demands.

At the other extreme was Judge Joseph Proskauer and the American Jewish Committee which rejected the Biltmore program completely.

In order to establish a common front to which all American Jews could subscribe, the Zionists prevailed upon Henry Monsky of the B'nai B'rith to call an American Jewish Conference which represented millions of Jews in New York in 1943. The Zionists were in the majority of the 502 delegates, but it was clear that in order to get Judge Proskauer and the American Jewish Committee to participate, there had to be an agreement to remain within minimal bounds which would be acceptable to him, a position that would have meant ignoring the Zionist issue. Abba Hillel Silver, however, broke the agreement, and in an impassioned address swayed the delegates to support statehood as the only viable way of rescuing European Jewry. He carried the day by 496 votes to four opposed. Silver's move had the effect of uniting American Jewry and in turn isolating the most rabid non-Zionists. The American Jewish Conference was probably of greater significance than the Biltmore program itself, for it demonstrated that the vast majority of the American Jewish community now was solidly behind the Zionist position. The American Jewish Committee could never again present itself as the voice of American Jewry.

Abba Hillel Silver's militant stand, however, brought him into conflict with the Washington office of the Jewish Agency headed by Nahum Goldmann and Louis Lipsky, who were minimalist in their approach and feared Silver's outspokenness. In 1944 Silver failed in his attempt to get Congress to pass a resolution not favored by Roosevelt in support of the Zionist position, and resulted in a split with Stephen S. Wise who maintained an implicit trust in Roosevelt. As a result Silver was forced to resign from the leadership and only returned to office a year later. It was only in October 1945 that on the third attempt the bi-partisan resolution of Congress for which Silver had worked was passed, but by that time it had little meaning. Zionist activity, nevertheless, did result in both political parties in the United States supporting the Zionist position in their platforms.

Circumstances now directed events more than men. The true horror of the Holocaust made the Zionist cause invincible. At the end of the war no Jew, not even Judge Proskauer, could fail to realize that a Jewish sovereign state was an absolute necessity. The new American President, Harry S. Truman, was also a much more forthright individual than Roosevelt had been on Jewish matters. Truman supported a demand for the immediate admission of 100,000 Jewish displaced persons into Palestine after the end of the war despite British opposition. Zionist pressure on Truman however, was often so great as to be counter-productive, and only the fact that Foreign Minister Ernest Bevin of Great Britain was more infuriating kept Truman from repudiating the Zionist program. The Jewish Agency leadership and the World Zionist Organization at times lost their nerve, and with Weizmann and Goldmann in the van, occasionally sought retreat from the Biltmore program. Silver and Emanuel Neumann led the Americans in attacks upon the defeatism of Weizmann and Goldmann at the Zionist Congress in 1946, in which America had the largest delegation. Despite an impassioned appeal by Weizmann for practical work instead of a political confrontation with Britain, the Congress supported the more militant position. Conflict with Great Britain was inevitable.

By 1945, the Zionist Organization of America was actually larger than Hadassah, and the number of Zionists in all Zionist groups in the United States was well over the quarter million mark. American Zionists ranks were now growing at an unparalleled rate, and the masses were solidly in the militant camp of Abba Hillel Silver and Emanuel Neumann. By 1947 it was obvious that even the anti-Zionism of the American Jewish Committee under Judge Proskauer was weakening. The refugee problem was so intense that it swept all along in favor of any policy which promised amelioration in the condition of the displaced persons.

Militancy, however, did not always mean the same thing to different people. Emanuel Neumann, vice-president of the ZOA, argued vigorously as a militant against assuming a policy of compromise in the hope of arousing a desire for conciliation on the part of the British and the Arabs. He felt that the Zionist position should be the fulfillment of the Biltmore program. Within Palestine itself the Irgun Zvai Leumi and the Fighters for the Freedom of Israel (the Stern Group) were engaged in open warfare with the British as their form of militancy. There were also those who believed that it was impossible to fight for the Biltmore program and accepted a retreat from that position, a group which included Weizmann, Nahum Goldmann and Stephen S. Wise. At the 1946 World Zionist Congress the forces around Abba Hillel Silver and Emanuel Neumann gained a dominant position, and the Congress proscribed the Revisionist groups in the United States such as the Hebrew Committee for National Liberation and the American League for a Free Palestine which supported the Irgun in the Holy Land. At the same time the Congress refused to send Chaim

Weizmann to a conference which the British had called in London because they wanted their militant position to be clear. Stephen S. Wise severed his official connection with the ZOA because they had taken the lead in rejecting the British invitation.

The British now had no alternative but to turn the problem over to the United Nations where the Jewish case was presented most eloquently by Abba Hillel Silver. By this time there were over 200,000 members of the ZOA and almost 250,000 members of Hadassah, with other Zionist groups showing similar growth. Every Zionist group in America was growing vigorously, and it was quite clear that Abba Hillel Silver was truly speaking for the masses of American Jewry and world Jewry.

Professor Israel Friedlander, an early Zionist, is reported to have said on at least one occasion that the greatest danger to Zionism would be the achievement of Zion. By that he meant that the creation of the Jewish state would deprive the Zionist movement of its principal *raison d'etre*. Ben Gurion shared that view. In 1948 that stage was reached. Israel was reborn, and the functions of the Zionist movement necessarily had to change. American Zionism was left largely with the two areas of concern, propaganda on behalf of Israel and fund-raising through the United Palestine Appeal. Even in this last area, however, Zionists soon lost control to the non-Zionist leaders of the United Jewish Appeal in a move that had the sanction of Israeli Prime Minister David Ben-Gurion. In a report published in May 1949, Judge Simon Rifkind reported that American Zionism had been transformed, almost overnight, from an organization with political importance into an adjunct of Israel, with its tasks limited primarily to creating a bridge between American Jewry and the Israeli government so as to funnel funds into the Jewish state. The rapprochement of the Israeli leaders with the non-Zionists, especially the American Jewish Committee, further weakened the influence of the Zionist movement in this country.

Yet during the three decades between the Balfour Declaration and the establishment of the State of Israel, there is little doubt that American Zionism played a crucial role in the redemption of Zion. At critical moments, the movement in the United States found that important functions were thrust upon it by the play of events, and it found the inner vitality and strength to respond to the challenge. It did so, for the most part, by eschewing rigid and doctrinaire ideological positions, and concentrating upon practical work and pragmatic responses to specific crises. Undoubtedly this lack of ideological commitment contributed to the decline of Zionist influence after 1948, but that may have been the price it had to pay for the practical successes it attained in the thirty years before Israel came into being.

Toward the Pittsburgh Program: Horace M. Kallen, Philosopher of an American Zionism

by Sarah Schmidt

Horace M. Kallen was a philosopher, an educator, a "scientific humanist," an "aesthetic prgamatist" — a man who, until his death in February 1974, was still active, lecturing, writing, and publishing. His career had been long and varied, stretching from the turn of this century when he first attracted the attention of his Harvard professors, who perceived unusual qualities of intelligence and sensitivity in this young Jewish immigrant. Those teachers — William James, George Santayana, Barrett Wendell, Josiah Royce — were also leaders of their time in American philosophy and literary criticism. The influence they had on young Kallen, combined with his own receptivity and perceptive empathy, gave him the start towards an unusually creative lifetime, combining contemplation and action in equal measure.[1]

Since the early years of his career, Kallen had addressed himself towards a wide range of problems of contemporary concern: an interest in minority cultures that can be traced back to 1908, when he first began to think about the "right to be different" that later became "cultural pluralism"; an interest in the environment and in ecological problems of human survival that began during World War I; an interest in man as consumer that derived from experiences with the labor movement during the twenties; and a lifelong interest in education, particularly adult education, that found its outlet in his 55 year association with the New School for Social Research. But there had been another, and special, side to Kallen's life, reflecting his position as a Jew living in America. "I have always regarded you as the foremost creative American Jewish thinker who demonstrates by actual example that it is possible to live with distinction synchronously in two civilizations," wrote Rabbi Mordecai M. Kaplan to Kallen in 1952, on the occasion of Kallen's seventieth birthday.[2] Kaplan's appraisal was correct, for Kallen did succeed in defining and in living his life both as an American and as a Jew from a single philosophical perspective — that of Hebraism, the source, according to Kallen, of both cultures. In so doing, Kallen arrived also at a unique definition of Zionism, one that fit in with his concept of Americanism, and one that, because it accurately reflected the needs of many American Jews in the early twentieth century, became the underlying philosophic basis for the 1914-1921 "Brandeis era" in American Zionism, leading ultimately to the expression of a particularly American orientation to Zionism, the famous Pittsburgh Program of 1918.

The three seminal phrases in Kallen's thinking and writing, phrases that came to him early in his career and that continued to dominate his work were 1) The American Idea, 2) Cultural Pluralism, 3) Hebraism. Because Kallen's understanding and definition of these phrases led to his formulation of the Zionist idea in rather unique terms, and because they undergirded his own committment as a Zionist activist and the success he had in influencing others to join the Zionist movement, it is important to clarify his use of them, and to see how they interacted to form his rationale for Zionism.

The American Idea is a phrase Kallen adopted from crusading transcendentalist minister Theodore Parker, who defined it in 1850 as "the idea that all men have inalienable rights, that . . . all men are created equal, and that government is to be established and sustained, for the purpose of giving every man an opportunity for the enjoyment and development of all these inalienable rights."[3] Kallen saw this American Idea as the national religion, an ideal to which all "*bona fide* Americans as citizens are committed." Gradually, applying the pluralism implicit in the teachings of William James to his experiences with different groups in the settlement house in which he lived and worked while a student at Harvard, and recognizing both his own sense of difference as a Jew and the discrimination experienced by a Negro classmate Alain Locke, Kallen began to emphasize in his own thinking the part of the American Idea which states that "all men are created equal." What did the word *equal* imply? In order to be equal did one have to be the same — or was the right to equality of greater significance if each person was free to express his own unique individuality, i.e., an "equality in difference"? The American Idea, Kallen concluded, "takes for granted that [men] are countless . . . multitudes of human individuals, each somehow different from all others. . . . It postulates that this difference, this singularity of the person, is *the* inalienable right. . . ." Men could be equal only insofar as they could be different; the greatness of the United States resided in the fact that its founders defined our system of government precisely to institute "an organization of liberties" dedicated to granting men the freedom to be different.[4]

As Kallen became more sensitive to the pressures faced by various immigrant communities in the early twentieth century in having to conform by Americanizing into the vast "melting pot" that surrounded them, he came gradually to expand this principle of the freedom to be different from individuals to social groups. Not only each person, but each group — each religion, each ethnic community — is different. "The American people . . . are a mosaic of peoples, of different bloods and different origins . . . varied in background and outlook as well as in blood," he wrote. The United States is not merely a union of "geographical and administrtive unities"; it is, also, a "cooperation of cultural diversities . . . a commonwealth of national cultures," aiming "through Union, not at uniformity, but at variety, at a one out of many." Kallen called this concept "Cultural Pluralism," comparing the United States to a symphony orchestra, where each ethnic group had its own "theme and melody" to contribute to "the symphony of civilization."[5]

A crucial point in Kallen's thesis was the distinction he made between nationality and citizenship. Politically, as citizens, we are all equal; yet the way in which each of us expresses ourselves, a way related to our "*natio*" or "nativity," is different. Kallen traced this concept of a "harmonious cooperation of nationalities" back to the prophets of Israel, "those champions and vindicators of social justice and international righteousness and peace . . . [whose] spirit . . . literally inspired the democracy of our America." These prophets enunciated what Kallen called the Hebraic spirit, a "living spirit which demands righteousness, expressed in all the different interests in which Jews, as Jews, have a share — in art, science, philosophy and social organization, and in religion." Kallen used the term *Hebraism* to refer to "all that has happened in Jewish history, both religious and secular"; Judaism stands for only one special aspect of Hebraism, that "which comprises the sentiment, theories, doctrines and practices which relate to God."[6]

The concept of Hebraism allowed Kallen to retain an identity with the community of Jews that fit in with his secular, humanist and scientific American education. At the same time he could reject the religious tradition for which his father, an Orthodox rabbi, stood, but which Kallen perceived as supernatural, i.e. not grounded in modern science. Most crucial, however, was the fact that it gave him a way to define the essence of being Jewish as the awareness of belonging to a well-defined ethnic group.

But if Hebraism was a culture, "the fruit and flower of the *whole* of Jewish life," then its expression, according to Kallen, had always been rooted in "the ethnic solidarity and geographical concentration" of the Jewish people. Until the end of the eighteenth century the majority of Jews, even in diaspora, tended to live together as homogeneous communities, living "an organic social life" and expressing their culture in their own way. In response to the forces of emancipation, however, the cohesive Jewish groups had begun to break apart, and Hebraism had started to die, unable to survive without an integrated community to sustain it. During the nineteenth century a "Jewish problem" arose, both for the non-Jews, who resented the stranger now free to live in their midst, and for the Jews, who were in danger of losing their identity.[7]

Kallen was personally quite sensitive to the issues he raised in this analysis, for without a living secular Hebraic culture he had no way to justify his own connection with the Jewish people. The solution he found for himself was Zionism, the then nascent movement to re-nationalize the Jewish people. For only if the Jews could live freely in their own land, he reasoned, could Hebraism thrive, enriching "the harmony of civilization" while preserving, at the same time, "that unique note" which expressed a distinct and creative Jewish individuality.[8]

In 1903, when Kallen became a Zionist, he began to work out for himself several reasons for a commitment to Zionism, rationales that addressed themselves both to his own needs and to the anti-Zionist rhetoric then common among American Jews and non-Jews. While some of his reasoning shows a relationship to Zionist themes found elsewhere, one addition entirely his own — the definition of Zionism in terms of cultural pluralism — had an original emphasis that would help to allay the most significant fear of the American Jewish community concerning Zionism, the charge it invited of dual loyalty.

Kallen's first cohesive expression of his Zionist rationale was a paper, "The Ethics of Zionism," which he delivered before the 1906 convention of the Federation of American Zionists. He began by rejecting two traditional Zionist positions — that Zionism is a charity to help free the masses from anti-Semitic persecution, and that Zionism is the fulfillment of an age-old religious instinct. Zionism, he said, needed a new rationale, one based on reason and on science, one that could show that the Jews deserved to live as a separate people in a country of their own. The Jew would have to prove his right to survive "by the vigor of his achievement and the effectiveness of his ideals, by his gifts to the world and his power for good in the world."[9]

In a rather elaborate exposition, Kallen then extended the Darwinian principle of survival of the fittest from the individual to the social group, and applied this principle to the history of the Jewish people. Longer than any other people of recorded history the Jews had survived, remaining "masterful and ever assertive . . . molding the Western soul and setting before him definite controlling ideas." The Jewish race, therefore, had ethically asserted its right to maintain its self-hood.

But to continue to do so, like the other nations of the world, it needed to have "permanent occupation of a definite territory." National self-expression would be possible only with a distinctive national life "under customs and law spiritually native." It was the duty of all Jews, but particularly those living in a free country like the United States, to support the re-nationalization of the Jewish people, for who better could understand that "each man in the human family [has] the right to live and to give his life ideal expression."

In his later writings Kallen returned often to the themes he had suggested in "The Ethics of Zionism." He began generally by defining the need for a Jewish state in much the same humanitarian terminology as, for example, his American predecessor Emma Lazarus, who conceived of a Palestine as a place of asylum for those subject to actual anti-Semitic oppression. But Kallen went beyond a mere philanthropic impulse. Financial aid, while capable of relieving immediate conditions, would never really remedy the position of the Jew at the mercy of the anti-Semite. In addition, dependence on philanthropy implied acceptance of a less than equal position, a "servile sufferance," and,

therefore, a "surrender of individuality and self-respect." Only if the Jewish nation would become self-supporting could it become, also, self-reliant enough to "fight back" against enemies from a position of strength; it would be the role of the American Jew to help the Jewish people to help itself.[10]

Kallen, however, did not stress this position in his writing and speaking. He called it "negative . . . a reaction [to] the relation of the Jewish masses to other European groups." Instead, he much preferred to emphasize what he considered the "affirmative" side of Zionism, " a program to actualize the impulse which the Jewish people feel, like the other peoples of the world, towards the realization of their characteristic potentialities in an autonomous group life having its appropriate social and cultural forms." Zionism, Kallen said, would give to the Jewish people an opportunity to "lay in Palestine the foundations of a new and living Hebraism." This Hebraism, expressed in a dynamic culture, could then "strengthen, and if need be, replace [Judaism's] failing supernaturalism."[11]

Kallen saw the rebirth of Hebraism going beyond the question of mere Jewish survival, however.

> To the Jews of the world it [is] . . . a program of self-help and social justice within Jewry; giving the same rights and responsibilities to both sexes, and actually trying out experiments in economic organization to abolish the exploitation of one man by another without abolishing the impetus towards individual excellence.
> To the nations of the world [Hebraism] . . . should carry into effect the social and spiritual ideals of the Hebrew prophets . . . it [should] reassert the prophetic ideal of internationalism as a democratic and cooperative federation of nationalities.[12]

Here Kallen was reacting to something close to his own experience, the cumulative impulse towards reform in the early twentieth century known as the Progressive Movement. The period between the Spanish American War and World War I was a time when the heretofore agrarian and commercial economy of the United States was shifting to become more urban and industrial. Many Americans expressed concern about the position of the individual within the country's increasingly industrial society, and began to seek ways to bring the government back to the people. Reformers spearheaded the enactment of new laws to destroy the urban political machines and their attendant corruption, to regulate public utilities and corporate power, and to ameliorate the lot of innocent victims of the new order, like the poor of the cities' slums. Their goal, said the Progressives, was to abolish special privilege through equal opportunity for all; their underlying motive was to restore to America the values on which it had been founded, the ideal of a democratic and humane society based on egalitarianism and on social compassion.

Kallen saw that the renationalization of the Jewish people would give them an opportunity to start afresh, to create a country based on "their ancient tradition . . . of social justice and fundamental economic democracy." Their entire state could constitute a reform, which for Kallen meant primarily economic reform, embodying new concepts of land and resource ownership and control and of economic cooperation. At the same time that the "Hebraic spirit" would be revitalized, thereby ensuring the survival of the Jewish people, so also would the traditional prophetic ideals have a new opportunity to flourish, making the Jewish state the living embodiment of a free and just social order. [13]

Kallen added still another facet to his Zionist reasoning, tying it in with the concept of cultural pluralism he had first hinted at in "The Ethics of Zionism." "Culture . . . constitutes a harmony, of which the peoples and nations are the producing instruments, to which each contributes its unique tone. . . ." Kallen wrote in 1910. If this is so, the Jewish people who have contributed "the Hebraic note [which] has given to the history of Europe an unquestionable coloring" deserve to have a land of their own where "this note may gain in strength and purity" and where the Jews "like that of any of the peoples of Europe may again be free to express itself characteristically in organized social life, in esthetic and intellectual activities." [14]

Implicit in this argument is the notion that Zionism does not mean the concentration of all Jews in Palestine. An individual Jew in the United States, for instance, could choose to live in America and to make his contribution to the "American symphony." At the same time, however, the Jewish people, as a national group, should be given the same right as other nations to express its culture in a land of its own, contributing, thereby to the "symphony of nations." [15]

Writing during the period of nationalist hysteria generated by World War I, Kallen took care to stress the values of American democracy. Because America, ideally, is both "liberal and liberating," it encourages "collective self-expression" of European-born groups "in their ancestral lands." American Jews, therefore, could participate in the American liberal tradition if they supported the Zionist cause. In turn, the inspiration the American Zionists would receive from the renewed Hebraic spirit would help them to contribute more successfully to the pluralist American culture. To Ruth Mack, a young would-be Zionist whose father, Julian, later was to become president of the American Zionist movement, Kallen concluded:

> It is not within the province of Zionism to gather all the Jewish people into one region. The movement is not philanthropic except incidentally. . . . Insofar as Zionism aims to make conditions free by insisting on the democracy and equality of nationalities it will improve the condition of all the Jews in the world.[16]

There were several points in Kallen's analysis of Zionism that made it especially attractive to well-educated, almost assimilated American Jews, many of whom had been either indifferent or hostile to the Zionist cause. In the first instance, Kallen, by defining Zionism in a way that went beyond philanthropy, and by putting it in the accepted American Social Gospel tradition of *noblesse oblige,* appealed to the instincts of those who wished to help their brethren but who denigrated charity as a means of perpetuating poverty and low status. During this period of progressive reform many Americans were helping new immigrants by setting up settlement houses and courses of education whose goal was to enable the immigrants to learn to help themselves. Now, Kallen said, a national state could do the same thing for the persecuted Jewish masses in Europe; the position of the Jews in Palestine would be "natural," and they could thrive, therefore, by their own efforts. Thus American Jews, if they became Zionists, could fill the same role for the immigrants to Palestine as their non-Zionist counterparts were doing for the immigrants to America, in a mode highly sanctioned by the majority American culture.

In addition, Kallen's insistence that the new state would grow on the base of a revitalized Hebraic spirit, incorporating the most just economic conditions and emphasizing both democratic principles and individual excellence, encouraged those who knew the need for reform in America but who were already despairing of its implementation in a large and complex country. Palestine was small, virgin territory for experimentation in the form and substance of government, a new chance to see if the school book ideal Jeffersonian principles of democ-

racy could be made to work in a world made different by modern
technology. The Progressive impulse, already dying in America by the
time of the first World War, could be brought back to life with the
success of the Zionist movement.

Most important, perhaps, was the blow Kallen's theory of cultural
pluralism gave to the ubiquitous charges of dual loyalty. Accepting the
assumptions of the pluralist theory meant accepting the implication
that "hyphenated" Americans were better Americans. "Our duty to
America, inspired by the Hebraic tradition — our service to the world .
. . — both of these are conditioned, insofar as we are Jews, upon the
conservation of Jewish nationality," wrote Kallen.[17] Though many of
the new Jewish immigrants from Eastern Europe may have found this
formula too subtle to grasp, it had great appeal for those whose needs it
met, those who were looking for some rationale that might help them
to maintain a Jewish individuality compatible with a commitment to
American ideals and culture. Kallen's arguments for Zionism gave
them, as it gave him, a means for becoming more American by becoming more Jewish. Instead of replying defensively to demands for assimilation, the Jews could provide an affirmative alternative that was both
proof of their patriotism and preserving of their identity.

The most important person to have been influenced by Kallen's
ideas was the "people's attorney," famous as the leader of many of the
Progressive movement's crusades, Louis D. Brandeis. Brandeis,
though he had never disowned his own Jewish identity, had been
fervent in his denunciation of the dual loyalties of "hyphenated"
Americans who kept alive "difference of origin" by "habits of living or
of thought."[18] Until 1910 he had had no real exposure to the Jewish
community; then, at the age of 54, he was called upon to act as mediator
in a strike among New York's mainly Jewish garment workers. Impressed by the ability to cooperate that he observed even between the
antagonistic employers and employees, and moved by their mutual
concern for social justice, Brandeis, an almost completely assimilated
Jew, began to take some interest in the question of Jewish survival. A
chance meeting with Jacob deHaas, Theodore Herzl's former English
secretary, helped him to learn something of the activity in Palestine to
renationalize the Jewish people; sympathetic to deHaas' description of
a prideful nation of Jewish pioneers, Brandeis felt himself increasingly
drawn to the Zionist cause. Yet he was still lacking the intellectual
rationale that might enable him to give up the assimilationist convic-

tions of a lifetime in order to take a more active role in the Zionist movement.

Kallen's ideas appear to have been the link Brandeis needed. In 1913, having read of Brandeis' interest in an economic project in Palestine, Kallen had contacted Brandeis and began to send him copies of articles he had written expressing his own Zionist formulations. Brandeis had been impressed favorably by Kallen's views which stressed the possibility of "a new state and a happier social order" in which exploitation and injustice might be avoided "by right beginnings." He arranged, therefore, to travel with Kallen on an overnight boat trip both were taking to the August 30, 1914 conference that had been called to organize a Provisional Executive Committee for the management of Zionist affairs during World War I.[19]

During the course of this trip Kallen presented to Brandeis a memorandum which he had prepared, at Brandeis' request, to explain his rationales for Zionism and to propose a blueprint for an ideal state that might be established in Palestine. Kallen's study discussed his concept of "the equality of the different" and the importance, to free men, of maintaining these differences. In it he argued that a new Jewish nation would revive the Jewish culture, and he defined and delineated Hebraism, "the mind . . . of the Jewish people." Kallen rejected the idea of Zionism as philanthropy, stressing that Palestine must be free from dependence on charity in order for the Jews to be able to express their "ethnic nationality" freely and autonomously. And finally, he showed how the American Jewish community was in danger of dying without a Jewish national homeland with which it could identify.[20]

Kallen's thoughts were new to Brandeis, for most of them were not part of the standard European Zionist ideology with which deHaas, for example, would have been familiar. Their effect on Brandeis and their contribution to Brandeis' decision to assume active Zionist leadership by becoming chairman of the Provisional Executive Committee can remain only a matter of conjecture. But the fact that shortly thereafter Brandeis was to repeat, almost verbatim, many of these same points in a Zionist philosophy of his own demonstrates, with considerable certainty, that they made a signficant impression on him.[21]

The influence of Kallan's concepts, through Brandeis' statements, went further, however. As Kallen admitted shortly before his death,

Now Brandeis took up the ideas . . . and after he identified himself with the Zionist movement . . . he presented in his own language the essential ideas. And in presenting those ideas, the conflicts he had imagined between Zionism and Americanism and that were emphasized so much by the [anti-Zionist] American Jewish Committee of those days . . . were simply nullified. Now that gave Zionism publicly a philosophical status in terms of what you might call the American faith, and gave it a public force that it couldn't possibly have had from me alone.[22]

Kallen, through Brandeis, thus became the philosopher of an Americanized Zionism, the intellectual who worked behind the scenes with a leader whose influence would remake the Zionist movement in America. From 1914 to 1921 American Zionism took on a different complexion, influenced mainly by Kallen's and Brandeis' perceptions as American Progressives rather than by European definitions and emphases. "The American Zionist view tended to crystallize in a formulation of the Jewish position less partisan, more scientific, more historical and more sociological than formulations made at the seat of the Jewish problem — in crisis in central Europe, and the American Zionist tended toward an attitude less ardent, more contemplative and more businesslike than that of the European," Kallen observed in 1921.[23] Indeed, it was this formulation that was to lead ultimately to the downfall of Brandeis-led American Zionism, when, in 1921, the masses of Eastern Europeans who had joined the movement during the wartime period rejected a Zionism that projected, in their eyes, too much of the American Progressive mode and too little of the European Zionist tradition. But for a few years, Horace Kallen's concept of the Zionist movement as the chance to effect in Palestine a state reflecting the highest goals of economic and social justice was the crucial one, leading finally to the quintessential statement of American Zionism as a Progressive, reform-oriented movement, the Pittsburgh Program of 1918.

On June 17, 1918 Kallen wrote to a friend in England, "During the last week, I have been engaged on a declaration of our economic and political principles. This declaration . . . will be presented to the Convention [of the Zionist Organization of America] in Pittsburgh the 23rd of the current month."[24] A copy of this declaration, in Kallen's handwritting, signed by him and noted as "1st corrected draft — 17/6/18," is in Kallen's files as "A Memorandum on the Principles of Organization of the Jewish Commonwealth in Palestine." The form and language of this memorandum make it quite clear that Kallen had the primary role in framing what has come to be known as the Pittsburgh Program, a series of seven principles that the delegates to the 1918 convention of the Zionist Organization of American adopted as their credo.

In the August 1914 memorandum that Kallen had submitted to Brandeis just prior to the formation meeting of the Provisional Executive Committee, Kallen had included an outline of the utopia he forsaw for Zion. The aim of the Zionist organization, as he saw it then, was to establish a state in which the government would facilitate the expression of the ethnic nationality of the Jewish people — its language, literature, religion, philosophy and art. He suggested, therefore, an international organization to work out "a carefully reasoned plan for the central control of all practical activity in Palestine." This organization would have five divisions: 1) a ministry of public affairs to be in charge of the "consistent development of the settlement, the establishment of industries, etc."; 2) a ministry which would apply uniform laws, "so as to maintain the practice of democracy and to avoid economic and social injustice"; 3) a ministry to develop a system of national education from grade school to a university; 4) a ministry of public health; and 5) a ministry to establish a Bureau of National Art.[25]

For some time the working out of the implications of this scheme occupied Kallen's mind. He wrote of it to Brandeis in 1915, and his concern with practical plans for the Jewish nation-to-be underlaid much of his efforts for the Zionist organization. Kallen had been influenced especially by the works of Robert Owen, a British socialist of the early nineteenth century, who held that the key to human progress lay in economic, not political, reform. This concept was close to that of many American progressive reformers, Brandeis among them, who had concerned themselves with various plans and regulations to ensure a more equitable distribution of wealth. Owen had devised, also, a form of a child-centered education, similar to that of progressive educators like John Dewey and Randolph Bourne. Kallen felt certain that in Palestine, a land with "no complicated or immemorial social structures," an area "fully within the limits of control," plans such as Owen had suggested could be put into effect. [26]

In 1917 the entrance of the United States into World War I seemed to precipitate a renewed lease on life for progressive ideas. Starting in late 1917, and continuing into 1918, the Wilson administration proposed several schemes for economic planning; the *New Republic* described the morale of the country as that "of a cooperative commonwealth." Kallen was not untouched by these developments. In addition, he took seriously what he construed to be the British promise in the 1917 Balfour Declaration. It seemed especially appropriate, therefore, to begin to formulate specific programs, along progressive reform lines, to ensure the economic and socially just development of Palestine.

Kallen's draft memorandum for the Pittsburgh Program makes explict the influence both the American Idea and Hebraism had on his thinking.

> . . . [T]he Zionist movement has been from its inception a movement to establish such a homeland on the principles of a social justice that will actually secure to each man his life, his liberty, and his happiness. The prophetic, Talmudical and legal traditions of the Jewish people rest on these principles; economic and social democracy, to be achieved through the proper control of natural resources and universal education, are the chief concern of the prophets; are the objective of the legislation of Deuteronomy and Leviticus and the intent of the living law of the people as recorded in the Talmud.[27]

One of Kallen's major published writings of this period, his 1918 "Constitutional Foundations of the New Zion," reflects, also, the way in which he applied his concept of cultural pluralism to the purpose of the Jewish nation-to-be. The function of the state, he wrote, "is to keep the ways of life open to the free movement toward the expression and fulfillment of their natural capacities by individuals and groups." Since "private ownership in community values" and "privilege of any sort" had been the greatest historic causes "of the arrest of the vital movement of the masses of men," the most important function of the state would be to abolish these where they might already exist, and, even more important, to prevent them from arising.[28]

Kallen's draft for the Pittsburgh Program made several concrete suggestions toward this end.

I. *The National Ownership of Land and Public Utilities*

(a) To insure to all the citizens of the homeland in Palestine the completest possible equality of opportunity and responsibility, we declare for the national ownership and control of the land and all its resources, and of all public utilities.

(b) We hold, however, that the most effective development and use of both the natural resources of the land and of public utilities is to be attained by the initiative of private cooperative enterprise under such leases as will secure the continuity of the undertakings. . . .

II. *Democracy: Economic and Political*

(a) Economic democracy: We delcare that the continuity of the great tradition of the Jewish people can be best maintained and the needs and conditions of modern enterprise met by the organization of all industrial, agricultural, commercial and finanical enterprises on a cooperative basis.

(b) Political democracy — (1) We declare for the political and civil equality, irrespective of race, sex, or faith, of all peoples inhabiting the land. . . .

III. *Education*

(a) We declare for the creation, in the Jewish homeland, of a system of compulsory, free, and democratic education.

(b) We declare for Hebrew as the medium of Jewish national instruction.

IV. *Recommendation to the Zionist Administration Commission*

. . . (b) As immediate steps we request:

1. The prevention of all speculation in land and land values. . . .[29]

With some minor changes in placement and wording, Kallen's "principles" for "the Jewish Commonwealth in Palestine" became the Pittsburgh Program, the visionary statement of one who measured the worth of Zionism in its extension of the principles of the American Idea to the new Jewish nation, an attempt to construct in Palestine a model democratic Jewish nationality, following the guidelines of Progressive reform. Equality irrespective of race, sex, or faith; national ownership of public resources and of public utilities; emphasis on the cooperative principle; concern with the inherent value of land and with the evil of speculation; stress on education — these were the themes of the Progressive reformers, even more, perhaps, than "the prophetic, Talmudic and legal tradition of the Jewish people."

It is not surprising, therefore, that the Pittsburgh Program was to be the cornerstone of the official program of the Zionist Organization of America only from 1918 to 1921. Like other of Kallen's ideas, the masses never really understood it; the American Yiddish press of the period, for example, ignored it.[30] The very fact that Kallen and the people who he influenced had been attracted to Zionism as an expression of American idealism distinguished them from both their Zionist colleagues abroad and from the European immigrants who had come recently to America.

The Europeans saw Zionism in a different light, as a response to Jewish tradition and as an expression of Jewish culture. Most of them, moreover, had suffered from overt anti-Semitism and were more cautious and less idealistic in pressing their claim for a Jewish state. As Leon Simon, a British Zionist intellectual who at this time was closely associated with Chaim Weizmann and Ahad Ha'am, wrote to Kallen,

> . . .There is . . . something refreshingly "far off" in the American way of looking at things. . . . Whatever ideas our lawgivers and prophets had, they were not 20th century American democrats. . . . [I]n relation to the present and the future the Program simply doesn't face facts. . . .
>
> [F]or the Zionist who is first and foremost a Zionist the essential thing is that we get the biggest possible run for our money in Palestine; and . . . in order to have the money wherewith to use our run we shall inevitably be compelled to avoid pushing doctrines to extremes. . . .[31]

The World Zionist Organization never accepted the Pittsburgh Program, despite much lobbying on its behalf, and the American Zionists of European background, who sided with Chaim Weizmann and who forced the Brandeis faction to resign in 1921, repudiated it by implication.

In 1972, two years before his death, Kallen recalled his role as a philosopher of an American Zionism.

> I was a radical, in the sense that I wanted action. I wasn't prudent — a radical in that sense, and . . . perhaps also impractical, because the commonwealth notion was regarded, and perhaps rightly, as an impractical notion. Although I say, perhaps rightly I feel, actually, wrongly. I think if we had started with it [the Pittsburgh Program] the whole history of the movement and its achievement might have been very different. But then, you know "what might have been. . . ."[32]

The fact that Brandeis shared Kallen's vision of Zion, and continued to remain committed to the Pittsburgh Program, was to become of primary importance in 1919-1921, when the confrontation between Brandeis and Weizmann went beyond the differences of opinion in the correspondence between two intellectuals, and represented a major clash of views between the two leaders of the Zionist world. Yet it was inevitable that Brandeis' perceptions of Zionism would continue to reflect his own background as an American progressive reformer, firmly supported by Kallen's cultural pluralist rationale that Jews needed a national life of their own primarily to realize more fully their "equality in difference."

The European Zionists sensed rightly that plans for a utopian economic democracy to be implemented by the scientific management methods stressed by the American progressive movement, plans which seemingly ignored the issues of Jewish nationalism and which made the question of Jewishness almost irrelevant, were alien and "un-Jewish." Kallen, Brandeis and their followers had become Zionists not because they were good Jews, but because they were good Americans and perceived Zionism as a way to strengthen their American values. Kallen had rejected the Jewish religious tradition, and his Zionist formulation was primarily an intellectual one, conceived "in terms of the philosophical pluralism with which [William] James was identified and in terms of the interpretation of the American tradition . . . by [literary historian] Barrett Wendell" rather than in terms of what he "had learned of Torah at home or in *Cheder*."[33] It was an ideal that allowed him to preserve his American identity with others in a pluralistic society at the same time that he could advocate a broader extension of the precepts of liberty and equality which he attributed to the American Idea. In America, a country that prided itself on its toleration of religious minorities, and that ideally encouraged equal opportunity for all, this positon had some logic. To the European Jews, however, whose national allegiances were always subordinate to their Jewish identity, and whose Zionism was a deeply felt reaction to the suffering which Jews had experienced because they were Jews, this formulation was absurd.

The significance of the Pittsburgh Program is that it defined precisely the perspective from which Kallen and Brandeis perceived their Zionism — a new way to apply Jeffersonian-like principles and practices of social democracy, a new opportunity to build an ideal "City Upon a Hill." Zionism was on a par with other reforms they sought in American life, except in this instance the reform would take place in a different locale as a model of what efficient planning would do. The land of Palestine was less important for its historic role as the Biblical homeland than for its small size, its scattered population, and its potential for experiment.

Kallen has recalled that he defined his Zionist stance from the perspective of a "practical idealist," a position he equated with the philosophic Pragmatism of his mentor, William James.

> The Brandeis program wanted to develop Palestine in an organized way by established methods which nevertheless would conform to the principles of the Pittsburgh Program. . . . Whatever [the American Zionists] did, day by day, and year by year, was a function of their image of a social setup, designed to turn it from an image into a fact.[34]

Indeed, from 1914 to 1921 the Zionist organization had pulsated with energy and with hope, in no small measure due to Kallen's quiet, behind-the scenes influence. His ideas, and Brandeis' leadership, helped to change the American Zionist movement from a small, rather inefficiently managed group to one that, with new definition and new direction, grew rapidly in numbers, financial resources, and influence. His approach to Zionism gave it a uniquely American cast that led during this period first to its rise, then to its fall. That Kallen's role has gone unrecognized for so long is a tribute to the modesty he exhibited in his lifetime. But it is well, that in memoriam, his valuable collection of papers has enabled us to give credit, finally, where credit is due.

FOOTNOTES

1. Alfred J. Morrow, "Introduction," in Horace M. Kallen, *What I Believe and Why – Maybe* (New York, 1971), pp. 10-11.

2. Mordecai M. Kaplan to Horace M. Kallen, August 7, 1952. Horace M. Kallen Papers, American Jewish Archives, Cincinnati, Ohio.

3. Kallen quoted the Parker definition in "The American Dream and The American Idea" in *What I Believe*, p. 60.

4. Kallen wrote about his settlement house experiences in a letter to Brooks Atkinson, April 20, 1957, Kallen Mss, and about his relationship with Alain Locke in "Alain Locke and Cultural Pluralism," *What I Believe*, pp. 129-133. He discussed these, also, in a series of personal interviews with the author, June 1972 — August 1973. See "The American Idea," p. 63, for the quote.

5. Kallen, "Democracy versus the Melting Pot," *The Nation* 100 (February 18 and 25, 1915): 190-194, 217-220. A more complete exposition of these ideas is in Kallen, *Culture and Democracy in the United States* (New York, 1924).

6. Kallen, "Democracy, Nationalism and Zionism," *The Maccabean* 31 (July 1918): 187, 175; Kallen, "The Distinction between Hebraism and Judaism," *The Maccabean* 23 (May 1915): 86; "Judaism and the Modern Point of View," *Judaism At Bay* (New York, 1932), p. 48.

7. Kallen, "The Distinction between Hebraism and Judaism," 86; Kallen, "Judaism, Hebraism, Zionism," *Judaism At Bay*, pp. 37, 40; Kallen, *Zionism and World Politics* (Garden City, New York, 1921), p. 71.

8. Kallen, "Judaism, Hebraism, Zionism," p. 41.

9. Kallen, "The Ethics of Zionism," *The Maccabean* 8 (August 1906): 61-71.

10. Kallen, *Zionism and World Politics*, pp. 47, 90; Kallen, "The Issues of War and the Jewish Position," *The Nation* 110 (November 29, 1917): 592.

11. "Dr. Kallen on Zionism," *The Maccabean* 25 (November-December 1914): 188; Kallen, "Judaism By Proxy," *Judaism At Bay*, pp. 76-77.

12. Kallen, "Zionism and the Struggle for Democracy," *The Nation* 101 (September 23, 1915): 379; Kallen, "Constitutional Foundations of the New Zion," *The Maccabean* 31 (April 1918): 97-98.

13. Kallen, "In The Hope of the New Zion," *International Journal of Ethics* 29 (January 1919): 455-456: Kallen, "Constitutional Foundations," p. 98. The degree to which Kallen's definition of Zionism reflected the influence of the Progressive movement is explored further in Sarah Schmidt, "Horace M. Kallen and the 'Progressive' Reform of Zionism," *Midstream* 22 (December 1976): 14-23.

14. Kallen, "Judaism, Hebraism, Zionism," *Judaism At Bay*, p. 37; Kallen, "In the Hope of the New Zion," p. 456.

15. Kallen, "Zionism and Liberalism," *Judaism At Bay*, p. 113.

16. *Ibid.*, p. 119; Kallen to Ruth Mack, August 4, 1915, Kallen Mss.

17. Kallen, "Nationality and the Hyphenated American," *The Menorah Journal* 1 (April 1915): 86.

18. Two good accounts of Brandeis' life and role in the Zionist movement are in A. T. Mason, *Brandeis: A Free Man's Life* (New York, 1946), and Melvin Urofsky, *A Mind of One Piece* (New York, 1971). The quotes are from a speech titled "What Loyalty Demands" in *Brandeis*, p. 442.

19. Kallen to Louis D. Brandeis, December 20, 1913 and August 27, 1914, Louis D. Brandeis Collection, Zionist Archives, New York.

20. Kallen, unpublished memorandum, "The International Aspects of Zionism," on which he added a handwritten note, "Copy submitted to Mr. Brandeis, August 29, 1914," Kallen Mss.

21. For an analysis of Brandeis' speeches and their use of Kallen's ideas and themes, see Schmidt, "The Zionist Conversion of Louis D. Brandeis," *Jewish Social Studies* 37 (January 1975): 18-34.

22. Interview with Kallen, July 1972.

23. Kallen, *Zionism and World Politics*, p. 133.

24. Kallen to Alfred Zimmern, June 17, 1918, Kallen Mss.

25. Kallen, "The International Aspects of Zionism," *ibid.*

26. Kallen, "Constitutional Foundations of the New Zion," pp. 98-99.

27. Kallen, unpublished memorandum, "A Memorandum on the Principles of Organization of the Jewish Commonwealth in Palestine," Kallen Mss. The complete text of this memorandum is reprinted as the appendix in my unpublished dissertation, "Horace M. Kallen and the Americanization of Zionism" (University of Maryland, 1973).

28. Kallen, "Constitutional Foundations," p. 100.

29. Kallen, "A Memorandum." For more details on Kallen's ideals and how they affected the Pittsburgh Program, see Schmidt, "Messianic Pragmatism: The Zionism of Horace M. Kallen," *Judaism* 25 (Spring 1976): 217-29.

30. Yonathan Shapiro, *Leadership of the American Zionist Organization*, (Urbana, Ill., 1971), p. 127.

31. Leon Simon to Kallen, August 3, 1919, Kallen Mss.

32. Interview with Kallen, July 1972.

33. *Ibid.*

34. *Ibid.*, August 1973.

Louis Lipsky and the Emergence of Opposition to Brandeis, 1917-1920

by Deborah E. Lipstadt

Organized Zionism in America faced a multitude of obstacles during its early years. Some of these difficulties can be attributed to problems which reflected the composition of the American Jewish community. The Federation of American Zionists (FAZ) was at its creation and for a number of decades thereafter an organization with leaders from one sector of the community and members from another. The organization drew its members from the ranks of the East Europeans. Its founders and leaders throughout the first two decades of its existence, with the exception of one short period, had their roots outside that community.

The federated structure of the FAZ also contributed to its difficulties, since individual Zionist societies fought FAZ attempts to exert strong national leadership. Reluctant to relinquish any of their own independence, they often ignored directives from the national office, rendering futile any attempts to centralize American Zionist activities. Active resistance and passive neglect of the central office by the member groups posed serious obstacles for the organization. The problem was compounded further by the existence of other national Zionist organizations, such as the Mizrachi and the Knights of Zion, which competed for members and duplicated activities. The World Zionist Organization refused, despite repeated pleas, to reorganize the FAZ as *the* American Zionist organization. The formation of the Zionist Organization of America (ZOA) in 1918 was a direct response to this bedlamic organizational situation.

The Zionists also faced the opposition of the *Yahudim*, the "uptowners", who were concerned that Zionism would foster doubts in American minds as to Jewish loyalties to America. Jewish patriotism, it was feared, would be questioned and all Jews — Zionist and non-Zionists — would be implicated. The "uptowners" continued to voice these fears even after the Balfour Declaration.

Prior to World War I the FAZ's membership never passed 16,000 and its coffers were rarely full. It is rather miraculous that, in the face of these varied problems, the organization was able to survive. It not only survived but laid the organizational and ideological groundwork for the mass movement which was formed in the wake of the war.

The FAZ's ability to continue functioning was due, in great measure, to a small group of individuals, some of whom were first-generation Americans born to Eastern European parents, and some of whom were immigrants who had come to this country at an early age. They immersed themselves in Zionist activities to the practical exclusion of all else, although they rarely occupied top-level leadership positions. On occasion, they actively protested the leaders' policies, but they did not attempt to wrest control of the organization from the notables. Only once during the first two decades of the twentieth century did they find the reins of the organization in their hands. Most of the time they functioned as office workers and lower echelon leaders without whom American Zionism could not have maintained even its most tenuous existence.

The members of this group, for whom Zionism became both an avocation and vocation, included: Bernard Richards, Abraham Goldberg, Charles Cowen, Senior Abel and Louis Lipsky. Rochester-born Lipsky, who emerged as their leader was at home in the Lower East Side immigrant world, but was not estranged from the uptown leadership.

Lipsky, who served as chairman of the Federation of American Zionists from 1911-1918, and as president of its successor, the Zionist Organization of America (ZOA) from 1921-1930, is an enigmatic character in the history of Zionism in America. Though he served as the editor of the *Maccabaean,* the house organ of the FAZ, lectured in many parts of the United States on behalf of this cause, wrote copious articles on the topic, led the organization longer than any other man, and was involved in much of the bitter dissension that characterized the early history of organized Zionism, his name today is unkown to many within the movement and those on its periphery. The attitudes towards Lipsky expressed by those within the Zionist organization and those outside it ranged from highly laudatory to extremely contemptuous. There were a variety of reasons for this sharp divergence of opinions.

Lipsky's hostility toward any organization, ideology or movement which sought to hinder Zionism was given free expression on the pages of the *Maccabaean* and in speeches before Zionist groups. He used no restraint in criticizing leaders of the Reform Movement, major benefactors of the Jewish community, or fellow Zionists if he believed their actions were detrimental to the course of organized Zionism in America. This earned him the enmity of powerful sectors of the community. Lipsky even earned the wrath of other Zionists because he publicly demanded that Brandeis relinquish his Supreme Court position and assume the leadership of the WZO. Many members of the Brandeis *coterie* never forgave Lipsky for asking Brandeis to step down, and for emerging victorious in the subsequent battle for control of the American Zionist organization.

Following the long imbroglio over the convening of an American Jewish congress in late 1916, until the summer of 1920 and the departure of the American delegation for the London conference of Zionist leaders, the gap between the East Europeans and the Brandeisians widened. After the London conference, Lipsky emerged as the leader of the opposition. Prior to it he fluctuated between the two groups, and it is clear that the factors which gradually led to Lipsky's alignment with Chaim Weizmann and opposition to Brandeis cannot be attributed solely to differences in Zionist philosophy. He gravitated towards this position slowly, and his alignment with the opposition could have been aborted on a number of occasions had the Brandeis administration actively attempted to keep him within the fold.

It was a combination of ideological, organizational and personal conflicts which ensured Lipsky's alignment with the opposition. From 1917 until he challenged Brandeis in 1921, Lipsky was increasingly isolated from the center of policy making, evidenced in a series of events in the 1918-1920 period. Lipsky's tactics upset the Brandeisians on various occasions, while the Brandeisian Zionist philosophy and style of leadership dismayed Lipsky.

Postponement of the American Jewish Congress

Lipsky had led the Zionist forces in the struggle to establish the American Jewish Congress, and after a long series of negotiations and

compromises, agreement was seemingly reached in 1916. Anxious that
the congress be convened forthwith, Lipsky immediately proceeded
with preparations for it. His tactics soon became the cause for controversy, and he was accused by the American Jewish Committee
(AJC) leaders of violating the compromises which had been laboriously
reached.[1]

A letter Lipsky wrote as chairman of the FAZ in June 1917 on the eve
of congress elections to Zionist societies caused the furor. He urged
consideration of a candidate's position on Zionism before voting:

> Every candidate seeking Zionist support should be asked to state his
> opinion as to how he stands with reference to the functions of the
> Congress. If he is in favor of a conditional, narrow program . . . *do not
> vote for him.* If he favors a free unlimited congress . . . *give him your
> vote.*[2]

It was important that Zionists ensure the election of delegates who
were sympathetic to the cause. In the compromise agreement provision "is made for the discussion of our Palestine interests in one
sentence, which is purposely rather vague but which may become
clearer if conditions arise that may make feasible the consideration of
what is involved in securing and protecting Jewish rights in Palestine."[3]

It is difficult to reconcile this letter with his subsequent actions at the
June 1917 FAZ convention. There, Lipsky "counseled" the delegates
to follow a policy of "strick adherence" to the agreement. He warned
those who complained about the compromises to refrain from a
"breach of agreement" and not to demand that the congress consider
the question of a national Jewish homeland.[4] His comments at the
convention contradict the statements in his letter in which he said that
the FAZ's interest in the congress was to "a large extent a Zionist
interest, and the Zionists, as a whole, should be invited to join in
making the Zionist decision, which should be morally binding upon all
organized and loyal Zionists."[5] His warnings to the delegates to adhere
to the agreement also conflicted with observation that "the Congress
should be permitted to become what the elected representatives of the
people want it to be. The peace agreement should not be interpreted
literally but liberally."[6]

In light of Lipsky's letter to Zionist societies, the AJC leaders were
convinced that his policy of "strict adherence" to the compromise was a

sham. They had cause to wonder if he was saying one thing and doing another. The *American Hebrew* juxtaposed his instructions to the delegates with the offical call to the congress. The contradictions were glaring. The paper accused him of "Zionising the congress".[7] Lipsky claimed that his statements did not constitute a breach in the peace agreement. He argued that even as the Zionist organization "unqualifiedly stands by the peace agreement" it had the right to "protect the interests of the Zionist movement by having as many Zionists in the congress as we can secure."

Lipsky wished to guarantee the defeat of any resolution inimical to Zionist interests. "A majority of delegates favorable to our cause is essential as a precaution against hostile action." Aware that some Zionist delegates might try to force a pro-Zionist resolution through the congress in violation of the compromises, he issued his warnings at the FAZ convention. Lipsky may have been technically correct. The agreement was "rather vague." However, his letter to the FAZ societies was certainly not within the spirit of the agreement.[8]

This issue never was resolved, but was overshadowed by a more immediate debate. In light of America's entry into the war, it was proposed that the congress be postponed until the termination of hostilities. Both the AJC and the Brandeisians advocated postponement. They were apprehensive lest the congress adopt pacifist resolutions which would cast doubt on the loyalties of American Jewry. Lipsky, however, opposed postponement.[9]

Initially, Stephen Wise agreed with Lipsky that "despite every difficulty, and there are great difficulties in the way, that the congress must now be held and gotten over."[10] Shortly after making this statement in September 1917, Wise changed his mind. His reversal was prompted by his attendance at a series of pro-congress rallies, where, hearing pacifist statements, he became convinced of the "menaces" inherent in holding the congress. Lipsky, present at many of the same rallies, and a number of the "workers" of the organization, actively fought postponement. Wise, therefore, suggested to Brandeis that: "we ought now to call a meeting . . . of our Zionist members of the Administrative Committee of the Congress and lay down the law to them — that is to say, make their vote for postponement mandatory, a matter of party discipline."[11]

In spite of the opposition the congress was postponed, which greatly vexed Lipsky. He believed that "from a moral point of view, the future of the Congress should be placed in the hands of the delegates." He was concerned about the implications of a decision based not on the "righteousness of our cause, but how, under the circumstances, non-Jewish public opinion would regard frank statements of Jewish views." It was indicative of the "resurgence of the *Mah-yomru-hagoyim* policy in Jewish life."[12]

It is noteworthy that Lipsky's criticism of a decision which was supported by Brandeis, Mack, Wise and Frankfurter appeared in the *Maccabaean*, although his remarks were printed after the decision had already been reached. The only practical effect of his action was voicing his disagreement with their policy; he had lost this fight but had not relinquished his independence.

The long-postponed congress was finally held in December 1918. Ironically, Lipsky was disappointed by the congress for which he had so arduously struggled. It had not been a great deliberative body, but resembled the annual convention of a national organization:

> It was not as deliberative as it should have been. There was too evident haste, as if the business had to be disposed of as quickly as possible. The discussions were to a large extent superficial and not illuminating . . . The delegates did not feel a sense of continuing responsibility, a responsibility to their constituency and a responsibility to the Congress itself.

He attributed the failure to the "chain of compromises" which had been made:

> Like every other political ideal, the Congress movement lost its original color by a chain of compromises, one leading into another, which reduced the Congress to the idea that there should be an assembly of American Jews to articulate the demands of the Jewish people, and then disappear.[13]

He failed to note that he had participated in forging the compromises responsible for its failure.

The Formation of the ZOA

The re-organization of the American Zionist organization from a federation of constituent societies to a direct membership organization, the Zionist Organization of America (ZOA), in 1918 constituted a fundamental change in American Zionism, with the national office's control over policy and activities increased considerably through membership geographically subdivided into districts. At the 1918 convention the re-organization proposal had to overcome significant opposition from local East European leaders and Yiddish journalists. They contended that the ZOA would mix those who had a strong commitment to Zionism with those whose interest was strictly philanthropic. "The English-speaking and the Yiddish-speaking would be put together in the same group; they would have little in common and would constitute a large army controlled by the center," as Jacob Fishman noted in the *Jewish Morning Journal*.[14]

Yonathan Shapiro contends that Lipsky and the "organization officers" supported the re-organization because it would "increase the power of the full-time party workers."[15] Shapiro's argument, though possibly correct, only partially explains Lipsky's support for the re-organization. Lipsky had long recognized the federation's organizational weakness, and re-organization would eliminate many of the obstacles that had frustrated him over the preceding two decades. At the 1917 FAZ convention, Lipsky had

> . . . pointed out that there were too many varying groups and societies in the movement and urged that uniformity of method and organization be adopted and individual allegiance and responsibility sought for. Individual affiliation should be the primary allegiance of the organized Zionist.[16]

In addition to the physical re-organization, Brandeis proposed that there be a change in the nature of Zionist activity. Increased emphasis was to be given to economic development of the *yishuv*. All activities which did not have the material benefit of Palestine as their objective would be curtailed. This included Zionist propaganda activities designed to inculcate in diaspora Jewry a sense of nationalism. This new orientation for Zionist activity would serve as one, though not the sole, reason for the Brandeis-Weizmann struggle. Although Lipsky eventually became the American leader of the Weizmann forces, initially he demonstrated no reservations about the increased emphasis on Palestine projects. He argued that this was an idea whose time had come:

> The time for discussion of academic theories has passed. All our thought is now to be devoted to arousing the Jewish people to the

need of practical action for Palestine. . . . If, today, we see our way clear to an investment in the anti-malarial campaign, we should pursue that object with a determined effort, but if sixty days from now that effort requires a larger investment, there should be no hesitation in overturning the budget in that respect, and taking up the larger burden where we see a larger burden must be taken up by us in order to succeed. At the present time irrigation is an inspiration. Tomorrow it may become a practical project. What is clear to us — or should be clear to us — is that we are actually entering upon the period of building.

In 1919, in fact, Lipsky echoed Brandeis' view of Zionist activities:

We should not deceive ourselves with beautiful ideas that we have no direct relationship with practical action . . . everything we do in Palestine must be conditioned by the hard material facts that exist.[17]

After Brandeis' departure from public leadership of the organization and his assumption of silent control, policy was set by Mack, Frankfurter, Wise, deHaas and a few others who were privy to the Justice's letters and memoranda. Most of the directives from Washington were transmitted via deHaas, the only one of the Brandeisians who devoted all his time to Zionism. Brandeis' associates wished to maintain a low profile, and with the exception of deHaas, most refused to participate in public gatherings or mass rallies.

This had a decidedly adverse effect on membership and fund-raising drives, which Lipsky was responsible for as secretary for organization. He knew that the absence of prominent leaders hurt the ZOA. Charles Cowen, acting executive secretary and a Brandeis follower, Blanche Jacobson, deHaas' secretary, and deHaas also complained about this situation. deHaas told Brandeis that: "Everybody is very much overstrained, Lipsky in particular as there is an incessant demand for speakers in connection with the campaign and men like Wise and Mack in particular are rendering us no service in that direction."[18] The administration's silent and tight control of Zionist policy laid the foundation for the first organized opposition to the Brandeisians. During the war, rule by directive had been tolerated; afterwards it was not.

Lipsky recognized the administration's shortcomings, but did not as yet join in the attacks on it. It had, he conceded, failed to observe democratic niceties, but

. . . whatever injustice there may have been in the criticism of the Zionist administration, it was, generally speaking, reducible to the charge that habits of action created by war conditions had been continued after conditions had disappeared.

This problem, Lipsky believed, could have been avoided had the Brandeisians not chosen to isolate themselves from the membership:

> The Administration gave the impression that it was not willing to shift its policies from that of the war period to that of the methods of the period of peace. Probably, if it had had time to take counsel, it would not have arrived at this conclusion, but so many of the important members of the Administration had estranged themselves by absence from the organization proper that they could not be made to realize that a new spirit had come over the Zionists.[19]

Lipsky was irked by the administration's failure to heed the warning signs of this dissension. In December 1918 at an executive committee meeting Mack had to defend the leadership's decision-making process. He admitted that key decisions were made by Brandeis, Wise, de-Haas, Frankfurter and himself without consultation with the executive, but argued that actions of a political nature could not be discussed in an open forum, and he included meetings of the executive in this category. Members complained that, on those occasions when the executive was given the opportunity to voice its opinion, it was not provided with the necessary background information.[20] The views of those outside the inner circle had been rendered ineffective.

Horace Kallen, far more closely aligned with the administration than with the party workers, was appalled by the course of events. In February 1919 he joined the protest, complaining that ZOA policy did not reflect the "choice of the Executive Committee but merely the will of a very few." A half year later Kallen complained again:

> Regarding the status of the Executive Committee, I am much troubled. There nobody had felt any responsibility. It had been through the year a rubber stamp for the actions of the Administrative Committee. Such a situation is not healthy, even in an eleemosynary institution.[21]

Lipsky tried prior to the 1919 convention to warn Brandeis about this growing discontent. He organized regional conferences in a number of cities in order to enable the membership to express its ideas to the leadership, and reported to Brandeis that at these gatherings he was often called upon "to help bring about a better understanding of the situation."[22] The top leadership paid no heed to the complaints and suggestions. Lipsky vented his frustrations to his wife, Eddie:

> The office here is going wrong. There is no one with any ability or understanding of the situation. Judge Mack has little Zionist sense and is waiting to and from Brandeis on every important question. Dr. Wise is away and is sore at Mack. Cowen goes about like a pouter pigeon, thinking of himself, bragging and making himself ridiculous and all this time the Zionists feel deep resentment and don't know at whom to vent their wrath. Lucky for us the Regional Conferences have brought about a better understanding, but to do this I had to go myself to most of them and answer all questions and explain and argue.[23]

In order to avoid dissent at the 1919 convention, Lipsky tried to rectify the situation. He asked Wise to cooperate:

> When are you returning to the city from our vacation? There are a number of us here who have talked over our Organization problems, and we would like to see you in order to have your cooperation in working out a plan of action to be taken in advance of the Chicago Convention. As things are now, the Administration is practically non-existent and somebody will have to take action in order that at least what is called the Administration should present a point of view to the delegates at Chicago.[24]

It is important to note that Lipsky wanted a change of procedure and not personnel. Neither he nor the more vocal critics called for insurrection. This, Lipsky believed, the Brandeisians did not comprehend:

> All the pent-up disappointment and vexations, all the personal animosities created, poured out in a disorganized desire to provoke and irritate the Administration, but not to displace it.

The administration dismissed the complaints voiced as excuses for the formation of an opposition. Brandeis and Mack failed to recognize that there was no cohesive opposition, but rather a general sense of discontent on the part of local leaders and office workers at having been shut out of the decision-making process:

> Coming to the convention unprepared for the outbreak of dissatisfaction, the Administration was also the victim of the circumstances. It misconceived the purpose of the insurgent groups. Instead of looking at their proposals with a benevolent eye, eager to pick the good out of the chaff of the impractical, it assumed for several days that the insurgents represented Administration opposition. In vain the insurgents disclaimed that they were opponents. In vain they sought to debate their propositions and to come to some understanding. The Administration seemed to think it an essential measure of protection to condemn everything that did not have its sanction in advance, although due notice had been given in the Regional Conferences of the sincerity of those advocating reform measures. In the last moments of the Convention a change of attitude was noticed with good results. . . .

> These Zionists included the best workers in the Districts, the most loyal workers and the most intelligent workers. Realizing the impossibility of the situation that had been created during the war, they wanted to have their views reflected in the views of the leadership. They wanted the leadership to be responsible, and consciously so. They felt that unless there was a free flow of views from the constituency to the Administration and vice versa, the Organization could not hold together. They were astounded to find the Administration unwilling to listen and branding their demands as opposition.[25]

Despite their astonishment, the opposition managed to hand the Brandeis forces their first defeat. The issue was a relatively minor one. However, the fact that they were able to overcome the administration was significant.

The 1919 ZOA Convention and the
Attempt to Ban Factions

The creation of the ZOA highlighted a problem which had long concerned Lipsky: separatist Zionist parties. Mizrachi, the religious Zionist group, was now the main area of contention. In 1917 Lipsky, as chairman of the FAZ, had ruled that organizations such as Mizrachi did not constitute a "separatist entity," and were not eligible for repre-

sentation on the committees of the Provisional Emergency Committee
for General Zionist Affairs (PEC). In protest, Mizrachi and a number of
other organizations, withdrew from the PEC. During subsequent
years little was done to resolve the problems inherent in the relationship between the FAZ or ZOA and other Zionist organizations, and in
1919 it was still a cause for debate.

The ZOA administration was intent on eliminating all non-ZOA
Zionist entities. The Brandeisians could then more easily control the
statements made in the name of American Zionists and avoid diaspora
nationalism. Concerned primarily about the bureaucratic difficulties
presented by separate organizations, Lipsky supported the administration. In 1919 he suggested to Brandeis that:

> Inasmuch as the Mizrachi actually wants to maintain a parallel or-
> ganization in every sense of the word in the U.S. and inasmuch as
> they present new demands whenever any new activity is to be
> undertaken . . . it would be of mutual benefit for the Mizrachi to go it
> alone and to leave our organization to carry its work without any
> interference without such entangling alliances that are continually
> wearing away our patience and make it impossible for us to carry out
> work in the right way. We are always at the mercy of an internal
> opposition which seeks the most favorable moment to gain advantage
> at the expense of the center . . . I can see before me a parallel
> organization operating in the U.S. not only nationally but also locally
> and this simply means the destruction of our district plan and con-
> tinuous bickering all along the lines . . .[26]

Lipsky was particularly upset by Mizrachi's timing of its fund-raising
appeals to coincide with those of the FAZ and then the ZOA. Mizrachi
engaged, according to Lipsky, in "tactics designed to confuse the mind
of the public." He warned societies to "safeguard the remittance of the
contributions" to prevent them from inadvertently going to Mizrachi.[27] He believed the ZOA would "serve" the "cause best by breaking with Mizrachi" completely. Lipsky was cognizant of the fact that
the Yiddish press and the rank-and-file membership were reluctant to
take these drastic measures. He recognized that "our own Zionists
could not see the differences between Mizrachi and ourselves . . . Now
that the idea of common action appears to be impossible, it becomes
our duty to explain the essential differences in our points of view."

Lipsky must have known that it was not "essential differences" of an ideological nature which hindered cooperation, nor Mizrachi's espousal of Orthodox Judaism which was an obstacle. The conflict was caused by Mizrachi's refusal to accept the FAZ or the ZOA as the ultimate authority in American Zionist affairs. He argued that:

> if the Mizrachi were willing to confine themselves to what may be called purely Mizrachi activities it would not be half as bad, but they declare that it is their intention to wield Mizrachi influence not only in education and religious matters, but also in economic, legal and each undertaking of the moment. Under such circumstances there is no earthly use in continuing an arrangement which practically means that the vitals of the ZOA are to be eaten up systematically by this party.[28]

In March 1919 the ZOA and Mizrachi severed relations. At the 1919 convention, in his report as secretary for organization, Lipsky spoke of "competition" with Mizrachi and introduced the administration's resolution "calling upon the World Zionist Congress to revoke the international charters of these factions and require them to merge with the general organization in every country." He knew that this would constitute a "radical step" for many members but believed the administration's stand "promoted Zionist unity and discipline."[29]

Yonathan Shapiro argues that this resolution, "the first major issue on which the Brandeis administration was defeated," was too extreme for the "Eastern European party workers" to accept.[30] Where did Lipsky fit in on this issue? His support of this measure was not a result of blind loyalty to Brandeis, nor does it indicate that he was generally aligned with the administration. Twenty years of organizational experience had convinced him that the measure was imperative. He had always favored investing the general Zionist organization — both the FAZ and ZOA — with the ultimate authority. His stand on this issue was in harmony with many others he had taken during previous decades.

There was, however, another reason for the resolution's defeat. Administration leaders had refused to appear before members and explain their policies, and no alternative leadership was even remotely available. Voting against an administration resolution proved the only way to express discontent with the leadership's style.

If one can speak of two organizational factions — the Brandeis administration and the East Europeans — at this time, then Lipsky

fluctuated between them. He understood the validity of some of the
discontent but felt that many of the attacks on the administration were
unwarranted. Those Yiddish journalists and local who had opposed the
ZOA's formation demonstrated a readiness to indiscriminately believe
all innuendoes and rumors about administration misdeeds. Lipsky
described the reports appearing in the Yiddish press as an:

> arrow poisoned by malice and shot through the Jewish world, dis-
> seminating irritation and unrest and doubt . . . It undermined the
> confidence of the Jewish people in the Zionist Administration. There
> was not a rumor, no matter how stupid, that was not believed. There
> was not a project, no matter how fantastic, that was not seriously
> discussed. . . . All spoke and all argued and all came to a conclusion,
> each one for himself, with the newspapers as the stirrers of the
> cauldron, until we were in the midst of a babel of sound without
> rhyme or reason, battering against the unfortunate Jewish problem.

Although the administration was defeated on this issue, the convention ended in relative harmony. The administration's "change of attitude" during the "last moments of the convention" helped, according
to Lipsky to save the situation. It was agreed that the entire Executive
Committee would be included in the decision-making process:

> Responsibility for the Zionist administration [would be in the hands
> of] the authority created by the constitution, to-wit: the Executive
> Committee . . . The Chicago convention had re-won for the Zionist
> organization the confidence of its constituency. It reestablished
> democratic methods of procedure.

In less than a year it would be apparent that Lipsky's predictions about
the re-establishment of "democratic methods" would be unfulfilled.[31]
    However, even if power had been returned to the Executive it
would not have solved the differences between the East Europeans
and the Brandeisians. Fundamental conflicts over the nature of the
organization and social and cultural differences proved fatal to ZOA
unity. Shapiro contends that the emphasis on increasing ZOA membership during this period was a result of the East European's conviction that there was a correlation between "the number of members in
an organization and the amount of funds the organization was able to
mobilize." He argues that unlike the East Europeans, the Brandeisians

were primarily interested in winning the allegiance of a few wealthy individuals who would bring other magnates in their wake. The East Europeans were concerned about increasing membership but so were the Brandeisians. It would be easier to attract wealthy philanthropists if the organization spoke for a vast number of Jews.[34]

The membership drive was Lipsky's responsibility. It was dogged work and Lipsky did not relish doing it. It began in January 1918 and continued for many months:

> The registration is going fairly well. The whole thing will last until November 2nd when I am going to take some days off. The country is waking up. We have had a great deal of publicity. I have been terribly lonesome. I have had to stop working evenings and with nowhere to go, and no one to talk to about matters other than Zionism, I have been feeling like a lost sheep. The registration work is all-engrossing and cannot now be left without my cooperation.[33]

Brandeis joined Lipsky in emphasizing the "value of numbers" and continued to do so, even after the London conference in 1920 when the organization began to devote the major portion of its efforts to investments in Palestine. From the Justice's chambers in Washington Lipsky received a stream of memoranda, suggestions and instructions regarding membership drives. "I think you will be interested to know that my department," Lipsky wrote to Brandeis, "is now engaged in setting up a plan for carrying out the idea expressed by you in Chicago with regard to captains of hundreds and captains of tens." When Brandeis wrote Lipsky to prod him to increase registration, Lipsky requested specific suggestions: "I . . . would appreciate it if you would let me know what you have in mind when you write about doubling membership before January 1st [1920]."[34] Many of Brandeis' suggestions were sent to deHaas who transmitted them to Lipsky. It is clear that Brandeis was personally concerned about the membership drive.[35]

Attempts to Win the Affiliation of German Jewish Leaders

In the months following the 1919 convention, differences between Lipsky and the administration increased. Lipsky was disturbed by their tendency to decide policy on the basis of *"mah-yomru-hagoyim."* This attitude resulted, in part, from the desire to attract wealthy German Jews to the Zionist standard. Since the Balfour Declaration and the end of the war the "uptown" community had demonstrated increasing interest in Palestine. Emphasizing diaspora nationalism would, the administration feared, alienate the "uptowners." Starting in 1917, Brandeis and his closest associates conducted meetings with Jacob Schiff to convince him to affiliate. If Schiff, considered the key figure, joined it would be easier to win other leaders of the *Yahudim*. Schiff stipulated that any cooperation on his part was dependent on Brandeis' "position on political Zionism." If he could be assured that political Zionism would be set aside he might be willing to cooperate.[36]

Lipsky did not participate in the sessions with Schiff, and his exclusion was intentional. Schiff's ideological and personal antipathy towards Lipsky was demonstrated in December 1919 when the wealthy philanthropist suggested that the Zionist organization and the Joint Distribution Committee (JDC) conduct a fund-raising campaign. He invited representatives of the two organizations to a conference to discuss the "possibility of an agreement between the two bodies whereby a joint drive for funds might be conducted in the city of New York and other cities of the U.S." Schiff informed Mack, who as president of the ZOA represented the Zionists, that the executive staff of the two organizations would be excluded in order to limit the size of the conference. Lipsky would, therefore, not be invited. Mack accepted this stipulation, but politely called attention to the fact that Lipsky was "in direct charge of all our drives and fund-raising efforts."

When Schiff sent Mack the list of participants, it became apparent that, while the "principal workers" of the ZOA had been eliminated, those of the JDC had not. In view of the "greatly increased number of participants from the JDC," Mack urged Schiff to send invitations to Henrietta Szold, Harry Friedenwald and Lipsky, all of whom were "elected officers of the organization." Schiff consented to add Szold and Friedenwald, but not Lipsky. Lipsky's presence began to assume mythic proportions. The Zionists were convinced that Schiff's tactics were "aimed specifically at Lipsky." Schiff threatened to cancel the conference if the Zionists failed to agree that "his judgement be respected."[37]

The Zionists debated whether to participate if Lipsky were excluded. Mack wrote Schiff that he did not wish to precipitate the conference's cancellation and, therefore, reluctantly accepted the magnate's demands. Aware that many Zionists opposed participation under these conditions, Mack added that despite the fact that "certain people have objections to Louis Lipsky," he

> is the elected secretary of the Department of Organization and as such in direct charge of all our drives and money-raising efforts . . . But more than that he is a member of the Administration and of the Executive Committee, and more than any other single man he has the unbounded confidence of the whole mass of Zionists of the country. I may say, too, that I personally have never found a more devoted and faithful worker than he is.

Schiff relented and invited Lipsky but admitted to Mack that his reluctance to have Lipsky present was not based on his concern about the conference's size but on his antipathy to Lipsky. "As you have it so much at heart I shall have an invitation sent to Lipsky, but I know that this will have at least no salutory effect upon the conference."[38]

Schiff's feelings can be understood in light of Lipsky's undisguised contempt for the AJC and its leaders. Lipsky had no reservations about his desire to put "a strangle hold" on the JDC. Mack's willingness to jeopardize the conference over Lipsky was not prompted by his concern for Lipsky; it was Lipsky's presence *qua* officer of the ZOA and not Lipsky *qua* Lipsky which was important to Mack. To permit Schiff to slight the organization was intolerable to the members and workers. Though the meetings between Schiff and Brandeis produced no results, Lipsky opposed the concessions supposedly necessary to attract Schiff. deHaas also was skeptical about these efforts and wrote to Brandeis: "I do not agree with Mack who would pour so much water in the Zionist wine that even prohibitionists would permit its use."[39]

It was not solely the fear of repelling Schiff which caused the Brandeisians to eschew mention of the nationalistic goals of Zionism. They periodically threatened to "get out altogether" should nationalist elements predominate, and their fear of being charged with dual loyalty was at times all-consuming. At the American Jewish Congress meeting Mack "explained away certain misconceptions prevalent regarding the Zionist aims, and declared an independent statehood for Palestine. . . . to be 'an impractical and impossible dream.' " "We are now stressing the word homeland," deHaas informed Brandeis.[40]

Prior to the Schiff conference on the joint drive, the Executive Committee met to consider the instructions to be given the ZOA participants. It was proposed that they be allowed to reach a final agreement with the JDC, using a set of executive-approved guidelines. Emanuel Neumann, who would emerge as one of the leaders of the opposition to Brandeis, protested this arrangement. Neumann, then 26 and education director of the ZOA, did not oppose the guidelines' contents. He argued that the executive should have the opportunity to review a final agreement. Lipsky, who participated in the formulation of the guidelines and who would be present at the conference, opposed Neumann. He moved that the Zionist representatives be authorized to finalize an agreement with the JDC. Neumann requested that, contrary to general procedures, it be specifically recorded in the minutes that he voted against the motion.

Lipsky, it seems, did not consider his actions to constitute a violation of his assurances to the delegates of the 1919 convention that the administration had "re-established democratic methods of procedure," and that decisions would no longer be made by a select few. One can only surmise whether Lipsky would have supported Neumann's motion had Schiff been successful in barring him from participating in the conference.[41]

The International Aspects of the Conflict

As 1919 drew to an end the Americans became increasingly distressed by the disorganization and inefficiency they believed prevailed in the world Zionist headquarters in London. The Europeans, in turn, were angered by the Americans' failure to commit themselves totally to Zionism. For the Europeans, as for the East European party workers in New York, Zionism was their whole life. They were not uncomfortable with strong expressions of diaspora nationalism. These organizational and ideological differences would form the basis for the Brandeis-Weizmann dispute.

These tensions already marked American-London relations when Chaim Weizmann decided to convene a *jahreskonferenz*, an international conference of the Zionist executive. The question of American participation in the *jahreskonferenz*, originally scheduled for the winter of 1920, was discussed by the ZOA Executive Committee in December 1919. Brandeis opposed participation because:

the dates set for this Conference made it impossible for the officers and other Zionists having business or professional obligations in this

country to attend, the summer being the proper time for such Conference; that the financial situation of the Organization was critical
and that if the leaders left for Europe now the success of the drive
would be jeopardized; that the American Zionists were doing their
full and highest duty by staying to insure the success of the drive; that
the failure of the drive would jeopardize the whole future of the
movement.

Though the time probably was inopportune for Americans, Brandeis' opposition was based on a fear that the conference might adopt
some policy which would be "contrary to the views of the [American]
Organization." The presence of an American delegate would imply
ZOA support of the policies adopted. "If the [American] Organization
communicated in writing its views with regard to proper Palestinian
policy such a statement would be compromised by what any American
representative might say or fail to say at the Conference."

Brandeis assured the executive that if the Americans opposed a
decision, it could be altered in subsequent gatherings. They should,
therefore, not be concerned about not participating. Lipsky did not
believe the Americans could protest policies adopted at a meeting
which they had boycotted. He rejected Brandeis' argument that the
Americans could not afford to spare the personnel:

> In an explanation of his vote Mr. Lipsky stated that he favored
> sending a delegation because the excuse that men couldn't be spared
> from the drive would only be a reflection on the poverty of American
> leadership; that if the Conference adopted policies contrary to our
> drive slogans, the drive would be seriously injured; that the absence
> of American representatives to protest formally and publicly against
> action contrary to our views would prejudice our case in any later
> attempt to secure revision; that our delegates would attend but not
> vote and publicly explain their refusal to vote.[42]

The conference was postponed until the summer months. In the
interim the Europeans petitioned for invitations to America. Brandeis
vehemently opposed such visits. As the chasm between the European
and American leaders widened, the Brandeisians feared that Weizmann, Sokolow or Levin would strengthen the American opposition.
The Europeans would, they feared, reinforce diaspora nationalism;
"intensify Zionism in America" among the "rank and file [who would]

be delighted" if the Europeans would "come here"; and above all, "repel Schiff and those who have lately started to come into line."[43]

The administration offered the Europeans a variety of technical excuses for their opposition to the visits. When Weizmann requested an invitation to visit America in 1920, he was told that the ZOA was embarking on a fund-raising drive. His visit would force the executive to neglect the drive. This seems illogical. Weizmann's presence in America would not have hindered a drive; it would have aided it. In May, a month prior to the American delegation's departure for London, Weizmann was told that his visit would disrupt departure preparations. Brandeis recognized that a visit by Weizmann was "inevitable" and mused that there might be "advantages" in allowing the European leader to come in May. The visit would have to be short because of the delegation's departure. Brandeis suggested that an invitation be sent with the stipulation that the Americans would not change their plans to sail on June 12th. The invitation was cabled to Weizmann on May 6th. His visit, had he left immediately upon receipt of the cable, would have been quite short. Weizmann probably understood the reasons for the invitation and decided to postpone his visit.

Nordau and Levin also wished to visit the United States. deHaas called these requests for invitations "rather clever manoeuvere[s]" by the "other side." Lipsky was disturbed by the "bewilderment" that pervaded American Zionists about the Yishuv's future. The Europeans' presence might dispel this sense of confusion. deHaas reported to Brandeis that:

> Lipsky was strongly in favor of Nordau's [and the other leaders'] coming here. Wise hesitated and believed it was impossible to get a permit owing to Nordau having written something rash in 1914. Mack wavered between the question as to whether or not his coming would help to raise money. Flexner was entirely opposed.

Brandeis had the final word on the matter: "Send them to Argentina."[44]

Lipsky believed a "state of depression" afflicted Americans Jews due to the failure of the Balfour Declaration to be implemented and the lethargy of the American Zionist movement. In April 1920 the ZOA executive discussed the British incarceration of Vladimir Jabotinsky, the Yishuv leader. Lipsky argued that Zionist-sponsored protest meetings would remove the "present state of depression and bewilderment

. . . due to the situation in Palestine." The Brandeisians opposed Lipsky's suggestion of rallies to protest the arrest. Bernard Flexner, with whom Lipsky would eventually differ on a wide range of issues, believed such gatherings conducive to rash pronouncements. "Mr. Flexner . . . argued that . . . no public meetings could be so controlled as to eliminate the possibility of intemperate and dangerous utterances." "Intemperate and dangerous utterances" was a euphemism for statements in favor of the nationalist claims of diaspora Jewry. deHaas claimed that "Jewish protests were always discounted and that for that reason our present silence was perhaps more effective than demonstrations." The Brandeisians relented on the condition that the administration "issue instructions to the districts all over the United States on the resolutions which are to be adopted at demonstrations." "Carefully prepared resolutions" were to be adopted at these meetings. Nothing was to be left to chance.[45]

On April 18th the discussion at the executive meeting concerned payment of the delegates' expenses. This was the first time that a sizeable American delegation would attend an international Zionist conference. Lipsky reminded those at the meeting that delegates to previous congresses had been those who chanced to be in Europe at the time and persons of sufficient means to travel abroad. This "unfortunate" situation would be rectified by payment of delegates' expenses. No one would be prevented from participating because of financial considerations. Bernard Flexner, who vehemently opposed Lipsky's motion, was willing to make an exception for those individuals "indispensable to the business of the entire delegation." Lipsky would have certainly been included in the delegation. His opposition to Flexner's motion was not, therefore, personally motivated. Financial ability, he argued, should not determine who would fashion Zionist policy.[46]

Despite the fact that the East Europeans and the office staff were not yet a monolithic opposition group, the tension between them and the administration members increased as the time for departure drew near. Events at the London Conference would cement those differences.

Conclusion

The struggle between the East Europeans and the Brandeis forces increased after the London 1920 Conference and continued until the

Cleveland Convention in June 1921. There, opposition forces were able to counter the charisma of Brandeis' name with that of Weizmann's and successfully defeat the administration. Lipsky assumed the leadership of the American Zionist organization.

It is possible that the opposition would not have emerged victorious in 1921 had the Brandeis forces correctly anticipated the extent of the feelings of discontent which existed among Lipsky and his followers. The Brandeisians might have weakened the opposition by allowing the East Europeans to participate actively in policy formation. They might have given them the *koved* they believed their due and avoided treating them as "paid employees." Brandeis might have, on occasion, communicated with them directly and not through deHaas, though, in fairness, it must be noted that Brandeis also communicated with his own lieutenants through deHaas. These personality differences must be seen as the major factor in the emergence of the opposition.

However, even if Brandeis, Mack, Szold, Frankfurter, Flexner and the other Brandeisians had treated the East Europeans in a more solicitous manner, the conflict would not have been completely resolved. None of the East Europeans — Lipsky in particular — would ever have become permanent members of the Brandeisians' inner circle. They feared the East Europeans' diaspora nationalism and wished to avoid being tainted by this policy. The East Europeans believed that the Brandeis forces had, in their desire to avoid controversy, excised much of the essential from Zionism. Major ideological and tactical compromises would have been necessary in order to avoid this conflict. Once Weizmann entered the fray, the Brandeisians faced a formidable opponent.

For a few years after this convention Lipsky remained the leader of the ZOA. By the middle of the decade, individual followers of Brandeis began to return to the organization. In 1930 they reassumed control on the condition that Lipsky relinquish his position in the ZOA. Lipsky did so, but remained closely tied to the organization. By the middle of the 1930's he was once again an active force in it. However, just as he had been eclipsed early in his career by Magnes and Wise, and, in later years, by the Brandeisians, now he was eclipsed in prominence and power by new leaders such as Abba Hillel Silver, and old ones such as Stephen Wise, whose friendship with Franklin Roosevelt and his outspoken battle against Nazism made him an increasingly popular figure in the American Jewish community.

With the exception of a short period immediately following Cleveland, in the eyes of the Zionist public Lipsky remained *one* of the leaders of the American organization, but never *the* leader. June 1921 may be said to have been both the pinnacle and the watershed of his power in the movement.

FOOTNOTES

1. Jacob deHaas to Louis D. Brandeis, May 11, 1917; Minutes of Provisional Executive Committee for General Zionist Affairs, May 20, 1917, both in Louis D. Brandeis Papers, microfilm copy at Zionist Archives and Library, New York.

2. Louis Lipsky, " 'Zionizing' the Congress: The Instructions to the Zionists," *American Hebrew*, June 15, 1917.

3. Louis Lipsky, "Zionists and the Congress," *American Hebrew*, June 29, 1917.

4. Louis Lipsky, "The Zionist Convention: Monday Afternoon Session," *American Hebrew*, June 29, 1917; A.H. Fromenson, "A Monthly Review of the Zionist World: Twentieth Annual Convention of the Federation of American Zionists," *The Maccabean* 30 (August 1917): 328.

5. Lipsky, "Zionists and the Congress."

6. Lipsky, " 'Zionizing' the Congress."

7. *Ibid.*

8. *American Hebrew*, June 22, 1917; Lipsky, "The Zionist Convention."

9. *American Hebrew*, October 12 and 19, 1917; Louis Lipsky to Stephen Wise, September 28, 1917, and Wise to Lipsky, September 29, 1917, Brandeis Mss.

10. Stephen Wise to Louis Brandeis, September 8, 1917, *ibid.*

11. Lipsky to Wise, September 28, 1917, Stephen Samuel Wise Papers, American Jewish Historical Society, Waltham, Massachusetts; Wise to Brandeis, September 29, 1917, Brandeis Mss.

12. Louis Lipsky, "Postponement of the Congress," *The Maccabean* 30 (November 1917): 390-91.

13. Louis Lipsky, "The American Jewish Congress," *ibid.* 33 (January 1919): 3-4.

14. Yonathan Shapiro, *Leadership of the American Zionist Organization, 1897-1930* (Urbana, Ill., 1971), p. 120.

15. *Ibid.*, pp. 120 ff., 123.

16. Fromenson, "Monthly Review," p. 328. Lipsky had proposed re-organization plans in 1906, 1907 and 1908, all of which had included provisions for direct affiliation with a national office.

17. Louis Lipsky, "From Words to Deeds," *The Maccabean* 34 (December 1919): 333-34.

18. Jacob deHaas to Brandeis, January 25, 1919, Jacob deHaas Papers, Zionist Archives and Library, New York.

19. Lipsky, "From Words to Deeds," p. 332.

20. Minutes of ZOA Executive Committee, December 29, 1918, Bernard G. Richards Papers, Zionist Archives and Library, New York.

21. Jacobson to deHaas, February 11, 1919, Brandeis Mss; Horace Kallen to Julian Mack, Horace Meyer Kallen Papers, American Jewish Archives, Cincinnati, Ohio. Kallen's description of the Zionist organization as an "eleemosynary institution" is indicative of the differences between the Brandeisians and the East Europeans. The full-time party workers in New York and London would probably not have described the Zionist organization as a charitable entity; for them it was a national liberation movement.

22. Lipsky to Brandeis, February 11, 1919; Cowen to Brandeis, May 20, 1919; Jacobson to deHaas, August 8, 1919, all in Brandeis Mss.

23. Lipsky to Eddie Lipsky, August 13, 1919, Louis Lipsky Papers, in personal possession of Eleazar Lipsky.

24. Lipsky to Wise, August 19, 1919, Wise Mss.

25. Lipsky, "From Words to Deeds," pp. 333-34.

26. Minutes of ZOA Administrative Committee, January 15 and 21, 1919, and Lipsky to deHaas, January 23, 1919, Brandeis Mss; Cowen to Brandeis, January 21, 1919, Wise Mss.

27. Lipsky to FAZ Affiliated Societies, January 1918, FAZ Records, Zionist Archives and Library, New York; Lipsky to Brandeis, February 27, 1919, Brandeis Mss.

28. Lipsky to Brandeis, January 24 and February 27, 1919, ibid.

29. Lipsky to deHaas, January 23, 1919, ibid., American Hebrew, March 7, 1919; Louis Lipsky, "The Zionist Convention at Chicago: Summary Report," [n.p., n.d.]; Lipsky, "From Words to Deeds," p. 332; Meyer Weisgal, "The Zionist Convention in Chicago," The Maccabean 34 (December 1919): 349.

30. Shapiro, Leadership, pp. 120 ff.

31. Lipsky, "From Words to Deeds," pp. 334-35.

32. Shapiro, Leadership. p. 123.

33. Lipsky to Eddie Lipsky, August 27, 1919, Lipsky Mss.

34. Brandeis to Lipsky and deHaas, September 26, 1919, deHaas Mss; Lipsky to Brandeis, September 29 and October 22, 1919, Brandeis Mss.

35. Lipsky to Brandeis, May 2 and 8, June 3 and 4, July 8, 10 and 16, 1918, February 11, September 23 and October 22, 1919; Brandeis to Lipsky, June 28, 1918, three letters; Kesselman to Brandeis, May 24 and 28, 1919, all in Brandeis Mss.

36. Memorandum of conferences at Library of Justice Brandeis on November 1 and 15, 1917, Julian William Mack Papers, Zionist Archives and Library, New York. Wise to Mack, November 19 and December 6, 1917, and to deHaas, December 6, 1917, and Mack to Brandeis, December 2, 1919, deHaas Mss; memorandum, "Schiff," n.d., Wise Mss; deHaas to Brandeis, November 23, 1917, Brandeis Mss.

37. Minutes of ZOA Executive Committee, December 14, 1919, Mack Mss; Mack to Schiff, December 3, 1919, and Schiff to Mack, December 4, 1919, Brandeis Mss.

38. Mack to Schiff, December 5, 1919, and Schiff to Mack, December 5, 1919, ibid.

39. deHaas to Brandeis, March 24, 1920, ibid.

40. American Hebrew, December 20, 1918; deHaas to Brandeis, June 19, 1918, deHaas Mss.

41. Minutes of ZOA Executive Committee, December 14, 1919, Mack Mss.

42. Melvin I. Urofsky, American Zionism from Herzl to the Holocaust (New York, 1975), pp. 266 ff; Shapiro, Leadership, pp. 139 ff.

43. deHaas to Brandeis, February 29, 1920, deHaas Mss.

44. deHaas to Brandeis, February 29, 1920, and to Mack, March 24, 1920, ibid.; minutes of ZOA Executive Committee, April 23, 1920, Mack Mss.

45. Ibid.

46. Minutes of ZOA Executive Committee, March 28 and April 18, 1920, Mack Mss.

From Merger to Autonomy: Hadassah and the ZOA, 1918-1921

by Carol Bosworth Kutscher

Following the 1911 World Zionist Congress, the Zionist movement emphasized the establishment of practical projects in Palestine. This coincided with the interest in financial contributions to such projects on the part of middle- and upper-class American Jewish non-Zionists, who would not commit themselves to the nationalist aspects of the Zionist movement, but were interested in Palestine projects for philanthropic, religious, or sentimental reasons.[1]

Recognizing this receptivity, Louis Lipsky, president of the Federation of American Zionists, formulated the idea of the Zion Associations for men and Daughters of Zion for women. Their goal would be: "to bring into our organization every Jew in this city who sympathizes with our ideal, especially . . . Jews of means." These "business and professional men and women" the FAZ felt, would be primarily concerned with fund-raising for "Palestinian institutions" with the "large burden of active attendance" at Zionist club meetings.[2]

Even less was required of the Daughters of Zion because the FAZ leaders believed that "the organization and propaganda of Zionism [would] interest women less than men." Therefore, the women did not pay the shekel to the World Zionist Organization, did not send representatives to the FAZ Conventions or World Congresses, and, in short, did not have "to pay attention to Zionist problems." Their sphere was "to initiate Jewish educational and agricultural enterprises and welfare institutions in Palestine."[3]

The men's Zion Associations soon disappointed Lipsky's hope that they would show the FAZ's "increasing influence among the wealthier classes here."[4] The Daughters of Zion, however, was to have a differ-

ent destiny. On February 23 or 24, 1912, the Hadassah Chapter of the
Daughters of Zion was established, incorporating Miss Henrietta
Szold's Harlem-based study group, which had started in 1907. Even at
this founding meeting, newly-elected president Szold spoke of select-
ing a "definite project." The women finally chose to set up a district
visiting nurses' settlement house in Jerusalem to care for the health of
Jewish women and children. The "Hadassah Plan" envisioned that this
project would give Zionist women a sense of long-term commitment to
a real goal and to their own Zionist organization, and also enable the
new women's organization to enlist the financial support of middle-
class American Jewish women, especially non-Zionists. The appeal
would be three-fold: humanitarian, woman-to-woman, and religious.
The Hadassah practical project, it was hoped, would in time become
the contribution of American Jewish womanhood to the development
of the Jewish homeland.[5]

From its inception, Hadassah was critical of the FAZ, and the
attitude was reciprocated. Miss Szold implied that the men indulged in
excessive "debate and deliberation" at the expense of action, while in
contrast "the most idealistic women are more inclined to practical work
than anything else." Miss Szold and other Hadassah women were also
dissatisfied with the peripheral and hostess roles they had formerly
assumed in Zionist activities, despite their constitutional equality in
the movement. Moreover, they accurately characterized the FAZ as
inefficient, ineffective, disorganized, and riven by party factionalism.
The women's organization, on the other hand, they viewed as the
embodiment of all that was modern, American, scientific, and productive.[6]

Hadassah leaders, in turn, were "particularly sensitive" to the assertion that the Hadassah chapters were mere "collecting agencies" for a
medical "charity" which was a "necessary evil," and that Hadassah's
work was "not Zionist, but only Palestinian."[7] Some FAZ officers
nettled Miss Szold by accusing Hadassah leaders of not being concerned with the Zionist education of members, and "were themselves
not interested enough in the issue to appear at the Executive Committee meeting" to discuss the issue.

Criticism of Hadassah by the FAZ became inevitable when the
women began to shape an organization which was not simply a FAZ
money-getting creature, but presumed to create its own policies,
goals, and membership and to criticize FAZ and World Zionist Organi-

zation inadequacies. In addition, Lipsky probably resented Hadassah's successful appeals to middle-class non-Zionist women. Hadassah's achievement in this area emphasized FAZ failure to enlist such forces among American Jewish men, despite Lipsky's claim to World Zionist leaders that the FAZ was enjoying "increasing influence among the wealthier classes here."[8]

Shortly after the outbreak of World War I, the Provisional Executive Committee for General Zionist Affairs (or PEC) was formed with Louis D. Brandeis its chairman. The PEC was intended to serve as the temporary agent for the world Zionist movement which was split and almost paralyzed by the war. The leaders of the PEC were drawn from among wealthy, prominent professional, business and community leaders, unlike those of the FAZ. The latter organization immediately subordinated itself to the PEC, though retaining a kind of autonomous existence with its own leaders and domestic policies.[9]

Although there is no evidence of significant and continual personal guidance of Hadassah by Brandeis, Miss Szold and other Hadassah officers admired him, and the women felt that at last American Zionism was being directed by a kindred spirit. Brandeis in turn, shared Hadassah's emphasis on "the highest American standards," self-reliance, a pragmatic approach to problem-solving, and "absolute integrity." the PEC had such confidence in Hadassah that in 1916, after an urgent cable from the Actions Comité, the PEC placed Hadassah leaders in charge of organizing a medical unit for the Jews of Palestine.[10] When the war forced the closure of the Hadassah nurses' settlement, the women requested, and Brandeis granted them, the status of official fund-raiser for the American Zionist Medical Unit (AZMU). The Unit thus became the new Hadassah "practical project." The bulk of the Unit's budget, however, was provided by the elite non-Zionist Joint Distribution Committee.[11] Despite mutual Hadassah-FAZ criticism and tensions, under "pressure of new business" Hadassah received a modern business office from the men's organization in the same building with FAZ, PEC, and Jewish National Fund offices.

The conquest of Palestine convinced many American Zionists early in 1918 that the organization of the American Zionist movement should be changed to fit these new conditions. The creation of the Third Jewish Commonwealth now seemed achievable. But in order to secure the millions of dollars as well as the human resources for this "historic, compelling task," the American Zionist movement had to widen its "area of influence" to include "all the Zionist sentiment and allegiance in the United States." Most significantly for Hadassah, Article XVI of the ZOA constitution called for the repeal of the existing constitutions of "all constituent organizations and all by-laws thereto, and all resolutions not in conformity with the provisions of this Constitution."[12]

During June 1918, Hadassah and the FAZ held separate conventions in Pittsburgh to consider the proposed reorganization. Henrietta Szold publicly favored the merger. As early as August 1917, she had said that, "we should tend more and more to merge our Hadassah work with the Federation work . . . [during] this . . . crucial moment in Jewish life and . . . Zionist history." At a PEC meeting a few weeks before the Pittsburgh Convention, Miss Szold told Brandeis that "the separation of men and women in Zionism is highly undesirable, and that Hadassah had served its purpose."[13]

Nevertheless, her conviction was less than complete. At the Hadassah subconvention itself, Miss Szold told the delegates that "there is something in the Hadassah movement that is different from any other idea in the Zionist movement" and therefore we "must hold together until this district plan works out . . . and then we will find out definitely whether we are to continue to hold together." The Central Committee as well believed that "for the present, at least, there should be distinct women's groups" since "the problem of bringing Zionism before the American Jews is one which demands peculiar treatment."[14] It was only a few weeks after the merger that Miss Szold confided, "the disintegration of Hadassah" deprived her of "the heart" to circulate Miss Seligsberg's Palestine letter among the Central Committee.[15]

Although Hadassah Central Committee had entered the new ZOA with expectations of retaining control over their Palestine work, it was not to be. Immediately after the ZOA Organizing Convention, a set of Hadassah Subconvention resolutions was presented to the Administrative Committee of the ZOA. The resolutions and the responses to them indicate clearly the sources of Hadassah's immediate disillusionment.

Resolution I(3) said that the Hadassah convention delegates "desire to maintain the identity of the Hadassah Chapters within the District, the specific objects of the Hadassah Chapters to be directed as heretofore by a Central Committee acting under the National Executive Committee or one of its Departments; these objects to be in line with the Palestinian work hitherto done by Hadassah. . . ." The ZOA reply was that the Chapters could be maintained within the Districts, but only as "individual units subordinated to the District. . . . The Central Committee shall henceforth constitute an advisory body, to be called on in connection with the work to be done by the Hadassah Chapters within the Districts, under the Bureau for the Propaganda of Zionism among Women."

The resolution also provided that in addition to individual dues to the ZOA, the Chapters would collect $1.00 per member, to "be applied as the Hadassah Central Committee may decide." The ZOA rejected this, stating that "the Central Committee, by accepting the ruling of the Zionist Organization . . . has no power to define the use to which shall be applied the extra dollar."

Resolution II recommended the creation of "a sub-department for the propaganda of Zionism among women" in which the Central Committee would be represented. The sub-department would direct "the specific Zionist or Palestinian work now done or in future to be done by groups of Zionist women." Hadassah thus intended to maintain control of its own Palestinian work and also to gain new power over any such work done by other organizations. The ZOA agreed to the creation of a Bureau for the Propaganda of Zionism among Women, but "to this the former Central Committee will act in an advisory capacity . . . while this bureau will direct the propaganda for Zionism among women in America, it *will not* have any relation to the Palestinian Bureau." The consternation of the Central Committee can be imagined when it received the news that it could no longer control its Palestinian work, that it could act only in an advisory capacity to the Palestine Bureau, and then only "insofar as it concerns itself with Palestinian supplies."

Resolution II recommended that "all the American activities of Hadassah be taken over by the various Departments to be created by the new organization," and in this Hadassah offered its full support to the ZOA. Through what must have been a deliberate misreading, the Administrative Committee of the ZOA, "in accordance" with this resolution assigned to the various departments not only the American work, but also "(a) the Palestinian work (midwife service, trachoma treatment, Polioclinic Children's and Convalescents' Hospitals, Medical Unit) and (b) the work done in America for Palestine (sewing circles, etc.)"

When the women formally resolved to consider themselves "members of the District" in the work of "organization, propaganda, shekel, fund collecting, education, etc.," the ZOA answer was almost rude. It maintained that this resolution "needs no discussion. We hope that not even an exhortation is necessary. Every Hadassah member will naturally do her duty as a Zionist in America. That duty is defined by the new constitution."[16] The members of the Central Committee suddenly found themselves to be without goals, and without authority. Even the means of communication were denied them, since Hadassah no longer maintained a separate treasury, and the Bulletin had been discontinued. The ZOA *Maccabaean* did not report in any detail on Hadassah's specific opinions or activities.

It seems ironic that Brandeis, who had so respected the practical achievements and character of Hadassah, and who had given it the responsibility of forming and directing it, should have called for the effective destruction of that unique Hadassah character through formation of the ZOA. It is interesting to note that the pro-Brandeis Hadassah leadership never seemed to resent him for this, but transferred their hostility to the Lipsky-led ZOA of post-June 1921.

Several Hadassah officers were given positions in the new departments, namely, the Palestine Supplies Division of the Palestine Bureau, and the Bureau for Propaganda for Zionism among Women. Both women, however, were subordinate to ZOA male officers Jacob deHaas and Louis Lipsky. Only Miss Szold was made the full secretary of a ZOA Department, that of Education.

If the majority of Central Committee members felt discontented, impotent and unappreciated in their new roles, it could be endured for a while, but once the war-time exigencies for concerted action by all American Zionists had passed, many of Hadassah's founder-leaders would no longer feel that they owed self-sacrificing loyalty or total organizational subservience to the ZOA. The Central Committee would no longer be content with their merely advisory status. They considered their position "anomalous": "a well-organized, well disciplined body of women, constituting a very large part of the total number of shekel payers in the United States, . . . a body of women who worked much harder than most of the districts worked" yet who could not elect their own representatives to the ZOA conventions and who, "*as a unit*" had to "obey the mandate of the Convention in which they *as a unit* had had no voice."[17]

As an added insult, during the summer of 1919, when Brandeis and deHaas were in Europe and Palestine, "without their knowledge" the New York office of the ZOA began sending AZMU funds to the WZO London office, "instead of direct to Palestine." The London office proved unreliable in forwarding the money promptly and regularly, so that the AZMU staff was forced to endure much anguish and criticism.[18]

The period of 1918 to 1921 found Hadassah's membership increasing in numbers, while membership in the ZOA declined after the wartime peak in 1918.[19] The influence of the Brandeisist leadership on world Zionism continued, however, and Brandeis moved to effect a radical change in the WZO organization. In April 1920, at a conference in San Remo, the World War I allies, Great Britain, France, and Italy, confirmed the Balfour Declaration and resolved to incorporate it into Britain's Palestine mandate. Brandeis maintained, therefore, that the political phase of the Zionist movement had ended successfully; new economic and financial requirements of practical upbuilding of Palestine were now paramount. Brandeis wished to replace most of the veteran world leaders with a small council of practical, financial experts, not necessarily Zionists.[20]

Brandeis's conception of specialized, separate instrumentalities for each financial need of the Jewish homeland was rejected by the London Conference in 1920. Instead, the plan for the Keren Hayesod, or Foundation Fund, was adopted. The Keren Hayesod was designed to raise $125,000,000 during a five year period in order to speedily lay the foundation of the Jewish National Home. The broad, general fund would cover all purposes, including immigration and colonization.[21]

In America, Hadassah was still growing and beginning to reassert itself, only two years after its voluntary submergence in the ZOA. In March 1920, publication of the *Hadassah Newsletter* was begun, just 19 months after the Central Committee had discontinued its *Hadassah Bulletin*. In April 1921, the Hartford Chapter organized a state-wide Connecticut Federation which held its first conference in December 1920, and the Junior Hadassah was established formally in the same year.[22]

At the June 1921 ZOA Cleveland Convention, the Brandeis memorandum on policies of reorganization of the World Zionist Organization and opposition to the establishment of Keren Hayesod in the United States was defeated by a majority of almost two-thirds.

With the resignation of Brandeis and 94 officers, Louis Lipsky became the effective leader of the ZOA.

The pro-Brandeisist Hadassah women however, did not resign when their male colleagues did. Hadassah had gauged how very divided it was into pro- and anti-Keren Hayesod elements, and realized that a serious rift could destroy the organization. The Hadassah Central Committee, and Miss Szold in Palestine, were quite clearly supporters of Brandeis. Their most general complaint seems to have been that "the Europeans" lacked what Miss Szold called the Brandeisists' "high standards of probity and efficiency." She wrote to her family that she was on the Mack-Brandeis side because of her bitter experience with Zionist offices in Palestine being run on "nothing a month." The AZMU had been one of the institutions which suffered acutely from faulty transmission of funds from London.[23]

Miss Szold blamed the Unit's distress upon London's sloppiness and indifference to maintaining high American standards, and she feared that if the Europeans got exclusive control, more of the same could be expected. As an example, she deplored Menachem Ussishkin's desire to put an ophthalmologist on the AZMU staff because he had once delivered a good speech on Zionism, not because he was a first-rate ophthalmologist. She accused the European Zionists in Palestine of being "politicians first and practical workers afterwards."[24]

Not only leaders of the Keren Hayesod met with her disapproval; Miss Szold accused its supporters of being "grasping, selfish, self-indulgent, without a thought or feeling for the public." Therefore, she believed that independent projects like the AZMU must be encouraged. They "raise the standard of work" in Palestine—not just of Zionist work or work for the Jewish National Home—but of work for Jews and Arabs alike. Only this could eventually force the Mandatory Government to support establishment of a modern Public Health Department. The Foundation Fund seemed like the supreme folly to Miss Szold because it was attempting the impossible, namely, to set up in five years, by an all-out effort of the Jewish people, "such a strong autonomous community, that the Mandatory . . . would . . . acknowledge our superiority in all Governmental Administration, and resign in our favor."

Miss Szold herself felt that her alliance with the Brandeisists was a "wrench." She had always been sympathetic to the Russian-Jewish elements in American Zionism, and had always considered Diaspora cultural work a vital part of Zionist activity. Yet she felt compelled to recommend that the World Zionist Organization now cut off aid to cultural work and concentrate all its funds on the purely economic development of the Jewish National Home until after the crisis had passed in the development of Palestine. Just recently, Arab rioters had killed Jewish settlers and looted their shops and homes. Only the creation of economic opportunities for Jewish immigrants as well as Arab inhabitants could prevent further blood-letting.[25] Furthermore, as she saw the Balfour Declaration losing much of its promise in the face of restrictive immigration laws, she believed that if Jewish money could improve the economy of Palestine, the Mandatory would no longer exclude Jews on the grounds that the land could not feed more people.

However neutral the Hadassah leaders may have wished to appear to the chapters, those who mistrusted and disliked the Keren Hayesod did attempt to win the membership over to the idea that Hadassah must "obtain the whole Medical Unit." The Central Committee did not mention unreliability as the reason. They made it, instead, a matter of Hadassah pride, asserting that "Palestine refuses to call this American health service anything but 'Hadassah,' " and because of this identification of American health service with Hadassah, "the organized women Zionists of America strive for the membership and financial strength that would enable Hadassah to obtain the whole Medical Unit."[26] The Hadassah leaders who wanted direct financial control of the AZMU came increasingly to be advised by the ousted Brandeisists, especially Julian W. Mack.

Now that the Brandeis leaders had resigned, Louis Lipsky asked the Central Committee to cooperate in raising funds for Keren Hayesod. The Committee refused, with only two of the nine members supporting Lipsky's request. Lipsky then wrote, on June 22, 1921, that the seven dissenting women must resign for disobedience to the ZOA. When they refused, the ZOA wrote that it was "dissolving" the Central Committee. "The Seven" were expelled from the business office in the ZOA building, deprived of ZOA funds, and accused of secessionism.[27]

The Central Committee Seven continued as leaders, for they felt that only the Hadassah convention which had elected them could remove them. Various chapters wrote to the Committee to state on which side they stood. Adherents of both factions threatened secession—Brandeisist Chapters from the ZOA, and pro-ZOA Chapters from Hadassah. The Brandeisists financed a new temporary office until the November 1921 Hadassah convention could elect new officers or confirm the original seven. This uncertain situation continued until the September 1921 World Zionist Congress in Carlsbad.

In Carlsbad, the details of the Keren Hayesod's workings were finalized. Miss Szold petitioned the Congress to permit Hadassah alone to finance and manage the American Zionist Medical Unit for the coming year. This request was refused, although the Unit's name was changed to the Hadassah Medical Organization. In light of the fact that the JDC and ZOA had provided a major part of the Unit budget, it may have seemed presumptuous for the seven to ask the ZOA and the World Congress to hand the Unit over to them. The implication was that the women could trust only themselves and the deposed Brandeis group to maintain the Unit on high American standards.

Nevertheless, Keren Hayesod was given the task of funding the Unit. Hadassah would no longer be able to solicit for their special purpose; all fund-raising would have to be for the Keren Hayesod, and Hadassah would have only indirect financial connections with AZMU. The Brandeisist Hadassah women were certain that this would spell disaster to their organization and to the Unit, for the Keren Hayesod was not bound to the Unit, and was not dedicated to its support and excellence as Hadassah was. To increase Hadassah fears, "many" delegates to the Carlsbad Congress seemed to regret that the Keren Hayesod had to fund the Unit at all, and wished that the *American Hadassah or the Brandeis-Mack group*" would fund it as before. This, the women felt, did not bode well for the future of the Medical Unit.[28] After the Congress, the ZOA leadership seemed firmly in control and Keren Hayesod pledged itself fully in support of the men's organization. As to Hadassah, the leadership stood in doubt as to the future of their earliest and most important project. Hadassah looked forward to its November convention in order to resolve the problems raised at Carlsbad.

At the convention itself, little time was spent in actually discussing either the Keren Hayesod or specific Zionist policies. It was as though the women had vowed not to permit these problems to divide the organization. Perhaps the anti-ZOA leaders really were not interested in all the legalistic acrobatics which came so naturally to the many lawyers in the Brandeis-Mack group. They cared only in preventing the Keren Hayesod from taking over full control of the Unit. Larger issues and implications seem not to have interested them.

Alice Seligsberg, former Hadassah representative with AZMU, was one of the most outspoken anti-ZOA officers. In her report to the Convention, she hinted, and in effect, threatened, that the opponents of the Keren Hayesod would leave Hadassah if forced to raise funds for the allegedly untrustworthy, irresponsible fund and that this would "break Hadassah" during the convention. Miss Seligsberg spoke frequently in terms of "conscience," "scruples," and "convictions." Emotional pronouncements seem to have been more frequent amongst the Brandeisists, possibly a product of their feeling that they were a minority on the defensive. The ultimate threat of their secession was never openly made. Rather, they presented aggressively partisan amendments and resolutions and in other ways hammered home their feelings.

On the other hand, there were voices espousing loyalty to the ZOA and WZO, and there was anxiety that anti-Keren Hayesod expressions might be "detrimental to the Hadassah Organization." Several times attempts were made to get amendments passed which would put Hadassah on record as loyal to the ZOA, but these proposals were only made after the introduction of resolutions which seemed to derogate the fund and the ZOA.[29]

In an apparent attempt to maintain Hadassah neutrality, Alice Seligsberg introduced a constitutional amendment to prevent Hadassah representatives on the ZOA National Executive Committee from discussing those aspects of the Keren Hayesod which did not directly pertain to the Medical Unit. After more discussions, this constitutional amendment was abandoned and in its place, the Resolutions Committee was asked to request of the ZOA that Hadassah be exempt for one year and perhaps longer, from the requirement to provide representation at meetings of the ZOA Executive Committee. The resolution "aimed to promote unity in Hadassah."[30]

During a discussion of the constitutional provision for the date of the Hadassah Convention, (the provision read that it should be held at the same time and place as the ZOA's "whenever feasible"), a delegate from Buffalo requested that "whenever feasible" be struck out. Others were also alert to the separatist possibilities in this provision. They did not blindly trust the anti-ZOA leaders to frame a constitution in the best interests of "the majority of us [who] are intensely interested in the Zionist activities" at the ZOA Convention, but who could not afford to attend two conventions at different times.

Resolutions were then passed to the effect that all Hadassah collections would be sent directly to the Unit, rather than through the Keren Hayesod. Since all Hadassah's contributions could be deducted from the fund's $100,000 medical budget, it would then be responsible for supplying only the remainder. Anti-Keren Hayesod women felt that they were making "a great concession" by these resolutions, but they certainly did not deserve to be called, as they were by Miss Szold, "a complete expression of loyalty to the present policy of the World Zionist Organization." Apparently, however, this concession satisfied the women who had wished to raise funds for the Keren Hayesod.[31]

Perhaps the essence of the anti-Keren Hayesod opposition was that according to the simple "Hadassah Plan," American Zionist women must work for the establishment and support of modern health services in Palestine. For them, Zionism *was* this particular practical work. It is probable that the fiscal irregularities and general unreliability of which the Seven accused the Keren Hayesod were largely rationalizations; what determined their stance was the nine-year-old Hadassah principle that the women's organization must concentrate on its own Palestine project when working as an organization. Individual members were, of course, free to raise money for any other Zionist or non-Zionist project.

Evidence of the primacy of the "Hadassah Plan" in the motivation of the Seven was their secret emergency plan to resign from Hadassah and form a new women's Zionist organization. If this became necessary, they would again devote themselves to a new practical Palestine purpose, for example, the vocational training of orphans.[32] The anti-Keren Hayesod Hadassah women could not see how collecting for the unspecific, variegated needs of the Keren Hayesod could fire the women's imagination and elicit their organized activity. Nor could it provide a sense of personal responsibility on an enduring basis.

The Central Committee Seven adhered ferociously to the idea of full control of the Unit, and of Hadassah finances, as the only basis of the organization's self-respect. Their self-image of doer, and practical mover, required that the Unit be a living embodiment of the tangible modern improvement in Palestine life brought about by efficient, thrifty American women. The Unit was the motive power which would lift the women's organization to national prominence and fame, after years of submergence in the ZOA. The women's desire for praise, authority and recognition as equals within the Zionist movement and among American women's organizations should not be underestimated. As Miss Seligsberg said, Hadassah wanted the recognition and the "power that those possess who hold the purse strings."[33]

As soon as these issues had been decided, Mrs. Gertrude Rosenblatt composed a cablegram to Henrietta Szold, "HADASSAH united for Medical Unit." Now Hadassah could devote itself almost exclusively to its special Palestine health projects without the distraction of fund-raising for the Keren Hayesod and other WZO funds.

Another important convention issue concerned the amount of membership dues, and the different purposes for which they should be designated. Some were willing to pay part of their dues to the ZOA and its districts. Others wanted to spend all dues on the Palestine work. Many delegates objected to doing anything more than paying the dollar shekel to the World Zionist Organization and perhaps a small portion of Hadassah dues to the ZOA. Some claimed that dues were so expensive that they kept interested women from joining. Furthermore, Hadassah was scattering its resources over many "administrations," and not leaving itself enough money for the Palestine purpose, for which, as one delegate thought, Hadassah had been organized in the first place.[34]

One delegate blamed this unwillingness to support the ZOA and its districts on the deep-seated, almost unconscious non-Zionism of many Hadassah women. "The great battle ideal to them is the philanthropy work." They are "staggered," therefore, when they suddenly realize that the extra dollar which Hadassah asked for dues was not going to Hadassah's work but to local administrative purposes.

The spectre of non-Zionism thus haunted Hadassah three years after it had merged with the ZOA! However, even the ardent "secessionists" on the Central Committee, those who fiercely criticized the ZOA and WZO because of the "corrupt" Keren Hayesod, were nevertheless anxious that Hadassah get full representation at ZOA Conventions, World Congresses and Conferences. Only this seemingly contradictory course of action could enable the women to exert any influence over ZOA and WZO policies, especially during this period of lack of harmony with the Lipsky administration. On the strength of this consideration, even the anti-Lipsky members finally agreed that 50¢ of

Hadassah dues would continue to be paid for district membership in the ZOA. Now of the $4 chapter dues, a total of $1 would be paid to the ZOA, and $1 to the World Organization.

These financial demonstrations of Hadassah loyalty to the ZOA were not sufficient to overcome the divisive elements in their relationships which produced the one significant convention failure. Hadassah had sought to achieve recognition by the ZOA as its sole agency for Zionist work among American women. This recognition was not granted and its competitor, the Keren Hayesod Women's Committee, remained an irritant for several more years.[35]

So that the animosity caused by Lipsky's dismissal of the Seven might not be revived at the Convention, there were no specific references to that incident. However, in order to prevent repetitions of dismissal for disobedience to the ZOA Constitution, the Convention resolved that "no outside power shall have the right to prevent" the "functioning" of Hadassah National Board members who are duly elected by and responsible solely to the Hadassah Conventions.[36]

The majority of Hadassah members, although in sympathy with the aims of Keren Hayesod, must have stood somewhat in awe of the Central Committee Seven who so resembled their male Brandeisist counterparts—an influential, prestigious, closely-knit group. The Central Committee Seven, and their sympathizers, had solid organizational and practical achievements to their credit; the pro-ZOA majority may have feared the consequences to the organization should the anti-Keren Hayesod Central Committeewomen quit Hadassah. Far better to risk ZOA and even WZO censure as "secessionist" or "separatist" than to lose such unquestionably talented and dedicated leadership. Nor were the ultimate goals of the anti-Keren Hayesod leaders uncongenial to the members; in effect, the leaders were calling for a return to the kind of autonomy in finances and Palestine work that Hadassah had possessed before the war compelled the submergence of Hadassah in the ZOA.

At the convention's conclusion, Miss Seligsberg and the various new officers expressed their feelings of pride and inspiration that Hadassah women could maintain their unity, although the men's movement had been deeply divided. Harmony within was a traditional ideal of American women's clubs; strife caused shame and must be concealed, with at least surface harmony before the eyes of the world.[37] The 1921 convention marked the beginning of Hadassah's rise to national prominence.

It demonstrated the validity and the viability of Hadassah's principle that women could best further Zionist goals by working within their own organization, doing practical work in Palestine. From this time on there could be no halting Hadassah in its rise to its eventual position of eminence—among American Jewish women, in the Zionist movement, and in medical work in the Jewish Homeland.

FOOTNOTES

1. Ben-Zion Mossinsohn, "Report on Zionism in the United States of America, to Actions Comite," July 2, 1912, p. 2, Records of the Central Zionist Office, Berling, Z3/754, Central Zionist Archives, Jerusalem.

2. FAZ Circular #12, August 1911, cited in Evyatar Friesel, *HaTenuah HaTsionit BeArtsot HaBerith BaShanim 1897-1914* (Tel Aviv, 1970), p. 287, n.20; FAZ Executive Committee Minutes, June 13, 1912, Central Zionist Office, Z3/755.

3. FAZ Circular #2, VIII/1911 cited in Friesel, *HaTenuah*, p. 175.

4. Louis Lipsky to Actions Comité, April 14, 1912, Central Zionist Office, Z3/754.

5. Gertrude Goldsmith Rosenblatt, "Notes on the Early Days of Hadassah, Extract from Diaries, 1911-1914," unpublished typescript, Henrietta Szold Papers, A125/3, Central Zionist Archives, Jerusalem; *Maccabaean*, (July 1913): 203-204, and May 1913, p. 139.

6. Carol Bosworth Kutscher, "The Early Years of Hadassah, 1912-1922," doctoral dissertation (Brandeis University, 1976), p. 134; *Hadassah Bulletin*, August 1918, pp. 8, 5; *Maccabaean*, May 1913, p. 138 and July 1913, pp. 203-204.

7. *Hadassah Bulletin*, June 1917; *Maccabaean*, May 1913, p. 137.

8. Henrietta Szold to jessie Sampter, October 29, 1917, Szold Papers; Kutscher, "Early Years of Hadassah," p. 148; Louis Lipsky to Actions Comité, April 14, 1912, Central Zionist Office, Z3/754.

9. Louis Lipsky, *Selected Works of Louis Lipsky*. Vol. I, *Thirty Years of American Zionism* (New York, 1927), p. 75.

10. Rose Jacobs, Introduction to Horace Kallen, *The Faith of Louis D. Brandeis, Zionist* (New York, 1943), pp. 2-4; *Maccabaean*, February 1917, p. 148; American Zionist Medical Unit Report, June 1916-June 1919 (New York, 1919), p. 5.

11. AZMU Report, 1919, pp. 7-8.

12. Jacob deHaas, *Louis D. Brandeis: A Biographical Sketch* (New York, 1929), p. 69; Louis Lipsky, "The District Organization Plan," *Maccabaean*, June 1918, pp. 158-159, and August 1918, pp. 258-260.

13. *Hadassah Bulletin*, August 1917, p. 15; *Maccabaean*, July 1913, p. 193.

14. Minutes of Hadassah Subconvention, 1918, Hadassah Archives, New York City; *Hadassah Bulletin*, April 1918, p. 8.

15. Henrietta Szold to Jessie Sampter, August 16, 1918, Szold Papers. Miss Seligsberg, helping to direct AZMU in Palestine, had been reporting on the Unit's progress in letters to Miss Szold.

16. *Hadassah Bulletin*, August 1919, pp. 1-4.

17. Alice Seligsberg, "Report of the Chairman of the Central Committee of Hadassah to the November 1921 Hadassah Convention," Hadassah Archives.

18. *Ibid*.

19. Yonathan Shapiro, *Leadership of the American Zionist Organization, 1897-1930* (Urbanna, 1971), p. 80.

20. Harry Sackler, "The Zionist Conference in London," *Maccabaean*, September 1920, p. 85.

21. I.A. Naiditch, "The Great Needs of the Hour," *Maccabaean*, September 1920, pp. 66-68, 99.

22. Donald Herbert Miller, "A History of Hadassah, 1912-1935," doctoral dissertation (New York University, 1968), p. 115; *Hadassah Newsletter,* February 1921, p. 4.

23. Miller, "A History of Hadassah, " p. 132; H. Szold to Julian Mack, June 5, 1921, and to her family, June 26, 1921, Szold Papers.

24. Henrietta Szold to Alice Seligsberg, July 16, 1921, p. 16, Szold Papers; Minutes of ZOA Convention, June 1921, Zionist Archives and Library, New York City.

25. Henrietta Szold to her family, June 22 and 26, 1921, and to Alice Seligsberg, July 16, 1921, Szold Papers.

26. *Hadassah Newsletter,* March 1921, pp. 1-2.

27. Miller, "A History of Hadassah," pp. 123-124, 128.

28. Seligsberg, "Chairman's Report."

29. Minutes of Hadassah Convention, 1921, Hadassah Archives.

30. *Ibid.;* A.H. Vixman, "A Word about the Convention Resolutions Adopted at the Hadassah Convention," *Jewish Criterion,* 1921, Szold Papers, A125/20.

31. Hadassah Convention Minutes, 1921; Henrietta Szold to Mrs. Richard Gottheil, October 26, 1922, Szold Papers, A125/20.

32. Alice Seligsberg, "Confidential Invitation to Pre-Hadassah Convention Meeting of Anti-Keren Hayesod Members," Hadassah Archives.

33. Seligsberg, "Report to the New York Chapter," January 1922, Hadassah Archives.

34. Minutes of Hadassah Convention, 1921.

35. Henrietta Szold to Mrs. R. Gottheil, October 26, 1922, Szold Papers, A125/20.

36. Miller, "A History of Hadassah," pp. 137-139.

37. Joseph Woodward, "Women's Clubs from a Reporter's Point of View," *The Club Woman* (December 1898) cited in William O'Neill, *The Woman Movement: Feminism in the United States and England* (Chicago, 1969), p. 145.

"Washington versus Pinsk": The Brandeis-Weizmann Dispute"

by Esther L. Panitz

"Washington versus Pinsk" is a convenient rubric with which to encompass all those divergent philosophies and beliefs which separated Chaim Weizmann from Louis Dembitz Brandeis in their respective pursuits of the Zionist dream. It is an appropriate slogan because in three words it sums up two differing orientations to life in general, and to Zionism in particular. It indicates an essential clash of wills and personalities, so that basically the same material with which each man had to work in fashioning a viable Jewish existence in Palestine was transformed into two separate entities.

It is practical to determine the true outside parameters in time for this Weizmann-Brandeis controversy, simply because it paraphrases many of the same differences which plagued the Zionist comprehensions of those early giants in the movement. Even after the crisis, when Justice Brandeis and his followers resigned *en masse* from the World Zionist Organization, these differences remained in theory, if not in practice, to plague all who would seek definitions for such imponderables as "who is a true Jew?" or "what is genuine Zionism?"

Various interpretations of Zionism have made such disputations as the Weizmann-Brandeis controversy inevitable. Did Zionism mean a world-wide spiritual awakening, or a physical, creative and political renascence in the Jews' own homeland, or both? How were the Zionist goals to be accomplished, through work in Diaspora which would stir the national consciousness of the Jewish people, or through political diplomacy based on the notion that the Jews already possessed nationhood? Or should the emphasis have been on cultural enlightenment abroad and settlement in Eretz Israel simultaneously?

77

In this connection it is well to remember the bases from which
Herzlian Zionism proceeded. According to that perspective, Jews
were perpetually and ineradicably aliens in all the lands of their
dispersion. Therefore it became necessary for them to leave those
countries where their very existence constituted an obstacle to the
social peace and stability of the environment. Herzl's original contribution to Zionism consisted precisely in crystallizing this theme. The
world would finally come to recognize the legitimacy of Jewish existence, only if the Jews were granted sovereign rights in a territory of
their own, one in which all the appurtenances of statehood would
ultimately be realized. To this end, Herzl insisted upon the need for a
charter legitimizing those rights.

For their part, Herzl's critics, the practical Zionists, were convinced
that settlement and colonization whether piecemeal, or at one fell
swoop, had to proceed at all costs. Though he never eschewed political
diplomacy, and in fact, became the Zionist diplomat *par excellence* in
the chanceries of the English-speaking West, Chaim Weizmann really
sided with the "practicians." It may well be that Weizmann's view of
Zionism was so much broader and deeper than Herzl's for two reasons.
First, Weizmann did come from Pinsk. All the age-old longings for a
return to Zion, made manifest through a resettlement of the land, were
his more uniquely than they were Herzl's. Herzl's notions of Jewish
redemption proceeded from the rootless misery of his people, Weizmann's from their nascent spiritual creativity. Second, Weizmann's
orientation to Zionism was bolstered by the views of his mentor, Ahad
Ha-am. One can, of course, argue cogently that for Ahad Ha-am
spiritual and cultural Zionism became an end in itself. He bore no
illusions about the return of Jews to their homeland. He was convinced
that the majority would remain in the Diaspora, and was therefore
intent upon securing other means than religion by which to maintain
the nationality of the Jews. For him, the Jewish ethos was to be
preserved by an educational means, an effort which in turn would
prepare the Jews for settlement in the *Yishuv*. Weizmann imbibed
enough of this well-spring of Ahad'Ha'amian thought to be
strengthened in his own conviction: that all the creatively intellectual
impulses in Jewish life had to be nurtured and fostered. But he was
impatient, and went beyond Ahad Ha-am. Weizmann would not wait
forever to return to the land. In coining the words "synthetic Zionism,"
Weizmann meant to draw upon the sources available to him to further

the Zionist ideal: the diplomacy of Herzl, the practical applications of colonization, and the creative intensity of Ahad Ha-am's cultural Zionism, its Diaspora nationalism.[1]

Such considerations were alien to Brandeis. This is no way impugns his love for the Jewish people, or his loyalty to Zion. But Brandeis' background was such that he would never have been able to consider the enormity of the choice among these options: cultural, practical, or diplomatic Zionism. By now, writers have detailed the ways in which the Justice came to Zionism, including his sympathy for the Jewish immigrant masses which the famous New York garment strike first awoke in him and his "conversion" to Zionist thought at the hands of Jacob deHaas, Boston editor and one-time secretary to Theodor Herzl in London. Brandeis' step-by-step ascendancy to assume the leadership of the American Zionist movement has also been carefully pinpointed. He brought to Zionism his own progressive philosophy, based on that American pragmatic premise that without men, money, and discipline nothing would ever be accomplished.[2] Incidentally, this also meant that whenever he chose to, Brandeis also resorted to diplomacy and practical work in resettling the *Yishuv*. Unfortunately, it was precisely when he had to spell out his pragmatic philosophy, or more accurately, when his followers spelled it out in his stead, that the crisis in his relations with Weizmann occurred.

In the beginning, all went smoothly.[3] At the very outset of the war, Weizmann's pro-Allied sympathies prompted him to urge Brandeis, and the American Provisional Executive Committee which he headed, to assume complete power over Zionist affairs. Despite the pro-German sympathies of the Jewish masses in America and the pessimistic evaluations of some European Zionists that the Allies were on the losing side, Weizmann sincerely believed that the future of Zionism lay with the western democracies. In this regard, his message to Brandeis struck a responsive chord, for there had never been any doubt as to the Justice's sympathies, and he was only too happy to comply with Weizmann's requests.[4]

In April, 1917, Weizmann informed Brandeis of a secret agreement between England and France which would have given France protectorate rights over northern Syria and parts of Palestine down to Lake Tiberias, while the rest of the country would be internationalized. This would have condemned the Jewish settlements in the north to an inhospitable French administration, while any hopes for a viable future for the rest of the country, insofar as Jews were concerned, would have been obliterated. Shortly before this dispatch, Brandeis also received other communications from Weizmann, James de Rothschild, and Joseph Cowen, which reassured him of the good intentions of certain influential Britishers as to the likelihood of securing a British protectorate, guaranteeing a Jewish National Home in Palestine. One of these messages went so far as to deplore what had been taken as precipitate action by American Zionists, urging the creation of a Jewish republic in Palestine. The burden of all these communications to Brandeis was for him to secure official governmental approval and popular Jewish support for the creation of a British mandate in Palestine, considered to be the first, indispensable requisite for the creation of a Jewish homeland.[5]

State Department opposition and President Wilson's hazy responses to Jewish nationalist ambitions made it doubly difficult for Brandeis to comply with this request. But comply he did, in spite of his position on the bench. Brandeis replied that American Zionists stood solidly behind their British colleagues. Brandeis later wrote that his talks with Balfour and his aides, during their visit to the United States, and with President Wilson, were encouraging. Historians, reconstructing Brandeis' conversation with the British minister agree that both men saw eye to eye on the "ethical purposes and practicalities of Zionism." Further, Brandeis himself insisted that Zionist sympathies on the part of American Jews would carry the day, despite opposition from American Jewish financiers or Jewish socialists.[6]

When Weizmann sent Brandeis an early version of the Balfour Declaration, the Americans objected to implications that non-Zionists and others might be dissatisfied with those governments to whom they had pledged allegiance as citizens. In this, Brandeis and his followers showed themselves to be as sensitive to the alleged imputations of disloyalty as some non-Zionists and anti-Zionists. Accordingly, they insisted upon eliminating any suggestions or nuances which might have shed doubts on the status of Jews as citizens in the democratic West. It has also been contended that Brandeis changed the words, "Jewish race," to read "Jewish people," though there may be sufficient evidence to prove that earlier Nahum Sokolow, obviously astute enough to realize the greater prudence inherent in the term "Jewish people" used that expression before Brandeis did.[7] In any event, American Zionists endorsed this formulation. Yet Brandeis, who earlier had acknowledged the indissoluble ties of "blood" among Jews, and later in communication with Cecil Spring-Rice, the British ambassador to Washington, continued to refer to them as members of the Jewish "race", seemed content with the new wording, which later became part of the Balfour Declaration.[8]

Yet no sooner had that famous proclamation been issued, than the rift between Brandeis and Weizmann began to widen. Its roots lay deeply imbedded in their different approaches to Zionist ends and means. More immediately, the divergences between Weizmann and Brandeis may also have resulted from differing American and British diplomatic comprehensions.

During the opening phases of the war, Secretary of State Robert Lansing had insisted upon strict neutrality for America in its relations with Turkey. Now that the Declaration had been issued, he cautioned President Wilson to keep silent and withhold his support. Though Lansing's request for presidential silence hinged in part on his animus towards the Jews, he also urged the President to stress the peaceful relations between Turkey and America. These countries were not at war with one another, and since Palestine was Turkish territory, it would not be fitting for America to intervene in any way. So successful was Lansing in tying Wilson's hands that it was not until ten months later, in August 1918, after Rabbi Stephen S. Wise had succeeded to the chairmanship of the Provisional Committee, that the President agreed to the tenets of the Balfour Declaration.[9]

Meanwhile, Weizmann and his European followers were eager to implement the Balfour Declaration. The British Foreign Office was also intent upon using this document to further its war policy. Both goals were uppermost in Weizmann's mind when he sent Aaron Aaronsohn, botanist, agricultural expert, the discoverer of wild wheat, and Jewish spy, to serve as liaison officer between Britain and the United States in Zionist affairs. Aaronsohn was personally accredited to Brandeis, and was instructed to spur Zionist interests on behalf of Palestine; Aaronsohn's mission also was part of a larger operation to insure Allied success. This was also true of the British decision to send an investigative commission to Palestine under Weizmann's auspices. Weizmann wanted American representation on this British-sponsored Zionist mission to Palestine, but Brandeis hung back. Weizmann decried his "changed attitude," while Brandeis reminded Weizmann of American neutrality. Indeed, he had no choice in the matter. Secretary Lansing refused to allow any American to participate in the Zionist mission in any official capacity, although in the end, an American assistant to the Zionists, Walter Meyer, did join the expedition.[10]

Brandeis' reticence to leave for Europe and Palestine did not grow from any diminished faith in the idealism that spelled Zion. Of this he was certain, even though at an earlier date he may have implied that American Jewry was not eager to share responsibility with the British in overseeing a Jewish settlement in Palestine. On the contrary, his hesistancy stemmed not from an official ruling, which he could hardly defy, but also from an interpretation of Lansing's neutrality. Clearly, the Secretary's attitude was also intended as a signal, disguising latent anti-Zionist prejudices. There were still Christian missionaries in Lebanon to be pacified; and American commercial interests in Palestine to be safeguarded. Viewed from the State Department perspective, issues of Jews and Zionism were miniscule matters. Official American involvement in such concerns would magnify them beyond their due proportions, or worse, would antagonize the Christian and Arab population in what were still Turkish territories.[11] Brandeis, with his close ties to President Wilson and his advisor, Colonel House, could do little else but advocate Zionist goals privately while publicly acceding to State Department policy. Weizmann, although equally close to the sources of power, was so much the Zionist and Anglophile, that when necessary he would clutch at straws to achieve his objectives. For this reason, he was chagrined at Brandeis' refusal to become involved in the Zionist Commission which went to Palestine in the spring of 1918.

Brandeis finally did visit Palestine in the summer of 1919, at the request of his aide and brilliant legal colleague, Felix Frankfurter, then representing the American Zionists at the Paris Peace Conference. At that time, technical advisors to the American delegation at the Peace Conference had been busy whittling away at Zionist proposals for a mandated settlement of the Yishuv. Therefore, Brandeis went to Palestine, and while abroad, tried to mend political fences both in Paris and London. Precisely because Brandeis was on the continent when the American delegation was being overwhelmed by floods of pro-Arab and pro-Christian propaganda, he was able to exert a strong Zionist counterbalance.

Lest we be betrayed into thinking that such bits and pieces were at best piecemeal offerings on the altar of Zionist implementations, it is well to remember that each of Brandeis' actions was complete in itself. Brandeisian thought was perhaps best perceived in the American Zionist Pittsburgh Platform, written in 1918. Its proposals sound, prophetically, like constituent aspects of Israeli society today. It called for the civil and political equality of all residents in Palestine, regardless of race, sex, or faith; it advocated public ownership of utilities and natural resources; it urged that land be leased to the whole people of Israel; it wanted to establish agricultural, industrial, commercial, and financial enterprises on a cooperative basis. Such provisos also guaranteed free education at all levels, and hoped to secure Hebrew as the national language.

European Zionists looked askance at this program. Its American, progressive tone evoked little sympathetic response from Jewish intellectuals on the continent, who were taken with notions of a Hebraic renascence. The very nature of the proposals downgraded the aspirations of affluent Jewish middle class entrepreneurs, who saw Palestine as another golden opportunity for investment, while it salved their consciences by guaranteeing a haven for persecuted Jews. "Men like Weizmann," we are told, would have had the battle for Zionism joined on issues other than the "social doctrines" inherent in the proposals of the Pittsburgh Platform. The document was also suspect in certain quarters, for it disregarded the concerns of the religious groups in the Zionist world, and ignored the yearnings of the Jewish masses, who, after all, were the human material in Weizmann's considerations of Zionism.[12] For him, these people were not merely so many thousands, whose homelessness was to be cured by pragmatically adept programs. "From the beginning," Weizmann wrote in his memoir, "I had looked upon Zionism as a force for life and creativity residing in the Jewish masses. It was not simply the blind need of an exiled people for a home of its own. I could not agree with Herzl that . . . the tragedy of Jewish homelessness, persecution and poverty, was sufficient to account for the Zionist Movement. . . . Need alone is negative, and the greatest productions of man spring from an affirmation. Jewish homelessness was not just a physical discomfort; it was also . . . the malaise of frustrated capacities. If the Jewish people had survived so many centuries of exile, it was . . . because it would not relinquish its creative capacities."[13]

Of course, when it came to philosophic abstractions, Brandeis was able along with the others to speak in terms of a reawakening and of reforging the Jewish spirit, the Jewish consciousness. But when it came to dealing with the people itself, the Jewish masses in Europe, Brandeis stood aside. He loved his people; on his first visit to Palestine he was emotionally stirred, as he had never been before. Yet as a leader, he was always *for* the people; he was not *of* them. For Weizmann, there was never any separation betweeen intellectual, psychological, and emotional comprehensions of Zionism and the Jewish people itself. This should be borne in mind when later on, Brandeis and the Americans accused Weizmann and his colleagues of garbling Zionist ends and means. Precisely because there were no demarcations for Weizmann, because he would not be immobilized over problems of dual allegiance, his practical plans for Palestine may have fallen short of ultimate expectations. It is true that Brandeis thought in Herzlian terms of settling the land, and Weizmann wanted a step-by-step fulfillment of the Zionists' dream. Weizmann was neither a Nordau, nor a Jabotinsky, nor an Ussischkin, and he was not prepared to accept a catastrophic view of Zionism which wanted to see the gates of Palestine opened at once to all of Eastern Europe's persecuted Jewish thousands. Yet he was prepared to take risks; for him, tomorrow would have been too late for the *Yishuv* to lead a normative existence. For him, then, everything else was prostrate before the Zionist dream. Simply because he gave all of his energies to the movement, sometimes with little heed to logic, he was subjected to bitter criticism.

When the war ended, Weizmann seemed beset by contradictory impulses towards Brandeis. On the one hand, he wanted the Justice to come to the Paris Peace Conference, to represent the Zionists, and to share the authority for world Zionist affairs. On the other hand, however, Weizmann felt that Brandeis failed to comprehend the impact of the Declaration correctly, and that Brandeis was mistaken in his belief that the document had solved the political problems confronting the Zionists.[14] Yet how could one like Brandeis, who in Weizmann's eyes was mistaken in his estimate of the Zionist situation, have shared the presidency of the World Zionist Organization with him? How could the two men work together when they held such divergent views of the movement?

What were those views, and why did they finally destroy the personal relationship between Brandeis and Weizmann? To say that Brandeis immediately wanted to apply business-like arrangements to make the *yishuv* a going concern, because the Balfour Declaration and the Mandate established at San Remo had cleared away preliminary obstacles, merely skirts the issue of his differences with Weizmann. At the heart of the matter is that both men viewed Zionism through different lenses. Brandeis came from an American milieu, and it would have been practically impossible for him to have acquired that inner national mystique, that tenor of Zionist times, so dear to Weizmann and the Europeans. Secondly, he recognized in Zionism American principles of equal justice for all and of social democracy, and it was most natural for him to emphasize these aspects of Zionism to the exclusion of others which held a special appeal for the suffering Jews of Europe. Brandeis' singular contribution was to identify these American tenets with the roots of Zionism, and with Judaism itself, and making that identification, to enlarge upon the dynamism of American idealism so that it could include the nationalistic aspirations of homeless peoples, such as the Jews. This meant, essentially, that for American Jews there were to be no accusations of dual loyalties.[15] For Brandeis, possible statehood in Palestine in no way impugned the allegiances of American, or other Jews in the Diaspora, ot their countries of origin or residence. In the knowledge that they were free citizens in a free land, American Jews would be able to contribute their best talents to the shaping of a national home in Palestine for the Jewish people. In Brandeisian terms, even if that home were to be transformed to a political entity in the distant future, charges of unfaithfulness to America were not to be laid at the feet of its Jews. Brandeis was undoubtedly influenced in his thinking by Horace Kallen, whose emphasis on cultural pluralism made it possible for various immigrant groups in America to nurture dreams of peoplehood for members of similar ethnic origins.[16] In this sense too, then, Brandeis never tired of thinking of his brethren as one people.

Yet he was also a practical men and his plans for radical alterations in the management of the *Yishuv* called for a total de-emphasis on the political and even on the nationalistic elements in the entity that was to become Israel. This naturally infuriated Weizmann and his colleagues, who viewed the Brandeisian economic schemes as tantamount to the destruction of Zionist principles themselves. Yet there are two factors to be marshalled in Brandeis' defense. His earlier battle to fashion a unified American Jewish Congress, one reflecting a valid Jewish consensus, strengthened his abiding belief in the need for compromise to achieve significant results.[17] He knew also that Palestine would first

have to become economically viable. After that, with success on the
wing, he would be able to deal with matters of the spirit, of the intellect
and of political yearnings. Furthermore, the disappointing lessons in
foreign policy revealed at Paris must have taught him the need to
emphasize only what could be counted as a practical achievement. If,
at the London Zionist Conference in 1920, he had declared that the
decision taken at San Remo to hand over the mandate to Great Britain
and the appointment of a Jew to the High Commissioner's post had
obviated all political issues, it was not that he was a trusting *naif* of the
Allied Powers. Rather, he saw the necessity to proceed in a *yishuv* that
desperately needed social and economic expansion.

When Brandeis had visited Palestine in 1919, he had been appalled
at the enormous need to modernize the country in order to make it fit
for human habitation. He was also outraged at the anti-Zionist orientation of the British governmental administration in the land. The Paris
peace negotiations had also revealed a progressive weakening of the
original Zionist proposals to establish a Jewish commonwealth.[18]
Brandeis, at the 1920 London Conference, therefore had no choice but
to downgrade all political aspects of the projected mandatory system.
Trying to salvage what he could, he wanted to emphasize the social and
economic development of the *Yishuv*. The tide had been running
against the Zionists, not was it even banked by the appointment of a
Jew, Sir Herbert Samuel, as High Commissioner for Palestine. Under
the circumstances, it may have been politically wise for the Justice
publicly to abjure any political considerations in the development of
the *yishuv*. At the same time, perhaps he honestly believed that the
issue of political battling to realize the Zionist dream was over; nothing
more could come ot it. When he said as much at the Zionist Conference, though, his words backfired. That in certain ways his London
Plan was an extension of the Zionists' earlier proposals to the Peace
Conference compounds the irony.

The Mandatory Power itself, for example, was to have a Jewish
agency which would act in an advisory capacity to it in "economic and
social matters, subject always to the control of the Administration."
The Zionists had called for a contractual agreement with the Mandatory Power, for free immigration, attention to developing agriculture
and industry on a cooperative basis, and a Jewish Council, to cooperate
with the Mandatory Power to oversee the actual administration of the
country. The Brandeis plan also called for the three-man executive,

with himself as an honorary member. The entire control of the Zionist Movement was to be vested in this group, which would then coopt industrial and financial experts, both Zionist and non-Zionist to form a seven man directorate, responsible for appointing governmental heads of administrative bureaus in Palestine. Eschewing all political policy, which was to be the exclusive domain of the High Commissioner, such management experts would then be responsible directly to the Commissioner and to the Zionist Organization for developing the Jewish National Home.[19]

All the earlier differences between the Europeans and the Americans, between Weizmann and his followers, and Brandeis and his aides, had been mere skirmishes. The London Plan signalled the opening salvo of the real battle between East and West. Logically, the Brandeis project presented at London proceeded directly from earlier proposals in the Pittsburgh Platform, in negotiations at Paris, and from the final arrangement at San Remo. Yet the Brandeis Plan rankled the Europeans, as no other scheme had, because it stripped the Zionist Movement of its emphasis upon a spiritual and cultural renaissance of Jewish values, it involved non-Zionists in the maintenance of the *Yishuv*, and it called for liquidating the Zionist Commission in Palestine. This Commission, by now a quasi-governmental agency of the Zionist Organization, and operative since 1918 with the sanction of the British Foreign Office, was the same Commission initiated under Weizmann's auspices, and whose opening sessions Brandeis had been forbidden to attend.

European Zionists believed eliminating the Commission would deny the validity of the Zionist Movement itself, for the Commission symbolized the governmental apparatus of the *Yishuv* and was its first political instrumentality approved by Britain. Its ultimate purpose was to facilitate the eventual establishment of a Jewish state. How could the Brandeis Plan have called for its abandonment? The Europeans, like everyone else, were not blessed with foresight; the Zionist Commission was only the forerunner of the Jewish Agency. The *Yishuv* ultimately developed its own political institutions, while the Agency attempted to deal with England.

Brandeis, too, could not have foreseen such a development at the time, but his motives in calling for the elimination of the Zionist Commission were clear. Brandeis, on his visit to Palestine the previous year, had been dismayed at the financial mismanagement, the parlous

physical conditions of the country, and its problems of large unemployment. He had also taken General Allenby's words to heart, that
before there could be any large scale immigration, the swamps would
have to be drained.[20] Brandeis was certain, then, that the Zionist
Commission was equal to all those tasks.

Though the Americans accompanying Brandeis to London presumably concurred in his estimate of the Palestine situation, they did not
oppose the decision of the Steering Committee of the London Conference. That body voted against Brandeis' program because it would
allow non-Zionists to assume control; yet Brandeis insisted that Weizmann himself was originally responsible for its main outlines. Presumably pressured by his European colleagues, Weizmann not only abandoned the Brandeis scheme without informing the Justice, but presented an alternate plan. This second arrangement supposedly
poached on the services of those very individuals (Lords Reading, de
Rothschild, and Alfred Mond) originally intended for the Brandeis-
inspired executive. Weizmann's plan called for a British Economic
Council, composed of affluent Jews, both Zionist and non-Zionist. The
Council was to engage in such financial and industrial undertakings as
were to have been the domain of the Brandeis secretariat. Both Weizmann's and Brandeis' plans proposed to create investment agencies
operating in Palestine on proper business principles. Both projects
recognized the emergency nature of the situation in Palestine, and
were willing therefore to facilitate long-term credit facilities, with
lowered interest rates, and were geared to the possibility that at the
outset, semi-public economic ventures might yield little or no returns
on capital funds.

To make matters worse, the Keren Hayesod, a Jewish Foundation
Fund, established by Weizmann and Sokolow at same London Conference, was to serve as a source of financial credit for the Economic
Council. Monies for this all-purpose fund, to be used for immigration,
colonization, health work, and educational services both in Palestine
and in the Diaspora, were to be raised through a tithing system on
individual incomes, and through returns on economic investments.
The American Zionists were so jealous of this British money power that
they even overlooked a European concession to their own arguments
against the fund. They had contended that to operate efficiently, the
Keren Hayesod should not commingle charitable bequests and interest on investments. As a matter of fact, in the financial undertakings of

the Economic Council, investment sources of the Keren Hayesod were reserved to the exclusion of incomes from donations. The Americans, however, refused to believe that such a condition prevailed. Indeed, when they heard that the Economic Council was to control those funds derived from investments, they viewed this as a nefarious plot to prevent the formation of a separate American Economic Council. So fearful were they of British competition, that at one point they even contemplated forming their own local committee or branch of the Council. Perhaps the idea was that if they could not effectively eliminate the Council, they had better join forces with it.[21]

It may well be that beyond the American criticism of the Council, lay the hidden fear of non-Zionist pressures. Benjamin V. Cohen, an American then serving as financial secretary to the Zionist Executive in London, urged Mack to restrict the Keren Hayesod in America to a donation fund. Like Julius Simon, a European Zionist leader with American sympathies, Cohen feared that wealthy industrialists would hesitate to become involved in any business venture which might be too closely associated with a purely Zionist appeal. For such potential clients, it simply would never do for the same source of monies to succor poor Jews, while it yet served as an attractive investment possibility.

Could it be that neither side was prepared to speak freely, that what was at stake was not necessarily a set of high ideals, nor even the means towards fulfilling the Zionist dream, but rather the competition of two groups of people for possible investments in Palestine?

Such ugly, unvarnished notions were covered over. Instead, both groups trotted out the old arguments which most closely approximated their understandings of Zionism. Once again, the Weizmannites saw themselves bedecked in the mantle of cultural Zionism, true to the spirit of Ahad Ha'am, while Brandeis and his followers were convinced they were the true descendants of Herzl. So bitter did their contentions become, that unfortunately neither group realized the paradox of its position. Brandeisians, who renounced political action and its implications, looked to Herzl, while Weizmannites, relying on all the tangential meanings of cultural Zionism, were yet absorbed with all the benefits to be derived from political nationalism, both in the *yishuv* and in the Diaspora.

It was therefore natural that accusations and counterclaims flew thick and fast. The Weizmannites complained that Brandeis' Palestine would be a Zion without Zionism, while the Americans regarded the Europeans as directionless people, who garbled ends and means in the pursuit of their Zionist goals. Such people, the Americans contended, with their *luftmensch* approach to practicalities, their pursuit of culture to the detriment of economic and social planning, would certainly destroy the Zionist Movement itself. It is tragic that the underlying hope of the Zionist dream—to create a Jewish National Home founded on prophetic idealism—to which both groups subscribed, failed to unite them.

Numerous postscripts to the rejection of the Brandies Plan served only to heighten the tension between the Weizmann and the Brandeis-Mack forces. After the London Conference, the Americans drastically reduced their subvention to the World Zionist Organization. Brandeis claimed that only straightened circumstances prompted this move; no one even thought of seceding from the Movement. But the Europeans were not convinced, and found justification for their skepticism in the dictum imposed by Brandeis once his program had been rejected: No American was to serve on the World Zionist Executive. Yet Brandeis' decision to keep Americans off the Executive was really honored in the breach; Weizmann himself was pressured into adding two European Zionists, sympathetic to the Brandeis point of view, to the Executive. These were Julius Simon and Nehemiah de Lieme, Governor of the Jewish National Fund.

By now, both groups had embarked upon a collision course, from which it would be impossible to retreat. In September, 1920, the World Zionist Executive, in an attempt to heal the effects of the London fiasco, urged the Americans to send Robert Szold, an attorney, to accompany Simon and de Lieme in an investigation of Zionist activities in Palestine. This three-member Reorganization Commission received *carte blanche* from Weizmann to effect any necessary improvements in the *Yishuv*. But the changes they proposed were so radical, that they went beyond the original Brandeis Plan rejected at London. Brandeis had allowed for low returns on quasi-public investments in Palestine, but the commissioners' score was orchestrated to achieve quick profitable returns. Most grating now to the Europeans, if not to Weizmann himself, was the proposal of the commissioners to eliminate Menachem Ussischkin's post as Director of the Zionist Commission. Ussischkin, who had long been a leader in the Zionist Movement, could claim credit for having converted large portions of

Russian Jewry to the Zionist cause, but the three-man Reorganization Commission seemed unmindful of his prestigious past. Instead, it charged him with a lack of strict accounting, with faulty budgeting, with mixing donation and investment funds, and with an unrealistic approach to demands imposed by limited resources. This meant that in the revised scheme of the Reorganization Commission, the *Yishuv* was not to expand through scattered colonization; contiguous settlement would guarantee better results. For much the same reason, intensive land cultivation was to replace the afforestation program. In its *Report*, the Reorganization Commission even anticipated British policy, and corroborated earlier Allied approaches when it warned against any Jewish immigration into Palestine beyond its absorptive capacity.[22]

For Szold, de Lieme, and Simon, the vision of Jewish self-sufficiency was so important that it would be foolhardy to conjecture whether or not their tactics might have helped the Arab cause. Ussischkin, however, had no doubts on this score. He felt that every post held by a Jew in the *Yishuv* was essential to the maintenance of the Zionist dream. He was fearful lest an Arab majority, led by an Arab-dominated adminstration, in turn catered to by a Jewish High Commissioner eager to appease the Arabs, would spell the demise of the *Yishuv*. He was not about to knuckle under to American obsessions for measuring achievements in terms of their productive or non-productive capacities. To him American arguments about costs, proper bookkeeping, the inviolability of funds earmarked for divergent purposes were completely irrelevant. At the same time he regarded the intent of the Reorganization Commission to cut educational efforts in the *Yishuv* to their bare minimum as self-destructive. Equally upsetting to him was the modified Brandeisian tone of the whole scheme. Here too there was to be only a small secretariat, shorn of true political power, responsible only to the High Commissioner, but capable of appointing heads of governmental bureaus.

For Weizmann such a plan would have spelled chaos. *The Report of the Reorganization Commission*, with its emphasis on meticulous accountability and its disavowal of political agitation, would have denied the Keren Hayesod a basis for its existence. No longer would it be able to serve as a collection agency, disbursing funds the world over, for a variety of needs. Its public relations work in the Diaspora would have had to be disbanded, since the *Report* called for the elimination of educational and political efforts in the Diaspora. The educational aspect of Zionism was as essential to Weizmann as it was to Ussischkin. By urging the latter's dismissal, the Reorganization Commission not only invited a revolution in Zionist philosophy and methods, but also struck indirectly at Weizmann.[23]

Weizmann had promised the Reorganization Commission plenary powers to effect significant changes, a fact which the three men never allowed him to forget. Unknown to them, however, Weizmann had concluded a secret agreement with Vladimir Jabotinsky, that fire-eating Zionist who had founded the Jewish Legion. By its terms, Jabotinsky would join the Directorate of the Keren Hayesod, and would later be opted onto the board of the World Zionist Executive, provided the Reorganization Commission lost its right to introduce changes into the *yishuv*, and Simon, the Brandeis-Mack choice for the Zionist Executive, lost his controlling vote as the American representative to the Keren Hayesod Directorate.

The Americans may have been appalled at how far apart they were in philosophy, orientations, and methods from Ussischkin, but they were livid with rage at the thought that Jabotinsky would have a decisive voice in the evolution of the *Yishuv*. He had fought with them and accused them of being minimalists in their approaches to Palestine.[24] But in the winter of 1921, Jabotinsky had been acclaimed a national hero for the defensive role he took against the Arab rioters in Jerusalem, and for the unjust sentence meted out to him. In turning to him, Weizmann was looking for a new source of strength to bolster the Zionist Movement, now short of funds, and deprived of American leadership on the world scene.

Events then rushed to their inevitable conclusion. The Americans, confirmed in their suspicions that Wiezmann engaged in double-dealing, tried to restructure native American Zionism on Brandeisian principles, limiting the ZOA to membership recruitment, organization, and investment work; educational tasks were to be abandoned, and contributions to World Zionist bodies were to be suspended. But in their passion for pragmatism, the Brandeis-Mack forces unwittingly forged an effective opposition party within the American Zionist ranks. Led by Emanuel Neumann and Louis Lipsky, the rebels then looked for help to Weizmann, who reached America in April 1921. He had come, ostensibly, to implement the establishment of an American Keren Hayesod, but instead, the stage was now set for the final confrontation in June, at the Cleveland Convention of the ZOA. There, with the Justice maintaining a discreet absence, the main segment of American Zionists, strengthened earlier by the activities of Weizmann's followers in this country, rejected the Brandeisian leadership.

Through the effects of the controversy continued to agitate the Zionist body, in time the movement did adopt many of the Justice's economic policies. The Brandeis group, after its resignation, continued to invest in Palestine. Furthermore, the creation of an expanded Jewish Agency in 1929 represented essentially Brandeis' earlier plans on behalf of the *Yishuv*. In fact, both Brandeis and Weizmann were forced to seek allies however they could; they had always to compromise in order to succeed. Their real tragedy then lay elsewhere. Whenever crises arose, they had to trim their sails to the prevailing winds, and their courses collided.

FOOTNOTES

1. "Zionism," *Encyclopedia Judaica*, 16: 1033-1162.
2. Melvin I. Urofsky, *American Zionism from Herzl to the Holocaust* (New York, 1975), pp. 114-24; Ben Halpern, "Brandeis' way to Zionism," *Midstream* 17 (October 1971): 12; Alpheus T. Mason, *Brandeis: A Free Man's Life* (New York, 1946), pp. 441-43.
3. Mason, *Brandeis*, pp. 451-53; Frank E. Manuel, *The Realities of American-Palestine Relations* (Washington, 1949), p. 168; Nahum Sokolow, *History of Zionism, 1600-1918* (New York, 1969 ed.), pp. 80, 82.
4. Leonard Stein, *The Balfour Declaration* (New York, 1961), pp. 198-99.
5. Sokolow, *Zionism*, pp. 56-57; Stein, *Balfour Declaration*, pp. 424-26.
6. *Ibid.*, pp. 506-509.
7. *Ibid.*, p. 369; Mason, *Brandeis*, pp. 451-52; Manuel, *Realities*, pp. 169-70; Sokolow, *Zionism*, pp. 124-25.
8. Louis D. Brandeis, *The Jewish Problem and How to Solve It* (New York, 1915), p. 6; Mason, *Brandeis*, p. 453; Stein, *Balfour Declaration*, p. 582.
9. Manuel, *Realities*, p. 172; Stein, *Balfour Declaration*, p. 586.
10. *Ibid.*, 579-81; Manuel *Realities*, pp. 192, 200, 201.
11. *Ibid.*, pp. 216-17.
12. Urofsky, *American Zionism*, pp. 239-40; see also article by Sarah Schmidt in this volume.
13. Chaim Weizmann, *Trial and Error, An Autobiography* (New York, 1949), p. 192.
14. Urofsky, *American Zionism*, p. 245.
15. Melvin I. Urofsky, *A Mind of One Place: Brandeis and American Reform* (New York, 1971), p. 102.
16. Sarah Schmidt, "The *Parushim:* A Secret Episode in American Zionist History," *American Jewish Historical Quarterly* 65 (December 1975): 125-26.
17. Urofsky, *American Zionism*, pp. 161-81.
18. Manuel *Realities*, pp. 228, 233, 236-49. Zionist representations at the Peace Conference itself had been handled poorly. Despite the efforts of Louis Marshall, Felix Frankfurter and other Americans, the various Zionist groups had been unable to form a truly united front. As a result, the final desposition of Palestine represented not so much any triumph of Zionist diplomacy, but the ability of Britain to impose its own interests on the settlement. What the Zionists failed to recognize throughout this time was that Britain wanted Palestine for its own purposes, and had

used the Zionists; as long as British and Zionist aspirations coincided, there would be no problem. When they did deviate, as was to happen shortly, Britain quickly showed that it would follow what it considered its own benefit, totally disregarding Zionist plans.

19. Walter Laqueur, *History of Zionism* (New York, 1972), p. 454; Howard Morley Sachar, *A History of Israel* (New York, 1976), pp. 124-25.

20. Manuel, *Realities*, pp. 246-47.

21. Esther L. Panitz, "Louis Dembitz Brandeis and the Cleveland Conference," *American Jewish Historical Quarterly* 65 (December 1975): 149.

22. *Report of the Re-Organization Commission of the Executive of the Zionist Organization on the Work of the Zionist Organization in Palestine* (New York, 1921).

23. Panitz, "Brandeis and Cleveland Conference," p. 149.

24. Laqueur, *History of Zionism*, p. 345.

The Specter of Zionism: American Opinions, 1917-1922

by Naomi W. Cohen

The year 1917 stands out as one in which the course of Jewish history was permanently altered.* First, Britain issued the Balfour Declaration, a statement of policy sanctioned by the other western powers which set the seal of respectability on Herzlian Zionism. Secondly, the Bolsheviks swept into power in Russia. Although sympathizers had hoped that the Russian Revolution would bring about the long-sought emancipation of over 5,000,000 Jews, it resulted instead in a new kind of tyranny.

More immediately, the two events evoked new expressions of anti-Jewish sentiment. The Balfour Declaration aroused disgruntled Arabs, missionaries, and assimilationists to mount a campaign against Zionism which ultimately affected Jewry in general. Opponents of the new Russian regime seized upon the participation of Jews in the revolution to accuse them of engineering the Bolshevik takeover. Judeophobes in different parts of the world had no logical qualms about finding parallels between Zionism and Bolshevism. Their task was facilitated by the *Protocols* fever which reached its peak between 1919 and 1921. Elaborating on the so-called plans of the Elders of Zion for world rule, propagators of the *Protocols* cited both Zionism and Bolshevism as proof of the menace of international Jewry. From then on, "Zionist" and "Bolshevik" enriched the vocabulary of anti-Semites.

In the United States not all anti-Semites were outspokenly anti-Zionist nor all anti-Zionists anti-Semitic. But the two were connected, as the following discussion of three anti-Zionist types will reveal. It

* I am grateful to Cyma Horowitz, librarian of the American Jewish Committee, and to her staff for their courtesies.

should also be remembered that anti-Zionism and certainly anti-Semitism were not foreign to the United States. Even before the Balfour Declaration critics of Jewish nationalism (mostly Jews) had linked the two streams of thought, arguing for example that a return to Palestine was an anti-Semitic ploy to get rid of unwanted economic competitors, or that sympathy with the goal of a restored Zion would raise the suspicion of the anti-Semites who always said that the Jew was a disloyal alien.[1] But only with the Balfour Declaration and the succeeding steps which led to the Palestine Mandate (1917-1922) did the menace of political Zionism appear more serious to its opponents. Their criticisms, in turn, if not intrinsically anti-Semitic, played directly into the hands of the Jew-baiters.

Americans who spoke out against political Zionism usually made two assumptions about the Balfour Declaration. In the first place, they claimed that the Declaration implicated *all* Jews, Zionist and anti-Zionist alike, irrespective of their personal viewpoints. Although the British statement promised that "nothing shall be done which may prejudice . . . the rights and political status enjoyed by Jews in any other country," the taint of Jewish nationalism rubbed off on the entire group. Secondly, like the Zionists, they interpreted the Declaration to be the license for statehood and not merely the right to "a homeland." Some critics insisted that they did not oppose a colonization movement in Palestine or the need to make Palestine a refuge for oppressed Jews. It was the distinct likelihood of a Jewish state, or at least the expectation that statehood was the next logical goal of organized Zionists, that aroused their bitterness.

This reading of the Balfour Declaration may not have led to an opposition so vehement had it not been set during the war and immediate post-war years. The intense Americanism generated by a crusade against the Hun, which sparked concentrated drives to Americanize the immigrant and which read hyphenate groups like the German-Americans and Irish-Americans outside the pale of civic loyalty, spilled over into the post-Armistice period. The war had been advertised to Americans as the way to make the world safe for democracy, but the shocks of readjusting to a peacetime economy and the collapse of Wilson's design for an effective League of Nations made Americans more antagonistic to and resentful of the outside world. Their unspent hatred of the German was channeled into a hatred of the foreigner generally and into an hysterical Red Scare. In the post-war period as during the war itself, national loyalty meant conformity to a monolithic concept of Americanism, a doctrine fashioned in the Anglo-Saxon mold which earmarked any display of political or ethnic separatism as outright dangers.

I

Sensitive to the mood of hyper-patriotism, Jewish liberals who opposed Zionism warned of the dire consequences of that movement for American Jewry. Political Zionism raised the specter of dual allegiance and of a hyphenated group of "Jewish-Americans." "Certain as the day follows the night," Jews would be considered a foreign group, or temporary sojourners, with separate political interests and with enemies who would advocate their exodus to Palestine.[2]

Jewish liberals and assimilationists no doubt were aware of the struggle which had engaged Jewish spokesmen for over a century to prove to their compatriots that American Jewry deserved neither the stigma nor suspicion of being alien, separatist or disloyal. Acculturated Jews for the most part were never convinced by Herzl's premise that a Jewish nation would reduce Judeophobia throughout the world, and they continued to act as if Jewish behavior had the power to moderate or contain the course of anti-Semitism. They liked to think that Jewish participation in the World War shattered charges of Jewish alienism once and for all.[3] Now along came political Zionism which, under the misguided benevolence of the Balfour Declaration, could only undo years of effort and increase hostility against the Jews.

The outspoken anti-Zionists of the assimilationist stripe neither contested the premises of American chauvinism nor attempted to allay the suspicions which, they charged, would be generated by Zionism. Instead they took the lead in attacking and discrediting Zionists for alleged un-American views and behavior. Some justified public sentiment against hyphenates and rejected out of hand Brandeis' oft-hailed statement that Zionism made for better Americans. As Professor Morris Jastrow asserted: "It is impossible to belong to two countries. . . . 'Allegiance must be perfect—cannot be divided. Either a Palestinian or an American.' "[4] These critics shuddered at the sight of Zionist flags and the sound of Zionist songs. Congressman Julius Kahn of California, who submitted an anti-Zionist petition to Wilson for presentation to the Peace Conference, lashed out repeatedly against the display of foreign symbols: "I maintain that the Jews in this country have the right to carry but one flag, the Stars and Stripes."[5]

It fitted the mood of the true-blue Americanism of the period to call Zionism a movement of foreign origin, which, like "un-American" separatist political clubs and labor organizations, appealed to the newer immigrants. Anti-Zionists warned that naturalized citizens had to remember that in their oath of allegiance they foreswore loyalty to any foreign ruler or nationality. Jews "who are real Americans," a writer in the *American Hebrew* declared, spurned Jewish nationalism. Simon W. Rosendale, former attorney general of New York, put it more forcefully: "There should be but little patience for these un-American Zionists. If they want a Palestinian Jewish State, let them . . . go to it."[6]

Jewish liberals called Zionism a reactionary movement because it seemed as if it sought to turn back the clock on the historical process of assimilation.[7] For the Jew to break down the walls of the ghetto in the wake of the French Revolution and to renounce his distinctive peoplehood in exchange for civil rights and social acceptance appeared quite logical. The more complete his freedom and concomitant advancement in politics, economy, and society the less justified was his retention of tribalistic, anachronistic usages or his desire for self-ghettoization. As long as the United States accorded him freedom and opportunity,[8] Zionism was a discordant quantity, alien to the spirit of progress and civilization which was in fact the American spirit. In short, Zionism, the insistence on clannishness and ethnic separatism, was on a philosophic level also un-American.

Ralph Boas, whose essays appeared in the *New York Times* and *Atlantic Monthly*, argued in this vein. He warned that Zionists with their emphasis on separate nationalities and their adoption of the German pseudo-scientific concept of race would transform America from a melting pot to a Balkan peninsula. The images he evoked for an America at war equated Zionism with the enemy and the deviant anti-patriot. "The world sees only dimly," he wrote in December 1917, "that the root of national romanticism which is upon us is the child of Kultur." And, "Zionists are continually heaping abuse upon the non-separatist, upon the man who has no desire to be different from other human beings." Boas and other assimilationist Jews sought to minimize the degree and danger of existing anti-Semitism; the fault, in fact, lay with the Jews who tended to be overly clannish. This faith in assimilation rested on the optimistic belief that the conditions and status of Jews throughout the world would continue to improve.[9]

Morris Raphael Cohen, the eminent liberal philosopher, further developed the equation "liberalism equals Americanism equals good" and "Zionism equals tribalism equals evil." Zionism feared most the American ideal of freedom, he claimed, for it had to reject the creed of individual freedoms in favor of the group. In his words:

> Nationalistic Zionism demands not complete individual liberty for the Jew, but group autonomy. . . . Indeed, how could a Jewish Palestine allow complete religious freedom, freedom of intermarriage and free non-Jewish immigration, without soon losing its very reason for existence? A national Jewish Palestine must necessarily mean a state founded on a peculiar race, a tribal religion and a mystic belief in a peculiar soil, whereas liberal America stands for separation of church and state, the free mixing of races, and the fact that men can change their habitation and language and still advance the process of civilization.

Parenthetically, Cohen added another dig at Zionist idealists, when he likened their alleged readiness to ignore the rights of the native population of Palestine to German oppression. For all these reasons, he said, Zionism was utterly incompatible with Americanism.[10]

American Jews who attempted consistently to follow the lines of nineteenth century liberalism in their attack on Zionism were caught in a logical trap. Their philosophy defended assimilation and internationalism, and they considered Zionism a child of darkness because it glorified a narrow nationalism. Yet, wasn't it equally reactionary to stand for chauvinistic nationalism, even when it was American, if the road to world progress lay through internationalism?[11] Most anti-Zionist Jews sidestepped the issue. Tailoring their liberalism to fit the American temper, they indicated a greater concern for their security and a concomitant desire to prove their unalloyed Americanism.

The voice of Reform Jewry echoed most loudly in the anti-Zionist liberal chorus. Unlike others who faced the issue only when the Balfour Declaration lifted political Zionism out of realm of fantasy into the world of *realpolitik*, American Reform had been fighting the ideas of the Jewish nationality and a return to Palestine since pre-Herzlian days. On theological grounds alone Zionism was unacceptable, since it squarely contradicted Reform's teaching that Judaism was only a religious faith and that the Jews had been scattered throughout the world by divine intent in order to propagate the message of the fatherhood of God and brotherhood of man. But from the beginning Reform argued too that Zionism was un-American. It was a movement born in Europe which smacked of ignorant immigrants, the ghetto, and hyphenated nationalism. It flaunted the American doctrine of separation of church and state because it involved Jews, members of a religious group, in a political or "state" question and because it stood for the establishment of a theocratic state. It libeled the United States by its exaggeration of anti-Semitism in the country and by positing a Jewish question where in fact none existed.

At the same time that they condemned Zionism, Reform spokesmen accused the movement of aiding the anti-Semites, particularly those who charged that Jews could never be rooted citizens. That did not deter the *American Israelite,* the mouthpiece of Reform, from moving into the enemy camp itself. When the *Dearborn Independent* began its "exposés" of the international machinations of world Jewry, the Jewish paper stated that Zionism validated the anti-Semitic cry of a "Jewish Peril."[12]

While evoking images about Zionism unpalatable to average Americans, Reform developed a theme that would be reiterated by other Jewish and non-Jewish critics of Zionism. It distinguished between Zionist and non-Zionist and made that distinction one of good versus bad Jew. Good meant God-fearing and above all unquestionably American. The *American Israelite* stated that "refined" American Jews rejected Jewish nationalism, and it noted smugly that all Jewish newspapers edited or controlled by native Americans were strongly anti-Zionist. When the paper wrote in May 1918 that "the large majority of American Jews, namely those who do their duty by their country, their community, their families, are without any particular interest in the Zionist movement," it was labeling fellow Jews who were Zionists—even Reform leaders like Stephen S. Wise and Judah Magnes—as undesirables in American society. Simon Rosendale summed up the determination to separate the good from the bad when he said, "You shall not press the . . . badge of Palestinian hyphenism upon the Reform Jew in America."[13]

Reform's opposition to Zionism between 1917 and 1922 was more than the outraged cry of liberals countering a movement dedicated to preserve rigid nationalistic lines and to stem the course of assimilation.

True, Reform criticized Zionism for fostering a narrow nationalism, but Reform compromised its own internationalist bent by its American chauvinism.[14] To attribute that to the traditional insecurity of a minority group is only partially valid. From its early development in the mid-nineteenth century Reform spokesmen, religious and lay alike, had emphasized the role that the United States played in their ideology. They found parallels linking America with the spirit of prophetic Judaism, and they believed that Reform's religious mission was destined to take root and flourish in America.[15] However, if Zionists had their way and changed the course of American Jewry's evolution, Reform's ideological structure would collapse.

For more mundane considerations, too, Reform could not permit a Zionist triumph. Were Zionism to succeed in capturing the loyalty of the majority of American Jews and in establishing its control over the community, Reform would lose the predominant position it held since the 1870's in Jewish religious and secular institutions. Zionists had already scored a major victory when they swayed American Jews to support the idea of an American Jewish Congress, and Reform spokesmen admitted that their opponents had the ear of the masses of Jews.[16] If that pattern persisted, the power of Reform in determining the allocation of communal resources as well as the very paths that the community chose to follow would be largely eroded.

American Reform felt seriously threatened—a fact which explains the near-hysterical pitch of its arguments and the alacrity with which its leaders criticized Zionism publicly, even allying themselves with non-Jewish critics and exposing the deep rifts within the Jewish community to the outside society. Determined not to permit Zionists to pose as the spokesmen of American Jews, some attempted to go further than verbal denunciations.[17] In 1918 a nucleus of rabbis proposed a special conference of Reform religious and lay leaders in the United States for the purpose of combating Zionism.[18] Laity joined rabbis again when Mr. Max Senior, Professor Morris Jastrow, and Rabbi Henry Berkowitz prepared the petition against Zionism which was signed by 299 Americans and presented by Congressman Kahn to President Wilson.[19] In 1922 Rabbis David Philipson and Isaac Landman testified before the House Committee on Foreign Affairs on the Lodge-Fish resolution expressing American satisfaction over the proposed mandate for Palestine which incorporated the promise of the Balfour Declaration. Both stated that Zionism accentuated the

alienism of the Jews and impugned their loyalty. The resolution itself
was un-American, since it appealed to the Jewish vote, a concept
whose existence and very legitimacy Reform had always denied.
Philipson, consistently among the most rabid of the anti-Zionists, also
criticized the resolution for marking a deviation from the nation's
traditional policy of non-entanglement in Old World affairs. Landman
fought the resolution outside the Committee's rooms too. As editor of
the *American Hebrew* he printed numerous opinions against Congressional action and against the un-American posture of Zionism.[20]

Jewish anti-Zionists had a sure weapon when they pitted
Americanism against Zionism. Another immeasurable advantage was
their influence with both the Jewish and non-Jewish communities.
They had the support of the prestigious *New York Times* and of two of
the oldest Anglo-Jewish periodicals in the country, the *American
Israelite* and the *American Hebrew*. They also counted in their ranks
men whose opinions were bound to be considered seriously by the
outside society. Julius Kahn, for example, was beginning his tenth
term in Congress in 1919 and was well known in American public life.
Another influential figure was Henry Morgenthau, loyal Wilsonian
Democrat who had served as Ambassador to Turkey and more recently
as head of the special investigative mission to Poland. Morgenthau was
party to the anti-Zionist petition, and in 1921 he wrote an article on
Zionism for *World's Work* that discoursed on the theme "Zionism is
the most stupendous fallacy in Jewish history." The article, which
lambasted Jewish nationalism while it glorified the "spiritual"
Americanism of anti-Zionist Jews, caused quite a stir in the secular
press. Like pieces by Morris Jastrow, Morgenthau's article supplied
material for Christian writers who joined the attack against Zionism.[21]

II

Some of the Christian opinion-molders who contributed to the
public critique of Zionism followed the line of Professor Albert
Bushnell Hart. Hart announced upon the appearance of the Balfour
Declaration that Jews now had to fish or cut bait, to choose which
country and nationality claimed their loyalty.[22] Thomas Nixon Carver,
a sociologist and colleague of Hart at Harvard, agreed that the Jew
could not divide his allegiance. His alternatives were territorial

separatism through Zionism or complete amalgamation and disappear-
ance as a distinctive group. If he chose separatism outside of Palestine,
he had to be prepared to pay the price—race hostility on the part of his
co-nationals.[23] Paul Scott Mowrer, foreign correspondent for a
Chicago newspaper, went further in defining what amalgamation en-
tailed. Since Judaism entwined religion with nationality, Jews ought to
discard certain religious practices—even be ready, he specified, to
intermarry with non-Jews—in order to be accepted fully in the United
States. He advised those Jews who could not prove their single allegiance in this fashion to make their way to Palestine.[24]

A professor of international law at Princeton, Philip Marshall Brown,
also cited Jewish hostility to intermarriage as an example of the undesirable effects of racial solidarity. He called racial solidarity the driving
force behind Zionism, and he suggested that the prominence of Jews in
the Socialist and Bolshevik movements derived from that same matrix.
Although Brown denied that Jews joined those movements from any
sinister motives, his choice of analogies was unfortunate. In the years
1917-1922 Bolshevism was anathema to proper Americans; if Zionism
drew from the same source, it was no doubt evil too.[25]

Doubtless very few of those who argued the either-or position on
Jewish versus American nationalism would have considered their opinions anti-Semitic. It was not the Jew they said they disliked as much as
group distinctiveness. To many well-meaning Christians in the United
States Jewish separatism had always been the major stumbling block to
harmonious relations with Gentiles and was responsible, more than
Christian prejudice, for anti-Jewish discrimination.[26] For their own
good, some advised, Jews had to look beyond the Jewish community
and show their readiness to participate on multiple levels of civic
activity. Accordingly, Zionism was an unwise course, for it merely
reinforced the undesirable traits of clannishness and, in turn, the
barriers between Jew and Christian.[27]

While responsible Christian criticism usually stopped short of attacking Jewish nationalists directly—it was Zion*ism* that caused the
Jewish problem[28]—Dr. Herbert Adams Gibbons was as harsh as the
Jewish liberals who denounced the "un-American" Zionists. According
to Gibbons, Presbyterian minister and journalist who had also taught
in a missionary college in Turkey, "the Zionist movement tends to
emphasize in the immigrant what makes him unfit for American citizenship." The immigrant had to submerge himself in American inter-

ests and build his life around American ideals, in short to copy the
Biblical example of Ruth. But an immigrant who came with the spirit of
Ahad Ha'Am, believing that he was part of a closely knit international
community linked in an attachment to Zion as a cultural center, would
always be an unwelcome alien. Because of the Zionists who under-
mined Jewish loyalty to the United States and disrupted American
unity, an anti-Semitic crusade like Henry Ford's could flourish. Gibbons differentiated between Zionists and other Jews—"We do not hold
in abhorrence the Jews, but we do hold in abhorrence the Jewish
nation"—and he urged the non-Zionists to fight the nationalists within
the Jewish camp.[29]   Clearly the distinction between the good anti-
nationalist Jew and the bad Zionist had taken root. If not primarily a
way to legitimize hostility or Jew-baiting, it provided nonetheless a
convenient peg on which to hang traditional complaints about the
Jewish group and an easy way for sketching the model of the ideal
Jewish compatriot. In 1919 the prestigious weekly, the *Independent,*
printed an editorial summarizing some pros and cons of Zionism. What
purported to be an objective account of the views of two individuals
concluded with the *Independent's* own value-ridden statement:

> On the whole the conservative Jews, who desire above all things to
> maintain the old Jewish faith and the Talmudic tradition, incline to be
> Zionists. The progressive Jews, the men who deprecate race distinc-
> tion and hostilities . . . would prefer to see Jews intermarry and
> amalgamate with their Gentile fellow citizens in Europe and in
> America, and are disposed to discourage the Zionist experiment. Yet
> the Zionist movement has also attracted the support of may of the
> radical Jews who see in it an opportunity to found a semi-socialistic
> state.[30]

With "progressive," "race hostilities," and "radical" as clues, it took no
superior wisdom to tell the good from the bad.

Unlike the Jewish opponents of Zionism, Christian critics concentrated more on depicting the evils of the Zionist movement in Palestine. Those who had lived in the Near East and had engaged in
government or missionary or newspaper work were the most outspoken. They agreed that Zionism, the attempt of a minority to gain
complete control over Palestine, would incite the justified hostility of
Muslim and Christian inhabitants who had their own histories and
aspirations, and they predicted pogroms, religious strife, and even war

between the white and brown races. The Zionists in Palestine were imperialistic, conniving with and pressuring their British protectors, trumpeting an aggressive and bombastic propaganda line, and ever seeking more land. Despite Zionist accounts of steps taken to establish amicable relations with the Arabs, the Jews were in fact ruthless exploiters of the natives. Backed by the power of co-religionists throughout the world, Zionists were unequal competitors for the older Palestinian inhabitants. They were undemocratic, for they sought control over the police power and immigration policies of the country even though they were a small minority. They planned to establish a Jewish theocracy, offensive to Muslims, Christians, and secular democrats. Furthermore, they made their settlements exclusively Jewish and maintained a gulf between themselves and the non-Jews. Indeed, the native Palestinians much preferred the tyranny of their former rulers, the Turks, to the tyranny of the Zionists. In light of this native opposition, a Zionist state could only be maintained with armed force.[31]

Not all critiques confined the specter of Zionism within the geographical boundaries of Palestine. Some charged that Zionism was involved with international Jewry, financed by Jewish money from around the world, and protected by a powerful Jewish press which carefully doctored the news. Edward Bliss Reed of Yale University interpreted Zionism as an outright conspiracy when he testified on the Lodge-Fish resolution of 1922. The Balfour Declaration was a secret document framed by British and American Zionists who kept some of its details hidden from the public. The Zionists enjoyed an inordinately strong position at the Paris Peace Conference, where they succeeded in drawing up the very favorable provisions of the mandate, and where they made plans for assuming control over the lands of Palestine. Weizmann and his crew in Paris were able to squelch the publicization of the anti-Zionist King-Crane Report, indicating, Reed hinted, their influence in American government circles. Although Reed was the most extreme—Abraham Goldberg of the ZOA likened his testimony to a page out of the *Protocols of the Elders of Zion*—other critics struck equally alarming notes when they linked Zionism with Bolshevism. Not only did that make the Jewish settlers "materialistic" and "atheistic," but it suggested that a Jewish Palestine would become the center for the spread of revolutionary propaganda out to destroy Christian civilization.[32]

These charges clearly illuminate the interrelatedness of anti-Zionism with anti-Semitism. Critics of Zionism in Palestine, American consuls among them, also distinguished between good Jews, the anti-Zionist religious groups, and the bad Jews, the Zionist pioneers.[33] But they did more. Their indictments of the Zionists bore the familiar trappings of the anti-Semite's brief against the Jew generally—materialistic, manipulative, exploitative, internationalist, separatist, radical anti-Gentile. The anti-Zionist adopted those ready-made images to attack the Jews he did not like; he had found, perhaps without planning, a respectable rubric for any latent Jew-hatred he may have entertained. He may have been opposed to Zionism for objective reasons, and, like Dr. Gibbons, many of his dear friends may have been Jews,[34] but his indiscriminate use of adjectives about the Zionists would make him indistinguishable from the anti-Semite. Indeed, from the 1940's on, when more and more Jews rallied to the Zionist cause and overt anti-Semitism grew socially unacceptable, the switch of anti-Semitism to anti-Zionism became a common phenomenon.

American critics of the Yishuv also evoked images calculated to turn their country and compatriots from supporting Zionism. Zionism was undemocratic and hence un-American. Its political success was predicated upon the denial of self-determination to the natives of Palestine and the oppressive rule which a minority planned to foist upon a far larger majority. It would deny the Palestinians their proper share of political power, just as it would deny them the right to bear arms, and force them to live under a Jewish theocracy. As such Zionism contradicted the principles of American government and betrayed the American war aims of self-determination, impartial justice, and liberation of small nations. Furthermore, a Zionist Palestine was imperialistic and Prussian-like, and hence a menace to world peace. If the United States were not dragged into a war begun by the hostility which Zionism generated, it might be forced into supporting a Jewish state by military means. Still another likelihood was that America and Britain would be compelled to use stringent measures to counter Bolshevism in Palestine before it infected the entire Near East.[35]

The prospects thus forecast were well calculated to impress a war-weary America, where Prussianism and imperialism were held responsible for the greatest calamity the modern world had suffered, and where Bolshevism, a product of that war, was seen to pose ominous threats to the survival of civilization. The apprehensive American would understandably shudder at the thought of a Jewish state which threatened his own security. He might also direct his resentment and suspicions against his Jewish neighbor who, even if not a Zionist, was somehow related to the troublemaking Bolshevik pioneers in Palestine.

Indeed, the anti-Zionist campaign of the immediate post-war period, particularly insofar as it latched on to the Red Scare, scored on several counts: it supported and thereby reinforced the anti-Zionist posture of the State Department, and it contributed to the anti-Semitic momentum in the United States.

III

To dyed-in-the-wool anti-Semites, Zionism was not all bad. Some responded the way Herzl said they would and welcomed a chance to get rid of undesirable Jews. The prime need according to extremists in the United States was to cleanse American life of Jewish corruption and perversion. The *Brooklyn Anti-Bolshevist,* which preached among other things that the internationalist, separatist, conspiratorial Jewish race was responsible for dragging the United States into the war, suggested that an exercise in statehood might even improve the primitive Jew:

> Let the unassimilated Jewish race return to its traditional homeland, there to undertake the cares and responsibilities of statehood, there to build up a nation by assimilating other races . . ., and to learn what independence and national dignity mean when they shall have risen above racial ties to the level of a modern state.[36]

The theme of removing the Jews to Palestine lost much of its appeal with the appearance of the *Protocols of the Elders of Zion.* Since the latter purportedly proved the existence of a plan to control the entire world, Jews would not be content with Palestine alone nor would a Jewish state remove the threats that Jewry still posed. The *Protocols* were introduced into the United States by 1919 and were published in several editions. Disclosed as a hoax not long thereafter, they retained their popularity in America thanks mainly to the labors of Henry Ford and his *Dearborn Independent.*[37]

In May 1920 Ford's newspaper began weekly "exposés" of the

Jewish menace, particularly as it manifested itself in the United States. Its object was to show how Jewish activities conformed to the program outlined by the *Protocols;* in this way the paper reprinted the actual test of the documents. By referring to books, articles, and statements by Jews and non-Jews, the *Dearborn Independent* tried to gain credibility for its account. The picture of the Jew which emerged over several years was well-calculated to influence a midwestern agrarian audience. The Jew personified all the prejudices and fears of the farmer who bitterly watched his political and social power shrink as urbanization swept the nation: the Jew was the non-producer who lived by financial manipulation; he was pro-British (symbol of hard money) and an international warmonger; through his base of power in the cities he spread the poison of secularization and sought to undermine Christianity; his sensuality and lechery purveyed through his domination of the theater, movies, and popular music corrupted social values; he was the arch-conspirator, the radical and Bolshevik, who plotted the downfall of the American order.

Zionism was bound up with the *Protocols* from the very beginning. The very word Zion in the title showed how some of the *Protocols'* first sponsors linked the spurious documents with the World Zionist Congress of 1897. The *Dearborn Independent* accepted that reading,[38] and it also culled words and sentences from the statements of political Zionists that could lend support to its overall presentation. Nevertheless, in Ford's campaign, Zionism was of secondary importance; it was significant only insofar as it reflected the designs and characteristics of international Jewry. The latter, operating from a base in New York, used Zionism, but its real aim was to take over the United States and not Palestine.[39]

According to the *Dearborn Independent* Zionism afforded tactical advantages to the Jewish conspiracy. It provided a platform for uniting eastern and western Jews.[40] More important, it served

> as a very successful public screen for the carrying on of secret activities. International Jews, the controllers of the world's governmental and financial power, may meet anywhere, at any time, in war time or peace time, and by giving out that they are only considering the ways and means of opening up Palestine to the Jews, they easily escape the suspicion of being together on any other business.[41]

But although a Jewish state in Palestine was not the true goal of the

Jewish nation, the power of the Zionists could not be underestimated. After all, members of the "International Jewish Banking Combine" like Lord Rothschild and Otto Warburg also participated in the World Zionist Organization. Herzl and Nordau had predicted the sequence of Jewish behavior and of important diplomatic events from 1903 to 1919, and the Zionists had succeeded in getting the approval of the Allies, the Peace Conference, and the League for their program. They, the Zionists or the Russian Jews, "decreed" the destruction of Germany during the war. At Versailles, they were even able to secure the rights of self-rule and "extra citizenship" for Jews in some European countries. The tentacles of the Zionists spanned continents; for example, there always was a close relationship between the Zionists in Russia and the Jewish Kehillah in New York. At present in the United States, "the Zionists . . . dictate the policy of American Jewry."[42]

If Zionists were really so powerful, and if Jews really controlled international finance, why couldn't they raise the large sums they wanted for developing Palestine? The *Dearborn Independent* had an answer for that too. The Jews arranged it purposely to confuse the gentiles and to get England, their protector, to shoulder the expense.[43]

The *Dearborn Independent* posited that Zionism was integrally related to Bolshevism. Both were the movements of Russian Jews, and both attracted Jews not for their philosophic tenets but because they posed threats to the "gentile scheme of things." Since Judaism felt threatened by the development of gentile nationalism, it followed two tracks simultaneously, one of gaining control of the gentile states through revolutionary upheaval and one of constructing a separate state in Palestine. The Jews themselves admitted that Zionism and Bolshevism coincided in a common loyalty to the plot of world Jewry:

> As the Jew is a past master in the art of symbolism, it may not be without significance that the Bolshevik Star has one point less than the Star of David. For there is still one point to be fulfilled in the World Program as outlined in the *Protocols*—and that is the enthronement of "our leader." When he comes, the World Autocrat for whom the whole program is framed, the sixth point may be added.

No wonder then that in personnel and methods the Jewish government of Palestine closely resembled Bolshevik rule in Russia.[44]

When the *Dearborn Independent* depicted the Bolshevist/Zionist specter in Palestine it relied heavily on articles (analyzed above) which appeared in serious journals. It reprinted a long excerpt from an essay by John P. Peters recounting how the aggressive and arrogant Zionists were shirking manual labor and were inciting the Arabs to riot. Like Dr. Gibbons, whose articles it praised, the *Dearborn Independent* also predicted that Zionism in Palestine was creating the conditions for another world war. Drawing from still another piece, this one by Albert T. Clay, the paper reported Zionist activities in Palestine "to illustrate the genius of the Jew when he comes to power." It thus repeated the charges that Zionists underhandedly were dispossessing the lawful owners of the land, that they were tyrannizing the population by insisting upon cultural conformity, and that with enmity toward the rest of the world they were pushing themselves into international politics. When the Jews were let loose in their own land, their age-old evil traits became even more pronounced.[45]

In addition to its weekly articles the *Dearborn Independent* printed a feature called Jewish World Notes, a melange of short news items reporting on Jewish activities. Many were innocuous in and of themselves, but they directed the already suspicious reader acquainted with the nefarious Jewish schemes to further details in the uninterrupted Jewish quest for power. They could also sharpen his fear of the imminent Jewish specter and justify his anti-Jewish hostility. For example, one item in the issue of September 25th, 1920, stated that Supreme Court Justice Louis D. Brandeis returned from London where he had presided at the Zionist Conference. The wording was innocent and could have been found in any Anglo-Jewish periodical, but in the *Dearborn Independent* the overtones were what counted. Read in the context of the newspaper's campaign the item said: here is additional proof that the power of the international Zionists had infiltrated high American government circles.

These news items hammered repeatedly at the Zionists in Palestine—how they deceived the Arabs, how Sir Herbert Samuel acted as their pawn, how they behaved on every level "like people who had just foreclosed a mortgage on a very desirable territory."[46] To spark the imagination facts were embroidered with suggestions. The following item, copied in its entirety, is an apt illustration of how the *Dearborn Independent* summed up its favorite accusations:

Jabotinsky, the Russian revolutionary Jew, who went to Palestine, organized the military body known as "The Jewish Legion," became implicated in the Easter riots at Jerusalem, was heavily sentenced by the British authorities and immediately released on the arrival of Sir Stuart [*sic*] Samuel, the Jewish governor of Palestine, is reported to be planning to visit the United States. He has sent his thanks to "the American press" for its sympathy with him during his brief imprisonment.[47]

Logically, Ford had no cause to denounce the Zionists for un-American behavior because all Jews were involved in the same world-wide conspiracy. According to the *Dearborn Independent*, Jewish spokesmen generally opposed complete Americanization just as they opposed any modern gentile state because it threatened the preservation of Jewish life. Furthermore, unlike other critics of Zionism, the paper did not usually distinguish between good and bad American Jews, and it lashed out at all elements, Zionist and non-Zionist, from the left-wing East Siders to the conservative patricians of the American Jewish Committee. In some instances the paper insisted that the core of the Jewish evil rested in "the squat, swarthy, anarchic Eastern Jew," who could not be completely controlled by the "better class" of American Jews. But the latter were also to blame. The leaders of western Jewry, who worshiped the Golden Calf, were cooperating with eastern or "Mongolian" Jews on Zionism in order to protect their financial interests from destruction at the hands of the revolutionaries. That explained, the *Dearborn Independent* said, why Chaim Weizmann, a Jew from Pinsk, wielded so much power over the American Jewish community.[48]

IV

The Jewish liberals, the respectable Christian anti-Zionists, and the *Dearborn Independent* found nothing qualitatively new in political Zionism. They all saw danger in the movement—for standing in the way of assimilation and social acceptance in the United States or for disrupting the post-war order—but Zionism merely reinforced prejudices and suspicions which they had long entertained. All three relied on traditional images of the undesirable Jew, for even the Jewish liberals structured their arguments on the base of the alien and clannish Jew.

Basic dissimilarities, however, precluded the possibility that these factions could ever consciously league together in a fight against a Jewish state. In the eyes of the Jewish liberal, the ones who would suffer most because of Zionism were the American Jews themselves. The moderate Christians agreed that Jewish security was endangered, but they added warnings about Zionist (and Bolshevik) threats in Palestine and to world peace. The *Dearborn Independent,* whose anti-Jewish pronouncements were adopted by other extremists,[49] preached that the victim of any Jewish scheme like Zionism was the gentile world. Moreover, only the Jewish liberals really believed that Jews could change their behavior and obliterate the unfavorable images reflected in Zionism. Jewish racial characteristics were immutable according to the *Dearborn Independent.* As for some of the moderate critics of Zionism, their use of anti-Jewish imagery in depicting Zionist activity in Palestine suggests that they too expected nothing different from Jews.

The fact that anti-Zionism was linked to traditional anti-Semitism had two important corollaries. First, it meant that Zionists were less likely to convince opponents of the merits of their cause no matter how effective a counter-campaign they mounted. Secondly, frightened by the increasing Judeophobia and overt discrimination of the 1920's, which led among other things to barriers against Jews in white-collar employment and in higher education, American Jews retreated increasingly from Jewish nationalist endeavors.[50]

Nevertheless, Zionists had no choice but to defend their movement, for they, like their Reform counterparts, were fighting for control of the American Jewish community. Under the leadership of Brandeis their prestige and power had soared during the war years; they could point to the Balfour Declaration and the formation of the American Jewish Congress as notable victories. But challenged after 1917 by a widening and more militant opposition and by serious internal rifts, American Zionism could easily slide back to a subordinate position.

In 1906 Richard Gottheil had stated that only Jews, not Christians, worried about Jewish nationalism.[51] An exaggeration even then, it could hardly be defended after the Balfour Declaration. However, since it would have done little good to contest the extremists and the others who spun their opposition out of deep-seated Jew-hatred,[52] Zionists focused principally on the Jewish liberals, men like Jastrow, Kahn, Morgenthau, and Philipson. Resorting frequently to ridicule and contempt, they denounced their Jewish critics for creating dissension within the community and thus aiding the Jew-haters. They fumed especially at the rabbis who had testified against the Lodge-Fish resolution, calling them Benedict Arnolds and Pfefferkorns. The charge that Zionism conflicted with Americanism was totally groundless. How could Zionism be called un-American when it numbered among its supporters prominent Christian government officials, civic leaders like Brandeis or Julian W. Mack, and Jewish soldiers who had fought in the American army? Since the Allies gave their support to Jewish national self-determination, and thus identified it with their wartime strategy, Zionism had become one with American patriotism.[53] On a deeper level Horace Kallen addressed himself to the issue of assimilation and argued that true democracy in the American spirit had to include freedom for different nationalities. By encouraging cultural pluralism America would be enriched.[54]

These protestations notwithstanding the Zionists themselves were shaken by the upsurge in anti-Semitism. A few ventured the opinion that anti-Semitism was a constant, irrespective of how Jews behaved, and like Herzl they suggested that a Jewish state would increase respect for the Jew throughout the world.[55] But many more lost confidence. They feared the effects that the concept of diaspora nationalism—which assumed greater prominence with the Brandeis/Weizmann split in 1921—might give rise to, and some felt impelled to leave the movement entirely. Those who stayed talked less and less of statehood, and, slowly, American Zionism was watered down to Palestinianism.[56]

Certainly, American anti-Semitism never prompted Zionists to argue that Jews had no future in the United States. From the very beginning of the movement, supporters had insisted that America was not exile, that it stood outside the Herzlian interpretation of the anti-Semitic world. Although they had more reason in the 1920's than ever before to change their stand, they stood firm. They insisted that a Jewish Palestine would not appeal to American Jews personally; the latter supported it only on behalf of oppressed Jews elsewhere.[57] By equating their movement with philanthropy Zionists tacitly admitted that the monolithic concept of Americanism was too difficult to combat or that it was in fact unimpeachable.

Unable to withstand the forces of American nativism which sustained their opponents, the Zionists were losers in the controversy over a Jewish state which raged from 1917 to 1922. But theirs was only a short-term loss, for ultimately they achieved both their aims, the establishment of a Jewish state and control of the American Jewish community. However they, indeed all Jews, still had to cope with another problem that persisted from that early period—the practice of anti-Semites to conceal their true motives under the guise of anti-Zionism.

FOOTNOTES

1. See for example, *Jewish Messenger*, February 9, 1877, March 13, 1891, July 24, 1896, August 18, 1899; Joseph Krauskopf, *Prejudice, Its Genesis and Exodus* (New York, 1909), p. 86.
2. Morris Jastrow, Jr., "The Objections to a Jewish State," *Menorah Journal* 4 (June 1918): 136; *New York Times*, February 6, 1919; Julius Kahn, "Why Most American Jews Do Not Favor Zionism," *New York Times*, February 16, 1919, sec. 7, p. 7; reprint of article by Rabbi Samuel Schulman, *New York Times*, November 25, 1917, sec. 9, p. 3; Jesse I. Straus in *American Hebrew*, March 14, 1919. When the *New Republic* (October 5, 1918) supported the idea of a Jewish state on the grounds that Jews could not contribute to mankind generally so long as "they dwell as aliens among more or less friendly peoples," anti-Zionists like Jastrow and Rabbi David Philipson blamed the Zionists for thus stigmatizing American Jewry. *American Hebrew*, November 15, 1918; David Philipson, *My Life as an American Jew* (Cincinnati, 1941), pp. 276-77.
3. See anti-Zionist statement to the Peace Conference, in Morris Jastrow, Jr., *Zionism and the Future of Palestine* (New York, 1919), p. 154.
4. *Ibid.*, pp. 120-1. Interview of Kahn, *American Hebrew*, February 7, 1919.
5. Quoted in *New York Times*, February 6, 1919. On the importance of the flag for Zionists see *Maccabaean* 31 (November 1918): 313.
6. Henry S. Hendricks in *American Hebrew*, January 31, 1919; Simon W. Rosendale to R. B. Sanford, September 4, 1918, printed in *Congressional Record*, 65 Cong. 3 Sess., Appendix, pp. 78-80, and cited in Stuart Knee, "Vision and Judgment: The American Critics of the Zionist Movement, 1917-1941, doctoral dissertation (New York University, 1974), ch. 3.
7. Cf. Walter Laqueur, *A History of Zionism* (New York, 1972), pp. 385-407.
8. Henry Morgenthau, *All in a Life-Time* (Garden City, N.Y., 1925), pp. 399-400.
9. Ralph P. Boas, "Program of Zionism Menaces Jewish Unity," *New York Times*, December 16, 1917, sec. 4, p. 4; Boas, "Jew-Baiting in America," *Atlantic Monthly* 127 (May 1921): 659 ff; H. G. Enelow, *The Allied Countries and the Jews* (New York, 1918), p. 87; Jastrow, *Zionism*, pp. 131-3.
10. Morris Raphael Cohen "Zionism: Tribalism or Liberalism?" *New Republic* 18 (March 8, 1919): 182-83.
11. Gilbert Seldes, "The House of Esau," *The Nation* 113 (October 5, 1921): 374.
12. Naomi R. Wiener, "Reform Judaism in America and Zionism, 1897-1922," M.A. thesis (Columbia University, 1949), esp. pp. 18-21, 84-6, 95-6, 102-3.
13. *Ibid.*, pp. 18-20, 100; *Congressional Record*, 65 Cong. 3 Sess., Appendix, p. 79. A logical consequence of Reform's dichotomy between Zionist and non-Zionist was the radical plan advanced by Isaac W. Bernheim, a leader of the Union of American Hebrew Congregations. Bernheim proposed a "Reformed Church of American Israelites" to consist of 100 per cent American Jews who did not want to be connected in any way with Zionists and who were willing to relinquish to the latter the name "Jew." Wiener, "Reform Judaism," pp. 33-4.
14. *Ibid.*, pp. 76-7.
15. *Ibid.*, pp. 96 *et seq.*
16. Morgenthau, *All in a Life-Time*, p. 392.

17. *American Hebrew,* January 17, 1919, April 28, 1922. The paper became anti-Zionist in 1919 when Rabbi Isaac Landman assumed the editorship.

18. *Correspondence on the Advisability of Calling a Conference for the Purpose of Combating Zionism* (New York, 1918).

19. Jastrow, *Zionism,* appendix.

20. *Establishment of a National Home in Palestine,* 67 Cong. 2 Sess., Hearings before the Committee on Foreign Affairs on H. Con. Res. 52, pp. 85-7, 99-116; *American Hebrew,* April 28, May 5, 12, 1922.

21. Morgenthau reprinted the article in his autobiography. "Zionism a Surrender, Not a Solution," *All in a Life-Time,* ch. 19; Charles Goldblatt, "The Impact of the Balfour Declaration in America," *American Jewish Historical Quarterly* 57 (June 1968): 467.

22. *American Hebrew,* February 1, 1918.

23. Thomas Nixon Carver, "The Choice Before Jewry," *Menorah Journal,* 5 (February 1919): 10-1.

24. Paul Scott Mowrer, "The Assimilation of Israel," *Atlantic Monthly* 128 (July 1921): 103-10.

25. Philip Marshall Brown, "Zionism and Anti-Semitism," *North American Review* 210 (November 1919): 656-62. Brown wrote: "The Jew is restless, and by nature detached from most nationalistic interests because of his sense of racial solidarity that militates against his taking deep root in any community. . . . This thing we term Christian civilization is something alien to him. He would readily welcome a new social order with enthusiasm and erect a new altar to an 'unknown' God." In another article, "Jewish Nationalism" (*American Journal of International Law* 103 (October 1919), Brown listed the alternatives open to the Jew: a national home, a gradual loss of racial identity, or (most unlikely) the acquisition of more tolerance than ever accorded to a separate race.

26. See for example, Philip Cowen, *Prejudice Against the Jew* (New York, 1928), pp. 46, 75, 83, 86, 93, 97, 104-5, 116, 117, 127, 132.

27. For example, H. N. MacCracken, "A University Problem," *Menorah Journal* 9 (October 1923): 228; Fiorello LaGuardia, in Reuben Fink, *The American War Congress and Zionism* (New York, 1919), p. 165.

28. John P. Peters, "Zionism and the Jewish Problem," *Sewanee Review* 29 (July 1921): 268, 294; Horace J. Bridges, *Jew-Baiting* (New York, 1923), pp. 5-6, 73-5.

29. Herbert Adams Gibbons, "The Jewish Problem—Its Relation to American Ideals and Interests," *Century Magazine* 102 (September 1921): 787-92.

30. April 19, 1919, p. 85.

31. Herbert Adams Gibbons, "Zionism and the World Peace," *Century Magazine* 92 (January 1919): 370-8; Edward Bliss Reed, "The Injustice of Zionism," *Yale Review* 9 (April 1920): 522-8; Albert T. Clay, "Political Zionism," *Atlantic Monthly* 127 (February 1921): 268-79; Anstruther Mackay, "Zionist Aspirations in Palestine," *Atlantic Monthly* 126 (July 1920): 123-7; Peters, "Zionism and the Jewish Problem," pp. 282-93; Brown, "Zionism and Anti-Semitism," pp. 660-1.

32. See n. 31 for references to articles by Reed, Clay, and Gibbons; *Establishment of a National Home in Palestine,* pp. 21-35, 42, 69-74, 80, 83; Mackay, "Zionist Aspirations," p. 127; *Catholic Month,* cited in Goldblatt, "Impact of the Balfour Declaration," pp. 473-4; *Literary Digest,* July 31, 1920, pp. 30-31; Selig Adler, "Backgrounds of American Policy Toward Zion," in Moshe Davis, ed., *Israel: Its Role in Civilization* (New York, 1956), p. 276. Frank E. Manuel, *The Realities of American-Palestine Relations* (Washington, 1949), pp. 199-200, 222, 291-3; Peters, "Zionism and the Jewish Problem," p. 286.

33. Adler, "American Policy Toward Zion," p. 276; Clay, "Political Zionism," pp. 269, 276; Gibbons, "Zionism and the World Peace," p. 374.

34. Gibbons, "The Jewish Problem," p. 788.

35. Clay, "Political Zionism," p. 272; Mackay, "Zionist Aspirations," pp. 125, 127; Gibbons, "Zionism and the World Peace," pp. 375-8; *Establishment of a National Home in Palestine,* pp. 22-34, 70, 83; letter of Reed to *New York Times,* April 16, 1922, sec. 7, p. 8.

36. *Brooklyn Anti-Bolshevist* 1 (June 1919): 5.

37. Herman Bernstein, *The Truth About "The Protocols of Zion"* (New York, 1971), ch. 4; Morton Rosenstock, *Louis Marshall, Defender of Jewish Rights* (Detroit, 1965), pp. 118-27.

38. Norman Cohn, *Warrant for Genocide* (New York, 1967), pp. 68-71, 103; *The International Jew* (Being a Reprint of a Series of Articles Appearing in *The Dearborn Independent* from May 22 to October 2, 1920) 1:93; *Dearborn Independent,* December 17, 1920. References are to *Dearborn Independent* (hereinafter referred to as D. I.) only for items not reprinted in the volumes of the *International Jew.*

39. *International Jew,* 1: 30-1; *D.I.,* October 23, 1920.

40. *International Jew,* 3: 117.

41. *Ibid.,* 1: 89-90.

42. *Ibid.,* 1: 87, 89, 131, 159; 2: 25; 3: 115; 4. 153; *D.I.,* October 29, 1921.

43. *Ibid.,* October 23, 1920.

44. *International Jew,* 1: 88, 233; 3: 115, 118-24; 4: 65-6; *D.I.,* January 22, July 9, December 17, 1921.

45. *International Jew,* 3: 119-25, 128-40.

46. *D.I.,* September 18, October 2, November 6, 1920, April 9, July 2, 1921.

47. *Ibid.,* October 16, 1920. Note: the Zionist leader is a Russian revolutionary; the Zionists are assuming military control in Palestine the Jews (or at least Jabotinsky) and not the Arabs were responsible for the 1920 riots; the Zionists, working in this case through Sir Herbert, are making a farce of British rule; Jabotinsky expects a welcome in the United States (why else would he visit?); the presss was kind to him because it is Jew-contolled.

48. *Ibid.,* July 2, 1921; *International Jew,* 3: 88-101, 117; 4: 54-66, 154, 179-91. The *Dearborn Independent* expressed some sympathy for the poor and devout Jew, and for "the poor Jew who suffers for the delinquencies of the rich exploiter of his race." 1: 45, 49. Nevertheless, the image of Jewish character and behavior was fashioned by the powerful Jews.

49. An anti-Semitic weekly in New York, *American Standard,* frequently cited or excerpted from the *Dearborn Independent.* The Ku Klux Klan also invoked the same anti-Semitic images. David M. Chalmers, *Hooded Americanism* (Garden City, N.Y., 1965), p. 110; Rosenstock, *Louis Marshall,* p. 204.

50. Stephen S. Wise spoke bitterly of "the most tragic symptom of Jewish life in the world today—a panicky, sickening, tragi-comic nervousness of Jews in the light of any attempt to bring Jews together, to make them take counsel together, to think and feel and act together." Wise, *Jewish Anti-Semitism—A Tragi-Comedy,* address delivered before the Free Synagogue, January 1, 1928.

51. *American Hebrew,* February 2, 1906.

52. Stephen Wise did write a public answer to Ford, *Maccabaean* 34 (November 1920): 107-9 and Professor Israel Friedlaender answered Gibbons' article in "Zionism and the World Peace—A Rejoinder," *Century Magazine* 97 (April 1919); 803-10.

53. *Maccabaean* 31 (June 1918): 143; (October 1918): 287-8; 32 (February 1919): 31-2; (March 1919): 66-7, 69-70; *American Hebrew,* February 14, 21 (letters to editor), 1919; *Jewish Tribune* in *Current Opinion,* (August 1921); 202; *New Palestine,* July 1, August 5, October 21, 1921, January 13, April 28 (editorial and excerpts from Jewish press), May 5 (editorial and report of Untermyer's address), May 12 (editorial and letter of Marshall to Lodge), June 2, July 14, 1922; Samuel Untermyer, "Zionism—A Just Cause," *Forum* 66 (September 1921): 214-27; David Werner Amram, "Answering Professor Jastrow," *Menorah Journal* 4 (June 1918): 147-8.

54. Horace M. Kallen, "The Issues of the War and the Jewish Position," *Nation* 105 (November 29, 1917): 590-92; "Democracy, Nationality and Zionism," *Maccabaean* 31 (July 1918): 175. Kallen specifically rebutted Morris Raphael Cohen in "Zionism: Democracy or Prussianism," *New Republic,* 18 (April 5, 1919): 311-13.

55. Amram, "Answering Professor Jastrow," pp. 147-8; *Dos Yiddishe Folk* in *Maccabaean* 34 (July 1920): 21-3; H. Dannenbaum in *New Palestine,* December 23, 1921; Elisha M. Friedman, "In the Wake of Zionism," *Menorah Journal* 4 (April 1918): 107 and "Anti-Semitism," *Menorah Journal* 8 (February 1922): 1-6.

56. Yonathan Shapiro, *Leadership of the American Zionist Organization, 1897-1930* (Urbana, 1971), pp. 118, 127, 129, 131-2, 165-6, 251. See defensive statements by Judge Julian W. Mack, president of the ZOA denying that Jews constituted a *political* nationality. *Jewish Exponent,* March 26, 1920; *Survey,* May 22, 1920.

57. Naomi W. Cohen, *American Jews and the Zionist Idea* (New York, 1975), pp. 11-12, 30-1.

Felix M. Warburg and the Jewish Agency

by Jerome M. Kutnick

Felix M. Warburg (1871-1937), scion of a famous German Jewish banking family and partner through marriage in the investment banking firm of Kuhn, Loeb and Co. was a leading philanthropist in the American Jewish community. In 1929, he and other non-Zionists joined with members of the Zionist movement to form an enlarged Jewish Agency for Palestine. Warburg's willingness to participate in an organization with Jews of divergent views and from different backgrounds was not in itself a new phenomenon. The German-Jewish leadership to which Warburg belonged comprised a powerful stratum of American Jewry. This group, mainly of Jews from Germany or native American Jews of Central European origin, had a long history of serving and then cooperating with Jews from other milieus.

In response to the influx of Jews from Eastern Europe, German Jews had established institutions to serve the needs of the immigrants, and supported the Educational Alliance, YMHA and other organizations eager to Americanize the immigrants. In 1902, although they themselves affiliated with the Reform movement, German-Jewish leaders reorganized the Jewish Theological Seminary. They sought an institution that could train Rabbis who were sufficiently traditional to attract East European Jews, yet modern enough to provide a religious alternative for immigrants rejecting orthodox Judaism. After the Kishinev Pogrom, German-Jewish leaders of the community founded the American Jewish Committee in order "to prevent the infraction of civil and religious rights of Jews in any part of the World."[1]

The German-Jewish leadership began to cooperate with Jewish leaders and organizations outside their tightly-knit circle. During the first World War, American Jewry organized relief for Jews in war-torn Europe, and the German-Jewish establishment in America joined with orthodox and Jewish labor leaders in creating the Joint Distribution Committee. After the war, under pressure of public sentiment, German-Jewish leaders participated with the more recently arrived Eastern-European Jews in a joint delegation at the Paris Peace Conference.

The German-Jewish establishment was active in Jewish communal affairs for a variety of reasons. While it was motivated in part by a sense of *noblesse oblige* and a feeling of responsibility, it also desired to prevent or at least modify what they perceived as the more radical political tendencies and cultural behavior of American Jews from eastern Europe.

Felix Warburg was an active member of this establishment. He helped persuade the different factions of American Jewry to form the JDC and served as its chairman from 1914 to 1932. In the decade after the first World War, he served on the managing boards or executive committees of the Bureau of Jewish Social Research, Council of Young Men's Hebrew Association, National Council of Jewish Social Service and was an officer in the Jewish Theological Seminary, Joint Distribution Committee and Jewish Welfare Board to name but a few.[2] By examining Felix Warburg's leadership in the Jewish Agency, one can better understand the constellation of motives of at least one member of the German-Jewish establishment, and possibly shed some light on how and why a leading non-Zionist like Felix Warburg devoted his energy and resources to the problems of Palestine.

Philanthropy was a major vehicle by which the German-Jewish leadership manifested its interest in Jewish affairs. Felix Warburg and Jacob Schiff (his father-in-law) were the foremost philanthropists of this circle. Their approach to philanthropy, however, differed greatly. Schiff (1847-1920), although an active member of Reform Temple Emanu-El, helped endow the Jewish Theological Seminary and Yeshiva Isaac Elchanan (today Yeshiva University). Notwithstanding his heavy business responsibilities in Kuhn, Loeb and Co., Schiff gave of his time as well as his money. As president of the Montefiore Home for Chronic Invalids, he visited that institution once a week for over thirty-five years. Schiff viewed his philanthropy as an important responsibility and religious obligation. At the beginning of each year in keeping with his understanding of the Biblical concept of tithe, he would transfer ten percent of his annual income to be distributed during the year.[3]

For Felix Warburg, however, philanthropy was not as much an obligation as a vocation. Unlike his father-in-law or for that matter his brothers Paul and Max, Felix Warburg was not interested in banking or high finance. Although he became the senior partner in Kuhn, Loeb and Co., he preferred to devote his energies to philanthropy. He felt that good causes needed people who could "get the honey even out of the sour flowers" and recognized his own special talent for persuading people with divergent views to work together in support of a worthwhile cause.[4] Warburg, a man of great charm, ebullient personality and gregarious temperament, enjoyed the comradeships of his philanthropic associations. He regarded "friendships formed in the common interests of an earnest cause the only ones that are worthwhile and of lasting value."[5]

As a young boy in Hamburg, Felix was taught to donate a tenth of his allowance to charity. Later as a grown man in America, he continued to support worthwhile causes. By 1929, he had been an officer or had served on the board of over fifty philanthropic associations. Warburg seldom verbalized his reasons for supporting one cause rather than another and did not consciously develop an ideology of philanthropy. In 1927, two years before he joined the Jewish Agency, Warburg wrote *Under the Seven Stars,* a 64-page memorandum on his interests and activities. These unpublished notes shed light on Warburg's views on philanthropy. They tend to confirm the non-ideological nature of his philanthropic endeavors. The leading Jewish philanthropist in America compared the problems his philanthropy sought to solve to stones strewn in one's pathway, which required someone to stop and remove them. He found himself "stumbling over problems right and left asking for solutions."[6]

But Warburg's interest in different causes was not strictly a matter of chance. His decision to enter the Jewish Agency for Palestine was due to more than the random encounters of a wealthy philanthropist with a worthwhile cause. He did not merely "stumble" into the Agency, but in August 1929, only after years of discussions and investigations, joined the enlarged Jewish Agency for Palestine.

The term "Jewish agency" originated in the Palestine Mandate of the Council of the League of Nations. Article four of the Mandate agreement recognized the need for:

an appropriate Jewish agency . . . for the purpose of advising and
cooperating with the Administration of Palestine in such economic,
social and other matters as may affect the establishment of the Jewish
national home in Palestine.

Although in 1922 the Mandate agreement stated that "the Zionist
organization . . . shall be recognized as such agency," it also called
upon the Zionist Organization to "take steps . . . to secure the cooperation of all Jews who are willing to assist in the establishment of the
Jewish national home."[7]

Even before the League of Nations had officially confirmed the
Mandate agreement, the World Zionist Organization was discussing
ways of securing such cooperation. At the London Conference of 1920,
American Zionists under the leadership of Louis D. Brandeis proposed
enlisting non-Zionists into the Zionist organization by dropping its
political functions. A year later the 12th World Zionist Congress proposed convoking a World Jewish Congress in order to organize World
Jewry on behalf of Palestine.[8] Chaim Weizmann, president of the
World Zionist organization sought an organization that would include
Jews who were prepared to help build Palestine but were unwilling to
affiliate with the Zionist movement. He believed however, that the
German-Jewish leadership in America, whom he recognized as "the
mainstay of the Joint Distribution Committee" and whose "philanthropies were manifold and generous" would neither enter the Zionist
Organization nor assent to the democratic machinery and implied
sovereignty of a World Jewish Congress. In February 1923, after
having the Zionist Actions Committee approve the idea of a "Jewish
responsible to a body representative of the Jewish people," Weizmann
went to America to interest the non-Zionist pillars of the community in
an enlarged Jewish Agency. It was during that trip that Weizmann first
met Warburg, laying the foundation for the latter's participation in the
Jewish Agency for Palestine.[9]

Warburg's interest in Palestine, however, preceded his meeting
with Weizmann. Judah Magnes, Felix Warburg's close friend and the
Warburg family rabbi had been writing Warburg about Palestine's
problems. Warburg was more concerned with "the terrible conditions
all over the world" than with "the problems of Palestine . . . whose
radius is small."[10] In time, however, perhaps due in part to Magnes'
influence, Warburg began to regard Palestine as "an important point
for inspiration" and a "place for scholarship and research." He con-

ceived a plan for sending newly ordained American rabbis to Palestine so "they may gain inspiration from what they may see" and donated $500,000 to help establish the Hebrew University in Jerusalem.[11]

In 1925, Warburg visited Palestine for the first time. Two years later, he together with other non-Zionists organized the Joint Survey Committee to examine Palestine's economic development. In August 1929, after having assured themselves that the reconstruction of Palestine was both economically feasible and a worthwhile cause, Warburg and other non-Zionists joined the Jewish Agency for Palestine.

The enlarged Jewish Agency was formally established on August 14, 1929, in Zurich, Switzerland. Warburg considered its inaugural session "a real picture of historic importance" and exulted at witnessing "so many different types of Jewish leaders together endeavoring to work hand in hand."[12]

According to the Pact of Glory (as the Agency Constitution was called), the Jewish Agency was to consist of three organs, the Council, Administrative Committee and Executive, each composed of equal members of Zionists and non-Zionists. On August 11, 1929, when the constituent meeting convened, Zionists and non-Zionists had not yet reached agreement on the terms of non-Zionist participation in the Agency and were still arguing over the ratio of Zionists and non-Zionists in the Executive. Warburg, however, was not too concerned. He expected that by ignoring political and ideological differences, "people would as quickly as possible forget who was appointed from the non-Zionists and who from the Zionists." Warburg spoke several times at the Agency's first session. His public statements at this gathering underscored some of his views on the Agency's function and how he envisioned his own role in the new body. Warburg paid tribute to Chaim Weizmann and Louis Marshall as the two Jewish leaders most responsible for creating the enlarged Jewish Agency. Upon accepting the chairmanship of the Administrative Committee, he promised to fulfill his responsibilities "so that Weizmann and Marshall, my foster parents in this matter, may be satisfied."[13]

Warburg did not look upon the Agency as a way of securing a Jewish national home but as an instrument to rebuild Palestine. Not sharing the Zionists' ardent desire for a Jewish national home or even understanding the nature of their striving, he was willing for the Agency to waive Zionist objectives in order to improve relations with the Arabs. He hoped to involve the Arabs in Jewish Agency work so that its efforts at developing Palestine "would be the hand to hand work of the whole population of that little country."[14]

Warburg's motivation for entering the Jewish Agency was clearly not nationalistic. He believed that the non-Zionist participation in the Agency demonstrated its intention to rebuild Palestine for non-Zionist reasons. But his expectation that the formation of an enlarged Jewish Agency would improve relations with the Arabs proved unrealistic.

On August 23rd, nine days after the ratification of the Pact of Glory, Arabs in Palestine began to attack Jews in Jerusalem, Hebron, Safed and other settlements. 133 Jews were killed and several hundred were wounded. These assaults, resembling the worst pogroms, were perpetrated not in Eastern Europe under a Tzarist regime, but in Palestine under the British Mandate, and grieved and enraged Jews throughout the world. Jewish communities protested British inaction and demanded that the Mandate Government stop massacres and restore order. As the violence ended, people tried to ascertain what had actually happened. Explanations varied as to the causes of the riots and opinions differed over what policies should be adopted. At the same time, Zionist and non-Zionist members of the Jewish Agency had to agree on a common coarse of action.

Warburg learned of the riots while still in Europe. He received a detailed account of the situation in Palestine from Col. Kisch, shortly before the latter's return to Palestine. Warburg was disappointed "that after the (Agency's) declarations of good feeling towards the Arabs and the expressed desire to live in peace with them this outbreak should occur." But he was not disillusioned. He considered himself still "the same old optimist and believed things will straighten out."[15]

During his return trip to America, he spent his days on board the S.S. *Homeric* taking stock of the situation. In a memorandum prepared on the boat, he wrote down his ideas on how to "prevent reoccurrences of these absolutely unnecessary, unconstructive and cruel outbreaks." Warburg wanted to end the discussions of "rights on one side and promises in regard to a national home for the Jews on the other side . . .", since "evidently the millenium of good understanding has not come and will not come by dwelling on the points of disagreement."[16]

While Warburg sailed homeward, American Jews were venting their anger at the British and Arabs. In New York City, 35,000 Jews marched to the British Consulate-General office; a restaurant owner Graubard formed the "Graubard batallion" to rush to Palestine and "put the Arabs in their place". Zionist organizations protested British policy, and the president of the ZOA accused England of not having "defended the justice and rights to Jews contained in the purpose of her mandate." The Zionist labor monthly, *The Vanguard,* assured its readers that even Great Britain "is not strong enough to thwart the united will of a great people."[17]

Warburg was also critical of the British administration of the Mandate. But while he admitted that "some officials accused of stupidity or negligence . . . ought to go", he urged Jewish leaders not to antagonize the Mandate authority. Warburg pressed for a more conciliatory policy. He and the Zionists differed on how Jewry should react towards England's administration of Palestine. Their disagreement, however, was not merely over policy but was concerned with the very nature of the Jews' relationship to non-Jewish society.

In 1929, the Zionist movement had not yet defined its nationalist objectives. Ideological lines were not so drawn that Jews opposed to a Jewish state would feel unable to participate in Zionist projects. But although Zionists did not concur on whether to focus their struggle on reviving the Hebrew language, resettling Palestine or attaining political sovereignty, they agreed that the Jewish people must be master of its own fate and should insist on its own solution of the Jewish problem.

Warburg and his non-Zionist colleagues invested in the Palestine Economic Corporation, endowed the Hebrew University and even contributed to the Zionist movement's *Keren Hayesod.* But although they supported many Zionist projects they did not share the belief that the Jews alone could solve the Jewish problem. Instead they sought to strengthen the liberal element of society and relied on humanitarian impulses to ameliorate the conditions of the Jews. Warburg regarded the non-Zionist proposals for cooperation and goodwill among Jews and non-Jews more hopeful of achievement than building up a Jewish home on bayonets. He considered Zionist objectives "impractical and foolhardy." Jokingly, he would tell his friends how a future Jewish state would have to send an ambassador to Kuhn, Loeb and Co. to negotiate its annual budget.[18]

When Warburg left Europe two weeks after the Agency's meeting, riots in Palestine had still not ended. Upon arriving in New York, he issued a statement stressing the Agency's willingness to compromise and the common desire of all people for good relations in Palestine:[19]

As I see it, we who are united in the Jewish Agency stand solemnly

pledged to the following guiding principle: no political ambition, but
cultural social and economic 'live and let live' for all. As for the Arabs,
. . . I am quite sure that the better part of the Moslem population
resents this uprising.

Warburg's statement elicited much criticism; Stephen Wise, for
example, expressed his "amazement . . . that certain men in the
forefront of Jewish life in America have intimated that the time has
come to renounce political ambitions." Isaac Landman, on the other
hand, publisher of the non-Zionist English-language Jewish journal,
The American Hebrew, wrote Warburg of his "shock . . . at the attack
of Dr. Wise (thinly veiled) on your honest and straight forward utter-
ance regarding the future aims of the Jewish Agency . . ." and
suggested having his paper expose the Zionists for "frustrating conciliatory measures towards the Arabs." Warburg may have shared
Landman's views on Zionist intransigence but he asked the publisher
to modulate his paper's criticism of the Zionists "so that it will in no way
jeopardize the progress of the upbuilding work in Palestine."[20]

On September 21st, Landman and Warburg discussed *American
Hebrew* policy, and soon afterwards *The American Hebrew* was less
critical of the Zionists. It no longer assailed "the arrogance of the
so-called Zionist revolutionaries (which) is doubtless a causative factor
behind the unhappy Moslem outbreaks." It even had positive things to
say about its erstwhile enemy, the American Jewish Congress, lauding
it for being "cautious where the welfare of the Jews of Palestine hangs
in the balance."[21]

On September 11th, one month after Zionists and non-Zionists had
assembled in Zurich, the Agency faced another major crisis. Louis
Marshall, the non-Zionist leader deemed most responsible for creating
the enlarged Jewish Agency and Warburg's "foster-parent in this matter" died on an operating table in a Zurich hospital. Felix Warburg,
wealthy American-Jewish philanthropist and the chairman of the
Agency's Administrative Committee, now became the leading non-
Zionist in the Jewish Agency.

In certain respects Marshall and Warburg seemed alike. Both men
were members of the German-Jewish establishment of the American
Jewish community. They had served together on the boards of the
Joint Distribution Committee, Jewish Welfare Board, American
Jewish Committee and numerous other organizations supported by
the German-Jewish establishment. While neither Marshall nor War-

burg desired a Jewish state, both men helped persuade other non-Zionists to join the Jewish Agency for Palestine. Nevertheless, despite their similar social backgrounds and common interests in Jewish affairs, Marshall and Warburg viewed Palestine and understood the Jewish problem quite differently.

Marshall, a prominent attorney and brilliant intellectual, had been influenced by Ahad Ha'am's conception of Palestine as the spiritual center of the Jewish people. Although Marshall did not accept the Zionist concept of a Jewish nation, he did consider himself part of the Jewish people and felt a responsibility for their fate and well-being. Warburg's interest in Palestine was to a large extent a product of his friendship with Judah Magnes. Like Marshall, he regarded Palestine as a spiritual and intellectual center. But Warburg perceived his commitment towards the upbuilding in Palestine in the same way he regarded himself duty bound towards other humanitarian causes.

Marshall's death worried many Zionists. During negotiations on enlarging the Jewish Agency, Zionist Organization memos had constantly referred to the American non-Zionists as "the Marshall Group." Col. Kisch, who had negotiated with the non-Zionists reported to the Zionist Executive about Marshall's "dictatorial position" and complained of the non-Zionists' inability to answer Kisch's querries without first consulting Marshall.[22] Zionists were also concerned about the leadership of their new partners in the Agency being transferred from Louis Marshall, who according to Weizmann, "had a very clear understanding of and a deep sympathy for the national endeavors of Jewish communities . . . [and a] devotion to Jewish matters," to Felix Warburg, whom some Zionists felt was "incapable of a complete understanding of our problem." At the same time they recognized that Palestine was "only one among the fifty-seven varieties of Warburg's philanthropic endeavors.*[23]

Although Warburg replaced Marshall as the leading non-Zionist, he did not consider himself as heir to Marshall or his policies. Rather after Marshall's death, Warburg no longer had "the possibility of consulting him continuously" and would "have to obtain wise counsel elsewhere."[24] But he still intended to remain in the Agency and perform his duties as he understood them.

* Warburg had a large screen containing fifty-seven different file cases built in his office. Each file case represented a different committee or board on which he served. Warburg would show this screen to his visitors and tell them, "I am like Heinz Pickles. I belong to fifty-seven varieties of committees."

Warburg continued looking for ways to bring peace to Palestine. He sent cables to the London Zionist Executive suggesting measures they should take. Sometimes his messages sounded like veiled threats as when Warburg, the largest private investor in the Palestine Economic Corp. wired the Executive that "investment in Palestine forthcoming only if Palestine entente restored." Warburg believed that the Jews could improve relations with the British by first clearing up their difficulties with the Arabs. He asked Weizmann to postpone his negotiations with the British Foreign Office and travel to Palestine "to get as many declarations goodwill Palestine from Christians and Moslems and give as many to them."[25]

Two incidents, however—Warburg's interview with the prime-minister of Great Britain and his involvement in the controversy over Magnes' proposals—demonstrate the difficulties Warburg's leadership encountered when his views clashed with those of the Zionists and Jewish public opinion.

When Ramsay MacDonald, Prime Minister of England, informed Weizmann of his willingness to meet a delegation of Jews in America in late 1929, Weizmann asked Warburg to arrange for a deputation. Weizmann was aware of Warburg's proclivity to avoid arguments and seek areas of agreement, and warned Warburg not to let his audience with MacDonald develop into mere goodwill gestures; Warburg should not "be put off with mere words or assurances."[26] The Zionist Organization of America also drafted a statement to be submitted to the British prime minister. After deleting nine of the ten references to "the Jewish national home" Warburg presented a modified version of the ZOA statement to MacDonald.[27]

At their meeting, MacDonald impressed Warburg as "most friendly and most sympathetic, full of genuineness and sincerity." Warburg read a prepared statement recalling American Jewry's investments in Palestine and outlining new enterprises being planned. His statement linked these investments "to the practical steps that will be taken by the Mandatory Government to restore confidence in the safety of life and property in Palestine." He also urged MacDonald "to maintain liberal principles of immigration . . . to encourage the close settle-ments of Jews on the lands . . . (and) to fix the status of the Jewish Agency."

After he had concluded his prepared statement Warburg discussed with MacDonald his own plan to prevent future riots. He suggested erecting an impartial broadcasting station to "counteract the spreading of false rumours," such as had driven "excitable people into a frenzy of fear." Warburg, however, heeded the London Executive's request and did not discuss his other idea with MacDonald. He did not suggest that Great Britain and the Jews participate in a project for the benefit of the Arab population that would demonstrate the advantages of living under the Mandate.[28]

The following Sunday, Warburg hosted MacDonald at his country estate, Woodlands. It was in a private conversation at Woodlands that Warburg suggested that MacDonald tell the High Commissioner of Palestine of Judah Magnes, "a party who might be helpful in bringing the English, Arab and Jewish population together." (When Warburg discussed Magnes with MacDonald on October 25, he did not know of Magnes' negotiations with St. John Philby for an Arab-Jewish peace agreement. Warburg learned of Magnes' activities on October 30 from a coded cable he received from his former secretary, Harriet Lowenstein Goldstein, who informed Warburg that "Magnes planning independent negotiations Arab and third person pro-Arab.")

Two weeks later Magnes himself told the High Commissioner of his negotiations with Philby for an Arab-Jewish agreement. Magnes' request that Warburg support these negotiations further enmeshed Warburg in political disputes between Zionists and non-Zionists concerning Jewish national aspirations for Palestine.[29]

Magnes cabled Warburg the tentative agreement he had achieved with John Philby, admittedly a friend of the Arabs. The Philby-Magnes plan would retain the Jewish Agency and Mandatory government and permit immigration based upon economic capacity. It would also establish a democratically elected legislature, which given the population figures of Arabs and Jews in Palestine in 1929, would probably result in an Arab parliament majority. Built-in safeguards, however, would prevent the legislature from contraveing international obligations or legislating acts detrimental to minorities and foreigners. "If you agree (with these proposals)," Magnes cabled Warburg, "take immediate action Weizmann. If not ask you not communicate Weizmann, Zionist Executive London, Zionist Organization Palestine, ZOA."[30]

Warburg transmitted Magnes' proposals and asked Weizmann not to discuss them with anyone outside his office. He told Weizmann he did not necessarily agree with the Magnes-Philby accord, but was delighted that Magnes was so active for peace and understanding. At the same time, Warburg privately criticized Magnes for his independent station. He told Magnes he neither approved nor disapproved of his agreement, but preferred having the various "treaties and proposals submitted to the (Agency's) sound minds concerned with these difficult problems."[31]

Weizmann ignored Warburg's request for secrecy and conferred with the Political Commission of the Jewish Agency on Magnes' negotiations. Weizmann believed that Philby had duped Magnes and that the negotiations were really "a trick to wipe out the impressions created by their [the Palestinian Arabs] atrocious behavior [the riots]."[32] However, when the plenary meeting of the Political Commission unanimously rejected the Magnes-Philby agreement, Weizmann warned the Commission not to disavow the proposal outright "as otherwise no money would be forthcoming from America." The Commission demanded that Warburg instruct Magnes to break off negotiations, and asked Weizmann to phone Warburg from London in order to explain why such action was necessary. Weizmann told Warburg he considered Philby untrustworthy and believed Magnes had made a grave mistake negotiating with him. At the same time, he assured Warburg that "he (Weizmann) is most anxious to get an understanding along the lines suggested and wants to take the matter up with the Prime Minister very soon." Warburg conveyed the Political Commission's orders to Magnes, but Magnes, instead of breaking off negotiations, went public. He revealed his plans for a political settlement in Palestine in the New York Times and called upon the Jews to "renounce all political ambitions in Palestine."[33]

Magnes' proposals aroused a furor within the American Jewish community. A public statement by James Rosenberg, a close friend of Warburg, calling upon the Jewish community "to stop all conversation (on the Magnes controversy) and have the matter left to Felix M. Warburg," did not help matters and perhaps served to further identify Warburg with Magnes' views. The ZOA sent a protest letter to Warburg urging him to repudiate Magnes. Communal leaders noted privately that unless Warburg disassociated himself from Magnes, cooperation between Zionists and non-Zionists within the Jewish Agency would cease.[34]

Warburg, however, refused to publicly denounce Magnes, but let it be known that he had asked Magnes to break off negotiations with

Philby. Privately, however, Warburg told acquaintances that while Magnes' proposals had "a good deal to recommend itself, the time and the place was ill-chosen." He admonished Magnes for having "driven a wedge among Jews," and explained to him that while "the agitation against you will die out," as far as Warburg's position in the community and in the Agency is concerned, "it has made things more difficult."[35]

After the 1929 riots, Warburg found himself in constant disagreement with the Zionists. Warburg believed that World Jewry was ultimately dependent upon the humanitarian and liberal sentiments of others. Accordingly, he urged the agency to demonstrate to others its desire for peaceful relations with the Arabs. The Zionists, while also seeking peace in Palestine, did not believe that such appeals would solve the Jewish problem. Moreover, while the Zionist movement had not yet determined its position on Jewish statehood or on Jewish political sovereignty, it was not about to waive that option or other nationalist objectives to placate Arab and other opponents of Zionism.

Warburg responded to the issues dividing him and the Zionists by ignoring the whole question of the different outlooks and beliefs. His avoidance of discussions on Arab rights and on the promises of a national home for the Jews prevented him from understanding the serious differences that divided the Arabs and the Jews.

In 1929, Warburg, because of his proclivity to avoid conflicts, compromised his own position. He restrained the non-Zionist press from embarking upon a campaign against Zionism, withdrew his suggestion for a British-Jewish project to assist the Arab population and even cooperated with the Political Commission's attempt to stop the Magnes-Philby negotiations.

Warburg joined the Jewish Agency with preconceived notions on how to promote peace and rebuild Palestine. Convinced that his plans for Palestine were for the general good, Warburg did not believe he was protecting vested interests. Rather, he felt he was devoting his own energy and resources to a cause that would benefit others. This philanthropic gesture on Warburg's part, his acceptance of a position of responsibility and leadership in the Jewish Agency, like philanthropy in general, was voluntary, and based on the whims of a philanthropist, subject to his personal recall.

Despite his opposition to Agency policies, Warburg did not resign from the Jewish Agency or become less active in Palestine affairs. Rather, Felix Warburg's non-Zionist leadership, by compromising on points of contention while ignoring fundamental differences set the tone of future Zionist—non-Zionist relations within the Jewish Agency for many years to come.

FOOTNOTES

1. Charter of the American Jewish Committee, November 11, 1929.
2. "National Jewish Organizations in the United States," in *American Jewish Year Books* 19-30 (1918-1929).
3. Frieda Schiff Warburg, *Reminiscences of a Long Life* (Privately printed, 1956), p. 52.
4. *Ibid.*, p. 100.
5. Felix M. Warburg, *Under the Seven Stars—Biographical Material* (1927) in Felix M. Warburg Papers, American Jewish Archives, Cincinnati, Ohio.
6. *Ibid.*, p. 35.
7. Mandate for Palestine, text in *Encyclopedia of Zionism and Israel*, 2: 757-60.
8. Ben Halpern, *The Idea of a Jewish State* (Cambridge, Mass., 1961 ed.), pp 188-89.
9. Chaim Weizmann, *Trial and Error* (New York, 1949), p. 307.
10. Felix Warburg to Judah L. Magnes, March 16, 1923, in Judah Leib Magnes Papers, microfilm copy at American Jewish Archives, Cincinnati, Ohio.
11. *Under the Seven Stars*, pp. 4, 48; interview with Edward M.M. Warburg, April 18, 1967, in Oral History Division, Institute of Contemporary Jewry, The Hebrew University of Jerusalem.
12. Warburg to Frieda Schiff Warburg, August 13, 1929, Warburg Mss.
13. Warbug comments in *The Jewish Agency for Palestine Constituent Meeting of the Council, Held at Zurich, August 11-14, 1929, Official Report* (London, 1930).
14. Minutes of Administrative Committee Meeting of Jewish Agency, August 13, 1929, Magnes Mss.
15. Warburg to Max M. Warburg, August 26, 1929, Warburg Mss.
16. Memorandum by Felix M. Warburg, on board *S.S. Homeric*, August 28—September 3, 1929, *ibid.*
17. L. Berg, "American Public Opinion on Palestine," *Menorah Journal* (October 1929); *Vanguard*, September 1929, p. 8.
18. Minutes of Administrative Committee, September 26, 1929, in Lee K. Frankel Papers, American Jewish Historical Society, Waltham, Massachusetts; David Farrer, *The Warburgs: The Story of a Family* (New York, 1975), p. 103.
19. *Jewish Daily Bulletin*, September 5, 1929.
20. Isaac Landman to Warburg, September 14, 1929, and Warburg to Landman, September 14, 1929, Warburg Mss.
21. *American Hebrew*, August 30 and September 27, 1929.
22. Fred Kisch to Chaim Weizmann, February 27, 1929, records of the London Office of the World Zionist Organization/The Jewish Agency for Palestine, Record Group Z4, Central Zionist Archives, Jerusalem, Israel.
23. Weizmann, *Trial and Error*, p. 308; interview with Emanuel Neumann, November 3, 1975.
24. Memorandum of conversation with Louis D. Brandeis and Bernard Flexner, September 19, 1929, Warburg Mss.
25. Warburg to Zionburo, September 17, 1929, in Maurice B. Hexter Papers, American Jewish Archives, Cincinnati, Ohio.
26. Weizmann to Warburg, September 24, 1929, Hexter Mss.
27. *Jewish Daily Bulletin*, October 13, 1929, and *Jewish Chronicle*, December 6, 1929.
28. Memorandum on deputation to MacDonald, *Jewish Daily Bulletin*, October 11, 1929; address to MacDonald, October 13, 1929, Warburg Mss.
29. Warburg to Judah Magnes, October 17, 1929, Magnes Mss.

30. Magnes to Warburg, November 1, 1929, *ibid.*

31. Warburg to Chaim Weizmann, November 4, 1929, Hexter Mss; Warburg to Judah Magnes, November 2, 1929, Magnes Mss.

32. Records of the Political Commission of the Jewish Agency, November 11, 1929.

33. Memorandum of conversation with Chaim Weizmann in London, November 12, 1929, Hexter Mss; *New York Times*, November 21, 1929.

34. *Jewish Daily Bulletin*, November 25, 1929; Zionist Organization of America to Warburg, November 21, 1929, Warburg Mss; Stephen S. Wise to Louis Newman, November 21, 1929 Stephen S. Wise Papers, American Jewish Historical Society, Waltham, Massachusetts.

35. Irma Lindheim to Judah Magnes, December 31, 1929, and Warburg to Magnes, December 4, 1929, Magness Mss.

The Roosevelt Administration and Zionism: The Pre-War Years, 1933-1939

by Selig Adler

Recent revisionist historiography has challenged many interpretations blithely accepted by a previous less critical generation. This inquest has included President Franklin D. Roosevelt's resignation to the slaughter of six million European Jews. Many of these innocents, it is argued, could have been spared had FDR made determined efforts to open the gates of the United States to shelter them.[1] The purpose of this study is not to retell this story, but rather to investigate Washington's half-hearted efforts to facilitate entry into the British mandate of Palestine. The Holy Land was the most feasible asylum for uprooted Jews, so many of whom subsequently perished at the hands of the Nazis. With the onset of war in 1939, political and military considerations multiplied the difficulties in maintaining an open door in Palestine. But during the years that elapsed from the beginning of the Nazi pogrom in 1933 to the outbreak of general war in 1939, how much effort did the United States expend in trying to persuade England to make maximum use of the Holy Land sanctuary?

Three assumptions can be made in answering this question. First, that since the domestic situation made a general lowering of the American immigration barrier politically impossible, Palestine remained the only alternative for large numbers of expellees at a time when all plans to create new havens of refuge proved abortive. Secondly, it is assumed that the Holy Land could have absorbed many more newcomers than the 42,000 who fled there during the five initial years of the Nazi inquisition.[2] The final supposition is that unrelenting American pressure could have kept the British from tightening the Palestine immigration quota during the pre-war years of Nazi aggression when the final doom of European Jewry was clearly foreseeable.[3]

Obviously had Palestine been put to full use, the Holocaust's grim toll would have been measurably reduced. Hitler did not implement his plans for genocide until early 1942, when he concluded that there was no place of refuge for the millions of unwanted Jews swept up as his legions pierced through the Jewish heartland of Eastern Europe. It is, of course, impossible to know if Hitler's verdict would have been for exile rather than annihilation had the Allies, during the early stage of the war, furnished transportation from the neutral Iberian ports to previously assigned retreats. But it is certain that if the doors of the Holy Land had been kept fully open prior to 1939 many who were ultimately machine-gunned or gassed would have been saved.

The blame for the American failure to act before the sands of time ran out has often been placed upon a covey of Near Eastern specialists within the State Department. These men, so the indictment reads, allowed their ingrained anti-Zionist bias to thwart the warm humanitarianism of the President. Since FDR could have reversed their decisions as he did many others made by his subordinates, any inquiry must originate with an analysis of Roosevelt's approach to the concept of a Jewish Palestine.

The President was a complex man who revealed few traces of his innermost thoughts. He was much more the expert mass psychologist and able politician than the creative diplomat. This was particularly true during the early New Deal years when he was so engrossed in lifting the paralyzing business depression that he had little time to spare for the Middle Eastern muddle. Because he regarded this region as peripheral to American vital interests, he allowed the State Department to formulate Palestinian policy. Meanwhile he used his expert powers of dissimulation to placate the harried Jewish leaders who sought his help. When pressed too hard by his Oval Office callers for concrete action, he would make glib promises which he usually failed to put into the executive pipeline.[4] Thus it was that while FDR made only faltering efforts to solve the refugee problem, his image in Jewish circles remained that of a warm friend whose helping hand was stayed by intransigent subalterns.

The archival remains readily expose the President's methods of operation. He steadily retreated from the stout endorsement of a Jewish Palestine that he had made prior to his 1932 election. After his inauguration, messages to Jewish groups would invariably emphasize that the Balfour Declaration had granted Jewish rights to a home in

Palestine without promise of exclusive occupation. As time elapsed the caveats to this position multiplied. Chief among them was an endorsement of the State Department's narrow interpretation of the 1924 Anglo-American convention on the Holy Land which held, contrary to Zionist arguments, that the United States' role in Palestine was limited to preventing changes in the operation of the mandate detrimental to the interests of American nationals.[5] As the Axis crisis ripened to the point where Britain's Middle Eastern bastions stood in jeopardy, the State Department grew fearful of arousing the Arabs by any kind words at all for Zionist aspirations. Inasmuch as all White House statements on Palestine were drafted by the State Department, their wording grew ever more bland.[6] Meanwhile, the President limited himself to glad-handing his Jewish visitors and patiently hearing out their problems. On rare occasions he did prove helpful. Thus in 1936 he pressured London not to curtail the Palestine immigration quota and at times he allowed the State Department to prepare rejoinders to Arab complaints against the Zionists.[7]

Such sporadic action nourished the idea in the Zionist camp that Roosevelt would have done much more but for State Department opposition. Only rarely before the news of Hitler's wartime genocide horrified the American Jewish community did any of its leaders openly question the President's benevolence. FDR even failed to protest vigorously the 1939 British White Paper which vitiated the Balfour Declaration by proposing to turn Palestine eventually into a land controlled by the Arab majority. Nonetheless, Rabbi Stephen S. Wise thanked Roosevelt for doing "all that you could do to avert this disaster."[8]

Jewish advisers among the White House retinue seldom prodded FDR on the Palestine issue. Samuel I. Rosenman, the President's major speech writer, cautioned his chief to give heed to non-Zionist Jewish opinion which Rosenman equated with majority sentiment.[9] More might have been expected of Felix Frankfurter, an experienced Zionist leader. But the Harvard law professor's correspondence with the President reveals no urgency on Jewish matters and where reference was made to Zionism it was often of a jocular nature. Moreover, Frankfurter was an ardent Anglophile who thought the administration correct in using restraint toward London on the Palestine issue.[10]

If the President was occasionally flippant on Zionist matters, he certainly gave the Jewish problem serious thought. He was fond of recalling that he had attended the Versailles Peace Conference where the victorious Allies had designated the Holy Land as the Jewish National Home. Sumner Welles, a close confident of the President, was probably correct in holding that Roosevelt regarded the Balfour Declaration as an act of international justice. But the President thought of a Jewish Palestine in terms of an autonomous enclave within a large federation of surrounding Arab territory, a view which concided with the long-held opinion of the State Department.[11]

This plan of bi-nationalism within an Arab federation was contemplated long before Hitler created an acute refugee crisis and nothing that subsequently happened to the Jews made sufficient impact to alter official Washington's opinion. Jewish pressure during the Nazi crisis resulted in talk of other solutions, but both the White House and the State Department clung to the notion of a bi-nationalist accommodation in a tiny portion of Palestine within the confines of a large federated Arab state. In the light of both Arab and Jewish opposition the plan was unworkable, and too rigid adherence to it proved an obstacle to more feasible solutions.

As the war skies darkened over Europe, the administration grew even more guarded in its policy toward Zionism. The President shared, to a far greater degree than ordinarily recognized, the all-pervading isolationist fixation of the 1930s.[12] He feared that a pro-Jewish stand might ensnare the United States into just the kind of foreign entanglement that he wished to avoid. The Middle East was a restive British sphere of influence, and Washington knew that London would not be amiss to sharing some of its vexations there. "A very wise old bird tells me," the President wrote in 1935, "that . . . the British would much like to involve us in some way—any way—in the world's critical problems."[13]

The President had additional reasons for his caution. A superb politician, he was not anxious to help fasten the label "Jew deal" upon his administration at a time when the phrase was popular in right-wing circles. With the Jewish masses safely in the Democratic coalition why provide ammunition for the American proto-fascists?[14] FDR, however, had to make some move as the Nazi vise tightened around the Reich's stepchildren. The President, of course, was helpless in the face of this tragedy but he was rightly expected to assume the humanitarian task of finding new homes for the swelling list of expellees. Roosevelt was never to come up with a viable solution for mass re-settlement of the displaced, but acting in character when faced with a thorny question, he flitted from one improvisation to another.

For three years FDR's principal effort on behalf of the wanderers was some gentle pressure on Britain to keep the Palestinian door ajar. But his hand was forced to greater effort in the dreary spring of 1938 when Hitler annexed Austria, adding Vienna's teeming Jewish population to the stream of homeless outcasts. He summoned a conference financed by private organizations with representatives from thirty-two countries. The conferees who assembled at the French resort of Evian les Baines in 1938 might well have been stalemated in any event. But their failure was made all the more certain by Roosevelt's prior declaration that no country, including the United States, would be expected to raise its immigration quotas.[15] This meant that any substantial diminution of the refugee horde could only come by increased outflow to Palestine. But this solution faded when the British representative at Evian ruled out even any discussion of a Zionist answer to the problem.[16] The Intergovernmental Committee on Refugees, set up at Evian, proved to be an exercise in futility, since it was neither properly subsidized nor endowed with sufficient power to function effectively.[17]

Roosevelt was not the man to rely on any single answer to a problem. Possibly to avert increased Zionist pressure on the White House he stepped-up the search for alternate havens. The President, an amateur geographer, had long been intrigued with the possibility of filling out-of-the-way lands with westernized peoples. He thus began to speak of several major settlements where Hitler's scapegoats might create a "self-sustaining civilization" of their very own.[18] FDR broached this idea to those of his Jewish visitors whom he knew to be non-Zionists, asking their aid in finding territorial substitutes for the Holy Land. At one time or another the administration flirted with the possibilities of some 666 different locations. These lands ranged from Baja California southward to thinly settled areas of Latin America, and then eastward to Roosevelt's favorite locale of colonial Africa.[19]

All of these castle-building schemes vanished into thin air. American geographers warned of the health hazard of the tropics, the lack of transportation in empty regions of the earth and the barren soils of these contemplated new Zions. There just seemed to be no new feasible place suited for the mass influx of urbanized Europeans. To have implemented Roosevelt's plan on even a limited scale would have cost more than either the western powers or the Jews of the free world were willing to pay. Nor were the American Jews enthusiastic about FDR's plans. Zionist eyes were fixed on the Promised Land while the uncommitted feared "re-ghettoization" in some forgotten corner of the globe.[20]

Thus the President found no suitable haven for the bulk of displaced Jews prior to the time when the advent of war greatly complicated his search. The subsequent tragedy lay in Washington's failure to recognize that Palestine was the only place outside of the United States able to absorb any sizable number of refugees. While the President must bear ultimate responsibility for this dereliction, his refusal to come to grips with political reality was strongly influenced by the adamant opposition of the State Department.

The State Department hierarchy of the depression years was a jerry-built structure not designed or staffed to deal with a world set in perpetual turmoil by the Fascist onslaught. The department's personnel remained imbued with the complacency of the quiet Coolidge years while its general demeanor was "suffused with habits of thought that reached back to a still earlier day."[21] The President was well aware of the department's shortcomings and he took into his own hands diplomatic matters he thought of prime importance. Inasmuch as Roosevelt did not place the Middle East in this category, the decisions in this area were made by unimaginative men devoted to precedent. This precedent had long been opposed to Zionism.

The New Deal Democrats who came to power in 1933 inherited from their Republican predecessors a bundle of anti-Zionists axioms formulated at a time when the refugee question was virtually non-existent. The primary postulate held that the Middle East was a British sphere of influence, a region where the United States had few vital stakes. A corollary added that any interference in the affairs of this area would be detrimental to the national interest. While conceding that official Washington had approved of the establishment of a Jewish National Home, the department argued that no one, including the Jews, was agreed on the precise meaning of this novel concept. Hence only London could define the terms of the Balfour Declaration while outsiders must approach the subject with "the utmost care."[22] Further, the department held rigidly to its rule that the requests of any religious group must be viewed suspiciously. Little wonder then, that

Jewish spokesmen considered the affable Roosevelt a friend who, like themselves, found it difficult to persuade the starchy State Department bureaucrats of the merits of the Zionist case.

Since the President relegated the Middle East to minor importance, decision-making in this area fell to Secretary of State Cordell Hull. This courtly southern gentleman knew little of places more remote than Western Europe and this limited knowledge compelled him to rely on the department's geographic chiefs.[23] Hull thus reflected the Near Eastern Division's position that the destiny of Palestine was in British hands, a fact not changed by the pressing refugee problem. Zionist representatives found communication difficult with this rigid man given to procrastination and endless consultation with his subordinates. Nor was Hull vulnerable to ordinary political pressure, since he correctly regarded himself as an elder statesman backed by a nationwide popularity.

Secretary Hull was prone to silence on sensitive issues, therefore it is difficult to reconstruct his assessment of the Zionist case. He probably felt the Jewish tragedy more deeply than he revealed, since he had personal reasons for his reticence. Correct in his public behavior to a fault, he feared that he might be accused of Zionist favoritism for his wife was of Jewish origin.[24] Further, unlike the President, the Secretary refrained from promising what he could not deliver and so he refused to talk both ways to Jews and Arabs.[25] Consequently, Hull confined his actions on Palestine largely to the protection of American nationals within the mandate, thus refusing to press London to facilitate Jewish entry into the Holy Land.[26]

Because Hull relied heavily upon the advice of his subordinates, their points of view are of unusual importance. His Under Secretary during the crucial years of 1937 to 1943, was Sumner Welles. Like FDR a Groton-Harvard man, Welles had been a page at the President's wedding and had long been his protegé. But the intimacy between the two men was more than social, for Roosevelt had the highest regard for Welles' diplomatic judgment, finding in him the creative foresight and sense of daring so lacking in Hull. Jewish deputies regarded the tall, austere and snobbish Welles as their truest friend in FDR's court, and this assumption has been handed down in Zionist lore.[27] This favorable image was sharpened by Welles' later writings, but while in office he had taken no positive stand for Zionism. Actually, he was less critical of British action in Palestine than some of his colleagues and it took him far longer than others to grasp the grim significance of the Nazi threat.[28] Moreover, the Under Secretary was the actual author of a number of White House statements on Palestine that proved deeply disappointing to men who dreamed of a Zion reborn.[29]

Welles' role in Palestinian affairs was dwarfed by the influence of the chief of the Division of Near Eastern Affairs, Wallace Murray. According to Secretary Hull, regional experts such as Murray appraised area developments and upon their verdict "the higher officials, from the President down" formulated their policies.[30] This dependency explains the unique influence of Murray. Any understanding of American policy toward Palestine during the New Deal years requires an analysis of this man and his outlook.

Murray (1887-1965) had begun his career in the Foreign Service whose personnel evaluated the local situation from their desks in the various consulates. A profile of these minor diplomats reveals some striking similarities. They were, by and large, products of small town America who usually capped their hill-top college educations with graduate work at a prestigious university. More often than not, they had entered government service after a stint of teaching, newspaper reporting or as veterans of the 1917 war. Most of the Middle Eastern hands at the State Department had served at various Moslem capitals before their assignment to Washington.

Murray's career conformed to this prototype. Following an assignment to Teheran he was called back to the State Department to man the Persian desk. By 1929 he was chief of the Near Eastern Division and part of the anti-Zionist clique formed to countervail President Woodrow Wilson's endorsement of the Balfour Declaration. Sheldon Whitehouse, one of Murray's predecessors had complained in 1920: "The Jews . . . think that . . . ducats wisely distributed will heal all sores. . . . The Moslem population [will] meet this insinuation with the curse 'Thy money perish with thee'."[31] This sentiment was fully shared by Allen W. Dulles (later of CIA fame) who headed the division from 1922 to 1926. Dismissing the Zionists as an "influential and a noisy group" he, in the face of all evidence to the contrary, doubted that Wilson had ever given his blessing to Zionist aspirations.[32] Dulles strongly influenced Murray's ideas on the Holy Land. Both men were wary of any American commitment in Palestine, both believed that Zionism was a minority movement and both lent a willing ear to the anti-Zionist arguments of American missionary and educational personnel domiciled in the Middle East.[33]

A scholarly pedantic man, incapable of small talk, Murray found the visits of concerned Jewish spokesmen taxing. The chief made little attempt to conceal his *sang froid* toward Zionism stressing always that Palestine was not the answer to the refugee problem. Part of Murray's prejudice was owing to an exaggerated fear of Communism. Forty years ago it seemed likely to many that a Jewish Palestine would result in a quasi-Marxist state and this Murray sought to prevent by doing his best to preserve British hegemony in the Middle East.[34]

Murray's fear of a Jewish Socialist state had some basis in fact. American diplomatic dispatches from Jerusalem regularly reported that native-born Palestinian Jews placed Marxist dogma above the bourgeois tenets of the general Zionists. The future would bring, it was predicted, a shift in a radical direction. Even Felix Frankfurter, then the archtype liberal, recognized the importance of sending American Jews to settle in Palestine in order to prevent a Bolshevist future there.[35] These anxieties eventually proved groundless, but they seemed very real to the more conservative members of the New Deal Administration. The Mapai's Anglicized name, the Palestine Workers' Party, had an ominous ring to it. It was not yet clear in FDR's day that Mapai's economic blueprint was essentially that of a Scandinavian mixed economy.[36]

For all these reasons Murray refused to press for the full utilization of the Palestine haven and he did his utmost to minimize its possibilities during the Nazi crisis. Because Secretary Hull relied so heavily upon him the net result was that the State Department took an anti-Zionist position. Nonetheless the Hitlerian terror, by creating ever increasing hordes of political outcasts, lent new logic to the Zionist argument. But Murray refused to budge, insisting that American treaty rights were severely limited to the protection of American nationals in the mandate. A broader interpretation of the 1924 convention with Britain, he warned, would place the United States in the precarious position of guaranteeing peace in Palestine.[37] Under this restricted interpretation Washington lacked any legal means of forcing London to open wide the Palestinian haven during the zero hour of modern Jewish history. This policy permeated upward from the Division of Near Eastern Affairs to the White House and downward to Murry's subordinates so many of whom he had personally introduced to the labyrinths of Middle Eastern statecraft.[38]

Unquestionably Murray was genuinely concerned lest an Anglo-American insistence on a Jewish Palestine would drive the Arabs into the welcoming arms of the Axis; Mussolini had already filled the Middle East with a large corps of Italian propagandists who threatened to undermine British control over the region. This threat seemed to be real because the Italian dictator concentrated naval and air units near the British linchpin of Suez. The formation of the Rome-Berlin Axis in 1937 brought the other Fascist power into the picture. Hitler, taking a cue from Imperial Germany, invited Arab students to study in the Reich and swamped the Moslem world with agents thinly disguised as businessmen. As the war clouds thickened over Europe, it seemed necessary for the free world to appease the Arabs in order to insure their neutrality in the coming conflict.[39]

Meanwhile Murray insisted, that despite the mounting toll of refugees, England could not afford to weaken her position in the Middle East by any concessions to the Zionists.[40] He complained that the American Zionists, representing at the most ten per cent of the domestic Jewish population, were frustrating all humanitarian efforts to relocate the political castaways under any plan which did not envision eventual Jewish statehood. He therefore urged his superiors not to press London on Palestinian matters but rather to step up the search for alternative locations.[41] By this time, the President had already broached such a solution to Jewish leaders but as we have seen nothing ever came of it.

Murray was unusually well informed on the inner workings of the Jewish Establishment. He did his homework faithfully as his marginalia on newspaper clippings, periodicals and intelligence reports on Zionist activities testify. He apparently believed that a majority of American Jews was hostile to the idea of a restored Holy Land commonwealth. Hence no Jewish group received so warm a welcome in the offices of the Division of Near Eastern Affairs as the old-line Reformers who viewed Judaism as merely a religion. Murray reported to Hull that Rabbi Morris S. Lazaron, originally a pioneer Zionist in Reform ranks, now understood that the movement had fallen prey to a "deleterious" secularism. "It may be," read Lazaron's statement which made the departmental rounds, "that God Himself has brought us to this place to show us that statehood is not the way."[42]

Murray's staff had previously researched widely to prove Rabbi Lazaron's point. The study concluded that while American Jewry was deeply concerned with the fate of the refugees, the greater number did not want the homeless settled in Palestine. The Zionists, the report explained, thanks to superb organization and propaganda had created the illusion that they represented prevailing opinion. American Jewry, however, was in the main non-Zionist for reasons of self interest, since statehood would spread anti-Semitism in the United States by creating the vexing problem of "dual allegiance."[43]

As Europe slithered toward war, Murray found an additional reason why Zionism presented a danger to American Jews. Palestine, he explained to Hull, was the keystone arch in the British imperial structure. London's Moslems were spread from Egypt to India and they might well make common cause with the Fascists. Then the balance of power in the Middle East would favor the Axis thus jeopardizing the vital interests of the United States with the finger of blame pointed to the Jews. Nor, he added, would free world support for Zionism be in the humanitarian interest, since it would lead eventually to the massacre of several hundred thousand Jews in the Holy Land by the surrounding millions of aroused Arabs.[44]

Murray's influence was particularly effective for a bundle of reasons. He solicited statements on the Arab point of view from American diplomatic personnel in the Moslem world and he widely disseminated this information.[45] Further, Murray was unusually well informed, for in a department where record-making was notoriously inept, he mastered the cumbersome system in use and was thus able to come up with much forgotten correspondence. With departmental anti-Zionist precedents at his finger-tips, he wrote bulky historical briefs indicting the Zionists for converting American declarations of sympathy for their movement into pledges of actual support. There was a certain validity to Murray's case, but he never would concede that the advent of Hitler had created an entirely new set of circumstances which mandated a re-evaluation of American policy toward Palestine.[46]

American Jews became slowly aware of Murray's unbending hostility toward Zionism and the extent of his influence upon his superiors. But it was not until 1943 that their complaints reached the President at a time when war made the choice of policy in the Middle East far less flexible.[47] By then, Murray had done incalculable harm to the Zionist cause by violating Secretary Hull's 1937 directive to his subordinates not to relay biased information or to take sides in controversial matters at issue in the department.[48]

These rules had also been violated by lower echelon American diplomatic personnel stationed throughout the Arab world. Secretary Hull, seldom a harsh critic of his subordinates, once described these Foreign Service careerists as a "stuff-shirt group of cane-carrying bureaucrats."[49] The animosity of American consular representatives in the Middle East to a Jewish Palestine stemmed more from a partiality to the exotic Moslems than from a hatred of their rivals in the Holy Land. The attraction of these consuls to Arab civilization was not accidental, since field officers were strongly encouraged to familiarize themselves with the local history and culture. This they did by mixing with the citizenry of their assigned posts, culling the native press and listening to radio broadcasts.[50] Therefore it is not surprising that they immersed themselves in the dominant milieu and understood its mood. Most of these officials were amateur Arabists and those assigned to Jerusalem seldom understood or sympathized with the fervor of the Zionist pioneers. In the fashion of the Moslem Palestinians, they regarded the European Jews as intruders bent on destroying a quaint way of life.

It is therefore not surprising that the consular despatches to the State Department were marked by a strong anti-Zionist bias.[51] Like Murray who shared their general background, American legates to the Holy City feared the Marxist orientation of some of the East European newcomers. Consul General Ely Palmer found the Zionists smug and over-confident of their military clout which, he explained to Washington, rested upon illegally obtained arms. There was, Palmer advised, only one way to prevent an armed collision in Palestine and that was by curtailing sharply Jewish emigration to the mandate.[52] Zionist leaders were, of course, not privy to consular correspondence, but they recognized in Palmer a determined opponent. When he left his post, they tried in vain to have him replaced with a man more sensitive to the tragedy that was enveloping the European Diaspora.[53]

Shortly after Palmer's transfer from Jerusalem, the consulate reported that the Haganah (a well trained semi-secret Jewish army) was determined to prevent by force the mandatory government's plan to make constitutional changes which would favor the Arab majority.[54] When London vacillated on this plan owing to Zionist pressure, the Arabs staged a prolonged labor strike in 1936 which brought new civil disorders. Washington was told by its official representatives in Jerusalem that the "cocky" Jews, supported by a global Zionist network operating out of London, had triggered the Arab uprising by insisting on legislative reforms partial to the Jewish minority. The American *chargé d'affaires* reported that the Haganah had instigated the violence in order to prove the Arabs incapable of self-restraint. The consulate predicted that the Jews would prevent the democratization of the mandate, since the organized Zionists carried more weight at Whiṭehall than the disorganized Arabs.[55]

The next permanent consul at Jerusalem was George Wadsworth. His tenure is important, because it coincided with the hectic pre-war efforts of the refugees to find asylum. Since Wadsworth had earlier taught at Beirut and had served his diplomatic apprenticeship in Lebanon, the Zionists were apprehensive about his transfer to Jerusalem. Their fears were well founded for he promptly cultivated the friendship of the Grand Mufti, an Axis protegé. Like his predecessors, Wadsworth advised against full use of the Holy Land asylum, telling his superiors that Palestine was already over-populated, plagued by scanty rainfall in rural areas with its cities unable to house any more urban-oriented Europeans. These admonitions were widely disseminated in Washington by the Division of Near Eastern Affairs.[56] At a time when hordes of Nazi victims were desperately trying to find shelter, Wadsworth argued that London should declare that the pledge made in the Balfour Declaration had been fulfilled and that the time had come to turn the mandate over to the Arab majority.[57] Wadsworth seemed far more callous to Hitler's outrages than the State Department. After Austria was incorporated into the Third Reich, he suggested to Washington that his experience in Jewish matters would make him particularly valuable in a diplomatic post somewhere in Greater Germany.[58]

So it was that the consular reports which Murray read with his usual diligence, served only to re-inforce his own appraisal of the Holy Land situation. This similarity of views was no mere coincidence, since Murray recommended the appointments to Middle Eastern posts of men who, like himself, had been trained for their jobs in the Moslem world.

For all of the above reasons, no effective action was taken by the Roosevelt administration to pry open the doors of Palestine while time still remained to save a substantial fraction of the entrapped. Once the dogs of war were unleashed in 1939, rescue operations became much more difficult. Yet even during the initial years of World War II, the Nazi allowed some sealed trains to reach neutral ports with the tacit understanding that their passengers would be shipped out of Europe. It is a fair guess that many more could have escaped the gas chambers had a feasible refuge been in existence.[59]

Whatever the merits of this speculation, it is clear that official Washington badly bungled the refugee problem. Since part of the burden of the presidency is to accept ultimate historical responsibility, the blame must fall upon Roosevelt. His reluctance to overrule the State Department during his first term is understandable, for his efforts were focused on business recovery at a time when the Axis threat had not yet developed. Moreover, the refugee crisis was initially confined to Germany whose half million Jews could possibly be absorbed by the western powers and the Palestinian immigration quota. This situation changed radically in 1938 when Hitler seized Austria and began the dismemberment of Czecho-Slovakia thus multiplying the list of expellees. To make matters even worse, anti-Semitism spread rapidly eastward setting in motion an exodus of Poland's three million Jews. By 1939 it was all but certain that the deteriorating international situation would lead to war and it should have been evident what this conflict would denote for European Jewry.

As chief exucutive of a great nation, a humanitarian duty fell upon FDR, *noblesse oblige*. Palestine was not the perfect solution to the refugee problem for the Arabs were there, but it was the best answer available. Thus the President expressed his private anger when in May 1939, a British White Paper pledged within five years to place Jewish immigration to the Holy Land at the mercy of the Arab majority. But he refused to intervene just when London was in such dire need of American support that a strong dissent from Washington would have probably forced a British reversal. FDR refused to take positive action for two major reasons. First, he believed that England was forced to appease the Arab world to insure Moslem support in the coming conflict. Second, the President's ardent efforts to arouse his country to the Axis peril was opposed by a powerful isolationist coalition united by hatred and suspicion of Britain. Hence FDR feared that a sharp reprimand to London would supply political ammunition to his avowed opponents.[60]

Viewed in historical perspective it would not have made much difference had Roosevelt forced England to keep the doors of Palestine fully open during the crux of the refugee crisis. Despite Allied efforts to placate the Arab nations, they remained on the sidelines in World War

II until a western victory was clearly portended. Nor would isolationist opposition to the President's pre-Pearl Harbor diplomacy been more vociferous because of any affirmative action that he might have taken on Palestine. The only measurable differences would have been to reduce the toll of the Holocaust and to have spared many of its survivors their pathetic wanderings until the 1948 emergence of Israel.

FOOTNOTES

1. Arthur D. Morse, *While Six Million Died: A Chronicle of American Apathy* (New York, 1968); Saul S. Friedman, *No Haven for the Oppressed: United States Policy Toward Jewish Refugees, 1938-1945* (Detroit, 1973); David S. Wyman, *Paper Walls: America and the Refugee Crisis, 1938-1941* (Amherst, Mass., 1968).

2. Wyman, *Paper Walls*, p. 33. According to David H. Popper, *The Puzzle of Palestine* (pamphlet, Foreign Policy Association, New York, 1938), p. 73, specialists on the ancient world hold that in classical times the region contained many more inhabitants than it did in the 1930s.

3. Document forwarded to the President by Under Secretary of State Sumner Welles, Nov. 28, 1938, PSF, Franklin D. Rossevelt Papers (Roosevelt Library, Hyde Park, N.Y.). See also Eliahu Ben-Horin, *The Middle East: Crossroads of History* (New York, 1943), pp. 175-176.

4. Statement of Loy Henderson, veteran State Department official to Selig Adler, Jan. 17, 1968.

5. Selig Adler, "The United States and the Middle Eastern Dilemma, 1917-1939," *The Maryland Historian* 7 (Spring 1976): 1-17.

6. *Ibid.*; statement of Judge Samuel I. Rosenman to Stephen S. Wise and Nahum Goldmann, Oct. 6, 1943, Abba Hillel Silver Papers (The Temple, Cleveland, Ohio).

7. Telegram, FDR to Stephen S. Wise, Oct. 12, 1938; the information on the 1936 intervention was added to the document by Marvin H. McIntyre, PPF 3292 and n.d., Official File 700: Palestine, Roosevelt Papers.

8. PPF 3292, May 22, 1939, *ibid.*

9. Rosenman to FDR, n.d., *ibid.*

10. Max Freedman, ed., *Roosevelt and Frankfurter: Their Correspondence 1928-1945* (Boston, 1967), *passim;* Frankfurter to Emanuel Neumann, Nov. 3, 1932, Felix Frankfurter Papers (Library of Congress) Box 86, Reel 2. For a more sympathetic assessment of Frankfurter's role, see Simcha Berkowitz, "Felix Frankfurter's Zionist Activities" (D.H.L. dissertation, The Jewish Theological Seminary of America, July 1971).

11. Sumner Welles, *We Need Not Fail* (Boston, 1948), p. 72.

12. Robert A. Divine, *Roosevelt and World War II* (Baltimore, 1969), pp. 1-23.

13. FDR to Robert W. Bingham, July 11, 1935 in Edgar B. Nixon, ed., *Franklin D. Roosevelt and Foreign Affairs* (3 vols. covering the period Jan., 1933-Jan. 20, 1937, Cambridge, Mass., 1969) 2: 533-554.

14. Henry L. Feingold, "Roosevelt and the Holocaust: Reflections on New Deal Humanitarianism," *Judaism* 18 (Summer 1969): 259-276.

15. Baltimore *Sun*, March 27, 1938.

16. Joseph P. Kennedy to Hull, Dec. 3, 1938. *Papers Relating to the Foreign Relations of the United States 1938 (cited hereafter as For. Rel.)* 1: 850-853; Wyman, *Paper Walls*, p. 49.

17. Henry L. Feingold, *The Politics of Rescue: The Roosevelt Administration and the Holocaust, 1938-1945* (New Brunswick, N.J., 1970), pp. 22-68; Wyman, *Paper Walls*, p. 51 ff.

18. Wyman, *Paper Walls*, p. 59.

19. *Ibid.*, p. 59 ff.

20. *Ibid.*, 58; Feingold, "Roosevelt and the Holocaust".

21. Donald F. Drummond, "Cordell Hull", in Norman Graebner, ed., *An Uncertain Tradition: American Secretaries of State in the Twentieth Century* (New York, 1961), pp. 184-209.

22. State Department Press Release, Oct. 14, 1938, *For. Rel. 1938*, 2: 953-955. The remarkable similarities between the Republican and Democratic approaches to Palestine and its problems are revealed in a statement of Secretary of State Henry L. Stimson at a press conference, Nov. 7, 1931, Frankfurter Papers, Box 85, Reel 1.

23. Drew Pearson and Robert S. Allen in Washington *Herald*, Feb. 19, 1938; Robert Bendiner, *The Riddle of the State Department* (condensed ed. New York, 1943), p. 60.

24. Anderson (Ind.) *Herald*, Aug. 29, 1943.

25. *The Memoirs of Cordell Hull* (2 vols. New York, 1948), 2: 1536.

26. Hull to Wadsworth, Aug. 17, 1937, *For. Rel. 1937*, 2: 905.

27. Dr. Nahum Goldmann in New York *Aufbau*, Dec. 15, 1967.

28. Arnold A. Offner, *American Appeasement: United States Foreign Policy and Germany, 1933-1938* (Cambridge, Mass., 1969), p. 269.

29. Joseph B. Schechtman, *The United States and the Jewish State Movement* (New York, 1966), p. 21.

30. Hull, *Memoirs* 1: 180-181.

31. Quoted in Frank Manuel, *The Realities of American-Palestine Relations* (Washington, 1949), p. 258.

32. *Ibid.*, pp. 277-278.

33. Memorandum, summarizing the division's point of view, prepared by J. Rives Childs in 1939, State Department Records (The National Archives), File 867N.01/1553 1/2.

34. Statement of Loy Henderson to Selig Adler, Jan. 17, 1968.

35. Wadsworth to Hull, June 8, 1938. State Department Records, File 867N.01/1101; Frankfurter to Robert Szold, April 17, 1919, Frankfurter Papers, Box 85, Reel 1.

36. Statement of Emanuel Neumann to Selig Adler, April 4, 1968.

37. Murray had made this case in a memo of March 19, 1930, and it was endlessly repeated by his division; State Department Records, File 867N.01/522. See also Childs' comprehensive memorandum cited in fn. 33, *supra*.

38. *Washington Post*, April 27, 1965.

39. Adler, "The U.S. and the Middle Eastern Dilemma".

40. Murray to Palmer, May 7, 1935, and to Welles, May 17, 1939, State Department Records, Files 867N.00/241, 867N.01/1599.

41. Murray to Welles, Dec. 12, 1938, *ibid.*, File 867N.01/1378.

42. Murray to Hull, May 19, 1939, *ibid.*, File 867N.01/1579.

43. Memo by Murray, Dec. 2, 1937. *For. Rel. 1937* 2: 921-922. In reaching their conclusions, the staff relied heavily upon the files of the anti-Zionist New York *Times*.

44. Memo, Murray to Hull, Feb. 9, 1939, State Department Records, File 867N.01.143 1/2. Murray later revised this memo with the intention of sending it to the White House but for some unknown reason it was withheld.

45. *Ibid.*

46. "Principal Factors Relating to Palestine," memo distributed by the Division of Near Eastern Affairs," Nov. 25, 1941, *ibid.*, File 867N.00/588.

47. Emanuel Celler to the President, Aug. 18, 1943, *ibid.*, File 867N.00/1985.

48. Radio broadcast by Secretary Hull. Sept. 1, 1937 in *Activities of the Department of State* (pamphlet, Washington, D.C., 1937).

49. Editorial, Washington *Star*, Feb. 20, 1938.

50. Statement of Foy Kohler in a speech at the National Archives, June 16, 1969.

51. This pattern was set by Otis A. Glazebrook, a former missionary, who was Consul General at Jerusalem at the time of the issuance of the Balfour Declaration. Selig Adler, "The Palestine Question in the Wilson Era," *Jewish Social Studies* 10 (October 1948): 303-334.

52. Palmer to Hull, April 4, 1935, Nov. 25, 1935, State Department Records, Files 867N.00/24 and 263.

53. Nixon, ed., *FDR and Foreign Affairs*, 3: 195-196.

54. Leland B. Morris to Hull, April 25, 1936, State Department Records, File 867N.00/283.

55. *Idem* to *idem*. June 6, 1936, *ibid.*, File 867N.00/31.

56. Wadsworth to Hull, June 21, 1938, *ibid.*, File 867N.00/407.

57. Wadsworth, quoted in Murray to Hull *et al.*, May 4, 1939, *ibid.*, File 867N.01/1535.

58. Wadsworth to Murray, May 16, 1938, *ibid.*, File 867N.01/1212.

59. Feingold, "Roosevelt and the Holocaust".

60. Selig Adler, "Franklin D. Roosevelt and Zionism—The Wartime Record," *Judaism* 21 (Summer 1972): 265-276; Adler, "The U.S. and the Middle Eastern Dilemma".

Toward Unity: Zionist and non-Zionist Cooperation, 1941-1942

by Isaac Neustadt-Noy

When war broke out in September, 1939, American Jewry anticipated a long and bloody conflict which would leave it in the position of the leading Jewish community in the world, and the only one capable of assisting those trapped by the war in Europe. They also suspected that this responsibility would not be relinquished after the war ended. Beyond this realization, little could be readily assumed, as the future of Jewish communities in Europe was highly uncertain and news reports concerning them were confused.[1]

Organizational response to the war demonstrates that the major factions in organized Jewish life all recognized the severity of the problem with which they were dealing. Nevertheless, they were not ready to yield their independence in favor of unified and coordinated action, at least in the early stages of the war. The perennial question of uniting the American Jewish community thus re-emerged in the context of responding to the war emergencies.

Major organizational shifts and changes that occurred during the war were specifically intended to meet the post-war challenge. The American Jewish Committee, for example, began concerning itself with problems of postwar reconstruction in 1940. It established the Research Institute on Peace and Postwar Problems as an independent venture after rejecting a World Jewish Congress suggestion for a joint enterprise. The Institute studied the "transitory and permanent changes brought about in Jewish life as a result of Nazi rule, including the proposals of Allied and neutral countries for postwar reconstruction," as well as "the question of Palestine in its Jewish and international aspects including the problem of Arab-Jewish relations." By establishing the Research Institute, the American Jewish Committee, accord-

149

ing to Naomi Cohen, indicated 1) a "belief in the ultimate destruction of the Nazi forces" and 2) "revised views about Jewish survival," reflecting disappointment with the "paper rights" granted to Jews by democratic governments that "could tolerate blunt discrimination and look the other way while the most inhuman acts were being perpetrated."[2]

A similar agency for postwar planning and research was the Institute of Jewish Affairs, which intended to buttress appeals for help to the United States and Allied governments with documentary proof and other data. Founded on February 1, 1941 by the American and World Jewish Congresses (the latter moved its headquarters to New York under the leadership of Nahum Goldmann), the Institute sought "to conduct a thorough investigation of Jewish life during the past 25 years with a view of establishing the fact of the present situation, determining its direct and indirect cause and suggesting the lines on which Jewish rights may be claimed in a postwar settlement."[3]

The Jewish Labor Committee too prepared itself for the ominous future. The J.L.C. cooperated with the American Federation of Labor in combating Nazism, and established its own Research Institute for Jewish Postwar Problems. Its contribution to unity of action within the community was an expression of willingness to "utilize a large part of the work of the research committees of the American Jewish Committee and the American Jewish Congress." Some organizational activities focused on immediate problems as well. The J.L.C., for example, founded a rescue committee as early as mid-1940, and was active in rescuing anti-communist Jewish and non-Jewish socialist leaders in lands that had fallen under Russian control with the partition of Poland after September 1939. Later, when the Nazi extermination of Jews began, the J.L.C. "concentrated its energies on saving as many individual lives as possible."[4]

The Agudath Israel, established in the United States in 1939, was yet another body whose attention was riveted on the war in Europe. Agudath Israel of America founded the *Va'ad Hatzala*, an Orthodox rabbinical relief agency "primarily concerned with the rescue of Jews destined for extermination." As a matter of principle, the American Agudath Israel opposed Orthodox participation in community umbrella projects, because they did not want to encourage activities which might legitimize non-Orthodox organizations.[5]

A heavy proportion of the researchers and counsel of all these planning organizations were themselves leading European scholars and Jewish activists who had come as refugees. In somewhat the same way, the Jewish Agency transferred personnel from its London and Jerusalem offices to participate in the current and long-range political work of Zionists in America.

As the miseries of European Jewry intensified, the non-Zionist public became increasingly concerned with the resettlement of Jewish refugees in Palestine. For the majority outside organized Zionist ranks, the issue of Palestine was transformed from an ideological to a humanitarian issue; rebuilding the land was essential to alleviate human suffering. Palestine as a viable project provided many non-Zionists with a vital sense of direction at a time of unprecedented emotional turmoil. Moreover, the admittance of Jewish refugees to the United States confronted the outright opposition of most Americans.[6] Thus, if unity could be effected within Zionist ranks, as well as the community at large, there was reason to hope for mass support for achieving the goal of a Jewish state.

The first step, therefore, was to unify the ranks of American Zionists. The war had catapulted the Americans literally overnight into a position of primary responsibility in the World Zionist Organization. At the 21st Zionist Congress in August 1939, W.Z.O. president Chaim Weizmann had already suggested the establishment of a Zionist umbrella body in the United States, to take over the duties of the Zionist Executive in London for the duration of the anticipated war. An Emergency Committee was constituted by four major Zionist organizations in the United States: the Zionist Organization of America, Hadassah, *Poalei-Zion* (the labor Zionists) and Mizrachi (the religious Zionists.) Among the leading figures who served on the twenty-four man Emergency Committee were Louis Lipsky, Stephen Wise, Solomon Goldman (president of the Z.O.A.,) Abba Hillel Silver and Robert Szold.

Unity as an abstract idea meant very little to most of organized American Jewry as long as it did not promise to enhance the particular interests of the individual organization. A rather long tradition of inter-organizational rivalry and mistrust had produced a chronic communal incapacity for unity. American Zionists were not much different from others in their attitude on this subject. They too considered the call for unity a means of enhancing Zionist interests and were reluctant to cooperate with other organizations on binding terms if such unity did not promise to serve their interests. The history of the St. Regis conference of May 1941 clearly illustrates this point.[7]

Convinced since the beginning of the war that the American Jewish community would now inherit world Jewish leadership, Chaim Weizmann, upon his arrival in America in April 1941, made considerable efforts to reach American Jewish leaders of all shades of opinion. His aim was clearly to direct the inevitable transfer of power into channels that would best serve current Zionist interests. He was able to convene a private luncheon conference of 33 leaders on May 25, 1941, at the Hotel St. Regis in New York City. Among the participants were Carl Austrian and Louis Kirstein of the American Jewish Committee, Stephen Wise and Louis Lipsky of the American Jewish Congress, Adolph Held of the Jewish Labor Committee, and Edward Kaufman of the Zionist Organization of America. Also represented at the St. Regis conference were Harry Lurie and Joseph Willen of the Council of Jewish Federations and Welfare Funds, the coordinating agency of the philanthropies and fundraising campaigns of local Jewish communities throughout the United States and Canada.

Weizmann began his remarks by stating that American Jewry had received the mantle of leadership from Europe; ". . . it is proper that at least the responsible members of this community, the only Jewish community which is not affected (by the war) and which is still intact . . . will have a great responsibility and great opportunity, and its voice might be decisive for the direction of Jewish history. . . ."

Weizmann pointed out the implications of this new responsibility:

> It is proper that we should try and see whether we cannot find a common denominator, perhaps the minimum which would satisfy people like my colleagues and myself, and perhaps the maximum which would satisfy the others who are not of the same way of thinking; but I think we could find a common platform (in regard to Palestine) in order that we should be able when the time comes, to speak with one voice.

Taking pains to demonstrate his realism, Weizmann stressed the limits of such a project: "I have no illusions that you can unite a people of millions, as there are always differences, but you can unite, probably, the active elements of Judaism." He further emphasized that the impetus for unity was humanitarian, and therefore something most Jews could agree on: "when this nightmare is over . . . those who will survive—and I count primarily the American Jewish community which still has a chance of survival . . . and the Palestinian Jewish community perhaps—we shall be faced with millions of Jews . . . four or five million, who will be thrown out of gear and will be upset, to say the least, economically, socially, and morally."

Weizmann proceeded to attribute the lack of unity to a lack of leadership: "there is a virile Jewish community here . . . it is a somewhat leaderless community. . . . It is affected by the same troubles as the world at large, which also has not enough leaders." Returning to his first theme, Weizmann emphasized: "This great virile Jewish community is faced with great responsibilities imposed on it by Providence. . . ." In the course of his long presentation, Weizmann built his argument gradually and carefully, avoiding any unnecessary confrontation with non-Zionist participants. He again emphasized, for example, the humanitarian commitment to Palestinian Jewry: "The sentiment for Palestine, apart from the slogans, is deeply rooted in American Jewry, and if properly handled there is nothing which American Jewry would not do for Palestine." For these reasons, Weizmann concluded, "I take the liberty of inviting you here . . . to see what is the minimum on which we can unite as far as the re-building of Palestine is concerned and directing this dust (the Jewish refugees at the end of the war) into Palestine."

Weizmann, treading carefully around controversial issues, compromised even the classical Zionist formulation of a sovereign Jewish state:

> What I believe we ought to achieve as a wide measure of autonomy in Palestine, are three things: 1) Autonomy of finance; 2) Autonomy of colonization; 3) Autonomy of immigration. . . . Now I went to the State Department, whose people are not particularly friendly. In fact, they are, to some extent, like the colonial administration. We say, either discard everything you have done, or else let us run our own business. That does not mean that we shall have an army or run our foreign affairs; that I should leave to a "Shabbas Goy."

Thus Weizmann assured a highly selective group of American leaders, Zionist and non-Zionist alike, that although Zionist aims envisaged rapidly turning Palestine into a refuge for millions of Jewish refugees, they fell short of establishing a sovereign country. Anticipating (in one possible interpretation) the formula later written into the Biltmore

Program, he proposed full autonomous powers for united Jewry to admit and resettle the surviving Jews in Palestine under a protectorate or trusteeship that would have ultimate power to maintain order.

It is difficult to determine whether Weizmann had really abandoned the belief in a Jewish state, or whether he was pragmatically dismissing the issue to gain non-Zionist support in an hour of great urgency. It is clear however that Weizmann's discussion of the Jewish state was meant to prepare his listeners for the central theme he was trying to "sell" them:

> The Jews have brought into Palestine something like one hundred million pounds. . . . How was this money found? Not by the Keren Hayesod or U.J.A. or U.P.A. A part of it did, indeed, and the American share is very respectable. But this public money paved the way in rendering Palestine safe and hospitable for the people. So the small man came in and a great many settlements were created by pioneering money, and after that, paved the way for three times as much private money. This will not happen normally because the private money does not exist any more, because the Jews, having been robbed, have no money, so that it will only be public money available now, and for that to happen there must be conditions different from conditions which have existed heretofore. These conditions are the minimum of autonomy of running our own show.

Weizmann thus was seeking unity among American leaders for a practical purpose—a coordinated fundraising drive to meet an unprecedented demand for financial assistance certain to come with the end of the war.[8]

Henry Monsky was the first to raise a question at the end of Weizmann's presentation: "What is the present status of the Jewish Agency so far as its actual function is concerned on this side?" Monsky deliberately raised the most sensitive issue of the entire meeting. Article 4 of the Mandate for Palestine as confirmed by the League of Nations in 1922 had provided for the establishment of a "Jewish agency . . . for the purpose of advising and cooperating with the Administration of Palestine in such economic, social and other matters as may affect the establishment of the Jewish National Home." The World Zionist Organization was provisionally recognized as the "Jewish Agency" until such time as it could "secure the cooperation of all Jews who are willing to assist in the establishment of the Jewish National Home." It was the Zionists themselves who had proposed that world Jewry as a whole be brought into the Jewish Agency, to bring in financial resources they could not themselves summon, and because world participation would give added substance to their claim to represent the general will of the Jewish people. But the attainment of unity had always remained problematic. "Notwithstanding the reasons which both Zionists and non-Zionists had for cooperating in the Jewish agency," Ben Halpern noted, "ideological conflict kept them divided for years after the end of World War I."[9]

Negotiations between the two groups had been carried on primarily by Chaim Weizmann, president of the W.Z.O., and Louis Marshall of the American Jewish Committee until a final agreement in 1929 established the expanded Jewish Agency as a more or less equal partnership of Zionists and non-Zionists. In the course of these discussions, Louis Marshall, the non-Zionist, had acted as a mediator between the pro-Weizmann and pro-Brandeis groups in America, enabling the latter to re-enter the Z.O.A. leadership. But the sudden death of Marshall in 1929 had severely weakened the basis for full cooperation between the Zionists and the non-Zionists. After a lingering period of deterioration, the partnership was tacitly allowed to expire in the late 1930s. Cooperation between Zionists and non-Zionists in the Jewish Agency had not been notably successful, and had often created more bitterness than unity.

In reply to Monsky's pointed question at the St. Regis conference, Weizmann admitted that the Jewish Agency was a non-functioning body since "the non-Zionists did not utilize their fifty per cent representation." He quickly added, however, that "perhaps one of the methods by which this unity for which I have been pleading can be achieved is to rebuild the Agency on the basis of organizational representation."

Monsky, however, was not anxious to rebuild a Jewish Agency which would naturally come under Zionist control. The constitution of the existing Jewish Agency provided for fifty per cent Zionist representation world-wide, and further stipulated that the charimanship of the Jewish Agency was secured for the president of the World Zionist Organization. Monsky instead proposed:

> . . . a committee of five, selected from this group or outside the group, to explore the possibility of an agency similar to, or having the function of, the Jewish Agency, on the basis of representation. . . . I propose this committee be organized for the purpose of creating a

basis of organizational representation which will mobilize the united
support of the American Jewish community to the up-building and
reconstruction of Palestine.

Thus, in lieu of an international Jewish Agency under constitutionally
guaranteed Zionist control, Monsky proposed an independent American union of organizations which under conditions prevailing in 1941,
would probably not be under Zionist control.

The Weizmann-Monsky exchange triggered a brief discussion on the
future status of the Jewish community in Palestine. At the end of the
discussion, Adolph Held, chairman of the Jewish Labor Committee,
threw his support to Monsky: "I agree that Mr. Monsky's motion is a
very good one, and we should like to make every effort to examine the
probabilities." At this point Morris D. Waldman, the powerful secretary of the American Jewish Committee declared: "I am very glad that
Mr. Monsky made the suggestion that he did, because I have deplored
the fact that the Jewish Agency did not function as it was intended to
function, and I should like to see an organized effort put forward to help
any constructive work in Palestine."[10]

It was obvious that the two major non-Zionist organizations, the
Jewish Labor Committee and the American Jewish Committee, were
behind Monsky's proposal, and not in favor of re-entering the Jewish
Agency. Held's prompt endorsement of the Monsky proposal suggests
that there had been a prior understanding between Monsky, Held and
Waldman regarding an alternative to reviving the Jewish Agency.[11]
Waldman's statement was followed by a discussion of the relations
between Jews and Arabs in Palestine. When the discussion ended,
Monsky returned to his proposal:

> There is not any very great difference of opinion as to forming a
> committee. Several of the gentlemen here have indicated that they
> approved of my suggestion. The committee, appointed by you, Dr.
> Weizmann, should be largely from non-Zionist organizations. It
> would be a mistake to have it a committee largely of Zionist organiza-
> tions.

The free hand Monsky was seemingly giving to Weizmann in choos-
ing the committee was completely inhibited by Monsky's insistence on
a non-Zionist majority. No opposition was voiced to the idea of building
up Palestine as a refuge for European Jewry. Monsky apparently

believed that since the conference was in favor of this, the way to implement it successfully would be through a non-Zionist majority on the proposed committee. Monsky might have felt that an umbrella project comprised of "largely non-Zionist organizations" would more accurately reflect the organizational power of the community in 1941 than would a Zionist-dominated one. If mobilization of the entire community was the goal, then clearly the Monsky proposal was the more effective means of achieving it. The Monsky proposal had all the ingredients necessary for success: unity was the acknowledged goal, based on the humanitarian concern shared by all, and reflecting the organizational complexion of the community as it existed at the time. Here was a banner around which they could all conceivably rally to mobilize the resources of the Jewish community.

Henry Monsky's proposal however did not succeed; the old rivalry between the Council of Jewish Federations and Welfare Funds and the national defense organizations complicated the issue. The C.J.F.W.F. regularly opposed umbrella projects such as that proposed by Monsky, for fear that the fundraising activities inevitably involved in them would cut into the Council's own fundraising role. This characteristic stance had been evident during the brief existence of the ill-fated General Jewish Council, a defense umbrella project founded in 1938 by B'nai B'rith, the American Jewish Committee and the American Jewish Congress in response to the rising Nazi menace. People such as Harry Lurie of the C.J.F.W.F. leadership were instrumental in undercutting the Council's efforts to solicit funds. It was not at all surprising, therefore, that Harry Lurie would throw the first monkey wrench into Monsky's machinery:

> There is not a good basis of cooperation between the Zionists and the non-Zionists. There is a situation of mutual distrust, and lack of confidence, and there is a relationship of friction between the various groups. I don't see how, on top of the situation, in which one group believes that it is opposed to Palestine, and so on, you can establish any working basis for cooperation in connection with a problem which is so complex. I think we would be deluding ourselves at this stage of our discussion.

Monsky was obviously upset at this turn of events when he retorted, "But you don't think that any harm would come from appointing such a committee?" Another member of the C.J.F.W.F., Solomon Lowenstein, then took the floor to fire another shot:

> When you begin to work on how you are going to handle this thing, it seems to me that you cannot ignore the matters in the mind of Mr. Lurie. All of us here have been involved in this discussion and we won't get anywhere by ignoring these factors. I do not believe that we are ready for the kind of committee suggested by Mr. Monsky. I think we are ready for a committee of 3 or 4, who could discuss the questions with you, Dr. Weizmann.

The third member of the C.J.F.W.F. group, Joseph Willen, was quick to caution the "Dr. Lowenstein's suggestions might be slower, but it might be more prudent to adopt them." Willen, an A.J.C. member as well as an ardent anti-Zionist objected on principle to non-Zionist cooperation with Zionists. It was clear that the C.J.F.W.F. people were trying to eliminate the Monsky proposal, while appearing only to modify it on the grounds of prudence.

Lowenstein's proposal of three or four members to meet with Weizmann fell far short of Monsky's intention. It not only assured in principle the constant supervision and tremendous influence of Weizmann over the three members of the committee, but also negated in practice the possiblity of further discussion during Weizmann's short and busy visit. The C.J.F.W.F. proposal, then, was not a viable alternative to the more comprehensive Monsky plan as a basis upon which the three powerful non-Zionist organizations might, for the first time, cooperate with the Zionists in attempting to form an American umbrella project for rebuilding Palestine.

With the stage set for a successful, working cooperation, it was the Zionists themselves who backed down. They were not interested in an umbrella project for work in Palestine which they could not control. This, certainly, is the impression given by Weizmann's surprising support of the C.J.F.W.F. block: "As far as Dr. Lowenstein's suggestion is concerned, nothing would give me greater pleasure than that, but my time in New York is running out quickly. I shall be back at the end of July and at that time I am perfectly willing to meet with a group."[12]

Throughout the St. Regis meeting, two ardent Zionists, Stephen Wise and Louis Lipsky did not intervene even once in support of the Monsky proposal. Their silence suggests that the Zionists were united and adamant in their refusal to join a unity project which would not come under their control. Furthermore, early in the General Jewish Council joint project in 1941, the Zionist-oriented American Jewish Congress headed by Wise and Lipsky had been outmaneuvered by Monsky and the American Jewish Committee as the two joined forces in fundraising, leaving the Congress behind. The results were devastating to the Congress' image and financial resources. At the St. Regis, Wise and Lipsky had no reason to trust Monsky, least of all in light of the support he received from the American Jewish Committee's secretary, Morris Waldman.[13]

Monsky's last recorded remark in the matter, which ended the discussion, smacked of bitterness: "I thought we could have a talk with a representative group around this table and see what could be developed." But his proposal was rejected in favor of Lowenstein's. The small committee which was appointed did meet occasionally with Weizmann, but made no significant progress beyond that of the St. Regis conference itself. No further progress occurred for almost two years, during which World War II raged brutally. When, in January 1943, another attempt to achieve unity was made, it was again Henry Monsky who was the initiator. The circumstances by this time, however, had changed dramatically.

It is of interest to note that Weizmann and Monsky had met prior to the St. Regis conference. On February 11, 1941, Weizmann, who expected to arrive in the United States the following month, sent a cable to his assistant, Meyer Weisgal, in which he confirmed a proposed meeting between himself and Monsky. Such a meeting indeed took place a month later, at which Monsky raised questions concerning the status of the Jewish Agency and its possible role within a future umbrella project. The meeting suggests that some understanding between the two leaders was achieved but for some reason did not materialize at the St. Regis meeting.[14]

The St. Regis conference failed primarily because the proposed plan for unity fell short of Zionist expectations of control in behalf of their special interests. Past rivalries among the American Jewish Congress, the American Jewish Committee, B'nai B'rith and the C.J.F.W.F. created an atmosphere of mistrust at the St. Regis which made the task of achieving unity all but impossible.

Shortly after the St. Regis meeting, Sol M. Strook, president of the American Jewish Committee, initiated another meeting with the Zionist leadership, this time at the Waldorf-Astoria hotel in New York City on July 10, 1941. It was preceded by a few hours by a closed Zionist preparatory consultation regarding the upcoming encounter. The Zionist consultation records reveal that Strook "was very anxious" to have a "complete discussion" between the Zionist leadership and "selected people representing the American Jewish Committee, meeting not *as* the American Jewish Committee, but as representing the point of view of the American Jewish Committee, and not as individuals; and that whatever shall emerge shall constitute the understanding between the Zionists as a body and the opinion represented by the American Jewish Committee." Strook further insisted that people "like Monsky and Held" should not participate in the meeting and in general seemed "very anxious to come to some kind of understanding."[15]

Given the alliance of the Committee, B'nai B'rith, and the Jewish Labor Committee, Strook's seemingly surprising move requires some explanation. The non-Zionist American Jewish Committee was not ideologically monolithic. Within this body, power struggles raged over the issues of Diaspora Nationalism and the Jewish Commonwealth, between anti-Zionists headed by Joseph Proskauer and moderates headed by Strook and his successor, Maurice Wertheim.[16]

Diaspora Nationalism refers to the conviction that "as a people, the Jews stood in need of creating for themselves social and cultural conditions that would enable them to retain their distinctive identity in the midst of the non-Jewish majorities of the countries where they lived." The Zionist idea of a Jewish Commonwealth, like Diaspora Nationalism, was predicated on the conception of and commitment to the "distinctive identity" of the Jewish people, rejecting the possibility of Jewish absorption into "the non-Jewish majorities of the countries where they lived." The Zionists however felt that this could only be achieved by a Jewish majority in their own homeland.

In the United States, where the rights of Jews "to retain their distinctive identity" as well as their equal status under the law was guaranteed by the Constitution, Diaspora Nationalism never became a salient issue. It was sustained, however, as a result of the activity of the Zionists in this country; they propagated the idea of Jewish national self-determination as a fundamental element in political Zionism. National self-determination was also intrinsic to the ideology of Diaspora Nationalism. This concept was disturbing to many American Jews for a variety of reasons, such as the fear that it would compromise their status as American citizens and possibly jeopardize the situation of European Jewish communities. In his memoirs, Morris Waldman wrote: "I came to the conclusion long before the outbreak of the war that the theory of national self-determination which was the product of the first World War, though noble in its motivation, was unrealistic and unworkable. Indeed, it helped to aggravate the very evils which were intended to be destroyed. It augmented and intensified the philosophical basis for hypernationalism whose most odious form was reflected in Nazism."[17]

There was no argument within the Committee regarding the opinion that both Diaspora Nationalism and Zionism were undermining the civil status of American Jews. Both anti-Zionists and moderates within the Committee agreed that public campaigns in favor of the two issues were likely to cast doubt in the mind of the non-Jewish public as to the loyalty of American Jews to the United States. It was, therefore, a sort of activity the community could well afford to do without.

Previously, during W.W.I., the Committee vehemently fought the idea of Diaspora Nationalism as formulated by the Zionist-oriented American Jewish Congress movement.[18] However, the moderates presently felt that an all-out public campaign against the Zionists, as demanded by the Committee's anti-Zionists was tactically unwise because it would leave the Zionists free to wage a noisy campaign in favor of a Jewish home land as a shelter for all Jews, including American Jews. Such a development would inevitably raise the specter of Diaspora Nationalism and would thus draw attention to the dangerous and embarassing issue. It was, therefore of vital import, from Strook's point of view, to reach an understanding with the Zionists; he was even willing to lend support to the idea of a Jewish Commonwealth, provided the Zionists would guarantee that a Jewish homeland and the struggle towards it would not affect American Jews in any way.

Time was clearly on the side of the Zionists, as the Jewish public, in the wake of the growing tragedy in Europe, became more and more sympathetic to the Zionist idea, if only for humanitarian reasons. The Zionists' awareness of this development lay behind their decision to undercut Monsky's efforts at unity at the St. Regis; they expected more favorable conditions in the near future. But the Zionists still needed the Committee's support as the latter was in a position to enable the Zionists "to establish a unified front and to do away with dissident voices." To this end, Weizmann had already promised the non-Zionists at St. Regis that "the question of a Jewish state, even in the attenuated form in which I tried to depict it, will not affect the position of the Jews here in America."[19]

Strook, sensing a basis for rapprochement between Zionists and non-Zionists decided to reach an understanding with the Zionist based on a limited recognition of the idea of a Jewish homeland, before the growing popularity of the Zionists within the community would make them unwilling to compromise. As the president of the Committee, he wanted to terminate the public debate over the question of Palestine and Jewish national revival. It was therefore important to dismiss people such as Henry Monsky, Adolph Held and especially Maurice Waldman, who followed Proskauer's inflexible stance in his attitude towards the Zionists. The Monsky-Held-Waldman alliance at St. Regis had, after all, been the major reason behind the failure to achieve unity. Furthermore, it had left the Zionists free to pursue their hazardous political course. Palestine, with all of its contingent problems, was not the worst possible response to the Jewish problem, if separated from the context of Diaspora Nationalism. The Zionists had no difficulty following Strook's line of thought. At the Waldorf-Astoria, prior to the meeting with Strook, it was argued that "Mr. Strook needs Palestine, from his point of view, just as much as we need it. As an intelligent man he understands the postwar problem of the Jews will not be settled merely by the end of the war. . . . He needs Palestine because he knows from experience . . . that it is the best place for Jewish colonies."

The Zionist leadership was consistent in its willingness to guarantee that the question of Palestine would not affect the civil status of American Jews. Weizmann, for example, argued: "They are frightened of what they call Goluth (Diaspora) Nationalism, which is to them the American Jewish Congress. For instance, they are frightened of Polish Jews demanding autonomy within Poland, or in Czechoslovakia. They will want us to guarantee them that no such horrors will be allowed in this country. Therefore it would be essential to tell them that we are concerned here with the Palestinian problem." Earlier in the meeting Weizmann declared:

> I look upon them, particularly the American Jewish Committee, as having today a nuisance value. Tomorrow it may be much more . . . if

they do not play with us . . . they will cause trouble and confusion and it will make our life and our work very difficult, for the reason that somehow the Goyim expect us to be united . . . that gives them (the A.J.C.) a tremendous power even with men like Churchill and Roosevelt.

As the rules of the game became clear to all the participants, the moment became ripe for a marriage of convenience. A major obstacle, however, was the Zionists' insistence that any understanding with the Committee would have to be binding and within a "disciplined" common organizational framework. Abba Hillel Silver put it bluntly when he argued that ". . . outside of organizational control they will be stumbling blocks," and that therefore ". . . in our discussion this morning with them, we should have it purely on organizational basis." Indeed that was the decision adopted by the Zionist leadership at the end of the Waldorf Astoria meeting.[20]

Strook was caught in a very awkward position. He could not unilaterally commit his organization to an agreement with the Zionists as he was already facing growing opposition there to his policy of rapprochement. The Zionists, on the other hand, made it clear that a noncommittal, unofficial understanding would not satisfy their needs, as mutual mistrust was far too deep to surmount in a non-binding arrangement. The need to have some written form of the much-sought rapprochement thus became all but inevitable.

Sol M. Strook never completed his mission. The man who did not have the "aggressive personality to gain wider recognition as an influential American Jewish leader" died suddenly on September 11th, two months after the Waldorf Astoria conference. He was succeeded by Maurice Wertheim, son-in-law of former Ambassador Henry Morgenthau. Wertheim followed Strook's political course, and continued negotiations with the Zionist leadership, ultimately drafting the "Cos Cob formula" of June 1942, which stated the Committee's willingness "to aid in securing the fulfillment of the original purpose of the Balfour Declaration." Potentially the "Cos Cob formula" could have been the most important break-through in relations between the Zionists and the American Jewish Committee since the Weizmann-Marshall rapprochement of 1929.[21]

Opposition to the Wertheim presidency, however, continued to mount within the Committee. The Proskauer-led anti-Zionist bloc finally ousted Wertheim; by publicly reversing the pro-Zionist policy, the short-lived hopes for Zionist-Committee cooperation were again brought to an abrupt end. Years later, in his memoirs, Proskauer wrote: "I could not understand how anyone could expect that a land, whose population in 1942 was two-thirds Arab and one-third Jewish, could then be organized as a purely Jewish state. I believed then, as I believe now, that the Biltmore Resolution showed a lack of proper sense of timing."[22] The collapse of the Zionist-Committee rapprochement had far-reaching consequences; unity was never achieved during the war years—not even in the face of the gravest tragedy in Jewish history.

In mid-1943, Henry Monsky's relentless attempts at unity were finally crowned with unprecedented success in the establishment of the American Jewish Conference. It was, up until that time, the largest umbrella body to be organized in the history of American Jews, and this time most of the Zionist leadership stood whole-heartedly behind Monsky. The growing general sympathy towards the Zionist movement in 1943 secured for its leadership what two years earlier at the St. Regis could only be assumed for the future: the Zionist control of a non-Zionist-initiated unity project.[23]

FOOTNOTES

1. *HaDoar*, September 8, 1939; *American Jewish Year Book* 42 (1941): 269-84; *Der Tag*, September 24, 1939.
2. Naomi W. Cohen, *Not Free to Desist: A History of the American Jewish Committee, 1906-1966* (Philadelphia, 1972), pp. 265-66; *American Jewish Year Book* 43 (1942): 84.
3. *Ibid.*
4. *Ibid.*; Melech Epstein, *Jewish Labor in the United States* (2 vols., New York, 1950), 2: 403-405.
5. *American Jewish Year Book* 48 (1947): 216; "Agudath Israel of America," *Encyclopedia Judaica*, 2: 426.
6. David S. Wyman, *Paper Walls: America and the Refugee Crisis, 1938-1941* (Amherst, Mass., 1968), *passim*.
7. Isaac Neustadt-Noy, "The Unending Task," doctoral dissertation (Brandeis University, 1976), pp. 1-132.
8. Minutes of the St. Regis Hotel Conference, May 25, 1941, in New York called by Chaim Weizmann, in Weizmann Archives, Rehovot, Israel, pp. 2-8.
9. Ben Halpern, *The Idea of the Jewish State* (Cambridge, Mass., 1969, 2nd ed.), pp. 179-80.
10. St. Regis Conference Minutes, pp. 8, 11.
11. The support of the J.L.C. and A.J.C. for Monsky was in line with the previous agreement between the American Jewish Committee and B'nai B'rith which had brought about the establishment of Joint Defense Appeal. Neustadt-Noy, "The Unending Task," pp. 78-132.
12. St. Regis Conference Minutes, p. 17.
13. Neustadt-Noy, "The Unending Task"; Cohen, *Not Free to Desist*, pp. 224-26.

14. Chaim Weizmann to Meyer Weisgal, February 11, 1941, Weizmann to Henry Monsky, April 11, 1941, Weizmann Mss.

15. Minutes of Zionist breakfast meeting at Waldorf-Astoria, July 10, 1941, *ibid.*

16. Cohen, *Not Free to Desist*, pp. 249-56.

17. Morris D. Waldman, *Nor by Power* (New York, 1953), p. 120.

18. Yonathan Shapiro, *The Leadership of the American Zionist Organization, 1897-1930* (Urbana, Ill., 1971), ch. 4; Cohen, *Not Free to Desist*, pp. 81-122.

19. Minutes of Waldorf-Astoria meeting, p. 2; St. Regis Conference Minutes, p. 17.

20. Minutes of Waldorf-Astoria meeting, pp. 3, 7, 9, 11.

21. Cohen, *Not Free to Desist*, pp. 239, 252, 149-53; see also Howard M. Sachar, *A History of Israel* (New Yori, 1976), pp. 160-62.

22. Cohen, *Not Free to Desist*, pp. 252-64; Joseph M. Proskauer, *A Segment of my Times* (New York, 1950), p. 237.

23. Neustadt-Noy, "The Unending Task," pp. 133-356, *passim*. Yet even then, "as a precaution that the Zionist cause should not suffer from such action, both [Monsky and Weizmann] agreed that in the event Dr. Weizmann found the calling of a national conference inadvisable, he should be at liberty to cancel the undertaking." Confidential memorandum on American Jewish Conference, Meyer Weisgal to Zionist Executive [1943], in Zionist Archives and Library, New York.

The Political Background of the 1942 Biltmore Resolution

By David H. Shpiro

The Biltmore Resolution marked a watershed in the history of the Zionist movement in that it set forth, for the first time, a clear political goal for the movement. During the first forty-five years of its existence, Zionism was forced, for a host of political reasons, to refrain from inscribing such a goal on its flag. And so, when in mid-1942, an American Zionist Conference adopted the resolution, urging that "the gates of Palestine be opened; that the Jewish Agency be vested with control of immigration into Palestine and with the necessary authority for upbuilding the country, including the development of unoccupied and uncultivated lands; and that Palestine be established as a Jewish Commonwealth integrated in the structure of the new democratic world," friends and foes alike were taken completely by surprise. What was the immediate background to the adoption of this particular resolution?

What caused such an about-face in Zionist policy at the most hopeless moment in the Second World War? What caused the Conference to convene in the United States and nowhere else, and what impact did the location of the Conference have on the spirit of the resolution? What role did American Zionists play in the adoption of the Resolution? An examination of the background and the developments that led to the convening of the Conference may afford us answers to at least some of these questions.

The entry of the United States into the Second World War, following the bombing of Pearl Harbor in December 1941, gave wings to an ideological current which had first come to the fore during the period of the First World War and which came to be called "Post-War Messianism" or "Post-War Millenarianism".[1] The proponents of this ideology viewed America's involvement in the "European War" as being not merely a military-political act by means of which America was coming to the aid of the democracies in "decadent Europe" in their war against Nazi Germany, but as an apocalyptic struggle, a battle of the "sons of light against the sons of darkness," in which all evil would be eradicated from the world.

All shades of American society were represented among the adherents of this ideology—from the Marxist left, in all its various colors, to the extreme nationalist right, each group with its own particular vision. Against this background it is easy to understand how Eleanor Roosevelt's naive declaration that "we are fighting this war so that every child in the world will have a glass of milk to drink each morning" could be greeted with resounding cheers. President Roosevelt's declaration that the United States was fighting "for the sake of a new world free from fear and want" became American policy with the adoption of the Atlantic Charter, which set forth the war aims of both Great Britain and the United States.[2]

Against this ideological background, there arose hundreds of organizations which set about planning various aspects of the "post-war world". Their common goal was to bring about, with the end of the war, a resolution of all of the world's problems, including hunger in India and the settling of Poland's borders. A directory published by the Council for Foreign Affairs in 1942 listed over 300 such bodies, many with names reflecting their vision of world-embracing importance, such as World Community Movement, World Federalists, World Citizenship Movement, and World Peace Association.[3]

Some were so bold as to plan solutions to economic and political problems by calling for regional cooperation. Others were dedicated to solving very specific international problems, such as unemployment, or served as advocates for the wider application of democracy. And many other bodies and organizations believed that advocating world peace, or cooperation, or religion, or free trade, or equality of rights, or the resolution of minority problems was the means for solving all of mankind's problems.

All of them, however, had a common denominator in their preoccupation with "post-war planning". This phrase seem to have had a magical effect, scarcely any organization or movement of a religious, social, economic, scientific or political nature in the United States did not find it necessary to incorporate these words into their aims. Most of these groups were of themselves not particularly significant, but collectively indicated the extent to which this trend of thought had gained currency.

As early as the fall of 1939, when war in Europe seemed inevitable, the United States Department of State began to plan America's foreign policy for the post-war period. A team of experts, the Advisory Committee on Problems of Foreign Relations concerned itself with America's interests in the post-war years and the future structure of international relations. The task, as Cordell Hull defined it in January 1940, was to create a stable world order based on law and the elimination of economic conflicts, social instability and wars.

Following the attack on Pearl Harbor and America's entry into the war, President Roosevelt established a public body called the Advisory Committee on Post-War Foreign Policy. The Secretary of State chaired the committee, and its members were chosen from the universities, Congress, the business world, the State Department and other government departments and agencies, assisted by a broad-based team of experts. Their working guidelines—the bases upon which every international problem touched on by the committee was dealt with—were set forth in three exceedingly succinct questions: "What does the United States want? What do other states want? How do we obtain what we want?" In 1942, the scope of the committee was broadened, and many of the independent research institutes were incorporated within it.[4]

Among Jewish organizations, the American Jewish Congress was the first to sponsor an institute for peace research. In February 1940, the Congress approached the American Jewish Committee, the Alliance Israelite Universelle, and the Board of Deputies of the Jewish Communities of Great Britain with the proposal to set up a body that would prepare a "Jewish plan" to be presented to the future peace conference. The American Jewish Committee rejected the proposal, and as a consequence by mid-1941, two parallel institutes for the study of Jewish problems in the post-war years had been created, one by the American Jewish Committee and the other by the American Jewish Congress.[5]

American Zionists did not remain oblivious to this general trend, and the names of Zionist organizations can also be found in the directory published by the Council for Foreign Affairs. However, the grave situation in which the Zionist movement found itself as a result of the

1939 British "White Paper," the outbreak of the war, the "Land Transfer Regulations," the forced removal of the "illegal immigrants" and the direct threat to the physical survival of the *Yishuv* did not allow much time for dealing with a subject that seemed to be so removed from immediate problems.

However, recognition of the importance of post-war political planning increased among Zionists when the range of activities of the Department of Public Relations of the Emergency Committee for Zionist Affairs was broadened and political activity initiated in Washington. The director of the Department, Dr. Emanuel Neumann, became impressed with the importance of post-war planning for Zionism as a result of the discussions he held with various departments and agencies. In these discussions, the experts emphasized the importance of formulating and presenting an all-inclusive Zionist plan for the solution of the Jewish problem, or as it was frequently referred to, the "problem of the refugees," following the war. At these meetings, representatives of the Emergency Committee emphasized the inseparable ties between the Palestine problem and the issue of the refugees.

When David Ben-Gurion came to the United States in September 1940, he became aware for the first time of the tremendous scope of the planning activities going on in the United States, and it made a very strong impact on him. On an earlier visit to London, he had already learned that the Royal Institute for International Relations, the famous Chatham House, had become a semi-official institution for the duration of the war and had prepared on behalf of the government research papers on the aims of the war. Unfortunately, Harold Billie, an anti-Zionist, had been appointed to head the department for Jewish affairs in that institution.[6]

Like Neumann and others, Ben-Gurion also came to the conclusion that political matters should not wait until the end of the war and the convening of a peace conference before presenting the Zionist position. There was an immediate need to formulate a clear and all-encompassing Zionist policy which could be brought before the Great Powers at the earliest possible moment.

Following discussions he held in the United States, Ben-Gurion decided that it was necessary to carry-out wide-scale economic studies to prove "by facts and figures" that Palestine could absorb masses of Jewish refugees following the war. Before he left America, he urged the Executive of the Jewish Agency to become involved in post-war planning for Palestine by redirecting the Institute for Economic Research of the Jewish Agency to deal with this subject.[7]

Immediately upon his return from the United States in the beginning of 1941, Ben-Gurion drafted a comprehensive political document which spelled out in detail what he believed the aim of Zionism should be at that time ("Guidelines for a Zionist Policy"). That aim, in his opinion, was to strive for a maximal Zionist solution to the issues that would have to be decided upon after the war came to an end: the question of political control over Palestine and the question of the Jewish world being destroyed in Europe.

To both these problems he offered only one solution: the establishment a government in Palestine under control of a representative body of the Jewish people to enable the rapid transfer and resettlement of millions of Jews in Eretz Israel where they would constitute a nation that could stand on its own feet. In an attempt to have these "guidelines" adopted as the official policy on the Zionist movement, Ben-Gurion brought them before the Executive of the Jewish Agency and also presented them before the Smaller Zionist Actions Committee; neither accepted his proposal.

Since Ben-Gurion had emphasized that his plan was based primarily upon the propaganda possibilities and the power of conviction afforded by the United States, he still had the option of turning directly to American Zionism. At the end of June 1941, therefore Ben-Gurion again set out for the United States, travelling a long and indirect itinerary which took him through Africa and to London. There he learned that there had been no change in Britain's policy concerning Palestine. The new Minister of Colonies, Lord Moyne, declared in Ben-Gurion's presence that "it was necessary to find a territory other than Palestine".[8]

Ben-Gurion was now strengthened in his conviction that it was hopeless to expect anything from Britain, and that Zionism should seek out new allies from among the "powers of tomorrow", Russia and the United States, who would be molding the post-war world. While in London, Ben-Gurion tried to interest the Soviet ambassador Maisky and the American ambassador Winant in his political plans.[9] The latter encouraged him to go to the United States to present his views before the Jewish public and the government.[10] In his baggage, Ben-Gurion carried with him the message he was about to deliver to the Jews of

America—an expanded English version of his "guidelines for a Zionist policy."[11]

Meanwhile, Chaim Weizmann had come to a similar realization of the need to formulate a new, Zionist political policy, despite his generally moderate approach and his belief in "gradualism". Since the fall of 1939 he had raised in various forums the demand that the western half of Palestine (or the majority of it) be transformed into a Jewish state; this, however, was merely a slogan whose substantive political content was given to frequent change. During that period, the general impression was that Weizmann envisioned Palestine as an autonomous unit within a Middle Eastern Federation, or alternatively, as part of the British Commonwealth.[12]

However, the factor which finally pushed Weizmann to urge that what he had for years referred to as the *Shem Hameforash"* (the unvocable name of God), i.e. a Jewish state, be declared to be the aim of Zionism, was what he believed to be the tragic certainty that by the end of the war there would be millions of homeless and broken Jews who would want to put Europe behind them and emigrate to Palestine. They would constitute the desired Jewish majority that was so necessary for the establishment of a Jewish state.

In formulating a new political policy, Weizmann relied primarily on two sources: the demographic theory developed by his associate and close friend, Louis Namier, concerning the numbers and condition of the Jews who would be left in Eastern Europe after the Allied victory; and his pointed discussions with the leaders of the various governments-in-exile in London concerning the possibilities for the Jewish survivors of the Holocaust finding acceptance in their countries when peace finally came. The conclusion that Weizmann drew from these discussions was that a third of the Jews living in Central and Eastern Europe, some 2,000,000 in number, would be forced to emigrate.

While Weizmann's and Ben-Gurion's proposals were being discussed in the inner forums in London and Jerusalem, discussions were also being held among the Zionists of America concerning Zionist aims for the post-war period. In the United States, the concern was less for demographic considerations and for the possibilities of *aliyah* in the post-war period than upon the need to devise an all-encompassing Zionist solution to the post-war "Jewish problem"—a solution which could be brought both before the Jewish public and which could find its place among all the other programs for the post-war world then being devised in the United States.

The first official Zionist body to act concerning post-war Zionist aims was the "National Conference on Palestine," the organization which sponsored the Untied Palestine Appeal in the United States. This decision resulted from the untiring efforts of the chairman of the American Appeal and the most "maximalist" of the American Zionist leaders, Dr. Abba Hillel Silver. As early as mid-1940, Silver had begun to argue for "maximal Herzlian Zionism" and at a conference held January 26, 1941, it was decided that "in the conditions which will prevail in post-war Europe, Jewry will be faced with the task of finding a home for large masses of Jews from Central and Eastern Europe . . . and only by large-scale colonization of these Jews in Palestine, with the aim of its re-constitution as a Jewish Commonwealth, can the Jewish problem be permanently solved."[13]

Prior to the adoption of this resolution, Silver had delivered an impassioned oration before the 1500 assembled delegates. Borrowing the words of the Irish nationalist leader Daniel O'Connor, "Agitate! Agitate! Agitate!" and the words of Danton, one of the leaders of the French Revolution, "Boldness! More Boldness! And Always Boldness!" Silver had declared that the time had come for the Jews of America to cease being silent. They should demand that the White Paper be repealed, that the gates of Palestine be opened wide for the refugees from Europe and that a Jewish Palestine be created upon termination of the war. To realize these goals the Jews of the United States should apply political pressure upon the Roosevelt administration so that it, in turn, would influence the British government in whose hands lay the fate of Palestine.

This was the very first call to political battle addressed to the Zionists of America by the man who was eventually to lead American Zionism in that battle. At the moment, however, it was a solitary cry in the wilderness—no direct action in that direction was then undertaken by any official Zionist body in the United States. But the echoes of that cry began to reverberate within the various Jewish communities. The delegates to the conference brought back the message to their home communities. Silver utilized the campaigns for the United Palestine Appeal, Keren Kayemet and Keren Hayesod and turned them into forums for political indoctrination, and there slowly began to develop a public pressure for the formulation of a clear Zionist policy.

As a result, in April 1941, the Office Committee of the Emergency Committee unanimously decided that "it was essential to formulate some kind of tentative program of Zionist post-war plans. Jews in this country want to know what we have in mind concerning the position of Palestine after the war, and it is important to be able to present some kind of plan, however vague."

To that aim a subcommittee was set up, chaired by Dr. Solomon Goldman, who had led the struggle against the White Paper in 1938-39. This appointment was only one example of the many "about-faces" that occurred among the Zionists of America in the early years of the war. At the 21st Zionist Congress at Geneva in August 1939, this very same Dr. Goldman had declared, in his capacity as president of the Zionist Organization of America: "Don't speak to the Jews of America about the ultimate aim [of Zionism]; they won't understand it."[14]

On June 19, the subcommittee presented its program before a plenary session of the Emergency Committee. In order to enhance the importance of the meeting, the members of the Zionist Executive who were then in the United States—Rabbi Perlzweig, Isaac Naiditch, Meir Grossman, Kurt Blumenfeld, Israel Marminsky and others— were also invited to attend. When he presented the "peace aims," Goldman emphasized the fact that the suggested program was an attempt to formulate a position for purpose of internal self-clarification only.

The Committee declared that *the* fundamental question for Zionist policy in terms of the political future of Palestine was whether the Zionist movement wanted to perpetuate the British Mandate over Palestine. The conclusion reached by the Committee was that "for obvious reasons" the Zionist movement should not. The creation of a Jewish state, as an alternative to the Mandate, was also dealt with by the Committee, but for various reasons it was decided to refrain from using this term and instead to use the phrase "Jewish Common-wealth." The Committee called for "the early reconstitution of Palestine within its historic boundaries as an autonomous Jewish Common-wealth," the granting of "full equality before the law" to all residents, and "autonomous rights" for the various ethnic and religious groups.[15]

During the stormy and tempestuous discussion following presentation of the program, the participants broke up into two clearly discernible, and opposing, camps. One claimed that the program was not sufficiently clear nor sufficiently maximalist; the other claimed that it

was too extreme. In the end, the subcommittee's program was neither
accepted or rejected. Because of the importance of the matter, the full
body decided to follow Isaac Naiditch's suggestion that a world Jewish
conference be convened in the United States to discuss and adopt an
official Zionist peace program.

Naiditch's suggestion to convene a world conference in the United
States was not an entirely new idea. Since the latter part of the 1930s,
Stephen Wise had been trying to convince the Zionist Executive to
hold a Zionist conference in America, but each time his proposal was
rejected on the formal grounds that the United States was too far away
from the centers of Zionist activity in Europe and Palestine. In fact,
however, both sides knew that a conference of this sort would be of
great value to American Zionism, in that it would grant it a legitimacy
as a third Zionist center—on par with London and Jerusalem—and this
neither the Zionist leadership in London nor in Jerusalem wanted to
grant to the Americans.[16] Now, however, circumstances forced the
leadership's hand.

Dr. Weizmann brought Naiditch's proposal for discussion before the
Emergency Committee.[17] The Chairman of the Committee, Louis
Lipsky, divided the discussion into two questions: Is the idea of convening a conference in the United States acceptable; and if so, what
should be the function and the authority of such a conference? A heated
discussion then ensued over these two questions. The Z.O.A., for
example, feared that such a conference would perpetuate the practice
of granting a "double vote" to the Palestine Zionists, a principle they
vehemently rejected since it denied to them the representation they
deserved in terms of their numbers. It was only upon the insistence of
Robert Szold that a compromise decision was reached, which favored
convening such a conference provided that equal representation be
accorded the American delegation.[18]

Other participants at the Emergency Committee meeting opposed
the proposal since, they believed, the conference would not have the
official authority to make any decisions on matters of internal importance to the Zionist movement, and this authority the Zionists of
America insisted be given to them. Instead they made a counter-
proposal: to convene, in the United States, a meeting of the Zionist
Executive—the supreme body of the Zionist movement in the period
between congresses. A meeting of this agency could then decide upon
convening a world Zionist conference, and could also endow such a

conference with the authority to determine Zionist policy. The decision that was finally adopted called for the convening of an extraordinary meeting of the Executive, with the participation of other Zionist delegates, to deal with the problems at hand. However, because of the blockade in the Mediterranean and the submarine war in the Atlantic, no practical steps could be taken at that time to convene such a meeting.[19]

Nevertheless, the public pressure applied by the "rank and file" upon all the branches of the Zionist movement did bring about results. The seeds sown in the January decision of the United Palestine Appeal and the deliberations that followed in its wake began to germinate. In May of that year, conferences of Mizrachi and the "League for a Palestine of Labor" (the public body of the Labor Zionists) both ratified the draft calling for the creation of a "Jewish Commonwealth."[20] The worsening of the situation on the North African front, the "Struma" tragedy and its aftereffects, and the steady stream of terrifying information concerning the fate of European Jewry living under the Nazi conquest—all combined to underscore the need for Zionist activity on a broad scale. The one body which incorporated all the Zionist factions—the Emergency Committee—was almost totally paralyzed, not only because of personal and party rivalries, but also because a clearly-defined and generally accepted Zionist policy was completely missing.

Events occurring beyond the sphere of internal Jewish affairs also pointed to the need for a clearly-defined Zionist policy. Britain attempted to take advantage of the idea of regional federalism, an idea favored by many of the post-war planners, by trying to create blocs of pro-British Arab states under the leadership of those loyal to Britain. Even though Palestine was not specifically mentioned in this context, Anthony Eden's speech at Mansion House in London on May 29, 1941, aroused American Zionism to the recognition of the danger to Zionism inherent in this position.

It then became clear that merely opposing British policy was not enough; a positive Zionist solution had to be offered. On September 2, a meeting of the Emergency Committee adopted a resolution opposing the incorporation of Palestine in any Middle Eastern federation. It was also decided that the demand for the establishment of an autonomous Jewish Commonwealth in Palestine be included in any public declaration of the movement. A few days later, the Zionist Organization of

America issued the following declaration at its annual conference, held
at Cincinnati:

> "We solemnly declare that the rapid resettlement and rehabilitation
> of the homeless Jewish masses can be effected only by the reconstitu-
> tion of Palestine, in its historic boundaries, as a Jewish Common-
> wealth. The solution of this otherwise insoluble problem can and
> should be achieved after the war under inter-governmental auspices
> and with inter-governmental assistance. There can be no substitute
> for Palestine as a permanent National Homeland."[21]

On November 2, a conference of Hadassah issued a similarly worded
declaration.

At the Z.O.A. conference, a dynamic new president—Judge Louis
Levinthal of Philadelphia—was elected to lead the organization, and in
his capacity as president he also served as chairman of the Office
Committee of the Emergency Committee. One of his first acts as
president was the decision to convening a meeting of all American
Zionists. After consulting with Chaim Weizmann, he asked Meyer
Weisgal to assume the task of organizing the conference, which was to
define the aims of Zionism, and mobilize American Zionism to large-
scale political and financial action. Levinthal recognized that by the
beginning of 1942, the ground had been well laid for a resolution finally
setting forth the political aim of Zionism.

FOOTNOTES

1. The herald of this ideological approach during the First World War had been President
Woodrow Wilson. During the years of isolation between the wars it remained frozen. For a
summary of this ideology as it was enunciated during that period, see R.W. Slosson, *The Great
Crusade and After: 1914-1928*, (New York, 1930).

2. The text of Section 6 of the Charter read: "After the destruction of the Nazi tyranny, they
hope to see established a peace which will afford to all nations the means of dwelling in safety
within their boundaries, and which will afford assurance that all men in all the lands may live out
their lives in freedom from fear and want". The Zionist Executive debated whether or not to
publish a reaction to the Charter, but because it was impossible to agree upon a clear formulation
of Zionist demands after the victory, no statement was issued.

3. R. Savord, *American Agencies Interested in International Affairs* (New York, 1942).

4. An official summary of all the planning activities in the sphere of international relations can
be found in the volume published by the State Department, Harley A. Notter, *Post-War Foreign
Preparation 1939-1945*, (Washington, 1949). A definition of post-war aims is on p. 151.

5. In fact, the American Jewish Committee had established a committee for peace research as early as the middle of 1940. On the activities of this committee, see Naomi Cohen, *Not Free to Desist* (Philadelphia, 1972), pp. 265-266; and Nathan Schachner, *The Price of Liberty—A History of the American Jewish Committee* (New York, 1948), pp. 132-135. Concerning the American Jewish Congress, see: *Congress Weekly* (Feb. 7, 1941): 4; (Feb. 21, 1941): 5-6; (March 28, 1941): 4; (Oct. 24, 1941): 5; and other dates. Some time afterwards, the Jewish Workers Committee and Agudat Israel in the United States established similar institutions; see *The Call* (December 1941): 3-5.

6. Ben-Gurion's report of his visit to London; Minutes of the Executive of the Jewish Agency, November 26, 1939.

7. A few days after his arrival in the United States, Ben-Gurion cabled Kaplan on December 3 requesting him to send him all the material in the possession of the Jewish Agency on the subject of post-war planning for Palestine. In a letter on April 28, 1942, to Dr. A. Ruppin, the head of the Institute of Economic Research, Ben-Gurion emphasized that "the work of the Institute is of inestimable political importance; since the primary political task in the United States was to convince government circles of the possibilities for the absorption of masses of people in Palestine." Records of the Political Department of the World Zionist Organization/The Jewish Agency for Palestine, Central Zionist Archives, Jerusalem, File S25/4754.

8. David Ben-Gurion, "On the road to the army and the State of Israel," a series of autobiographical articles in *Davar* (1966); no. 25.

9. David Ben-Gurion to Chaim Weizmann, November 13, 1941, Chaim Weizmann Papers, Weizmann Library, Rehovot, Israel; Ben-Gurion to Maisky, October 13, 1941, in the David Ben-Gurion Archives, Sde Boker, Israel.

10. *Davar* article No. 28. Winant even got him the "priority" needed to sail for the United States and met with him on his last day in London. (David Ben-Gurion's Diary, November 11, 1941, Political Dept. Records, S25/1023.

11. The phrase is not merely a literary flourish. Upon his departure, Ben-Gurion's baggage was searched by the British authorities, and the document was found and photographed. From that time onward his plans were known to the British and as a consequence he was considered by the Foreign Office to be a "dangerous individual". See Records of H.M. Foreign Office, Public Record Office, London, E. 6946, F.O.371/31380.

12. See, for example, Weizmann's article, "The Jewish Problem in the Coming Reconstruction," *New York Times*, August 13, 1941.

13. For the complete text of the resolution, see *The New Palestine* 32 (January 31, 1941): 22.

14. 21st Zionist Congress, Stenographic Report, pp. 114-15.

15. Minutes of the Emergency Committee, June 19,1941, in Zionist Archives and Library, New York.

16. This desire was defined by an American Zionist leader, in a paraphrase of the famous statement, thusly: "We are looking for an American place under the Zionist sun."

17. Even before the discussion, Emanuel Neumann had clarified the matter with Sumner Welles and received the authorization of the State Department concerning the granting of entry visas for those delegates who would come from abroad. At the same time, Welles hinted to Neumann that it would be worthwhile to discuss the implications of convening "such a gathering" on the overall political situation, in particular the repercussions it might have on the Arabs of the Middle East, a region where the military situation "still gave room for worry." (Neumann's report on the conversation, Emergency Committee Minutes, August 5, 1941).

18. *Ibid.*

19. Some two years later, the Executive of the Jewish Agency came to the conclusion that a gathering of this sort in Palestine was a necessity, and it too did not take place for the same reasons. (See the cable of the Executive of the Jewish Agency to the Emergency Committee, July 20, 1943).

20. For the text of the decision, see *New Palestine*, 32 (September 19, 1941).

21. *Ibid.*

A Tradition of Anti-Zionism: The Department of State's Middle Managers

by Phillip J. Baram

While it is a truism that the Department of State has long been unfriendly to Zionist ideology, the reasons for, and the nuances within, that attitude have rarely been examined, especially during World War Two, the embryonic period of America's great-power role in the Middle East. In the period 1942 through 1945, approximately a dozen men in the middle-echelons determined Middle Eastern policy-making and planning. This "core group," chiefly career diplomats with a few hired academics, came from the Division of Near Eastern Affairs (NEA), the Foreign Service (FS), and the postwar planning apparatus of research and planning committees.

The Division of Near Eastern Affairs

NEA, though it had gone and would continue to go through various mutations in structure and responsibility, covered the following countries as of 1944: Greece, Turkey, Iraq, Palestine, Transjordan, Syria, Lebanon, Egypt, Saudi Arabia and all other countries of the Arabian peninsula. By always grouping Palestine with its geographic neighbors, the Department classified and defined the Holy Land as strictly part of the "Arab world." By implication, therefore, that which was non-Arab in Palestine was inherently foreign, there by special privilege or sufferance, not by right. Naturally, the more Palestine became non-Arab, the more foreign, the more of an anomaly and a problem it became. That it was being populated by East European Jews, those perennial square pegs who fitted nowhere, added to the problem. Yet rather than accept such a trend towards Palestine's re-Judaization as a new reality, as it did so many other trends in the name of *realpolitik*, the State Department opposed it all the more, since such a trend violated its basic "definition" of Palestine.[1]

Wallace Murray, who became NEA chief in 1929, was a careerist and non-specialist in the traditional mold. He became unique, however, in the degree of his area expertise, and in his long tenure in NEA. He remained the Department's senior expert and main policy-initiator on the Arab Middle East and Palestine (not to mention the other countries under his purview) with scarcely any interruption, until after the Yalta Conference in February 1945. He then was appointed to a post he had looked forward to as a culmination of his career, the ambassadorship to Iran, where he served until June 1946. After retiring for health reasons, Murray was affiliated with American business interests in the Middle East, and also served on the board of the anti-Zionist American Council for Judaism.[2]

Murray's affinity for American Council for Judaism ideology was longstanding. "If the establishment of a Jewish State in Palestine would solved the Jewish question," he once declared, "there might still be some justification for a continuance of Zionist agitation. It is, however, open to grave doubt that the majority of American Jewry has any such belief." The latter had come to the United States voluntarily to become good American citizens, and did not like movements like Zionism, which, he said, "involves primary loyalty to a foreign political cause."[3]

Murray's closest associate was Paul H. Alling, assistant chief of NEA from 1934 to 1942. Previously, Alling had held foreign service posts in Beirut, Aleppo and Damascus. When Murray was elevated to adviser on political relations in March 1942, a post equivalent to assistant secretary, Alling moved up to become the ninth NEA chief. After the Yalta Conference, Alling served as an adviser to the American delegation at San Francisco and other conferences. Desiring a post abroad, partly to get away from the ulcer-causing Palestine problem, he served as diplomatic agent and consul general at Tangier, and then as America's first ambassador to Pakistan before his death in 1949.[4]

Both in the prewar and wartime periods, Alling and Murray appeared to have worked harmoniously and to have shared the same views, though it has been said that Murray was often dependent on Alling for the finer points in a given policy's rationale. Alling seems to have been less outspoken than Murray, more the intellectual and proper gentleman who got on well with all. Alling's personal friendships, like those of many others in NEA, included Presbyterian mis-

sionaries and Y.M.C.A. officials active or once active in the Middle
East. In contrast to Alling's calm temperament, Murray had an explosive temper which, with his clipped British accent, rankled some of his
subordinates, not to speak of visiting Zionist delegations.[5]

A third key member of NEA was Gordon P. Merriam who had taught
at Robert College (Constantinople) in the early 1920's and had been
one of the Department's first Arabic-language officers. He had held
vice-consul posts in Beirut, Damascus and Aleppo, and for a longer
period, until 1935, in Cairo. Merriam became an assistant chief of NEA
in May 1940, and was chief of a newer, smaller division of NEA at its
inception in January 1944, when Alling became Murray's deputy director of the Office of Eastern and African Affairs. Merriam remained a
principal in NEA until his retirement for health reasons in 1949.
However, as early as 1946, he felt the Department's "battle" for
Palestine was being lost to the Zionists.[6]

Of lesser import, though actively engaged in some of the policy
problems in the region, were Foy D. Kohler (Merriam's assistant chief
in the NEA), John D. Jernegan, William L. Parker, and Evan M.
Wilson, who in the last two years of the war was the desk officer for
Palestine. George V. Allen and Henry Villard, though dealing with
northern-tier countries and Africa respectively, functioned as di-
visional chiefs and also had periodic influence in NEA.

Murray, Alling, Merriam and their subordinates were all career
officers of very similar social and intellectual background. When
World War Two began, they were, moreover, in the prime of life,
confident of themselves, their values, and their understanding of the
American national interest in the Middle East. The negative corollary,
however, is that the men of NEA were all of like mind. Their collective
mindsets, despite individual differences in temperament, had been
nearly completely, and imperviously, made up before the war with
respect to positions the Department should or should not take on basic
Middle Eastern questions.

In essence, the Department viewed American national interests in
the Middle East as a pursuit of private profit and national prestige. If
these materialized, it was expected that there would be greater prestige for the Department itself both within the government and in the
public mind. To achieve such great-power status, the Department
from the late 1930s on espoused a Wilsonian doxology which included
the principles of an economic open door, national self-determination

for native majorities, and anti-European imperialism. By 1943, the Department had crystallized these goals and begun work to ensure that the postwar Middle East would be a region free of Axis and Anglo-French hegemony, free of Soviet encroachment, and also free of Zionist political agitation. Indeed, the Departmental consensus held that with such obstacles removed and with sovereign Arab states established, the chances were excellent that American influence would be dominant in the area.

The Foreign Service in the Middle East

Before the war, American consular and diplomatic activity in the region was limited, and there were more private than official interests represented there. Religious, educational, and philanthropic ventures characterized these private interests in the 1920s, while archeological, commercial and petroleum interests came to the fore in the 1930s.

Step by step, World War Two changed much of that. During the period September 1939–December 1941, in addition to regular consular activity, foreign service work emphasized extensive reporting of local events, especially of Axis influence. During the early war years, consular activity region-wide decreased markedly (with the exception of work on behalf of ARAMCO in Saudi Arabia). The decline was due to wartime restrictions on shipping, trade, and currency exchange, and to the evacuations of American nationals. Conversely, diplomatic activity greatly increased, particularly in light of Allied offensives, so that as of December 1942, the Middle East became the first "liberated" or "postwar" area of the war.[7]

Parallel to the Department in Washington, Foreign Service officers also moved to the center of the diplomatic stage, consulting, cooperating and competing with other American missions to the area, and, of course, with British, French, Arab and Jewish diplomats. Because of America's increasing power and prestige, even routine conversations between an American chargé in Damascus, for example, and a local nationalist or a French administrator necessarily took on a new dimension of seriousness to everyone, local or not, interested in Syria's future.

By the closing months of the war, America's overall diplomatic activity in the Middle East was considerable. Foreign Service officers fostered and exploited their opportunities whenever possible; and, knowing that their views would be compromised and stalled back in

Washington, they pushed their views on the Department all the harder.

While the size and activities of most consulates expanded in the late 1930s and during the war years, in contrast, the staff size of the Jerusalem Consulate, which dealt with Palestine and Transjordan, hardly changed, consisting throughout the war years of a consulate general, two consuls, and two to three vice consuls. Also symptomatic of the low priority of the Jerusalem post was the fact that the Foreign Service had by the war years a number of junior and senior officers fluent in Arabic, but none in Hebrew or Yiddish. Similarly, on its planning committees, the Department in Washington had a number of experts on Arabic studies, Orientalia and Islamica, but none in any serious sense of the word on Judaica or Zionism. This, despite the fact that the Department and the media considered Palestine a critical area and despite the fact that more American private capital, not to speak of American citizens, was concentrated in Palestine from the 1920s onward than in all the Arab countries *combined.*[8]

In terms of middle-echelon personalities at the helm, the earlier description of the principals of NEA is also applicable to the leading Foreign Service officers. They were a small group of intelligent professional careerists dedicated to the American flag *and* to their Arab "constituency," among whose western-educated upper classes they had lived for long periods. Interacting smoothly with each other and with, in Washington, Murray, Alling, Merriam, and later Loy Henderson, they knew one another on a first-name basis, rotated posts periodically, were fully acquainted with all local leaders and foreign diplomats, and by the outbreak of war were generally in the prime of life, with their values, convictions, self-confidence and biases well established.

The Principals in the Foreign Service in the Middle East

In terms of status, longterm influence, and intensity of personal involvement, the most important officers in the region were Alexander Kirk, George Wadsworth, Harold B. Hoskins, William Eddy, and Loy Henderson. Also important during the war, though less so in my view, were Lowell Pinkerton, consul general in Jerusalem; James Moose, Jr., chargé and minister in Judda, also consul in Damascus; and Ray Hare, chargé in Cairo and Jidda. Others, like Foy Kohler, Parker Hart and William Porter became rather prominent in the Department after the war. Indeed, all these lesser principals had more of a role, if only in terms of making the first drafts of the dispatches signed by their chiefs of mission, than the formal sources give them credit for.

Kirk, a pre-World War One graduate of Yale and the Harvard Law School, from February 1941 to December 1943, was envoy extraordinary and minister plenipotentiary to Cairo, and until July 1943, to Saudi Arabia as well. Partly due to his consular background in several of the world's major capitals, and to his intimacy from 1941–1943 with Egypt and Saudi Arabia, Kirk was ever the *realpolitiker* concerned with large strategic questions, like how the United States should secure a monopoly on Saudi oil and replace British economic hegemony in Egypt. His advocacy of a strong policy was, role and background apart, a direct projection of his character as well. His values included jaundiced views of the British, Zionists and Russians, and an aggressive devotion to the "open door" which probably outdid anyone else's on the Middle East scene, including Secretary Hull's. Kirk of course was "pro-Arab," but does not appear to have been as much an Arabophile as other careerists. There was the exception in the person of Ibn Saud, before whom Kirk, like everyone else in the Department, did obeisance. Oil, and the mystique built up around the Saudi king, had much to do with that.[9]

George Wadsworth as a young man taught at the American University of Beirut, 1914-1917, and for the rest of his life was affectionately connected with that institution. Wadsworth entered the Foreign Service in 1919, and from 1935 to 1941 was consul-general in Jerusalem, where he cultivated an already developed abhorrence for East European Jewish immigrants to Palestine. As of October 1942, he was the diplomatic agent and consul general in both Syria and Lebanon; in September 1944, his rank was raised to minister.

Like Kirk, Wadsworth was responsible for two Arab capitals, and like Kirk again, he was a strong personality, though more blustery and something of a maverick according to the prep-school and corporation standards of the Foreign Service. Indeed, he periodically embarrassed NEA, Secretary Cordell Hull, and later Acting Secretary Joseph C. Grew, by going beyond instructions in his zealous and open espousal of independence for the Levant and in his diatribes against the French and the Zionists—both of whom tried, unsuccessfully, to get Hull and Grew to remove him. The British Foreign Office, in contrast, was exceedingly pleased with Wadsworth's appointment; and during the

1943 showdown between the ranking British and French representatives, Sir Edward Spears and General George Catroux, Wadsworth worked especially closely with his bridge partner, Spears, both as sympathetic listener and advocate, urging the British to take action.[10]

Harold B. Hoskins, born in Beirut of Presbyterian missionary parents and one of the few members of the Department who knew Arabic from childhood, graduated from Princeton in 1917, and saw service with the U.S. Marines. At the start of World War Two he worked for the Department's Foreign Activity Correlation Division and as executive assistant to Assistant Secretary Adolph Berle Jr. Holding the military rank of lieutenant colonel, Hoskins subsequently headed several special missions to the Middle East relative to organizing propaganda for the Office of War Information, surveying the moods in various capitals, and sounding out Ibn Saud on the possibility of a meeting with the Zionist leader, Dr. Chaim Weizmann.[11] In between these wartime assignments, Hoskins, as it were, freelanced; at various times he was on military duty, lobbied on Capitol Hill for pro-Arab, anti-British, anti-Zionist support, and participated as adviser in Departmental operational and planning meetings. He also served as a Departmental liaison to the President and to the Joint Chiefs of Staff.

While not typical of the Department's professionals, Hoskins was a constant presence whose views carried weight. From another angle, while he shared much of the upper-class social background of regular officers and was on excellent terms with Sumner Welles and President Roosevelt, Hoskins was an outsider who was always chafing at what he felt was NEA's bureaucratic timidity and its personnel's over-concern for their careers. He appreciated the fact that most Foreign Service officers were not, as he was, independently wealthy and therefore could not be too independent-minded. Still, he felt wartime made it incumbent to break out of the mold and take new risks. For its part, NEA felt Hoskins was too pushy. Temperament apart, he and the Division were in agreement on most positions.

There were two exceptions, however. NEA disagreed with his repeated thesis that the Department should view the Middle East the way the British supposedly did, as a dynamic *whole*, rather than as—in his interpretation of the Department's viewpoint—a static collection of separate nation-states. Also, earlier than anyone else in the Department, Hoskins had recommended another "bold" approach, namely, that some 500,000 Jews be brought into Palestine in due course, in order to bring the Jewish total into parity with the Arab total (Jews and

Arabs to number approximately one million each). Thereafter, Palestine would be off-limits to Jewish immigrants who, suggested Hoskins, should be steered towards the ex-Italian colonial area of northern Cyrenaica (Libya) for their possibly Jewish state.

It is probably fair to say that over the span of the war years, NEA, and the Department generally, inched towards accepting Hoskins' Churchillian "cut-the-Gordian-knot" approach to Palestine, but they never really accepted Hoskins' large view as a policy the Department should support and take responsibility for implementing.[12]

Hoskins' cousin, Colonel William Eddy, had much the same kind of temperament and background: boldness, missionary parents, Princeton, the Marines in World War One. In the interwar period, however, while Hoskins had entered business, Eddy had become an academic, first as chairman of the English department at the American University in Cairo (1923-1928), and later as president of Hobart College, New York, in the late 1930s. Then, having left an unsatisfying college presidency and having reenlisted in the Marines in 1941, Eddy became prominent in the Office of Coordination of Information and its successor, the Office of Strategic Services.

Eddy was probably the nearest thing the United States had to a Lawrence of Arabia. He was *the* great and personal friend of the Arabs and expressed their point of view, especially Ibn Saud's, with unceasing advocacy, always assuming that American and Arab interests were one and the same. His dispatches from Jidda—particularly from June to September 1945, the twilight period of the war and crucial formative period of the postwar—were ever urging immediate and massive aid to the king, and predicting dire consequences otherwise.

Eddy's interest went beyond keeping Ibn Saud on the American side for oil or anglophobic reasons; it was far more dramatic and historically symbolic than that. Suggesting a monumental rapprochement â la Saladin and Richard the Lion-Hearted, Eddy wrote of the Ibn Saud-Roosevelt meeting in February 1945, that it represented a "moral alliance," "cemented" between the modern world's equivalent of a Defender of the Moslem Faith and the Arabian Holy Cities sacred to 300,000,000 people, and the head of a great Western and Christian nation. Moreover, the meeting, he said, represented a mutual breakthrough, Saudi Arabia emerging from its isolation, the United States asserting itself unilaterally and manfully in the Arab world, without looking over its shoulder at the British or the Jews.

Roosevelt's death shortly after the meeting was thus a grave setback to Eddy and to the bilateralism he had helped on both sides of the water to nurse. Another setback occurred later, when Truman accepted the partition of Palestine; symbolically, Eddy resigned (October 1947) from the Department in protest. Living or dead, Eddy's heart was always in the East. In 1962, when he died, he was, at his request, buried in his birthplace in Lebanon (Sidon), with only the words "U.S. Marines" on his tombstone.[13]

From 1938 to 1943, Loy Wesley Henderson had been a principal in the Department's European Division. Wishing to advance, but not, in his phrase, desiring to jump over other Foreign Service officers, he took advantage of an ambassadorial opportunity in Baghdad which no one else apparently wanted, although Iraq was outside his area of experience. In due course he became directly familiar with the Arab world and increased his reputation for dedicated work and quality of reporting. On the bases of these high marks and his friendships with Wallace Murray and Undersecretary Grew, Henderson became Murray's successor as director of the Office of Near Eastern and African Affairs in April 1945.

Henderson's prominence, in terms of the Department's Middle East policy-making, thus began very late in the war years and is essentially postwar. But his short wartime role was a large one; also his personal and ideological closeness to Murray highlights the nearly unmodified continuity of policy within the Department. Yet in his personal manner, if nothing else, Henderson was somewhat less anti-Zionist than Murray had been, and somewhat more opposed to Britain, France and Russia. On the first point, Henderson expressed "great respect" (as invariably have most careerists interviewed and researched) for Zionist "moderates" like Stephen Wise and Chaim Weizmann and of course the noted "spiritual" Zionist, Judah Magnes.[14]

In addition, Henderson's objections to the proposition of a Jewish state appear to have been less sweeping than in the case of other Foreign Service officers. Still, he felt a Zionist state in a partitioned Palestine would be impractical—economically unviable and militarily indefensible, requiring American intervention and blood to protect it—and that such a state would be a liability to American interests by alienating the Arab-Moslem world, and by introducing into the conduct of foreign policy the presumably dangerous and inappropriate precedent of domestic ethnic politics.

Some three years later, when Truman was supposedly forced by American Jewish voters to recognize the state of Israel, the evil ways of domestic ethnic politics seemed confirmed to Henderson. Nonetheless, it is worth noting that Henderson and his staff drafted Truman's famous letter of instant recognition in May 1948, notwithstanding the conventional view that the Department was surprised and chagrined at Truman's rash action. As a professional, Henderson apparently felt that loyalty to the Chief overrode one's own wishes and values. And secondly, Henderson was apparently concerned that alleged Jewish power and privilege in America (an absolute Departmental fixation in the 1940s which the realities of European death camps and later displaced-refugee camps did nothing to offset) would hurt the Department. That is, if the battle royale, in the "Jewish influenced" media between Zionist sympathizers and the Department became too intense, his career and health, and the careers and health of his colleagues, might well be ruined.[15]

The Middle East Units of the Postwar Planning Apparatus

Within the postwar planning apparatus created after Pearl Harbor were several divisions and committees which concentrated on American long run plans, chiefly for Eastern and Central Europe and for the Middle East. Working with the veteran middle managers of NEA, and to a lesser extent with the Foreign Service, these consisted in 1942-1943 of the Territorial and Political subcommittees, and the Division of Special Research. In 1944 and thereafter, the main Middle East unit was the Interdivisional Country Committee on the Arab Countries.[16]

The planners who were most closely and continuously involved in the wartime research, drafting, initiating, and follow-up advocacy of postwar solutions for the region were but two in number: Dr. Philip W. Ireland and Professor William Yale. Smaller and briefer roles were played by others, like Wilbur White, Jr. (on Syria and Lebanon), Christina P. Grant (on Syria, Lebanon, and Saudi Arabia) and Halford L. Hoskins (on the Suez Canal). On the top of the planning apparatus were men who also had expertise on the Middle East—notably Isaiah Bowman. But it was Ireland and Yale whose province was Middle East planning, and who therefore were the principal middle managers for the region within the planning apparatus.

Ireland had been an instructor at the American University of Beirut in the 1920s, and after receiving graduate degrees from Oxford, Cambridge, and the London School of Economics, taught Middle Eastern history at Harvard, Johns Hopkins and the University of Chicago. In July 1942, he entered the Department as an assistant in the Special Research Division, soon becoming an active participant in the two subcommittee meetings. Subsequently, he was acting chairman of the Interdivisional Country Committee of the Arab countries, assistant chief under Philip Mosely of the Division of Territorial Studies (heir to the divisions of Special Research and of Political Studies), special assistant to Loy Henderson, and assistant to the American delegation to the San Francisco Conference in the spring of 1945.

Ireland directed the research and analysis on the Middle East and was the main spokesman for Middle East researchers, serving as their liaison to the subcommittees and to NEA. His own personal research focused on Libya, Syria, Lebanon, Arab federation, together with intermittent studies of an historical or advisory nature, usually co-authored with Yale, on a diversity of topics, such as the roots of the Middle East's problems, Zionist pressures, and the desirability of sending American "advisers" to the region after the war.

While academically and linguistically qualified, Ireland, somewhat of a dandified and anglicized personality, was always quite abrasive and dogmatic. He had a reputation for being overly sensitive, officious, and an "odd duck." One former colleague, while fully sharing Ireland's views, including his absolute anti-Zionism, expressed the view that though practically everyone in the Department treating the Middle East was an anti-Zionist, Ireland was one of the Department's few anti-Semites. His tendency during planning meetings to equate Zionism with Nazi *lebensraum* suggests that his anti-Zionism was a passion, perhaps a mania, and not simply an intellectual thesis.[17]

William Yale, born in 1887, was with Wallace Murray, who was born the same year, the oldest Middle East expert in the Department, and indeed, had begun Departmental service earlier than Murray. Yale, the son of a wealthy upstate New York family, was hired by the State Department during World War One as special agent on the Middle East and liaison to General Allenby's British forces. He later served as a technical adviser to the King-Crane Commission, and then as an assistant to the American delegation at the Paris Peace Conference of 1919. Though quite young and not an Arabist or political scientist by training, Yale achieved these glamorous if distinctly peripheral roles largely by a combination of school ties, family connections, and plain happenstance.

In the interwar period, Yale cultivated what was, as he himself recognized, a strong emotional and intellectual interest in Jews (anthropological and historical more than religious). It was an interest which fluctuated between strong sympathies (for "gentle" Sephardic Jews, for assimilationist and liberal German-American Jews, for socialist Bundist Jews) and strong antipathies (for "arrogant" East European Jews, for capitalist Jews, for political Zionists of all stripe and American Zionists lobbyists especially). Psychologically, he seems to have acquired some of the dislike of Jews which his father had, as Yale acknowledged, though social environment doubtlessly helped, given the anti-Semitic pseudo-anthropology and discriminatory practices so pervasive at schools like Yale University when he graduated.[18]

During 1941 Yale sent several lengthy, and unsolicited, memoranda from the University of New Hampshire (where he was teaching history) to then Assistant Secretary Berle, admonishing the Department to beware of Zionist machinations. Whether these were factors in his reemployment by the Department is hard to say; in any case, his World War One memoranda were familiar to the Department, and at the end of 1942, he was recruited to come to Washington by Philip Ireland. Once ensconced in the planning apparatus, and put in charge of planning for Palestine, Yale always spoke as the elder expert who "knew" Jews and Zionists like nobody else. His tone was always Catonian, his attitude that of the watchful bulldog. His abiding thesis was that if the Department did not watch out, the Zionists would manipulate American foreign policy during and after World War Two—as they allegedly had done during and after World War One, when they supposedly managed to make support of the Balfour Declaration into an American policy.

Besides Palestine, Yale also did occasional planning for Transjordan and Saudi Arabia. Moreover, unlike other researchers, he was a regular, and vocal, member of the Territorial and Political subcommittees and the Interdivisional Committee on the Arab countries. At such meetings his Zionophobia was unsurpassed, even by Ireland and Wadsworth. As researcher and drafter, his written output was also extraordinary. There is far more from Yale's pen on Palestine in the documentation of postwar planning than there is by any other author on any other Middle Eastern country or combination of countries.

It is also noteworthy that with Ireland and Harold B. Hoskins, Yale was one of the few Departmental officers who was willing to fight fire with fire and engage in extra-Departmental covert maneuverings and lobbying against Zionists. For example, one of Yale's brainstorms (endorsed by NEA) was to contact prominent Jewish anti-Zionists, be they ultra-orthodox, socialist or assimilationist. (Yale was especially fond of the latter two, and was in periodic personal contact with officers of the American Council for Judaism, like Lessing Rosenwald and Rabbi Morris Lazaron.) Yale wanted to generate a native Jewish "popular front" against the efforts of the Zionist Organization of America which was seeking, apparently successfully, to convert American Jewry to the cause of Zionism.

Yale's "philo-semitism" and anti-Zionism went hand in hand during the war. He expressed positive admiration for non-Zionist Jewish leaders as well as earnest sympathy for the age-old Jewish problem and for Jewish suffering under Nazism; and he ardently detested Nazism. But he nonetheless stoutly resisted the occasional plan that came to the Department's attention for the rescue of Jewish children from the crematoria by, for example, transshipping them via Iran and Iraq to Palestine. His "objective" view was that to call such efforts humanitarian was to play into the hands of the Zionists, since it was clear that the more Jews in Palestine, whether children or adult, the more Zionists, and the more Zionists, the more probable was the emergence of a Jewish state.

Immigration into Palestine, except token amounts, was thus anathema to Yale. When Truman did not adopt this view, which every echelon and relevant Department division had accepted and initialed, and when the President urged that the British give 100,000 Jewish Displaced Persons entry certificates into Palestine on humanitarian grounds, Yale resigned in pique and frustration, and returned to his wife and to the University of New Hampshire.[19]

Conclusions

Superficially seen, the prewar and wartime responsibility of NEA, of Foreign Service officers in the Middle East, and the Middle East planners consisted of a moderate level of middle-management functions, namely: researching the facts and reporting the news, presenting drafts of prospective trends, policy alternatives, and recommendations to the upper echelons, after which NEA would convey the upper echelons' and President's ultimate decisions and advice back to the field officers. *De facto*, however, middle management's role was larger. NEA was one of the oldest Departmental geographic divisions, with a staff of great continuity and longevity. Its seniority and respectability were high, as instanced by the fact that NEA people were editorially prominent in the in-house *Foreign Service Journal.* The upper echelons of the Department had confidence in them. Furthermore, because the upper echelons were usually preoccupied with other matters, they tended to accept the views of NEA as the last word in unbiased reporting and expertise.

Seen from close up, therefore, NEA and its associates represented architects of Middle East policy, not merely humble draftsmen or messenger-boys. They were, moreover, "pushy," prodding advocates of the economic open door in the Middle East, of postwar American hegemony, and of full-fledged self-determination for the region's Sunni Arab majority—as well as intelligence-gatherers and respected "middle" managers.

It is noteworthy that these men all had difficulty coping with American political life. Insulated and inbred, elitist and upper-middle class, the middle managers viewed Congress and public opinion in general, and the growing public approval of the idea of a Jewish state in Palestine in particular, with consistent disdain. This negativism towards the American *hoi polloi* is paradoxical, because overseas the Department of State was usually beating the drums of anti-imperialism, majority self-rule, and other democratic principles. Indeed, whenever the Arab "world" seemed to talk violently or hold street demonstrations on a non-local issue, NEA and its Foreign Service liaisons, "alarmed" and "impressed" (and perhaps personally frightened), acted as if that world was a democratic electorate and they were its messengers and representatives. Regardless of the merits of the issue agitated over, they would instinctively urge the Secretary to placate the clamor for the sake of the American national interest and (left unsaid) for their own sakes.

However, if *American* public opinion seemed to clamor for something, the Middle East experts' instinctive reaction was to turn a politely attentive but deaf ear. It did this out of the conviction that not only was Congressional and domestic opinion ephemeral, "uninformed," divided, and corrupted by special pleading and election "politics"—but that even if it were none of these things, public opinion, as a political science abstraction, did not and should not have a tangible role in the formulation of American foreign policy.[20]

Finally, it should be underlined that despite the wartime increase in

Departmental staffing and the growing attention paid to the Middle
East by the Department as a whole, the pilots, so to speak, at the
controls of NEA remained remarkably continuous and homogeneous.
It has been said that while presidents come and go, the Department of
State, and therefore foreign policy, remain the same. By the same
token, one could add that while Departmental secretaries and upper
echelons come and go, the middle echelons, and therefore foreign
policy, remain the same. Certainly this was true of NEA, where
throughout the prewar and wartime periods, and only to a somewhat
lesser extent the immediate postwar period, too, the *same* very small
group of middle managers, with their mindset of fixed anti-Zionism,
held sway.

FOOTNOTES

1. Information on NEA's evolution collated from Graham Stuart, *The Department of State: A
History of Its Organization, Procedure, and Personnel* (New York, 1949), p. 216; *American
Foreign Service Journal* [AFSJ] 10 (1933):16; *Register of the Department of State 1941* (Washing-
ton, 1942, renamed *Biographic Register* as of 1943), p. 24; and Department of State *Bulletin*, 10
(January 15, 1944):57.

2. *Biographic Register of the Department of State 1945; New York Times*, April 28, 1965,
15:2.

3. Murray to Sumner Welles, November 27, 1942, Records of the Department of State,
National Archives, Washington, D.C., File 867N.01/11-2342.

4. *Biographic Register of the Department of State 1945; New York Times*, January 19, 1949,
27:1.

5. Information on Murray and Alling collated in part from interviews with William Yale, June
10, 1971, and July 29, 1971; Loy W. Henderson, July 28, 1972; Gordon Mattison, July 31, 1972;
Evan M. Wilson, August 8, 1972; Gordon P. Merriam, August 23, 1972; Lt. Col. Harold B.
Hoskins, August 31, 1972; Dr. Emmanuel Neumann of the Zionist Organization of America,
October 31, 1972.

6. *Biographic Register of the Department of State 1945*; interviews with Loy Henderson, July
28, 1972; Evan M. Wilson, August 8, 1972; Gordon P. Merriam, August 23, 1972; and wartime
memoranda and correspondence of Merriam in the *Foreign Relations of the United States* [FRUS]
series.

7. For an overview of Department of State philosophy and activity in the Middle East in the
prewar and wartime periods, see in particular chapter 2 in Phillip J. Baram, *The Department of
State's Views of the Middle East Through 1945: Emerging Positions Prior to World War Two,
Wartime Policies, and Plans for the Postwar Period* (doctoral dissertation, Boston University,
1976), scheduled for publication in 1978 by the University of Pennsylvania Press, as *The
Department of State and the Middle East 1919-1945: The Pursuit of Power.*

8. For capital investments and nationals from the United States, see Baram, *op. cit.*, chs. 5,
13.

9. *Biographic Register of the Department of State 1945*; interview with Ray Hare, former
chargé under Kirk, August 4, 1972; and the correspondence in 1941-1943 between Kirk and the
Department, in the *FRUS* series. For instances of obeisance to Ibn Saud, see Kirk to Hull, May
19, 1942, *FRUS* (1942), 4:570.

10. *Biographic Register of the Department of State 1945; New York Times*, March 6, 1958, 27:1; interviews with Ray Hare, August 4, 1972, Gordon Mattison, July 31, 1972, and Joseph Satterthwaite, August 7, 1972.

For an illustration of the affection, or localitis, of Wadsworth regarding the Levant, see his remarks, "Friendship in American-Levant Relations," at a dinner in his honor given at a New York Syro-Lebanese Club, December 9, 1945, printed in Department *Bulletin* 13 (1945): 940-941. On the Department's efforts to periodically restrain him, see Murray to Wadsworth, September 15, 1944, State Department Records, 890E.00/9-1544 OS/D; also Grew to Wadsworth, May 11, 1945, *FRUS* (1945), 8:1073.

11. In this last instance, Hoskins was a sort of rival to Ibn Saud's senior English adviser, H. St. John B. Philby. Though the evidence is contradictory, Philby had apparently broached the idea of a meeting to Weizmann and to Churchill, who in turn recommended it to Roosevelt and to the Department of State (which, like the Foreign Office, and the Jewish Agency, too, was highly dubious from the start). The basic idea was to arrange a trade-off between Weizmann and Ibn Saud—Jewish financial assistance in return for Arab non-interference in Palestine, with in addition Britain's grooming of Ibn Saud as a "boss of bosses" in the Arab world.

12. *Biographic Register of the Department of State 1945;* interviews with Loy Henderson, July 28, 1972; Ray Hare, August 4, 1972; Evan Wilson, August 8, 1972; Gordon P. Merriam, August 23, 1972; and Hoskins, August 31, 1972. Also, from Hoskins' correspondence with Roosevelt and the Department, particularly Welles, 1942-1945, in the *FRUS* series; brief descriptions of Hoskins and other Foreign Service officers can be found in Freya Stark, *Dust in the Lion's Paw: Autobiography 1939-1946* (New York, 1961), pp. 182 ff.

13. *New York Times*, May 5, 1962, 27:2; interviews with Evan Wilson, August 8, 1972, and Harold Hoskins, August 31, 1972; also, R. H. Smith, *OSS, The Secret History of America's First Central Intelligence Agency* (New York, 1972), p. 46; William A. Eddy, *FDR Meets Ibn Saud* (New York, 1954), pp. 42-43; and Eddy's correspondence with the Department in the *FRUS* series for 1944-1946.

14. It may be noted that this respect was based on empathy for Weizmann and Wise's "style," and not their ideological objectives. Both Zionist leaders, being somewhat anglicized gentlemen of the old school, struck a more responsive chord with very proper gentlemen like Henderson. In contrast, his vitriol was typically reserved for "activists"—who were in addition "ungentlemanly"—like Abba Hillel Silver and David Ben-Gurion; and later, for the so-called Jewish grey eminence at the White House, Truman adviser David Niles.

15. *Biographic Registers of the Department of State;* interview with Henderson, July 28, 1972; Gordon Mattison, July 31, 1972; Evan Wilson, August 8, 1972; Gordon Merriam, August 23, 1972; Dr. Emmanuel Neumann, October 31, 1972; Herbert Feis, *The Birth of Israel: The Tousled Diplomatic Bed* (New York, 1969), pp. 45, 61.

On the closeness of Murray and Henderson and the praise and grooming extended by the former to the latter, see Henderson to Murray, November 4, 1944, *FRUS* (1944), 5:631-633; and Murray's personal and confidential reply, November 4, 1944, State Department Records, 867N.01/11-1644, in which Murray wrote that Henderson's "telegrams provided us with exactly the ammunition which we needed to drive the point home of Arab anti-Zionism and the danger to America's stake in the Arab world." Also, note Murray's extraordinary praise, in Murray to Stettinius, November 7, 1944, Stettinius Papers, Alderman Library, University of Virginia, Charlottesville, Virginia, Box 217, Folder "NEA (Mr. Murray) 1/44---."

16. On the composition, evolution, and interaction of the sub-committees, see Harley Notter, *Postwar Foreign Policy Preparation 1939-1945* (Washington, D.C., 1949), pp. 92-108, 117-122, *passim*. On the research aspects of the planning apparatus, see *ibid.*, pp. 151-153, 520, Appendix 22; also, P. Baram, *op. cit.*, ch. 1, 14.

17. His publications include: *Iraq: A Study in Political Development* (New York, 1938); "The Near East and the European War," in *Foreign Policy Reports* 16 (March 15, 1940):2-16; and Ireland, ed., *The Near East: Problems and Prospects* (Chicago, 1942). Information on Ireland based on *Biographic Register of the Department of State 1945*, and interviews with William Yale, August 20, 1971, Loy Henderson, July 28, 1972, Gordon H. Mattison, July 31, 1972, Harry Howard, August 3, 1972, Ray Hare, August 4, 1972, Evan Wilson, August 8, 1972, and Gordon P. Merriam, August 23, 1972.

18. Illustrative of this background and spirit of the times was his essay, "Non-Assimilation of Israel," *Atlantic Monthly* 130 (1922): 276-278. Its pseudo-anthropological theme was that the "Jewish" attitude towards women was gross and indelicate compared with the chivalrous "Christian" attitude.

19. Interviews with Yale, June 10, 1971, July 29, 1971, August 25, 1971, August 26, 1971; Yale Papers, Mugar Library, Boston University (folios since 1945; also, marginalia in Yale's book collection on Jews, the Middle East, etc.); Yale Papers, Houghton Library, Harvard University (mainly originals of his drafts and memoranda, as postwar planner 1942-1945; also, correspondence, planning-committee minutes, etc.); and from Yale's memoranda on Palestine in the Harley Notter Papers, National Archives. Yale's published works include several articles and his opus, *The Near East: A Modern History* (Ann Arbor, 1958). On Yale's prewar memoranda to the Department, see, Yale to Berle, March 12, 1942, and March 23, 1942, State Department Records 867.01/1800. For an example of Yale's counterlobbying (trying to block the publication of a pro-Zionist ecological study, W. C. Lowdermilk, *Palestine: Its Decay and Restoration*), see Yale Papers (Harvard), Box 2, Folder 8/H; and Lowdermilk, Transcript, vol. 1, pp. 187-192, Oral History Collection, Columbia University. For his communications with Jewish anti-Zionists, see Yale Papers (Harvard), Box 3, Folder: Personal Correspondence and Related Matters.

20. E.g., see J. Rives Childs' disdain for Roosevelt, and for Hull, too, who supposedly played politics on Palestine to get Jewish support, in Childs, *Foreign Service Farewell: My Years in the Near East* (Charlottesville, 1969), pp. 104-109. For Hull's own irritation with Rooseveltian politics, see Hull, *Memoirs* (New York, 1948), 2: 1536-1537. Also, see Breckinridge Long's watchdog efforts to keep Congress and the newspapers out of any Departmental decision on Palestine and oil, notably in February-April 1944, in Long Papers, Library of Congress, Box 200, Folder: Palestine 1944, and Box 201, Folder: Petroleum 1944. The Department's tendency to ignore public opinion when possible was confirmed in interview with Merriam, August 23, 1972, and from letter of October 15, 1971, from H. Schuyler Foster, former Public Opinion Studies officer in the Department. To all the above, *cf.* Harry Truman's famous rebuttal: "The difficulty with many career officials in the government is that they regard themselves as the men who really make policy and run the government. They look upon elected officials as just temporary occupants." Truman, *Memoirs* (Garden City, New York. 1956), 2:165.

Rifts in the Movement: Zionist Fissures, 1942-1945

by Melvin I. Urofsky

When Lord Cornwallis surrendered to George Washington at Yorktown in 1781, the British military band sadly played "A World Turned Upside Down." For American Jewry in general, and for the Zionists in particular, the world of the early 1940's indeed seemed askew. In Europe, the centuries-old veneer of civilization had been shattered, and while millions of men, women and children were being brutally butchered to satisfy a lunatic's mania, the democratic nations of the world stood by passively. In America, an overwhelming majority of American Jews endorsed the Zionist goal of a Jewish state in Palestine, yet the voice of this majority seemed to be drowned out by the hysteria of the anti-Zionists on one side, and by irresponsible chauvinism on the other. The Zionists managed to do a great deal of good, solid propaganda work building up sympathy and support in the community and in Congress. But they failed to ignite the community, failed to transform the pent-up energies and frustration into an active, irresistible force, and only part of that failure can be attributed to anti-Zionist cliques in the State Department or a wily, double-talking president or even to headline grabbing factions within the community. Perhaps one of the saddest chapters in Zionist history can be found in the bitter infighting that took place during the Second World War, a fight not only over methods, but also over leadership. It is impossible to say that had these battles been avoided, American Jewry would have been a more potent force in world affairs; but it is quite evident that a long, drawn-out internecine strife sapped American Zionism of the strength and unity needed to face the terrible challenges of a world gone mad.

By mid-1942 the rough outline of the battle had been sketched in, and even though the Biltmore Conference marked a shift in power from one group to another, as well as a change in goals and tactics, it would be several years before the changeover would be complete, a process elongated far more than necessary by the egotism of the principal characters. The decision at Biltmore to seek the creation of a Jewish state after the war marked the decline in influence of Chaim Weizmann in the world movement and of Stephen Wise on the American scene, with the concurrent rise of David Ben-Gurion and Abba Hillel Silver. Unfortunately, unlike a political election, the winners could not be quickly determined, nor would there be an orderly transition of power. In the years following Biltmore, it seemed at times that Zionist leaders were fighting each other as much as they fought outside opponents. It is a complicated tale, yet its outcome materially affected the post-war struggle for a Jewish state; it also prefigured the later transformation of American Zionism after the creation of Israel.

The outbreak of the second world war had far less impact upon the world Zionist movement than had been the case in 1914.[1] At that time the bulk of Zionist strength came from continental Europe, especially Russia and Poland; English and American federations, as well as the *Yishuv*, were relatively weak in comparison to the Hovevei Zion of eastern Europe. By 1939, however, Hitler and Stalin had already destroyed much of continental Zionism, and the centers of gravity within the movement had shifted to a thriving Palestinian settlement and to potentially strong and affluent organizations in Great Britain and America. Zionist leaders in both Palestine and England recognized, however, that the free world's power now resided in the United States, and sought to establish a more visible and effective Zionist presence in this country. At first, the World Zionist Organization limited itself to creating the Emergency Committee for Zionist Affairs. But then Chaim Weizmann, the president of the WZO, impatient with what he saw as American indecisiveness, moved to establish an American base for himself. In 1941 he directed Meyer Weisgal to open an office of the Jewish Agency in New York, and the following April created an "office of the President of the W.Z.O. . . . to act as a liaison with the various agencies, Zionist, non-Zionist, governmental, scientific and otherwise."[2]

Weizmann's motives went beyond a desire to improve Zionist efficiency. In the 1930s the Jewish Agency Executive in Jerusalem had emerged as a rival center of power within the Zionist movement, and

David Ben-Gurion used his position as chairman of the Agency Executive to challenge Weizmann's authority. According to Ben-Gurion, Weizmann ran the Zionist Organization as a personal fiefdom, in which all division heads reported only to the president and were not accountable otherwise. The fiery Palestinian also sought so-called "procedural" safeguards, purportedly designed to prevent Weizmann from engaging in his unique brand of personal diplomacy without consulting other Zionist officials. As Yehuda Bauer notes, "the debate was not in the least procedural." What Ben-Gurion sought was nothing less than undivided leadership in Zionism, a leadership based in the *Yishuv* and not on the world Zionist apparatus. The two men also differed on their view of the relative importance of America. Ben-Gurion believed that in the end, the United States would be the decisive influence in securing a Jewish state, while Weizmann clung to his faith in Great Britain. They also drifted apart on the meaning they attached to specific goals, such as a timetable for creating a state after the war, and the transfer of some two million Jews from Europe to Palestine. For Weizmann, such slogans might be useful in political games, but he had grown too old and weary to believe that they could be anything more than that in a cynical world. Ben-Gurion, on the other hand, seized upon them as banners around which to rally Jews. He realized that American Jews would labor endlessly for a specific task, even a visionary one, while they had little patience with theory, and even less with those who did not believe in their own dreams.[3]

Both Ben-Gurion and Weizmann came to the United States in early 1942, and the differences in their approach soon manifested themselves in the negotiations preliminary to the Biltmore conference. For Weizmann, a declaration in favor of a Jewish commonwealth could be little more than a tactical propaganda step, a political demand on which to base future negotiations with the British. The Crown, he believed, would always listen to reason, but would not negotiate if confronted with an ultimatum. For Ben-Gurion, statehood meant just that, not a negotiable item which could be whittled away or ignored when convenient. Statehood was more than a slogan, and much to the surprise of many Americans, Ben-Gurion had already begun to talk privately about the possibility of having to fight England after the war in order to secure a Jewish state.[4] After Ben-Gurion had his way at Biltmore, a weary Weizmann went to the Catskill resort of Grossinger's to rest, and while, there, called his old friend Judge Louis

Levinthal, president of the Z.O.A., to come and visit him. As the two men sat in the secluded bungalow, they discussed the implications of Ben-Gurion's threatened warfare against Weizmann's beloved England. Still grieving over the death of his son Michael, an R.A.F. pilot, Weizmann said: "B.G. wants to be Bar Kochba. I don't want to be Bar Kochba. Maybe he's right, but I don't want to be a Bar Kochba. We've waited so long, fighting for our position, we'll wait a little longer. We don't want bloodshed."[5]

Anyone aware of the inner anguish Ben-Gurion later underwent as head of the Jewish armed forces in the Israeli War of Independence could testify that the last thing he wanted was to spill blood. But part of Ben-Gurion's genius lay in his sense of timing, his instinct for the right move at the right time. He sensed, he knew, that by 1942 the time of accommodation had passed; he did not seek the struggle so much as accept its inevitability. But, in typical Palestinian fashion, he moved to consolidate his position in a blunt, even brutal, manner. Weizmann's moment in the sun had passed, and now he should be pushed aside as quickly as possible. On June 11, 1942, Ben-Gurion wrote to Weizmann demanding that he step down from Zionist leadership. He accused the aging leader of having completely failed to harness the potential strength of American Jewry, and through his private and secretive leadership, of fostering disunity in Zionist ranks. The movement could not continue to be governed this way; either Weizmann must step down, or Ben-Gurion would refuse to work with him any longer.[6]

Ben-Gurion may have been right in his analysis of the situation, but he completely misjudged the emotional support that Weizmann commanded within Zionist ranks, the result of decades of devoted service. Even in America, where he had antagonized the old Brandeis group for more than two decades, Weizmann had become a familiar figure on his annual pilgrimages to this country in search of funds for Palestine. Although eventually most of the American leadership would align themselves on Ben-Gurion's side, in mid-1942 he was still an unknown quantity.

Stephen Wise tried to make peace between the elder statesman and the young lion, an attempt that within a few months he would recall with more than a trace of irony. Ben-Gurion and Weizmann agreed to meet in Wise's study, together with a handful of key American leaders—Louis Levinthal, Robert Szold, Louis Lipsky, Meyer Weisgal, as well as Nahum Goldmann. There, in a painfully embarrassing scene, Ben-Gurion, in a two-hour tirade, accused Weizmann of play-

ing a lone hand, of making serious political mistakes, of even preventing the creation of a Jewish army. Hayim Greenberg, the veteran
Labor Zionist leader, walked out of the room with tears streaming
down his cheeks, and murmured to Weisgal: "I never believed I would
live to see the day when such an outrageous discourse would be
delivered by a leader of the Palestinian labor movement." Weizmann's
reply, while much briefer, hardly added to the tone of the meeting; he
declared that Ben-Gurion suffered from hallucinations, and that the
whole affair added up to nothing less than political assassination.[7]

For once Ben-Gurion's sense of timing failed him. Four years later,
with American backing, he repeated essentially the same charges at
the Zionist Congress in Basle and forced Weizmann's ouster as head of
the WZO. But in 1942 the Americans did not yet know the Palestinian
leader well enough to trust him with the fate of the movement. Even
the Brandeisists in the group re-affirmed their personal confidence in
Weizmann; this, however, led Weizmann to misgauge completely the
tenor of American Zionists. He misread a vote of personal confidence
into a mandate, and over the next few years made one error in judgment after another in trying to direct the movement in America. And
just as Ben-Gurion had come to challenge his leadership, so another
young Turk arose to overthrow the Wise regime in American Zionism.

Stephen Samuel Wise had been a major force in American Zionism
ever since the founding of the Federation of American Zionists in
1897.[8] During the Brandeis administration, Wise had counted as one
of the jurist's chief lieutenants and spokesmen. When Hitler came to
power in the early 1930s, Wise had been among the few, the very few
to recognize that the Nazis meant what they said, that the Hitler
regime posed a real threat to European Jewry, and he had organized
countless protests and rallies to try to pressure the Germans into
leaving Jews alone. But Wise's importance far transcended Zionist
affairs, for he was also an important secular reformer as well as a mover
and shaker in Jewish communal life. Wise had been the first child labor
commissioner in Oregon, and later became a leading advocate of union
rights and labor reforms. From the time he settled in New York in 1907
he had been involved in good government campaigns on both the city
and state levels. In an age which still admired oratory, Wise had
perhaps the finest speaking voice of his time, a voice that could always
be found in support of the rights of minorities, of the downtrodden, of
those whom an industrial society had dealt a poor hand.

But Wise never neglected his Jewish responsibilities, and he had a major impact on American Jewish institutions and life. Perhaps Wise's most important work came in the democratization of Jewish life in America. He more than any other man led the fight against the aristocratic *shtadlanim* of the American Jewish Committee during the first world war, and organized and led the American Jewish Congress from its founding in 1916 until his death more than three decades later. During the 1930s he put together the first truly representative international Jewish body, the World Jewish Congress, which not only fought Hitler but took the lead after the war in securing billions of dollars of reparations for Nazi crimes against European Jewry.

Despite all this work for democracy in Jewish life, for new modes of congregational life and rabbinic training, for social justice and reform in civic affairs, Wise never lost his touch for the individual person. He was a man who held few grudges in his life, and his love of mankind and of his people flowed out and touched all who knew him. Nahum Goldmann once wrote: "Not only did he love the Jewish people, he loved every individual Jew. He would turn his hand to finding help for a poor refugee, arranging for the adoption of an orphan, or providing for a destitute widow as willingly as solving a great social problem. This explains his unsurpassed popularity with the Jewish masses of America. Other Jewish leaders may have been more revered, feared or admired than he, but none was so beloved."[9] This love enabled Wise to brush off the vitriol thrown by a Peter Bergson or a Ben Hecht, but it could not withstand an assault from within the Zionist movement led by Abba Hillel Silver.

Silver had once been the *wunderkind* of American Jewish life, but one whose promise as young man developed into extraordinary accomplishments as he grew older.[10] A brilliant orator as well as a respected scholar, he had at an early age become rabbi of the immensely prestigious and wealthy Temple Tifereth Israel in Cleveland, Ohio. From all reports, Silver was as devoted a rabbi to his congregation as Wise was to his; the two men also shared great involvements in their respective civic lives and in Jewish affairs, although where Wise had been a pioneer, the younger Silver would frequently rejuvenate an ailing, lackadaisical organization. Both men were among the few committed Zionists within the Reform rabbinate, and shared a devotion to the growth and well-being of the *Yishuv*.

But there the similarities ended. Where Wise was warm and open to the entire world, Silver was cool and closed except to his closest associates. Where Wise's opponents respected him, some of Silver's allies could not stand him personally. Wise acted on the grand stage, taking on giants, but was often a sloppy administrator, leaving many details to his loyal associates. Silver was an administrative and organizational genius, but also knew how to delegate responsibility and authority. He gave his subordinates free hands in their areas of responsibilities, but if they failed to perform their tasks satisfactorily, he would be mercilessly harsh with them. Like Ben-Gurion, Silver thought the time for a change had arrived, and like the Palestinian, would be blunt, even brutal, in seeking that change. Nahum Goldmann, even though oftentimes an enemy of Silver, has summed up his strengths and weaknesses accurately: "Above all he had unyielding strength of will. He was a typical autocrat, possessing the authority and self-confidence to command but not the flexibility to understand his opponent. He was an Old Testament Jew who never forgave or forgot and who possessed no trace of the talent for keeping personal and political affairs separate. Once he had adopted a movement or an idea, he served it with utmost devotion, and he was a loyal friend to all those who followed his orders absolutely. Anyone who fought him politically became his personal enemy. He could be extremely ruthless in a fight, and there was something of the terrorist in his manner and bearing."[11]

For Silver, Wise's greatest sin lay in his willingness, indeed his commitment to work within established routes. Wise, who for years had fought the *shtadlanim* of the American Jewish Committee, had to some extent become one himself. His fame and prestige, built upon a lifetime of service, gained him easy access to the inner offices of mayors, governors, congressmen, senators, and even the president of the United States. While Wise had no compunctions about utilizing these contacts to help Jewish and Zionist causes, he did shy away from forcing confrontation with men he considered his friends and allies. Saddest of all, Wise trusted them, especially his "great and good friend," Franklin D. Roosevelt, and could not believe that the president was playing a double game. Silver, who was a Republican and deeply distrusted Roosevelt, condemned Wise as naive, and in speech after speech warned American Zionists "to put not their trust in princes." Silver wanted an aggressive campaign to force politicians out into the open, to put them on record for the casual promises so "sincerely" made in private. But Silver's battle also extended to the

World Zionist Organization, which he felt was interfering, and doing so unwisely and ineptly, in political activities in this country. As a result, Silver became allied with David Ben-Gurion, while Wise and Chaim Weizmann, who had once been bitter foes, now joined together.

Silver had originally been reluctant to take a leading part in day-to-day affairs, partly because he realized that his innate militancy would be out of tune with the established leadership. But his speech at the Biltmore conference had impressed many people, and ironically enough, Chaim Weizmann made the first move to draw Silver into the inner circle. "Silver seems the most suitable," wrote Weizmann, and "would be prepared to take the part assigned to him, if it can be done with dignity and without friction, which is, I confess, not altogether easy to achieve."[12] Weizmann's concern grew out of the resignations of three key people from the Emergency Committee, David Petegorsky, Meyer Weisgal, and Emanuel Neumann, who all objected to the committee's disorganization and its lack of leadership and initiative.[13] Moreover, Weizmann and other Euopean leaders felt that American Zionists in general, and the ZOA leadership in particular, did not appreciate the gravity of the situation in Europe nor were capable of dealing with it.[14] Weizmann's early efforts to interpose a WZO presence in the United States had only fed Ben-Gurion's charges that he had been playing a lone hand. At Stephen Wise's urging, both for tactical reasons as well as to placate Ben-Gurion, the WZO expanded its American office to include all of its executive members from the United States, as well as a number of new American Zionist figures, including Silver.[15]

While Ben-Gurion refused to be pacified, he soon discovered that in Silver he had an ally who shared his impatience with the WZO, who believed in the necessity for a Jewish state after the war, and who stood ready to agitate and fight for that goal. For Ben-Gurion the hope of the Zionist movement lay in winning over the American public and government, and Weizmann's continual demands for moderation and caution could delay, if not actually defeat, the realization of an independent Jewish state. Silver also opposed such a hesitant approach, and from the time he went on the Emergency Committee spoke consistently for a bolder, more active stance by American Zionists.[16]

Silver came to partial power with the re-organization of the Emergency Committee in August 1943 into the American Zionist Emergency Council. Weizmann and other WZO leaders had been frustrated since the beginning of the war with the Emergency Committee's inability to pull together the various Zionist groups in the United States. As late as mid-1943 the Committee had not established a Washington bureau, nor did it even have a resident representative in the nation's capitol. Moreover, the lack of leadership had allowed Ben-Gurion's advocates, in Weizmann's opinion, to take far too militant a stand in interpreting the Biltmore platform.[17] Stephen Wise, the nominal head of the Emergency Committee, confessed to Weizmann that the burdens of the office exceeded his physical capacities, and he would welcome a younger man, like Silver, taking over.[18] After protracted negotiations, Silver agreed to become co-chairman with Wise of a reorganized Emergency Council, which would be recognized by the WZO as *the* representative agency of American Zionism. The Council consisted of 26 people, representing the four major Zionist groups, together with members of the smaller factions. Even the fringe groups, such as Hashomer Hatzair, Achdut Avodah, and the Revisionists were invited to send observers, so that the Council could claim that no one had been excluded. From the time he took over, however, Silver found himself fighting simultaneous battles within the Zionist camp. On the one hand, he opposed what he saw as the unwarranted and dangerous interference of the world organization in American affairs, and on the other, he had to overcome his colleagues' cautious approach to political activity.

Prior to the re-organization of the Council, the Jewish Agency Executive had established a political office of its own in Washington in May 1943, with Nahum Goldmann and Louis Lipsky in charge. The office had been created not only to fill a void in the Zionist campaign, but also to head off what Weizmann saw as a heretical tendency of American Zionists to ignore the world movement, a habit that had had such disastrous consequences after the first world war.[19] Weizmann promised the Council that this office would "closely cooperate" with it, but in fact Goldmann hardly ever consulted with Silver, and seemed determined to establish himself as the "Jewish ambassador" to the American government. By October 1943, Silver felt that either Goldmann had to agree to abide by the authority of the Council, or that the office should be abolished. At a stormy meeting at the Dorchester House in Washington on October 12, a reluctant Goldmann agreed, neither for the first nor the last time, to clear all his future appointments with government officials with the Council office.[20] Within a month, however, the two groups were again working at cross-purposes, one office setting up meetings without informing the other, bombarding confused congressmen and bureaucrats with contradictory viewpoints, and trading accusations regarding who had broken the agreement.[21]

The fight involved more than the mere "clash of temperaments" that Meyer Weisgal reported. Goldmann insisted that only the Jewish Agency had the prerogative to deal with foreign governments in matters relating to Palestine, and the proper function of any "local or national" Zionist group should be propagandizing Zionism's goals, particularly among non-Jews. Emanuel Neumann, speaking for Silver, sharply contested this view, arguing that only American Zionists as American citizens could legitimately deal with the American Government; the proper role of the Goldmann office would be contacts with foreign embassies. (The State Department indirectly supported the Neumann-Silver approach; Wallace Murray directed that any contact between the Department and the Jewish Agency should be made via the British embassy.) By January 1944, Neumann believed a showdown inevitable, and urged Silver to consolidate his forces within the ZOA in anticipation of a fight.[22]

The Zionist Organization of America was, in fact, the key to power at that time within American Zionism, despite Hadassah's larger membership. The women's group preferred to stay out of the internal political fighting, concentrating its efforts on maintaining its medical and social service program in Palestine. Hadassah had partisans of all factions on its board, but because of their remarkable loyalty to Hadassah, for the most part they kept the Wise-Silver and Ben-Gurion-Weizmann feuding out of their ranks. Whichever group could provide leadership, real and effective leadership, would find Hadassah ready to help.[23] The ZOA, on the other hand, thrived on the politics, and Silver recognized that unless he could establish a power base within that organization, he would have no leverage on the Emergency Council. Although Silver had made a bid for full control of both the Emergency Council and the ZOA, he had failed to secure it. The compromise gave him more effective power than Wise within the Council, due to his second role as chairman of its executive committee, but Israel Goldstein, at that time an ally of Wise, became president of the ZOA in September 1943.[24] Silver's perception of the situation proved accurate when matters came to a head in late 1944.

The battle began over efforts to secure a congressional resolution calling for the rescission of the White Paper, with a number of Council members urging caution while Silver called for "an active and vigorous attack." When the War Department managed to kill the proposal in committee, a number of Zionist leaders wanted Silver to soft-pedal the campaign, especially in an election year. Silver reacted angrily, and wrote Weizmann that "quiet diplomacy" would not bring any results, and that the alleged goodwill of government leaders could not be counted upon to produce concrete results. As for the election, the presence of five million Jews might yet prove more effective in securing action than backstairs pleading, and to prove his point, Silver, together with Robert A. Taft, managed to get the Republican Party to adopt a strong pro-Palestine plank in its 1944 platform.[25]

Throughout the spring and summer of 1944, relations between Silver, a Republican, and the ardently pro-Roosevelt Wise grew more tense, and Silver time and again suggested, not very tactfully, that the elderly Wise should retire and stop interfering with Silver's efforts to discipline the Council into an effective organization. The strain between Silver and Goldmann, who was allied with Wise through the World Jewish Congress, also increased, as Goldmann, with Weizmann's encouragement, continued to play a lone hand in Washington. Silver wanted the Goldmann operation closed, as he found his own work "becoming increasingly hampered and embarrassed."[26] With some heat, Silver complained that on all occasions he had kept the London office informed of developments in America, not only out of courtesy, but so that an overall Zionist policy could be created. But Goldmann acted as if he were the Jewish Agency incarnate. "Nobody has authorized him to speak on those basic Zionist policies," Silver declared, "and his actions and opinions are subject to no quick review by the parent body."[27] When Goldmann in late August saw Secretary of State Stettinius without first consulting Silver, the Cleveland rabbi exploded. Goldmann had created a situation in which it was impossible for the Emergency Council to function effectively, he announced, and then submitted his resignation from the Council.

The other members of the Council, and indeed the entire Zionist organization, reacted wildly to this unanticipated turn of events. The Council failed to convince Silver to withdraw his resignation, even after it passed a resolution directing that all contacts with any official of the American government could be made only after clearance with the

Council's executive committee. Cables shot across the Atlantic, urging the London office to take action, and Goldmann agreed, once again, not to act without consulting Silver.[28] Ben-Gurion personally urged Silver to stay on, that at such a critical point in Jewish history he could not withdraw. Finally, after Goldmann formally repeated his pledge of cooperation, and the peacemakers within the ZOA had soothed everybody's egos, Silver consented to resume his post.[29]

At first glance, the August resignation might appear as a tempest in a teapot: a strong-willed, self-important Silver picking up his marbles because of the conduct of an equally spoiled Goldmann. But beneath the surface larger issues simmered. Weizmann at any time could have broken the impasse by ordering Goldmann, whom he had personally selected to head the Washington office, to obey the Council's directives. But Weizmann, seeing his base of power in Europe and Palestine eroding, hoped to preserve control of American Zionism despite the rise of a younger, more aggressive leadership; Silver and his friends were unwilling to be guided, or manipulated, by a man whom they no longer trusted. Silver and Ben-Gurion would not be able to oust Chaim Weizmann from the WZO presidency until the Zionist Congress in 1946, but they were not going to cooperate in his minimalist policy, a policy they believed totally unsuited for the times. Similarly, Stephen Wise, despite his age and growing physical impairment, did not want to yield power either. During the resignation episode he was notably reticent in urging Silver to return, and Emanuel Neumann thought he detected a fair amount of manipulation by Wise's supporters, Robert Szold and Israel Goldstein, in turning the situation against Silver.[30] In London, Weizmann also remained silent. In Stephen Wise he knew he had a friend, even though they had quarreled during the Brandeis split; in Silver he saw a rival.

The "reconciliation" hardly deserved the title. Goldmann "consulted" for a few weeks, and then began to keep his own counsel. Wise actively worked for Franklin Roosevelt's re-election, much to the chagrin of Silver, who thought that while the Zionists should lobby both parties, they could not afford to play partisan politics. At an Emergency Council meeting, Silver argued that "it was not proper for a Zionist spokesman appearing on Zionist business to give the impression that the whole Zionist movement was tied to the Democratic party."[31] To add insult to injury, Wise had not even informed Silver of his much publicized meeting with Roosevelt until afterwards. Then, when Silver wanted to test Roosevelt's sincerity after the election by reviving the congressional resolution against the White Paper, he found Wise actively working to block him. An anguished Sol Bloom complained to Israel Goldstein that he did not know what to do. One moment Rabbi Silver tells him to go ahead with the hearings, and the next Rabbi Wise tells him to delay.[32] Within the Council, friction built to an intolerable level as advocates of the two men traded charges of "dictatorship" and "cowardice." Silver grew more and more secretive, refusing to discuss matters with any but his most trusted associates, and on several occasions acted as single-handedly as he had accused Goldmann of doing. Even Hadassah felt that the situation had gotten completely out of hand, and had to be resolved one way or another.[33]

Stephen Wise made the first move on December 12, 1944, resigning as chairman of the Council in protest against Silver's alleged dictatorialness and insulting manner. After Wise had defended his conduct in meeting privately with the president, the Council voted to refuse his resignation, a clear-cut vote of confidence in him, as well as a slap at Silver. On December 28, after a lengthy meeting, the resignations of both Silver and Wise were accepted. After pausing just long enough to tender appreciation to Silver for his devoted service to the cause, the Council then proceeded to elect Wise as sole chairman and Rose Halprin of Hadassah as treasurer, and reorganized the structure to give Wise complete control of the Council and its activities.

Silver, licking his wounds, retired to Cleveland, sorry that against his better judgment he had ever agreed to join the Council. Left to his own devices, it is doubtful that he would have tried to regain control of the American Zionist apparatus. But the uproar in the Jewish press, and the activities of his friends soon convinced him that while he had been outvoted on the Council, he had the support of the lay leadership. The editorials in the Jewish press for the most part eschewed attacking Wise so much as endorsing the Silver position. The *Jewish Morning Journal* (December 22, 1944), for example, declared: "At this moment we cannot afford to indicate lack of confidence in an outspoken Zionist policy—even when such a policy encounters difficulty," while *Der Tag* (December 23, 1944) opined: "Only an aggressive, dynamic policy can lead to success, and Rabbi Silver is clearly the man to be entrusted with such a policy." Philip Slomovitz, in the Detroit *Jewish News* (January 26, 1945) wrote that Silver "is a consistent and vigorous fighter for justice for Jewry and Palestine, and the Zionist constituency will surely reject any plan to eliminate him from leadership."[34]

Silver's friends, heartened by this response, made their first move

when two of the Council's leading staff members, Harry L. Shapiro and
Harold P. Manson, resigned, and together with Abraham Tuvin,
Harry Steinberg, and, of course, Emanuel Neumann, created the
"American Zionist Policy Committee" to lobby among the rank-and-
file for Silver's return to leadership. They began to issue statements not
only defending Silver, but directly attacking Wise, and they portrayed
the struggle as one between militancy and non-militancy, between
democracy and *shtadlaniuth*. At the Policy Committee's urging, local
Zionist sympathizers organized debates on the issues, and flooded the
Emergency Council with telegrams and petitions demanding Silver's
recall. At a ZOA administrative council meeting on January 7, 1945,
Israel Goldstein, Judge Morris Rothenberg, James Heller, and Louis
Levinthal defended Wise, while Emanuel Neumann and Jacob
Fishman presented the Silver case. While Neumann was making his
presentation, Wise interrupted to charge Silver's lieutenant with car-
rying on a "sewerage campaign." Neumann slowly turned, offered the
opinion that Wise was taking advantage of his years, and then left the
platform amid much applause. But when the vote came calling for
Silver's return, it lost 30 to 66.[35]

The Wise group, aware that the situation had gotten completely out
of hand, began searching for alternatives. While Wise stood ready to
resign, neither he nor his colleagues wanted Silver or one of his
designees in power. Strangely enough, they thought they could promote Meyer Weisgal, Weizmann's closest friend in America, but a
person totally unacceptable to the Silver coalition. Weisgal was willing, but the mere mention of the plan raised such a storm of protest that
it died immediately.[36] As the controversy dragged on through the early
months of 1945, the political activities of the Council came to a
standstill; only the pro-Palestine propaganda work, by now routinized
and handled by staff members, continued to give the organization any
semblance of life. Members of the WZO tried to find some solution,
only to realize that the situation no longer left room for compromise.[37]
Finally Chaim Weizmann decided that he would have to come to the
United States personally, and he sent out cables to the leading pro-
tagonists asking them to make peace, before his arrival if possible, or
failing that, to accept his mediation.[38]

The Policy Committee, in the meantime, worked feverishly generat-
ing support for Silver through a constant stream of newspaper articles,
speeches, and testimonial dinners. Ostensibly, the Committee aimed
at winning over the ZOA, the key to power in the American movement;

in fact, it had set itself up as a rival to the Emergency Council, and had the active backing of the Mizrachi and the Labor Zionists.[39] When Weizmann arrived on the scene in April, he found American Zionism completely split, and his efforts at peacemaking only yielded a growing criticism of his own policies. He urged American Zionists to unite so they could act, only to find himself under attack for lacking any positive program. When Hayim Greenberg, the head of Poale Zion, resigned from the Emergency Council on June 15, the Wise group recognized that their coalition could no longer survive. Accepting the inevitable, they appointed a three-man committee to work out a peace agreement with Silver.

In effect, it was a total capitulation. Although the final plan kept both Wise and Silver as co-chairman, few people failed to recognize that this sop merely preserved face for the defeated Wise faction. Silver now had the effective power; he controlled appointments to the executive committee, which he chaired, and a majority of the other officers as well as the key staff people, all came from the Silver bloc. At a meeting on July 12, Abba Hillel Silver listened quietly as the Emergency Council adopted the peace plan, and then gave what was, for him, a relatively conciliatory speech. "I do feel a sense of personal satisfaction at this moment," he said, "a sense of vindication. Beyond that I have no other feeling than that of profound gratitude that we have found our way back to comradeship and the possibility for united action. I hope we will all turn our backs on what took place in the last few months, and that we shall begin to think of ourselves not in terms of friends or foes, or as members of this group or that group, but in terms of comrades working in a common cause."[40]

And there was work aplenty to do. Even as Silver took over the leadership the American public was trying to adjust to the great events of the previous months. On April 12, Franklin D. Rooosevelt had died; a month later, the Germans surrendered. Even before the war in the Pacific had ended, Harry S. Truman, once a little-known senator from Missouri and now president of the United States, had convened the United Nations conference at San Francisco. And in the pages of *Life* and other pictorial magazines, the American people could see the brutal evidence of the efficacy of Hitler's "final solution." Now, in a world where one change crowded in upon another, the Zionists might find the opportunity to create their homeland in Palestine. Unity had not come a moment too soon.

FOOTNOTES

1. See Melvin I. Urofsky, *American Zionism from Herzl to the Holocaust* (Garden City, N.Y., 1975), pp. 119-21.

2. Mayer Weisgal, . . . *So Far, An Autobiography* (Jerusalem, 1971), p. 167; Chaim Weizmann to Stephen Wise, April 29, 1942, Records of the American Section of the World Zionist Organization/The Jewish Agency, Central Zionist Archives, Jerusalem, Israel, Z5/1216.

3. Yehuda Bauer, *From Diplomacy to Resistance: A History of Jewish Palestine, 1939-1945*, tr. by Alton M. Winters (Philadelphia, 1970), pp. 236-37; Walter Laqueur, *A History of Zionism* (New York, 1972), pp. 544-45.

4. *Ibid.*, pp. 239-43; interview with Rose Halprin, March 23, 1973.

5. Interview with Louis Levinthal, December 22, 1972.

6. David Ben-Gurion to Chaim Weizmann, June 11, 1942, and to Stephen Wise, June 19, 1942, both in Chaim Weizmann Papers, Yad Chaim Weizmann, Rehovot, Israel.

7. Stephen Wise to David Ben-Gurion, June 22, 1942, and memorandum of meeting, June 27, 1942, *ibid.*; interview with Louis Levinthal, December 22, 1972; Weisgal, . . . *So Far*, p. 175.

8. This sketch of Wise is drawn from a number of sources, but primarily from his autobiography, *Challenging Years* (New York, 1949), and from interviews with Justine Wise Polier, James Waterman Wise, Nahum Goldmann, Emanuel Neumann, Morton Berman, Golda Meir, Israel Goldstein, and Meyer Weisgal.

9. Nahum Goldmann, *Sixty Years of Jewish Life: The Autobiography of Nahum Goldmann*, tr. by Helen Sebba (New York, 1969), p. 124.

10. Unfortunately, there is no biography of Silver. I was fortunate to have read the manuscript of an autobiography he began, but which he did not finish, through the courtesy of his son, Rabbi Daniel Jeremy Silver; I also benefitted from interviews with Jacques Torczyner, Emanuel Neumann, and others. See also Leon I. Feuer, "Abba Hillel Silver: A Personal Memoir," *American Jewish Archives* 19 (November 1967): 107-26.

11. Goldmann, *Sixty Years of Jewish Life*, pp. 227-28. A story repeated by several sources holds that during the height of the controversy, Wise met Silver at a Zionist gathering, and stopped him in the hall. "Rabbi Silver," he reportedly said, "I am an old man, and have had my moment in the sun; you are a young man, and will have your proper share of fame. It is not necessary for you to attack me." Silver did not respond; he just turned on his heel and walked away.

12. Chaim Weizmann to Louis Namier, June 27, 1942, Weizmann Mss. Ironically, Stephen Wise at this time also considered Silver a most able man, and wanted to involve him more in the Zionist leadership. Wise to Lavey Bakstansky, September 29, 1942, in the Stephen Samuel Wise Papers, American Jewish Historical Society, Waltham, Massachusetts.

13. Memorandum, David Petegorsky to Emergency Committee, March 30, 1942, in the Harold Manson Papers, Archives of The Temple, Cleveland, Ohio; Minutes of the American Zionist Emergency Council, April 14, 1942, in the Zionist Archives and Library, New York; Meyer Weisgal to Stephen Wise, April 23, 1942, American Section Records, Z5/1216.

14. Chaim Weizmann to Berl Locker, June 3, 1942, Weizmann Mss; Weizmann to Stephen Wise, June 20, 1942, Wise Mss.

15. Stephen Wise to David Ben-Gurion, and Chaim Weizmann to Wise, both on July 6, 1942, Weizmann Mss.

16. Meyer Weisgal to Gershon Agronsky, July 29, 1942, in the Meyer Weisgal Papers, privately held, Rehovot, Israel, used through the courtesy of Meyer Weisgal; AZEC Minutes, July 8, 1942.

17. Doreen Bierbrier, "The American Zionist Emergency Council: An Analysis of a Pressure Group," *American Jewish Historical Quarterly* 60 (September 1970): 85; Chaim Weizmann to Berl Locker, July 15, 1942, and to Blanche Dugdale, January 8, 1943, Weizmann Mss.

18. Stephen Wise to Chaim Weizmann, February 10, 1943, and Weizmann to Abba Hillel Silver, June 21, 1943, *ibid.*

19. Notes on meeting of September 1, 1942, *ibid.*; Arthur Lourie to Leo Lauterbach, April 13, 1942, Records of the Organization Department of the World Zionist Organization, Central Zionist Archives, Jerusalem, Israel, S5/693; Urofsky, *American Zionism*, ch. 7.

20. Joseph B. Schechtman, *The United States and the Jewish State Movement: The Crucial Decade, 1939-1949* (New York, 1966), pp. 87-88; memorandum of meeting, October 12, 1943, Manson Mss.

21. Abba Hillel Silver to Nahum Goldmann, November 5, 1943, *ibid.*; Goldmann to Silver, November 9, 1943, American Section Records, Z5/653.

22. Meyer Weisgal to Chaim Weizmann, February 7, 1944, Weisgal Mss; Schechtman, *U.S. and Jewish State Movement*, pp. 87-88; Emanuel Neumann to Abba Hillel Silver, January 18, 1944, Manson Mss.

23. Hadassah National Board Minutes, 1943-1944, *passim*, in Hadassah Archives, New York.

24. Israel Goldstein to Abba Hillel Silver, August 2, 1943, in Israel Goldstein Papers, Israel Goldstein Archives, Jerusalem, Israel; Stephen Wise to Nahum Goldmann, August 4, 1943, Wise Mss; AZEC Minutes, August 26, 1943; Arthur Lourie to Leo Lauterbach, September 10, 1943, Organization Department Records, S5/693; Goldmann to Moshe Shertok, September 16, 1943, Records of the Political Department of the World Zionist Organization, Central Zionist Archives, Jerusalem, Israel, S25/237; interview with Israel Goldstein, September 12, 1973.

25. AZEC Minutes, October 5, 1943; Abba Hillel Silver to Chaim Weizmann, March 3, 1944, Weizmann Mss.

26. Meyer Weisgal to Chaim Weizmann, April 6, 1944, *ibid.*; Abba Hillel Silver to Emanuel Neumann, July 17, 1944, Manson Mss: AZEC Minutes, August 14, 1944.

27. Abba Hillel Silver to David Wertheim, August 25, 1944, Manson Mss.

28. AZEC Minutes, August 28 and 31, 1944; David Wertheim to David Ben-Gurion, September 1, 1944, Moshe Shertok to Ben-Gurion, September 2, 1944, Nahum Goldmann and Louis Lipsky to Ben-Gurion, September 7, 1944, all in Political Department Records, S25/1971; Meyer Weisgal to Chaim Weizmann, September 7, 1944, Weizmann Mss.

29. David Ben-Gurion to Abba Hillel Silver, September 17, 1944, Political Dept. Records, S25/1971; Meyer Weisgal to Chaim Weizmann. September 23, 1944, Weizmann Mss.

30. Emanuel Neumann to Chaim Weizmann, September 28, 1944, *ibid.*

31. AZEC Minutes, October 12, 1944.

32. Maurice Boukstein to Meyer Weisgal, December 5, 1944, Political Department Records, S25/1971; Sol Bloom to Israel Goldstein, December 13, 1944, Goldstein Mss.

33. For a detailed, although biased, account and chronology of the events beginning at the end of October 1944 until their denouement the following summer, see the draft of a proposed pamphlet, possibly drafted by Herman Shulman, in the Goldstein Mss, file 1614g [hereafter cited as Silver/Wise memo].

34. See also "The Crisis in American Zionism," *Jewish Spectator*, January 1945; *Jewish Morning Journal*, December 28, 1944 and January 1, 1945; *Der Tag*, December 30 and 31, 1944; *American Jewish World* (Minneapolis, Minn.), January 5, 1945, and *Jewish Daily Forward*, January 11, 1945.

35. Abba Hillel Silver, *Vision and Victory* (New York, 1949), pp. 72-73; *Jewish Morning Journal*, January 8, 1945; Silver/Wise memo; *New Palestine* 36 (January 19, 1945): 82-83.

36. Stephen Wise *et al.* to Chaim Weizmann, cable, January 9, 1945, Political Department Records, S25/1971; Meyer Weisgal to Weizmann, January 10, 1945, Weizmann Mss.

37. Nahum Goldmann to Moshe Shertok, January 31, 1945; Bernard Joseph and Goldmann to Shertok, [January] 1945; David Wertheim to Joseph, February 5, 1945, and Shertok to Goldmann, February 8, 1945, all in Political Department Records, S25/1971.

38. Chaim Weizmann, cables to Abba Hillel Silver, Meyer Weisgal, Stephen Wise, and Louis Lipsky, all February 15, 1945, Weizmann Mss.

39. Meyer Weisgal to Chaim Weizmann, March 9, 1945, *ibid.*; Israel Goldstein to Herman Shulman, March 12, 1945, Goldstein Mss.

40. Silver/Wise memo.

The 1943 Joint Anglo-American Statement on Palestine

by Monty N. Penkower

"I am leaving this country with a heavy heart," wrote Chaim Weizmann in a last letter before departing America for London at the close of June 1943. His depression came not from a contemplated Anglo-American statement on Palestine, secretly under discussion, for its significance had been casually dismissed by Under Secretary of State Sumner Welles in a conversation with the Zionist leader a few days earlier. Rather, Weizmann's efforts during more than a year's stay in the United States seemed to have accomplished little. The Allied powers had not heeded his anguished cry to save the Jewry of Europe. More than two million of his people had already been exterminated in the inferno of the Third Reich, and yet the Anglo-American conference at Bermuda, especially convened to consider the "refugee problem" the previous April, persisted in maintaining a calculated conspiracy of silence. The word "Jew" did not appear at all in the final official communiqué and the American delegation bowed to British insistence that Jewish immigration to Palestine remain limited under the White Paper of 1939 to another 29,000 souls by March 31, 1944. If that quota were maintained, reasoned the President of the World Zionist Organization and the Jewish Agency for Palestine, the most obvious haven for the one people marked for death in World War II might soon bear on its gates the inscription: "NO MORE JEWS NEED ENTER HERE."[1]

Confronted by this "absolutely impossible position," the ailing advocate of Zionism brooded over another uncertainty: could the movement itself meet the challenge of this darkest night in Jewish history? With Europe cut off and American Jewry possibly facing a period of moral impoverishment and greater assimilation, what would sustain and bring new life to the 500,000-strong *Yishuv* in Palestine? The Jewish State, called for by the New York Biltmore Resolutions of May 1942, and confirmed by Palestine's recognized Zionist bodies a week after Rommel's forces had broken at el Alemein in November, could not be considered within the realm of immediate fulfillment. As long as the British Colonial and Foreign Offices remained hostile and continued to exercise a baneful influence on the Near Eastern desk of the American State Department, Arab-Jewish tensions would mount; as a result, counsels of despair and disaster were already being voiced in Palestine. Weizmann and David Ben Gurion, Chairman of the Jewish Agency Executive, had already fallen out in mid-1942 over differences in tactics and temperament. It did not ease matters that a small clique of Reform rabbis had recently banded together under an anti-Zionist banner emblazoned the American Council for Judaism; and had not the highly influential, non-Zionist American Jewish Committee only the previous January broken with a twenty-five year tradition by not endorsing either the Balfour Declaration or the Jewish Agency when the Committee advocated an international trusteeship for Palestine after the war's end? In a tired and possibly reactionary post-war world, permeated with the poison of anti-Semitism, the dream of Zionism would be extremely difficult of attainment. Moreover, the world would be freed from pressure to solve the "Jewish question," given the effectiveness of Hitler's own solution.[2]

And yet, Weizmann, the embodiment of the dreams of the Messianic people, would not permit despair to blight tender shoots of hope. The Jewish Commonwealth would not come overnight, but come it would. Straws in the wind seemed to indicate that at long last a change was taking place in the "congealed state" of Zionist affairs, at "dead point" ever since the Chamberlain appeasement policy of 1939. Just before departing for the United States in March 1942, Weizmann had unexpectedly heard from Winston Churchill himself that after the war the British Prime Minister, together with President Franklin D. Roosevelt, would carry out a concurrent plan to make Arabia's King Ibn Saud "boss of the bosses" of the Middle East and establish a Jewish State in Palestine. A private message from Churchill in November 1942, on the twenty-fifth anniversary of the Balfour Declaration, hinted that "better days will surely come for the suffering people and for the great cause for which you fought so bravely." A month later, in the company of the Jewish Agency's Nahum Goldmann, Weizmann showed this cable to Under Secretary Welles, who seemed impressed and approved talks on the post-war status of Palestine with the Near Eastern specialists of the State Department.

These conversations in January and March 1943 raised the Zionists' case for a Jewish State in Palestine numbering at least two million more Jews and suggested the possibility of a Weizmann-Ibn Saud encounter after the Anglo-American governments had paved the way.[3] In May 1943, this situation took a turn for the worse, when Zionists found out that a State Department envoy, Lt. Col. Harold B. Hoskins, had returned from a trip to the Near East warning that continued pronouncements on behalf of a Jewish State would antagonize Arabs and probably lead to a large-scale Moslem revolt. But Weizmann took heart when Lord Halifax, steadfast advocate of appeasement and the White Paper when Foreign Secretary in 1939, and currently British Ambassador to the United States, hinted for the first time of a possibility of revising the standing British policy. He was also cheered by Welles' private assertion to Stephen Wise (chairman of the American Emergency Committee for Zionist Affairs—AECZA) that the American government had not approved the White Paper, and by the public affirmation of the British Minister of Information—a close associate of Churchill—that the Prime Minister's "friendliness to the Zionist cause" was "well-known" and that Britain had "a solemn obligation to the Jews which will be fulfilled." Finally, and most significantly, Welles took Weizmann to see the President on June 11, at which time Roosevelt agreed to the need for an Arab-Jewish conference at which he and Churchill would be present. The President made light of the Arabs' contribution to the democratic war effort, and seconded the possibility that Jews could help contribute financially to Arab advancement in the Middle East as a whole.[4]

The time had come for Weizmann to dig a tunnel "from both sides" and marry the Anglo-American alliance to the Zionist cause. "On the whole it was a satisfactory interview," wrote the Zionist leader to the sympathetic Secretary of the Treasury, Henry Morgenthau, Jr.; Welles later expressed his great pleasure that for the first time the President had not only displayed sympathy for the Zionist cause, but "came down to business." Welles himself indicated agreement with Weizmann's reasoned call for a Jewish State in an earlier article in *Foreign Affairs*. As for reports of Hoskins' "propagandizing" Senators and Congressmen with his personal views, the Under Secretary promised he would make sure that it stopped. In like vein, Welles would see that a planned Anglo-American declaration, designed to allay Arab unrest by postponing a decision on Palestine until after the war, would come to nothing. Thus assured, Weizmann thanked Welles for his help and understanding, and reminded his new ally that a firm decision in the near future by the two greatest democracies on behalf of a Jewish Palestine—especially in the face of the inevitable Allied victory—with the legitimate rights of the native Arabs protected, would surely bring Arab consent. The Zionist spokesman, armed with renewed energy, once again packed his bags and left on June 29, 1943, to resume battle in London for the one cause which had been his relentless master these many years.[5]

I

Had the chief architect of the Balfour Declaration known fully of the genesis and current standing of the planned joint statement which Welles had lightly dismissed, he would not have boarded the plane at LaGuardia in such hopeful spirit. Exactly one year earlier, members of the State Department's Near Eastern division, worried over reports from their representatives abroad that Zionist agitation for a Jewish army to defend Palestine against a possible breakthrough by Rommel's advance on Alexandria was undermining the Allied war effort, had drafted a declaration setting forth for the first time the United States government's attitude toward the Middle East and Palestine in particular. To counter Axis broadcasts, which constantly identified the Allied cause with Jewish domination of the Middle East and, by contrast, promised Arabs their independence and total elimination of the Jewish National Home, this June, 1942, draft affirmed the principles of the Atlantic Charter[6] and expressed a desire that a political solution for Palestine be reached through agreement between its Arab and Jewish communities. At the time, Roosevelt turned down the suggestion on the ground that it would "automatically stir up trouble at a critical moment," but the department's Advisor on Political Relations Wallace Murray, Chief of the Division of Near Eastern Affairs Paul Alling, and Assistant Secretary of State Adolf Berle ultimately succeeded in obtaining the President's approval for an American mission to the Near East, primarily to "gain more active support of the peoples of this area" for an Allied victory[7] Lt. Col. Harold B. Hoskins, formerly of the War Department's Office of Strategic Services and then Executive Secretary to Berle, left in November 1942 as Roosevelt's personal representative on a trip which would have significant repercussions on Anglo-American relations in the area and especially on the Palestine dilemma.[8]

While Roosevelt and the department awaited Hoskins' findings, State's Near Eastern division tried to mute the growing pro-Zionist publicity which was causing the Palestine cauldron to boil. It did not help, in the division's opinion, to have Wendell Willkie return from a global trip (including the Middle East) on behalf of the President and announce that "the doors of Palestine must be opened to the Jewish peoples of Central and Eastern Europe after the war," or for prominent individuals and Senators to endorse full-page advertisements of the Committee for a Jewish Army—organized by Peter Bergson and other members of an Irgun delegation from Palestine—an army to be composed of 200,000 stateless (European) and Palestinian Jews. Particularly worrisome was the declaration of 63 Senators and 182 members of Congress in December 1942, after the American and British governments had publicly confirmed reports of the massive extermination of European Jews by Hitler's minions, that "millions of homeless Jews" should be enabled in the post-war period to reconstruct their lives in Palestine.[9]

To shift this focus, Secretary of State Cordell Hull used the anniversary of the Balfour Declaration to urge a wider objective: "We must have a world in which Jews, like every other race, are free to abide in peace and honor." Wallace Murray quietly introduced his superiors to the binationalist views of Judah Magnes, president of the Hebrew University, and applauded the stand of Morris Lazaron, one of the major forces behind the American Council for Judaism. Hoskins' preliminary report, with its warning that "a very bloody conflict is in the making" unless a joint Anglo-American statement were to rule out in advance any Allied military support for extremists on either side, only confirmed the Near Eastern Division's fears.[10]

State's British counterparts, custodians of the Palestine mandate since 1920, shared these anxieties. High Commissioner for Palestine Harold MacMichael cabled his view that due to Zionist "maximalist" aims, the "critical period in Jewish politics" would come when "we are winning the war but still have our hands full." After reading Hoskins' report, he recommended that Britain restate clause four of the White Paper: "His Majesty's Government therefore now declare unequivocally that it is not part of their policy that Palestine should become a Jewish State." Foreign Secretary Anthony Eden tried unsuccessfully to get a sympathetic Myron Taylor, former U.S. delegate to the 1938 Evian Conference on refugees and currently Roosevelt's representative to the Vatican, to speak out against Zionist agitation.[11] On February 24, 1943, the day Hitler publicly reiterated his intention to exterminate all of European Jewry, Eden repeated in Commons his government's sympathy with "any movement among Arabs to promote their economy, cultural or political unity." A month later, he told Parliament that he viewed repatriation of Jews to their former homes in Europe as "the best way to solve both the immediate and post-war problems." Thus, when Secretary Hull urgently pressed the question of the 60,000-70,000 threatened Jews of Bulgaria during his visit to Washington at the end of March, Eden advised caution about offering to take all the Jews out of a country like Bulgaria: "If we do that, then the Jews of the world will be wanting us to make similar offers in Poland and Germany. Hitler may well take us up on any such offer and there simply are not enough ships and means of transportation in the world to handle them."[12]

Hoskins' final report of April 20 led State to chart a clear policy, one which, if adopted, would establish an American position regarding Palestine for the first time since the days of President Wilson and the Balfour Declaration. With American security officers in North Africa concerned at Arab hostility and "the seeds of a possible third World War" contained in mounting Arab-Jewish tension, curtailment of the Zionist cause was necessary. To win the wartime support of the sixty million Arabs in the area, Hoskins urged that the Allies immediately issue a brief declaration that "no decision altering the basic situation in Palestine should be considered until after the conclusion of the war. When the matter is considered, both Arabs and Jews should be fully consulted and their agreement sought." The son of Christian missionaries to Syria and vice president of the board of trustees of the American University of Beirut—two classic sources of pro-Arab sentiment—Hoskins had joined Murray's abortive effort of the previous June in already advocating these views; his long-range plan for Palestine now gave preference to the Arab cause as well.[13] Hoskins' colleagues in the department received the report from a missionary preaching to the converted. Assistant Secretary Berle, while approving an Office of War Information official's suggestion that Congressmen say something about Arab independence for foreign consumption, tersely advised his superiors regarding possible measures to save Europe's Jews: "The Jews in this country invariably push the cause of Palestine. The dangers in this of course are too well known to need discussion."[14] On May 7, Cordell Hull forwarded Hoskins' report to the White House with the suggestion that the proposed Allied declaration on Palestine be approved. Back came Roosevelt's notation: "CH OK FDR." Shortly thereafter, Brigadier General Patrick J. Hurley, another Roosevelt emissary to the Near East, went further than Hoskins in sympathizing with the Arab federation views of the Iraqi Prime Minister as an antidote to Zionist "imperialism." On May 26, FDR replied to an April message from Ibn Saud, strongly opposing Zionism, with a confidential reassurance along the lines of Hoskins' suggested declaration on Palestine.[15]

While State and the President were arriving at this consensus, the British found themselves divided between the Colonial and Foreign Offices and some members of the Cabinet. High Commissioner Mac-Michael backed a post-war reconstruction plan for Palestine which clearly favored the Arabs, while Colonial Secretary Oliver Stanley informed Parliment that the White Paper stood to ensure stability in the Middle East. Churchill, on the other hand, after receipt of a personal letter from Weizmann attacking that policy as appeasement, advised his War Cabinet on April 28: "We are free, as a new government, to review the entire field at the end of the war. I should expect that American pressure for a new declaration would be very strong, and President Roosevelt to be in entire agreement with me on the subject." The ex-Italian possessions in Libya (Eritrea and Tripolitania) should be examined as potential Jewish colonies affiliated, if desired, with the Jewish National Home in Palestine. "We've treated the Arabs very well" in Iraq, Transjordan and Syria, yet except for Ibn Saud and Abdullah, they "have been virtually no good to us in the present war. . . . They have created no new claims on the Allies should we be victorious." The Secretary for India (Leopold Amery), despite the threat that some seventy-eight million Indian Moslems would side with the Arabs over Palestine, applauded Churchill's plan, but recommended partition of Palestine with a loose Syria-Palestine federation to give the Jews "a definite area" along with the two former Italian colonies. Stanley remained unconvinced, and cautioned his colleagues that every effort must be exerted to "avoid an explosion" in Palestine.[16]

Eden's memorandum of May 10 went further in warning of trouble throughout the Middle East, and suggested that perhaps the time had come to speak with the American government for a joint declaration. Most influential was the fact that the Foreign Office's highest ranking Middle East diplomats had met with their military counterparts in Cairo at the same time and jointly recommended a public reaffirmation of the White Paper's basic principles with American support, if possible.[17]

Even as Halifax advised Eden to undertake this effort "at the highest level," Roosevelt and Churchill began discussing a mutual policy for the Jewish refugee question and the much Promised Land. Before the two leaders met in Washington in May, the President, while accepting the Bermuda Conference's recommendation to set up temporary camps in North Africa for Jewish refugees currently in Spain and Portugal, cautioned Secretary Hull against sending "large numbers" of Jews there: "That would be extremely unwise." To prove his point, after Churchill had expressed his continued interest in Cyrenaica and Tripolitania (with the support of his close friend Bernard Baruch) at a White House dinner on the 17th, Roosevelt gave the Prime Minister two memoranda by the State Department's Isaiah Bowman which opposed large-scale settlement of Jews in Libya for fear of a violent reaction in the Arab world.[18]

Roosevelt's views in these matters owed a great deal to Isaiah Bowman's influence. As early as November 1938, with the support of Secretary Morgenthau, FDR had asked Bowman, the territorial specialist in the United States delegation to the Paris Peace Conference of 1919 and president of Johns Hopkins University, to explore possibilities for mass settlement of refugees in northern South America. Chairman of the State Department's Territorial Committee and Post-War Advisory Council during 1942-1943, Bowman commanded a responsive audience in Berle, Murray, Alling and Taylor when deprecating the absorptive capacity of Palestine and focusing on Angola as the best location for a large-scale post-war settlement. The President's request now afforded Bowman the perfect opportunity to "join the different parts of the Jewish question": "Keep the Palestine question or Libyan settlement in abeyance, so far as possible, until the end of the war," he advised Roosevelt. Not only was future settlement in Palestine limited, but "unwise propaganda statements" asserted that the advent of a Jewish State would strengthen specifically Jewish culture in those countries where Jews were already established. Roosevelt expressed shock upon being informed of these Zionist claims, but his chief advisor on world geography suggested to "let him holler," because "extravagance of this sort would in time defeat its own ends."[18a]

At a White House luncheon on the 22nd, Roosevelt and Churchill showed their different colors. Jews, thought Bowman, should be spread out thin all over the world to avoid Gentile antagonism. FDR suggested this to Churchill at a luncheon on the 22nd, much as he had experimented with four or five families each in Marietta County (Ga.) and at Hyde Park. Shifting to the subject of Palestine, Roosevelt remarked on the unsuccessful effort of world Jewry's large charitable contributions to balance the country's export-import deficit, and he seemed to advocate a solid Arab bloc around the southern and eastern shores of the Mediterranean. Churchill, however, "cussed out" the various Arab leaders, especially their failure to come through with substantial aid to the Allied war effort, and he spoke of the possibilities of Transjordan for the Jews. Hearing this, Vice President Henry Wallace joined in with a reminder that if half of Jewry might agree with Roosevelt's "slow amalgamation" views, the other half "would be very vehemently in favor of Zionism." Informed earlier by Weizmann and various specialists of exploratory schemes for a Jordan Valley Authority (JVA) project along TVA lines to include an immigration of at least one million Jews, Wallace now embellished on Churchill's cursory remark: an irrigation dam could support many people in the area, especially given Transjordan's large size and limited population.[19] No permanent policy for Palestine was decided upon by the end of the Prime Minister's visit, yet these first talks on the subject between the two leaders of the West helped set the stage for what was immediately to follow.

The United States government made its major diplomatic moves in June. Reminded that State's draft for an Allied joint declaration on Palestine incorporated substantially the gist of his May letter to Ibn Saud, the President approved the Hoskins statement on June 8. The next evening, the Secretary of State cabled the Ambassador to England, asking that the text be submitted to Eden for review: the time had come to end "serious distraction from the war effort" caused by the Palestine problem. The Foreign Secretary, receiving the text on the afternoon of June 11, doubted that any good would be done by drawing attention to the tension in Palestine in this way. And as for Zionist political agitation in the United States and its spiral effect on increasing tension, this matter certainly did not "lie within the competence of HMG to control." Three days after Weizmann's talk of the 11th with Roosevelt, Churchill was informed of the President's wish to send Hoskins to Ibn Saud to see whether "any basis of a settlement can be found." On the 26th, Eden presented a paper to the War Cabinet in favor of a joint Anglo-American statement, since securing an Allied declaration would take time, some Allies might oppose it, and others had little interest in the subject. Three days later, Hull received word that while the Foreign Secretary doubted that Ibn Saud's views would allow for an Arab-Jewish settlement on Palestine, no British objections existed to the Hoskins trip provided that he not suggest territorial alternatives in other Arab countries, that the talks be purely exploratory and not in any way prejudice the interests of other Arab countries, and that the visit be carried out as unobtrusively as possible.[20] That same day Weizmann, unaware of what had come to pass, left for London.

II

The issuing of a joint Anglo-American statement on Palestine met with the unanimous approval of a British War Cabinet otherwise divided on a policy for the future of the country. Only days after the American proposal had been received, the British Minister of State, Middle East, provided details to the Colonial Office about the strong, illegal Jewish military organizations in Palestine, and he called for retention of the White Paper to calm Arab opinion and avert an "explosion." Minister of Production Oliver Lyttleton (first proponent of some joint declaration a year earlier when Minister to the Middle East), warning of dangers to British imperial interests, foresaw the need of "effective occupation" of Palestine for "a long time." On July 2, the Cabinet concluded that a joint Anglo-American statement should include a refusal to accept any forcible change in the status of Palestine or its administration. Taking a strong lead, Churchill beat down suggestions for the disarming of Jews and the need to consult Mac-Michael regarding Jewish immigration before going beyond the termination date of the White Paper. But he failed to obtain his colleagues' approval to mention past British pledges to the Zionists and his attack on the White Paper from the opposition benches in May 1939, as a "breach of faith." Churchill supported partition (as did Amery), and he wrote to Eden that a special Ministerial Committee (set up on the 12th to recommend a final policy) should take the findings of the Peel Commission as its starting point, in addition to considering the southern Negev and the two ex-Italian colonies. Until the committee reported, extremism on both sides could be dampened with the proposed statement. Accordingly, Eden returned a revised draft to Hull on the 14th incorporating the cabinet's emphasis against the use of force. Three days later, the Secretary cabled his British opposite that Hoskins' mission to Ibn Saud would "conform fully" with British wishes. Roosevelt approved the final joint statement on the 19th, Hull wired Eden on the 22nd suggesting a simultaneous release, and the British signaled their approval twenty-four hours later. The scheduled time and date: July 27, at 12 o'clock noon, Eastern War Time (U.S.).[21]

The Zionist camp, heartened by Welles' assurances a month earlier that the U.S. government would not do anything to prejudice Zionist aims, had looked forward to some successes in July. A Jewish Agency office had just been opened in Washington, and the book proposing a JVA and explaining how it would make possible large-scale Jewish colonization in Palestine was about to appear. Contacts with Soviet representatives seemed to be promising for future diplomatic relations. An American Jewish Conference, whose elected delegates (representing some one and a half million Jews) were 80-85 percent Zionist, would meet in a few weeks to enunciate Jewish post-war concerns. Weizmann, encouraged by his visit to the United States, immediately took a strong Zionist line in talks with the Colonial Secretary and the Minister to the Middle East, spoke at his first press conference of finding "sympathy and understanding everywhere" in the highest American government circles, and cheered a close friend by his outspokenness against the Colonial Office's "chronic obstruction" and his characterization of the Arabs as "professional political saboteurs."[22]

But nagging rumors in Washington about an official statement enjoining silence as to Jewish claims in Palestine continued to breed dark suspicions that would not down. Nahum Goldmann, now directing the Agency's Washington office, discovered that Welles was totally unaware of Hoskins' propagandizing Senators and Congressmen with his personal views, and he questioned the wisdom of sending this prejudiced observer of limited standing to Ibn Saud. Welles' departure for a month's vacation in isolated Bar Harbor left the perturbed Zionists with no key link to the State Department and Roosevelt just when a New York newspaper source leaked that a statement by the government was imminent. Senator Mead (D., N.Y.), at the Agency's request, made inquiries at the State Department, only to hear from Assistant Secretary Dean Acheson that while he thought no statement was to be issued, all such matters were being handled by the White House.[23] Taking the cue, and as a last measure, Stephen Wise secured an interview with the President on July 22 to ascertain the truth.

It would not be the last time that Wise placed his implicit faith in the individual most revered by Jews in those dark years. "A most satisfactory talk with the Chief," he wrote Weizmann a day later. Roosevelt had praised Weizmann and agreed to the World Jewish Congress' plan, then pending with State and Treasury, for depositing its blocked funds in Swiss banks to rescue Jews in Nazi-occupied Rumania, Czechoslovakia and France. Most significantly, the President "seemed completely in the dark" as to a rumored official statement enjoining silence on Palestine, and "I think I made him feel" that it would, "far from solving any problem, deeply pain, even wound," great numbers of Jews everywhere who looked to Palestine as "that greatest hope and the only sure refuge for their homeless people. I believe that he will see to it that the statement be not issued, if it was in contemplation." As to FDR's confidential news that he had invited Ibn Saud's heir for a visit, Wise had warned against Emir Feisal's making any statement in this country about the Jews of Palestine, for it would certainly evoke most acrimonious discussion.[24]

Zionists' joy at this report soon reverted to doubt when Wise gave confused and different accounts of his interview at the White House to various individuals, and they finally persuaded Samuel Rosenman to check and make a cautious inquiry. Roosevelt's chief speech writer and close associate heard a very different story: Yes, Wise had inquired, and he (Roosevelt) had replied that a very salutary statement was to be issued, perfectly innocuous from the Zionists' point of view. Told to allay anxieties among the Jews, Rosenman did so; his version naturally led to Zionist consternation. Goldmann rushed to Isaiah Berlin, the British Embassy's observer on Jewish affairs, to be told that if, as it seemed, Rosenman's story was correct, agitation would only serve to irritate FDR. Goldmann departed in gloom, and spread the word to a very worried group of Jewish officials in Washington (Benjamin Cohen, Felix Frankfurter, David Niles, and Morgenthau). It did not calm Goldmann any to hear that a cable from Welles (responding to Wise's telephone call after his talk with Roosevelt), while assuring that he had immediately contacted Hull, who said he would go to the President, indicated no surprise on the Under Secretary's part. Wise, who on the 23rd had written Roosevelt of his "real comfort" for the interview's reassurance, now confessed his great fear of the outcome to Goldmann. Berlin and his colleagues at the Embassy, convinced that it was "now or never" and that "delay would automatically invite intrigue," were therefore dismayed to receive a sudden call from the State Department on the 27th, saying that the declaration had been postponed for a week.[25]

In fact, the delay arose out of Secretary Hull's desire to secure War Department support for the draft declaration, a tactical move which by all past indications seemed to ensure the triumph of State's cause. Already the past December, the Chief of the War Department's Military Intelligence Division had warned that propaganda by the Zionist "militant minority group" and pro-Zionist statements by prominent U.S. officials *"must be stopped at once,"* or "we most certainly will alienate" the Moslem world and threaten the security of American troops in the Middle East. For the same reason, the department accepted the views of General Eisenhower and the Allied headquarters in North Africa in opposing the Committee for a Jewish Army's suggestion to raise a Jewish Legion from native French and European refugee Jews located in the area. On April 30, 1943, a confidential study by the department's Middle East section of Military Intelligence, embracing a totally pro-Arab position, concluded that the Cameroons be given the Jews as a refuge, that the United Nations should guarantee European Jews against any further persecution after the war, and that Palestine might follow Judah Magnes' plan or become a Holy Land for Jews, Christians and Moslems with a Swiss cantonal system of government. Disregarding the continuing Holocaust and its effect on European Jewry's desire to immigrate to Palestine, the report optimistically ended with the certainty that the Zionist leaders, under the present circumstances in Palestine, would "have enough humanitarianism to accept the half loaf." A memorandum in the files of the O.S.S. (Hoskins' former employer) also suggested that the Holy Land, denied the Jews as a center for mass settlement, be treated as "the common possession of devout men everywhere . . ."; "more tolerance on the part of Gentiles and less clannishness on the part of Jews" would remove the "world Jewish problem" after the war.[26] The Joint Chiefs of Staff consistently opposed the Bermuda Conference's recommendation to establish camps in North Africa for Jewish refugees because of alleged Arab unrest, and only a personal appeal from Churchill (with Eden's approval) finally obtained Roosevelt's approval in early July for a small, temporary camp in French territory there.[27]

Major General George V. Strong, to whom State's Murray and Alling turned for support at Hull's instructions on July 26, vigorously pressed the War Department to approve the joint statement. Strong, head of War's G-2 intelligence division, had warned Assistant Secretary Breckenridge Long at the time of the Bermuda Conference in April that the proposed movement of 3,000 Jewish refugees to North Africa might "result in the death and destruction of several hundred thousand American soldiers," because of Arab disaffection all along the American route of communications; this should "preclude any further consideration of the matter." The fear of a possible Moslem "Holy War" against troops in that area also led him to have State ask for the deletion of "Jewish Commonwealth" and Palestine as a "home for the Jews" in a speech by Secretary of the Interior Harold Ickes. Hearing now of the department's interest in a request from the Army favoring the joint statement on strict security grounds, Strong showed the statement to Acting Secretary of War Robert Patterson and suggested that he hold a press conference explaining the War Department's interest. Patterson, not in the habit of meeting with the press, preferred to sign any letter drafted by Strong to the Secretary of State with Chief of Staff George C. Marshall's prior approval. Strong then composed a letter in the presence of Murray and Alling for Patterson to send Hull the next day. This draft, given Strong's views, went much further than the proposed declaration by specifically warning that "continued agitation in this country for the immediate establishment of a Jewish State in Palestine constitutes a grave danger to the United Nations war effort"; it concluded that the War Department would appreciate any action which State might take to discourage agitation tending to prejudice military security in the area. The military chiefs and General Marshall (so State was informed) approved this draft, which then received Hull's informal acceptance as "adequate" to meet the situation. Patterson, however, toned down Strong's draft considerably on the 27th. Although noting the effect which disorders in Palestine would have on the war effort, his letter made no mention of agitation in the United States or intimated that War would appreciate action by State to dampen such agitation. Discouraged, Hull, who on his own had sent Hoskins to report to various Senators for this purpose and had pushed off the joint statement to the 28th, now decided that a second delay to August 3 might gain the support of Secretary of War Henry Stimson (returning to Washington from vacation).[28]

Hull's efforts, which continued during the last days of July, appeared headed for success. A Secretary of State who had long been overlooked in Roosevelt's personal conduct of foreign policy and who suffered regular attack in the press (particularly over the recent Darlan affair), Hull would not move on such a sensitive issue without the War Department's full consent.[29] He called Stimson and asked him to discuss the matter with Patterson, with the object of having Patterson's letter revised along the line of General Strong's harsher draft. Stimson indicated that he had a luncheon engagement with Patterson and would take the matter up at that time. Meanwhile, Welles called Hull from his Maine retreat and indicated continued Zionist concern. On the 29th, Congressman Sol Bloom, Chairman of the House Foreign Affairs Committee and a delegate to the Bermuda Conference, relayed the message of his worried Zionist constituents in a visit to the Secretary. After reviewing the Near Eastern division's file on the subject, the Jewish Congressman, who questioned but finally acquiesced to the White Paper policy at Bermuda, approved and even suggested strengthening the declaration. At the same time, he recommended that a person like Sam Rosenman meet in New York with outstanding Jewish leaders to explain the military necessity for issuing the joint statement. Hull approved this idea in a memorandum to the President the same day, and supplied a sheaf of pertinent documents to make his point. As Roosevelt was about to depart to Hyde Park for the weekend, he informed State that he would take all the papers along for discussion with Rosenman.[30]

His conversation with the President that Saturday, July 31, 1943, and other talks which followed, gave Rosenman the full picture at last. Roosevelt showed his guest State's file, including the text of the joint statement, Strong's draft, and Patterson's letter. As for the motivation behind the declaration, the President mentioned that both he and Churchill had been "incensed" by the full-page advertisements of the Committee for a Jewish Army and particularly the demand of the Revisionist New Zionist Organization during the Prime Minister's May visit to Washington, "Mr. Churchill, Drop the Mandate!" Though that broadside, which attacked the Colonial Office for obstructing the

Jewish effort in Palestine and quoted the late Lord Wedgwood's view that America should accept the Mandate, had been publicly criticized by Weizmann in London as "most unfortunate," the two leaders had neither forgotten nor forgiven. The statement was being pressed at the instance of the War Department, Roosevelt said, and he asked Rosenman to consult Strong and Murray and tell influential Jews to mute Zionist clamors. On August 3, Rosenman received military reports on the Middle East from Strong, who was particularly convinced that Palestine stood on the eve of violence. All "shivered" in Washington at the assertion by Moshe Shertok, head of the Jewish Agency's Political Department, in the *New York Times* of July 30, that Palestinian Jewry would be capable of "deeds of despair if driven to extremes of exasperation by a decision to persevere in what is to them a cruelly unjust policy." After Murray repeated Strong's theme with the aid of consular Middle East cables, Rosenman received State's blessings to discuss the matter with "competent" Jewish leaders in New York over the weekend.[31]

By an ironic twist of fate which Hull and the Near Eastern division could not have foreseen, the information in Rosenman's hands led to a vigorous counter-offensive. Now armed with all the facts, Rosenman and other high-ranking Jewish officials like Justice Frankfurter privately argued that the intended statement would succeed only in exciting the Jews, gaining liberal support to their cause, and providing grist for the mills of the Administration's enemies—precisely the reverse of what the statement sought to accomplish. An unexpressed fear also seized this circle that such a public outcry could ultimately stir up anti-Semitism by charging all Jews with playing politics in a time of crisis. When combined with the Zionist sympathies of Ben Cohen and Frankfurter and the appreciation of Rosenman and David Niles of the need for continued Jewish immigration to Palestine, this reasoning led him to warn Wallace Murray that "they could *not* stifle Zionist discussion in the United States."[32]

In another quarter, Herbert B. Swope, a Jewish anti-Zionist working with War Department public relations, had seen the file and reacted rather like Rosenman. Publication of the statement, he feared, would be the very thing to set the Jews of Palestine off. The Jews would be blamed for the ensuing bloodshed and obstruction of the Allied war effort, and the resultant wave of unpopularity would overtake their co-religionists in this country. Bernard Baruch, his long-time employer, heard from Swope and agreed that this would increase an already rising anti-Semitism in the United States. Swope sought out Patterson with the argument that his department should avoid "a political brouhaha of the first order." Baruch had a talk with his old friend Cordell Hull in the same vein.[33]

Rosenman's report had also come to the notice of Secretary Morgenthau, who had heretofore been kept informed of the general state of Zionist affairs by Weizmann and his close associates Meyer Weisgal and Josef Cohn. Morgenthau, converted to a pro-Zionist stand since 1941 as a result of his secretary's influence and his steady contacts with Weizmann and other leading Zionists, returned from a vacation and met privately with Weisgal and Cohn on the morning of August 3. After hearing their information about the statement, the true facts of the Haganah and the contribution of Palestinian Jews to the Eighth Army, he asked about the reports that asserted the imminence of outbreaks in Palestine. Weisgal replied that these highly exaggerated reports were "engineered" by "obstructionists." Although Hoskins' report had predicted an outbreak soon, none had occurred since its writing, and, after all, no riots had taken place when Rommel neared Alexandria. British forces presently in Palestine could take care of any trouble—if they desired—and, moreover, the Jews could handle the situation. The appeal fell on receptive ears: had not Morgenthau privately assured Zionists the previous October that Roosevelt and Churchill were "friends" and that, in his opinion, a Palestine settlement need not be postponed to the end of the war? Accordingly, he emphasized to his listeners that he wished, not to ameliorate the statement, but to suppress it entirely—the matter affected all Jews. Weisgal agreed that the lid had to be kept down to prevent "terrific outbursts." Morgenthau: "This never does much good, because of the anti-Semitic feeling in this country." Weisgal: "That was always the trouble. The Jews were damned if they did, and damned if they didn't." The Secretary ended by asking the two Zionist emissaries to remain in town for twenty-four hours in case he would need them; he suggested that they get a detective story and sit down and read it. He then rose from his chair and said, "Now let me get to work, I am not discouraged."[34]

While Morgenthau advanced on his front, Stephen Wise was kept informed the same day by Frankfurter and Rosenman. Frankfurter's telephone call referred to Patterson's letter and the hostile attitude of

Hoskins, Isaiah Bowman, Myron Taylor and especially General Strong. Rosenman took an evening flight to New York and from ten to midnight gave Wise a full account of his activities. His principal task was to calm troubled waters for the President, and, wanting to stop Bergson's Committee for a Jewish Army advertisements, Rosenman then put forward a striking proposal: he would call a meeting in Washington. Hull might be there as co-host, and either Strong or Patterson would be invited from the War Department. The Jewish representatives should be Wise, Joseph Proskauer of the American Jewish Committee, Henry Monsky of B'nai B'rith and Adolf Held of the Jewish Labor Committee, together with one or two representatives from Peter Bergson's Committee for a Jewish Army. Having done everything he could a month earlier to prevent the success of maverick Bergson's Emergency Committee to Save the Jewish People of Europe, including an intercession with Welles which convinced Myron Taylor not to attend, Wise's response was immediate: "It would be very bad to have any such honor done to the Jewish Army people." If authority were given to the Zionists, "we might be able to deal with them." It would be best if there were no statement, as the reaction would be "a very bad one" and, if the statement appeared, hundreds of thousands of Jews would feel they had lost a friend in FDR. But the fact remained, Rosenman retorted, that the military spoke of the need for several divisions in Palestine, because of the attitude contained in Shertok's statement of July 30. If the joint statement were suppressed, could the American Zionists guarantee that there would be no more "wild statements" by Shertok or others in Palestine? Perhaps it was not too late even now, Roosevelt's emissary also suggested, for Zionists to react to the anti-Churchill May advertisement. Wise, an Anglophile who had privately deplored the "idiocies" of that broadside, agreed to give his visitor an answer regarding the proposed meeting the following evening.[35]

Across the seas, Shertok, whose warning about "deeds of despair" had so frightened General Strong and others, left Cairo on August 3 expecting the joint statement any day. An accidental remark by the Middle East Minister Resident's *chef de cabinet* that Zionists would have a chance to state they had no intention of forcing the Palestine issue during the war raised his suspicions and led to a public reaffirmation—"provided no adverse commitments are taken in the meantime." C. L. Sulzberger, who chose to feature Shertok's comment about "deeds of despair" in his *Times* story for July 30, indicated to Shertok and his readers that an Anglo-American declaration on post-war Middle East and Palestine policy was about to appear. This, and his dispatches on August 1-2 predicting bloody civil war in Palestine, similar to earlier columns in May along State Department-Foreign Office lines, seemed part of the "scheme" (Morgenthau's word) to prepare the public for the joint statement. Wise hurriedly wrote Secretary Hull on the 3rd requesting consultation prior to any *fait accompli*, while Shertok warned his colleagues in London before flying to Ankara to try and help bring 1,000 Bulgarian Jews to Palestine.[36]

The first encouraging news for the Zionists came the next morning, exactly the twenty-four hours Morgenthau had indicated to Weisgal and Cohn. Calling them to his office, the Secretary of the Treasury said that publication of the statement had been postponed and, in his opinion, "it was a three to one shot" none would appear. State would not demand it unless pressure from War became very strong, and he could assure them that no such pressure would be forthcoming. "He had not done very much except to stiffen the backs of a number of people"; Rosenman had done "a very good job" and would present an "altogether reasonable" proposal to Dr. Wise. The Secretary went on to explain that his line of attack had been based on the proposition that the British "Governor of Palestine" should be asked squarely: "Can you, or can you not, keep the peace in the country?" The British, after all, had not asked this government for a joint statement about India to keep the peace. This argument met with Weisgal's full approval, and Morgenthau saw his visitors out by expressing interest in seeing if the militant Bergson could be gotten out of the United States and in their contacting him on any future problems.[37]

The dénouement came a day later with the War Department's reply to Secretary Hull, bringing victory to the Zionists. Patterson, while hearing from Swope, had already expressed his doubts to Hull. Stimson, who listened to Morgenthau's arguments, had lent his name to the advertisements of Bergson's Committee for a Jewish Army almost from its inception. Most important, as for G-2 intelligence reports and General Strong's warnings, the Secretary could recall that two years earlier he had sharply disagreed with that division's defeatist views about Britain and its contempt for Churchill as warlord. On August 5, he telephoned Hull to say that he had investigated the military situation in the Middle East, had considered Strong an "alarmist" in the matter, and had decided that the War Department did not regard the Palestine security situation so serious as to warrant any action from a military point of view. Hearing that War did not propose to take the matter up, Hull thanked Stimson and said that that ended it so far as State was concerned. The following day, the Secretary of State cabled Eden the War Department's conclusion and added that, accordingly, "no basis now exists, so far as the United States is concerned, for issuing the statement."[38]

The statement had been postponed, but the Zionists were hardly yet out of the woods. Hull's explanation of War Department objections (to be repeated in his memoirs) did not satisfy Halifax, and the ambassador warned the Foreign Office of this "sinister indication of the power of Jewish pressure groups in this country." For support he pointed to Drew Pearson's *Washington Post* column of August 9, with its (somewhat distorted) description of Hurley, Hoskins and Berle being outmaneuvered by Rosenman and Wise. "A shocking example of American methods," wrote Eden, and his staff prepared a memorandum for Churchill emphasizing the continued military need to issue the declaration. General Strong rushed a report marked "SECRET" to Chief of Staff Marshall, cautioning that any Allied policies which would antagonize the 370 million Moslems from Casablanca to Manila might well prove disastrous to the main supply routes to Russia, Allied security in North Africa, Asia and the Middle East, and—"certainly not least important"—Allied interests in the huge oil reserves in the Middle East. The "only logical and militarily safe course," he concluded in trying to recoup his loss, was to announce an official U.S. government policy along the lines of the intended statement.[39] With postponement continuing to hang like the sword of Damocles over Zionist heads despite Pearson's article, Weizmann tried to see the American ambassador in London. Emanuel Celler of New York rose in Congress to charge: "The joint statement will, with its 'Silence, please,' drown the clamor of the tortured Nazi victims pleading for a haven of refuge." Seen in this context, the Mandatory government's attempt to link the Jewish Agency to local arms thefts in a highly publicized trial of two British soldiers seemed another manifestation of a well-laid plot to discredit Zionism in America and "pave the way for its liquidation." Shertok privately feared that some idea might also be at work to justify in advance the continuation of British rule in Palestine at a time when the White Paper policy appeared to be seriously questioned by various British and Arab officials.[40]

And so, as in the past, the final decision rested with Roosevelt and Churchill, then meeting in the Citadel at Quebec to decide on a cross-channel invasion of Nazi-occupied Europe the next spring. On August 6, Under Secretary Welles had sent Stephen Wise a cable from the Jewish Agency and World Jewish Congress' representatives in Geneva: "The number of victims has reached about 4,000,000." (Secretary Hull had been told by the Polish Ambassador in Washington two days earlier that half of the Lublin province, with a Jewish population of over 1,000,000, was undergoing daily "liquidation.") Wise immediately appealed to FDR and Churchill to "take substantive action now to save European Jewry after a year of inaction which has doubled the toll of Jewish victims." Congressman Celler publicly asked the President to plead with the Prime Minister "to do the needful" in immediately opening the gates of Palestine: "Yours is the opportunity to be the voice of all conscience." The AECZA's Arthur Lourie met at the Citadel with Churchill's Principal Private Secretary, John Martin (his friend from the days of the Peel Commission), and argued that issuance of the statement would be attacked by liberals, as well as Jews, as "an intolerable interference with rights of free speech," especially at a time when the extermination of European Jewry was going relentlessly forward and Arab leaders were gathering freely in Cairo to discuss Arab federation and Palestine.[41]

Aware of these varied considerations, Roosevelt and Churchill sat down on August 22 to discuss the British agenda, including point four: "Joint Statement on Palestine. American proposal which we approved and want, and they have now abandoned. Can it be reexamined." Eden had handed Hull, the previous day, the Foreign Office's memorandum noting the forthcoming American Jewish Conference, Arab federation talks, large-scale thefts of arms by Jews in Palestine and the possible link to the Jewish Agency, concluding: ". . . the need for some sedative joint statement is as urgent as ever." The President, awaiting Hoskins' report about Ibn Saud's views on an Arab-Jewish conference and worried about growing anti-Semitism in the United States, tended in his single focus on military victory to relegate the complex Palestine problem to the need for stability in the Middle East. As for the Prime Minister, a month earlier he had strongly approved of a cable from his close friend, Prime Minister of the Union of South

Africa Jan Smuts, favoring a Palestinian Jewish State as part of a larger Arab federation, other areas like Libya accepting some Jews, or the adoption of both courses, in recognition of the highly valuable war effort made by Palestinian Jewry. Now, turning to the statement, the President favored—if any declaration were to be made—a shorter text to the effect that, in view of military considerations, the Palestine question could not be taken up at present. The Prime Minister wished it said, in any case, that British policy would not be decided by sporadic acts of violence. Finally, the two agreed that this question should be held "in abeyance" and discussed further between the two governments from month-to-month as the war situation developed. Any decision on the matter was left to the light of these further exchanges.[42] A few days later, Roosevelt and Churchill departed the Citadel, with no word to the world about saving European Jewry.[43]

III

The fate of the joint Anglo-American statement did not alter the perspective of the U.S. and British governments *vis-à-vis* Palestine in the months to follow. The American Jewish Conference, roused by the oratory of United Palestine Appeal Chairman Abba Hillel Silver, demonstrated American Jewry's strong support for a Jewish Commonwealth in Palestine, and Silver (now selected as Chairman of the AECZA's Executive Committee) began pressing for commitments from Congress and the two political parties without putting his "trust in princes." Weizmann remained more reserved, trusting in Churchill and especially worried lest Roosevelt be provoked sufficiently to issue the dreaded joint statement at any time. Palestinian Jewry continued in growing numbers to rally around the feisty Ben Gurion in opposition to the Mandatory power, while the more militant Irgun raised the banner of armed revolt in early 1944.[44] But the Jewish cause had no friend in the State Department once Welles, who alone had favored a Jewish State and opposed the joint statement, resigned in mid-August in a showdown over various matters with Hull.[45] Wallace Murray and Isaiah Bowman, having found British views similar to their own while working for the joint declaration, came to a meeting of minds with their opposite numbers in the Foreign Office during a visit to London the following April. The Near Eastern division prepared a memorandum favoring an international trusteeship for Palestine, to be run by Christians, Moslems, and Jews on world population ratios which argued badly for the Jews. Roosevelt's thinking was moving in a similar direction, and his personal objection (and those of the War and State Departments) effectively killed Jewish Commonwealth resolutions in Congress during 1944.[46] If the intended joint declaration represented the first significant intervention by the American government since Wilson's day regarding the future of Palestine, the United States' growing need for oil, officially recognized with the formation of the Petroleum Reserves Corporation in July 1943, introduced an additional, crucial factor, statement or no statement: increased interest in maintaining friendly relations with Ibn Saud (a point both Hoskins and Hurley—who numbered Sinclair Oil among his former clients— emphasized to the President) and the resultant development of a new and independent role for the nation in the Middle East.[47] Winston Churchill, Zionism's most highly placed friend, did report the outline of the Ministerial Committee's generous partition plan to Weizmann in October 1943, and a year later promised his support to the Zionist leader for a good partition and a post-war Jewish immigration of one and a half million over the next ten years. But the Colonial and Foreign Offices, with the concurrence of the British Chiefs of Staff, continued to regard such views as aggravating Arab fears, and by the close of 1944 both departments had succeeded in stalling final acceptance of the committee's partition report.[48] As a result, postponement produced a stalemate all round at the war's end, with strife mounting in the Holy Land.

For the enigma of Palestine was "a mere bubble in the stream," as Isaiah Berlin wrote to the Foreign Office, forgotten in the flood of the Allied war against Germany. Hitler's paranoid rantings to the contrary notwithstanding, the Jews were anything but a powerful international force. Having no state of their own—the Zionists had always grasped this—Jews could conveniently be considered expendable in the war years.[49] The democracies' silence about the rescue of European Jewry and Palestinian Jewry's war contribution was also exemplified dramatically in the joint statement, even though that statement did not appear. Indeed, the silence surrounding the joint statement extended beyond the political arena; it eluded the searchlight of history.[50] Roosevelt had asked Celler "not to make waves," and indicated that he had a secret agreement with Churchill whereby Jews could secretly enter Palestine despite the White Paper. There was no truth in this confidence, intended merely to calm the Congressman, Celler discovered months later. In point of fact, the State Department continued to assure Arab leaders privately until the war's end, *precisely* as Roosevelt had cabled Ibn Saud in May 1943 along the lines of the proposed joint declaration. Pressures on the President, especially by Congressional reaction to the activities of Peter Bergson's newly formed Emergency Committee to Save the Jews of Europe and by Secretary Morgenthau's discovery of State and Foreign Office delay in granting licenses for blocked funds abroad to save Jews, forced Roosevelt to create the War Refugee Board in January 1944. The board's valiant efforts proved that much could have been done earlier. Yet it was a case of too little and too late for the victims of the *Einsatzgruppen,* vicious Axis collaborators, and the crematoria. The White Paper remained in force, and only 52,000 Jews reached the shores of Palestine during the war (including 12,000 "illegals" allowed to remain) within its limited quota of 75,000.[51] Adolf Hitler had won his war against the Jews: the 4,000,000 victims reported in August 1943, were joined by an additional 2,000,000 when the Third Reich's *Götterdammerung* sounded. Against his determination and the failure of his opponents to meet the unparalleled crisis of the Holocaust with extraordinary measures, the Zionists' rare success regarding the joint statement ultimately counted for nought. It would be up to the post-war world, stricken by a guilty conscience after the event, to try and make some amends.

FOOTNOTES

I wish to express my appreciation to the National Foundation for Jewish Culture and to the Memorial Foundation for Jewish Culture for fellowships during 1974-1975 and 1975-76, respectively, which aided considerably in completing research. For their comments on an earlier draft of this article, my thanks to Professors Henry L. Feingold, Joseph Lowin and Michael Popkin, and to my father, Rabbi M. S. Penkower.

1. Weizmann to Wise, June 25, 1943, Z5/1215, Central Zionist Archives, Jerusalem (hereafter CZA); Stanley memo, August 31, 1943, Foreign Office records (hereafter FO) 371/35038, Public Record Office, London (hereafter PRO); Henry L. Feingold, *The Politics of Rescue, The Roosevelt Administration and the Holocaust, 1938-1945* (New Brunswick, 1970), Ch. 7; Weizmann statement, June 11, 1943, Minutes of Office Committee, American Emergency Committee for Zionist Affairs (hereafter AECZA), Zionist Archives, New York. The official British historian for this subject agrees that Arab approval of Jewish immigration to Palestine after March 1944 was "most unlikely." Llewellyn Woodward, *British Foreign Policy in the Second World War* (London, 1962), p. 388.

2. Weizmann-Halifax talk, May 7, 1943, Z5/1377, CZA; Weizmann statement, June 11, 1943, Office Committee, AECZA; *Contemporary Jewish Record* 6 (February 1943): 3-4. For a recent summary of the Biltmore Resolutions and their immediate relationship to internal Zionist politics, see Michael Bar Zohar, *Ben Gurion* (Hebrew), I (Tel Aviv, 1975), pp. 440-61.

3. Weizmann statement, June 14, 1943, Office Committee, AECZA; Weizmann to Wise, June 25, 1943, Z5/1216, CZA; Chaim Weizmann, *Trial and Error* (New York, 1949), p. 427; Halifax to Weizmann, November 2, 1942, Z5/1442, CZA; Welles-Weizmann-Goldmann talk, December 4, 1942, Z5/1377, CZA; State Department memorandum of January 19, 1943 talk, 867N.01/1-1943, State Department records (hereafter SD), Record Group 59, National Archives, Washington, D.C.; *Foreign Relations of the United States* (hereafter *FRUS*), 1943, 4:757-63.

4. Hoskins-Goldman talk, May 11, 1943, Z5/372,CZA; Halifax-Weizmann talk, May 7, 1943, Z5/1377, CZA; Welles to Wise, May 12, 1943, Z5/1410, CZA; Welles-Weizmann-Goldmann talk, May 18, 1943, Z5/1377, CZA; *Palcor*, June 4, 1943; Roosevelt-Weizmann talk, June 11, 1943, 867N.01/1933½, SD. It should be noted that the State Department's published version omits Roosevelt's disparaging comments regarding the Arabs, as well as Welles' observation that Ibn Saud's demand to stop further Jewish immigration to Palestine was "childish." *FRUS*, 1943, 4, pp. 792-794.

5. Weizmann statement, June 14, 1943, Office Committee, AECZA; Weizmann to Klotz (for Morgenthau), June 15, 1943, Morgenthau Diaries, vol. 642, pp. 75-79, Franklin D. Roosevelt Library, Hyde Park, New York (hereafter FDRL); Welles to Roosevelt, May 19, 1943, PPF 8084, FDRL; Nahum Goldmann interview with author, May 8, 1977; Chaim Weizmann, "Palestine's Role in the Solution of the Jewish Problem," *Foreign Affairs* 20 (January, 1942): 324-338; Stanley memo, August 31, 1943, FO 371/35038, PRO; Weizmann to Welles, June 25, 1943, Z5/1444, CZA.

6. The war objectives of the Atlantic Charter, a joint statement by Roosevelt and Churchill in August 1941, included Anglo-American respect for "the right of all peoples to choose the form of Government under which they will live." *FRUS*, 1941, 1, pp. 367-369.

7. *FRUS*, 1942, 4, pp. 538-540, 543-544, 25-26. To the same end, George Wadsworth, a firm anti-Zionist who had served during the 1930's as Consul General in Jerusalem, was appointed Diplomatic Agent and Consul General to Lebanon and Syria. *FRUS*, 1942, 4, 664ff. For Wadsworth's views at the time, which emphasized the "higher interest" of Christendom in Palestine, see Wadsworth to Henderson, January 31, 1943, 867N.01/1-3143, SD. His bias would continue throughout the decade.

8. Both Churchill, the British Foreign Office and the U.S. Joint Chiefs of Staff *only* approved that an American representative be sent to Cairo to discuss the proposed mission with British authorities there, an important point overlooked by Secretary Hull in his autobiography. *FRUS*, 1942, 4, pp. 32-36; Cordell Hull, *Memoirs* (New York, 1948), 2, p. 1532. (Hoskins was certainly not representing the Pentagon, an assertion made in Gabriel Cohen, "Churchill and the Establishment of the War Cabinet Committee on Palestine (April-July 1943)," *Zionism* 4 (In Hebrew) (1975): 259-336.) But the President, entertaining wider ideas, overlooked these reservations.

9. *Jewish Telegraphic Agency*, November 2, 1942; Peter Bergson interview with author, June 22, 1972; Edwin Johnson statement, *Congressional Record*, January 14, 1943, 89, pt. 9, p. A125; *FRUS*, 1942, 4, pp. 549-550. The Republican 1940 presidential candidate's account of his world tour, the spectacular best-seller of 1943, would go on to praise Zionist achievements in Palestine and castigate British imperialism in the Middle East. Wendell Willkie, *One World* (New York, 1943), pp. 15-36.

10. *FRUS*, 1942, 4, pp. 548, 557-558; Murray to Hull, December 18, 1942, 867N.01/12-1842, SD; Judah L. Magnes, "Toward Peace in Palestine," *Foreign Affairs* 21 (January, 1943): 239-249; Magnes to Untermyer, March 5, 1943, Magnes Archives, Jerusalem, file 234. Murray, most blatant anti-Zionist in the State Department since the 1930's, expressed great fears of Zionist affiliation with Communism, thought it best that Jews renounce political Zionism and opt for post-war settlement in Angola, and refused to grant recognition to the Washington office of the Jewish Agency. Murray-Goldmann talk, January 7, 1943, Robert Szold MSS., Zionist Archives, New York, Box 167; *FRUS*, 1942, 4, pp. 553-556; Murray to Welles, January 18, 1943, 867N.01/1837, SD; *FRUS*, 1943, 4, pp. 787-788.

11. MacMichael to Stanley, November 21, 1942, FO 371/31380, PRO; *FRUS*, 1942, 4, pp. 551-553; Machmichael to Casey, January 23, 1943 (in memo of March 31, 1943), FO 371/34965, PRO. Although Taylor supported the return of Jews to their former homes after the war and had indicated to Eden his displeasure concerning Zionist "extremist claims," he and Welles (over Murray's objections) sidestepped Eden's overture as "subject to misinterpretation or distortions"

which would harm the Allied cause. Peterson minute, October 23, 1942, FO 371/31379, PRO; Murray to Welles, January 18, 1943, 867N.01/1837, SD. For the Evian Conference, see Feingold, *Politics of Rescue*, Ch. 2.

12. *Jewish Telegraphic Agency*, February 24, 1943; *House of Commons*, Parliamentary Debates (hereafter PD), volume 387, February 24, 1943, column 139; *FRUS*, 1943, 4, p. 764n.; *House of Commons*, PD, volume 387, March 3, 1943, column 518; *FRUS*, 1943, 3, p. 38. Also see *FRUS*, 1943, 1, pp. 140, 143. Eden's 1943 statement came shortly after the Iraqi Prime Minister submitted an Arab federation plan (without a Jewish State) at the request of the British Minister Resident, Middle East. Woodward, *British Foreign Policy*, p. 388. Indeed, the Foreign Secretary's subordinates approved notifying the Iraqi minister in Washington of their support for the view of the State Department's Paul Alling that Arab propaganda be encouraged in the corridors of Congress. Memo of March 17, 1943, FO 371/34955, PRO. Concurrently, Eden informed American Jewish representatives that their wanting the Allies to approach Germany for release of Jews was "fantastically impossible." Shertok report, April 14, 1943, S25/10086, CZA.

13. Hoskins April 20, 1943 report, Confidential Files, State Department, Box 5, FDRL.

14. Parker to Berle, March 24, 1943, and Berle reply, April 16, 1943, Operation Plans Division files, War Department records, RG 165 (hereafter OPD, WD), National Archives, Box 1264; Berle memo, April 20, 1943, Breckenridge Long MSS., Library of Congress, Washington, D.C. (hereafter LC), Box 202; Breckenridge Long Diary, April 20, 1943, LC; Murray to Welles, April 23, 1943, 867N.01/1855, SD. When Rommel threatened Alexandria, Berle had advised Zionists to renounce all aspirations to a Jewish State in Palestine, evacuate most of Palestinian Jewry to Saudi Arabia and Africa, and settle after the war for a token "Vatican State" in Palestine and a haven in the highlands of Ethiopia. Emanuel Neumann, *In the Arena, An Autobiographical Memoir* (New York, 1976), p. 159.

15. *FRUS*, 1943, 4, pp. 773-788. Ibn Saud, prodded by the Foreign Office, had gone beyond an interview for *Life* (May 31, 1943) opposing a Jewish State to write his stronger letter to Roosevelt in the vein of an earlier (unanswered) communication of November, 1938. Eyre minute, May 6, 1943, FO 371/35033, PRO; *FRUS*, 1938, 3, p. 994. At a cabinet meeting two weeks later, immediately after receiving Weizmann, Roosevelt described Ibn Saud's message as "a fine letter." Harold Ickes Diaries, June 12, 1943, LC.

16. MacMichael to Stanley, April 19, 1943, Colonial Office records (hereafter CO) 733/449/76221, PRO; *House of Commons*, PD, volume 386, February 3, 1943, columns 863-867; Stanley to Churchill, April 10, 1943, FO 371/35033, PRO; Weizmann to Churchill, April 2, 1943, S25/7569, CZA; Churchill note, April 28, 1943, FO 371/35054, PRO; Amery to Churchill, April 29, 1943, Prem 4, 51/11, PRO; Stanley memo, May 4, 1943, CAB 66, WP 43 (192), PRO.

17. Eden memo, May 10, 1943, CAB 66, WP 43 (200), PRO; Douglas Newbold, *The Making of the Modern Sudan* (London, 1953), pp. 326, 331; Middle East War Council memo, May 19, 1843, FO 371/34975, PRO. For Eden's disagreement with Churchill on the White Paper and the approach to Ibn Saud, see Eden to Churchill, March 3, 1943, and Churchill reply, March 9, 1943, FO 371/35033, PRO. Earlier, Morris Lazaron's proposed Anglo-American declaration on Palestine (conforming to Hull's October, 1942, statement and recognizing Palestine as a Holy Land for Christians, Moslems and Jews) had met with Foreign Office disapproval because of its very limited reference to Arabs and its implication of continued Jewish immigration. Halifax to Eden, February 8, 1943, and FO staff minutes, FO 371/35032, PRO; Lazaron to Halifax, March 15, 1943, Lazaron MSS. ,American Jewish Archives, Cincinnati, Box 3045. By May, Lazaron echoed the State Department-Foreign Office line. Lazaron to Berger, May 14, 1943, American Council for Judaism Archives, State Historical Society of Wisconsin, Madison, Box 70.

18. Halifax to Eden, May 27, 1943, FO 371/35035, PRO; Roosevelt to Hull, May 14, 1943, OF 3186, FDRL; *FRUS, Conferences at Washington and Quebec*, 1943, pp. 345, 183; Bowman to Roosevelt, May 22, 1943, PSF Postwar, Box 98, FDRL.

18a. November 16, 1938, Morgenthau Diaries, vol. 151, pp. 32-35, 70-78, FDRL; Harley Notter Mss, Boxes 55 and 59, SD; Bowman to Roosevelt, May 22, 1943, PSF Postwar, Box 98, FDRL; Bowman to Taylor, June 23, 1947, Myron Taylor Mss, FDRL.

19. *The Price of Vision, The Diary of Henry Wallace, 1942-1946*, John Blum ed. (Boston, 1973), pp. 210-211, 188, 276-277. Wallace, when Secretary of Agriculture, had accepted the suggestion of Justice Brandeis (most influential of Zionists) that Walter C. Lowdermilk, Assistant Chief of the Soil Conservation Service, stop off in Palestine on his way to study Chinese land use for the U.S. government in 1939. Subsequently, the JVA idea, proposed by Lowdermilk on his return, was popularized with Zionist financial backing. Tamara De Sola Pool interview with author, February 19, 1976; Neumann, *In the Arena*, Ch. 15.

20. Hassett to Roosevelt, June 7, 1943, OF 700 Palestine, Box 3, FDRL; *FRUS*, 1943, 4, pp. 790-792, 795-796; Eden to Halifax, June 11, 1943, FO 371/35035, PRO. Foreign Office doubts about the efficacy of Hoskins' mission to Ibn Saud were confirmed by their receipt of the Saudi Arabian record of that monarch's conversation with Roosevelt's emissary, Brig. General Patrick Hurley. May 24, 1943 memo, FO 371/35164, and Willkley to Eden, June 19, 1943, FO 371/34959, PRO.

21. Casey memo, June 17, 1943, CAB 66, WP 43 (246), PRO; Lyttleton memo, April 3, 1942, Prem 4, 52/5, PRO; Lyttleton memo, June 23, 1943, CAB 66, WP 43 (265), PRO; July 2, 1943 cabinet conclusions, CAB 65, 92/43/2-3, PRO; Churchill to Bridges, July 7, 1943, and Amery to Churchill, July 2, 1943, Prem 4, 52/5-II, PRO; Churchill to Eden, July 11, 1943, Prem 4, 51/11, PRO; *FRUS*, 1943, 4, pp. 797-801. A Colonial Office recommendation to have the joint statement refer to the Biltmore Resolutions was turned down by the Foreign Office on the assumption that the U.S. government would not favor this inclusion. Battershill memo, June 15, 1943, CO 733/75862/444/14B, PRO. The British drafts for the joint statement are given in Nathan Katzburg, *The Palestine Problem in British Policy, 1940-1945* (in Hebrew)(Jerusalem, 1977), pp. 23-26.

22. Berlin memo, July 3, 1943, FO 371/35036, PRO; Walter Lowdermilk, *Palestine, Land of Promise* (New York, 1944); Weizmann reports, Minutes of Jewish Agency Executive, London, July 5-6, 1943, Weizmann Archives, Rehovot (hereafter WA); *Review of the Yiddish Press*, July 1943, American Jewish Committee Archives, New York (hereafter AJC); Stanley-Weizmann talk, July 8, 1943, and Casey-Weizmann talk, July 15, 1943, WA; *Palcor*, July 16, 1943; Richard Meinertzaghen, *Middle East Diary, 1917-1956* (London, 1959), pp. 187-188. The British Minister Resident, M.E., remained unconvinced. Richard Casey, *Personal Experience, 1939-1946* (New York, 1962), pp. 139-140.

23. Welles-Wise-Goldmann talk, June 21, 1943, Z5/666, CZA; Goldmann interview with author, March 14, 1974; Halifax to Eden, July 6, 1943, FO 371/35036, PRO; July 17, 1943 memo, Z5/665, CZA.

24. Wise to Weizmann, July 23, 1943, WA; Wise to Morgenthau, July 23, 1943, and Morgenthau to Wise, July 30, 1943, Morgenthau Diaries, volume 652, pp. 228-231, FDRL; Roosevelt to Wise, August 14, 1943, OF 76-C, FDRL.

25. Berlin to Malcolm, August 9, 1943, FO 371/35037, PRO; Wise to Roosevelt, July 23, 1943, 867N.01/7-2343, SD; Wise to Goldmann, July 27, 1943, Stephen Wise Mss., American Jewish Historical Society, Waltham (hereafter Wise), Box 109.

26. Halifax to Eden, August 1, 1943, FO 371/35036, PRO; Haynes memo, December 9, 1942, G-2 files, War Department records, RG 165, Federal Records Center, Suitland (Md.), Pal 3800; Handy to Patterson, December 13, 1942, and Patterson to Bergson, January 17, 1943, OPD, WD, Box 830; "Memorandum on the Arab-Jewish Question," April 30, 1943, OPD, WD, Box 1264. (Hoskins' plan followed identical lines, just substituting Cyrenaica for the Cameroons. See above, note 13.) July 25, 1943, #41702-S report, OSS records, RG 226, National Archives.

27. FRUS, 1943, 1, pp. 296-299; Eden to Churchill, June 15, and 18, 1943, Prem 4/51/4, PRO; *FRUS, Conferences at Washington and Quebec, 1943*, pp. 345, 631, 321, 324. While numerous delays occurred in establishing the Marshal Lyautey camp at Casablanca, the opportunity for Jews escaping from Nazi-held countries dwindled. Eventually, only some 650-700 (rather than the anticipated 6,000-7,000) arrived from Madrid during May and June, 1944, and the camp closed in November. The 432 Sephardic Jews from Salonika were sent to a Greek colony in Palestine; about half left to join Jewish settlements nearby, with the remainder sent back to a reluctant Greece. "Report on Middle East Camps," pp. 28-33, UNRRA records, United Nations Archives, New York, Box 2755.

28. August 16, 1943 memo, 867N.01/1919½, SD; Ickes Diary, March 14, 1943; Long memo, April 22, 1943, Long MSS., Box 203; Long Diary, April 21, 1943; June 1949 memo, 867N.01/1857½, SD; Strong draft, July 26, 1943, OF 700 Palestine, Box 3, FDRL; Murray to Hull, August 17, 1943, 867N.01/1908½, SD; Patterson to Hull, July 27, 1943, Samuel Rosenman MSS., Box 9, FDRL.

29. For Hull's inferior position, see *Navigating the Rapids, 1918-1971. From the Papers of Adolf A. Berle*, Beatrice Berle and Travis Jacobs, eds. (New York, 1973), pp. 431, 437-438, and 440; Ickes Diaries, March 6, 1943, and August 15, 1943. Hull also would have remembered that the Joint Chiefs had not approved Hoskins' mission in toto the previous winter. See above, note 8. General Marshall, in addition, had replied to a complaint of Sen. Edwin Johnson, Chairman of the Committee for a Jewish Army, that Hoskins' statements and appearance in uniform before gatherings of select Congressmen were indeed unauthorized by the military and that steps had been taken to curb such activities. Peter Bergson interview with author, June 22, 1972.

30. Murray to Hull, August 17, 1943, 867N.01/1908½, SD; Hull to Roosevelt, July 29, 1943, Watson to Roosevelt, July 30, 1943, and Roosevelt to Tully, July 30, 1943, Rosenman MSS., Box 9. For Bloom at Bermuda, see Feingold, *Politics of Rescue*, pp. 198-199.

31. W (Wise) report, August 4, 1943, Nahum Goldmann MSS., CZA, Z6/18/6; *New York Times*, May 18, 1943; *Jewish Telegraphic Agency*, July 16, 1943; *New York Times*, July 30, 1943; Murray to Hull, August 17, 1943, 867N.01/1908½, SD.

32. W (Wise) report, August 4, 1943, Goldmann MSS., Z6/18/6. Rosenman had previously participated in drafting the American Jewish Committee's January, 1943, Statement of Principles, which had the approval of Ben Cohen and Sumner Welles. Zionist-non Zionist Confidential files, November-December, 1942, AJC.

33. Berlin to Malcolm, August 9, 1943, FO 371/35037, PRO. Baruch had earlier favored large-scale settlement of post-war refugees (Jews and others) in Africa, while Swope preferred Alaska. Baruch to Benson, January 24, 1939, Baruch MSS., Firestone Library, Princeton, volume 44; Swope to Ickes, October 25, 1939, *ibid.*, volume 46. Rosenman approved of Baruch's plan at the time on the ground that "it is no solution to create a world ghetto instead of many local ones." Rosenman memo to Roosevelt, December 5, 1938, PPF 64, FDRL.

34. Henrietta Klotz interview with author, March 14, 1977; Josef Cohn interview with author, June 8, 1976; Morgenthau-Cohn-Weisgal talk, August 3, 1943, Z5/666, CZA; Morgenthau-Locker talk, October 27, 1942, Z4/302/25, CZA. Weisgal could have added that Moslems had not revolted against British rule in India and had remained quiescent after the British take-over of Iran and Tunis, while the pro-Nazi Arab revolt in Iraq had been put down with limited British forces. See "The Arab Myth," *New Palestine* 33 (May 21, 1943): 3; "Dangerous Illusions," *Zionews* 14 (May 1943): 7. For the later public rebuttal by the Zionist leadership to the Hoskins report, see memo of February 14, 1944, Abba Hillel Silver Archives, The Temple, Cleveland (hereafter Silver), file 4, drawer 2.

35. W (Wise) report, August 4, 1943, Goldmann MSS., Z6/18/6; Wise to Goldmann, August 4, 1943, Wise MSS., Box 109; Wise to Frankfurter, May 19, 1943, *ibid.*; Welles to Taylor, June 23, 1943, Myron Tylor MSS., FDRL. Rosenman and Niles repeated to Roosevelt the probable effect of the statement on the 1944 elections, Minutes of Jewish Agency Executive, London, August 23, 1943, WA.

36. Shertok report, Jewish Agency Executive, Jerusalem, August 22, 1943, CZA; *New York Times*, July 30, August 1-2, and May 5-8, 1943; Morgenthau-Cohn,-Weisgal talk, August 3, 1943, Z5/666, CZA; August 2-3, 1943, Minutes of Office Committee, AECZA.

37. Morgenthau-Cohn-Weisgal talk, August 4, 1943, Z5/387, CZA. Morgenthau's reference to Rosenman's proposal indicates that these two (and probably other) Jews in Roosevelt's circle favored the get-together of Jewish leaders to dampen Zionist agitation. Goldmann, however, supported Wise's view that the Bergson group should be left out of the discussions. Goldmann to Wise, August 5 and 8, 1943, Z5/1216, CZA. Because of Wise's objection to Bergson's presence, the meeting never took place. Bergson, however, managed to avoid military draft or deportation, and shifted his propaganda activities to the rescue of European Jewry.

38. Stimson Diaries, April 17, 1941, Stimson MSS., Yale University, New Haven. (And in June, 1940, immediately after the fall of France, Strong—then head of the U.S. War Plans Division—had proposed halting aid for the Allies and focusing on hemispheric defense. Maurice Matloff and Edwin M. Snell, *Strategic Planning for Coalition Warfare, 1941-1942* (Washington,

D.C., 1953), p. 191.) Murray to Hull, August 17, 1943, 867N.01/1908½, SD; *FRUS*, 1943, 4, p. 803; Hull to Rosenman, August 6, 1943, Rosenman MSS., Box 9. It is, therefore, in error to claim that War Department fears led to the ultimate decision regarding the Joint Statement. James MacGregor Burns, *Roosevelt: The Soldier of Freedom* (New York, 1970), p. 397. Burns is also imprecise in his interpretation of the subsequent Quebec conference, as I explain below.

39. Hull, *Memoirs*, 2, p. 1533; Halifax to Eden, and Eden minute, August 2, 1943, FO 371/35036, PRO; *Washington Post*, August 9, 1943; Strong memo to Marshall, August 5, 1943, U.S. Joint Chiefs of Staff records, National Archives, RG 218, 092. Palestine. The State Department had also suggested a postponement of the joint statement in return for delaying the American Jewish Conference (or at least soft-pedalling Palestine in its resolutions), but the Zionist leadership refused the *quid pro quo*. August 12, 1943, Minutes of Office Committee, AECZA.

40. Weizmann to Winant, August 12, 1943, Z4/14.885, CZA; Celler statement, August 12, 1943, 867N.01/1934, SD; Neumann to Friedrich, August 27, 1943, Silver Archives, file 4, drawer 1; Shertok to Locker, September 13, 1943, Z5/1217, CZA.

41. Welles to Wise, August 6, 1943, Wise MSS., Box 66; July 26, 1943 London cable, Cordell Hull MSS., LC, Box 61; *Jewish Telegraphic Agency*, August 20, 1943; Celler statement, August 18, 1943, 867N.01/1918, SD; Martin-Lourie talk, August 17, 1943, Manson files, Silver Archives.

42. FRUS, *Conferences at Washington and Quebec*, 1943, pp. 919, 1116, 930-932; Smuts to Churchill, July 22, 1943, and Churchill to Smuts, July 24, 1943, Prem 4, 52/5-II, PRO; Churchill memo, July 26, 1943, CAB 66, WP 43 (337), PRO; Woodward, *British Foreign Policy*, p. 391; Eden memo, September 1, 1943, FO 371/35037, PRO. The Near Eastern Division expert who had reported his fears in 1918 to then Secretary Lansing regarding a "nationalistic Jewish state, particularly of a Communistic nature," sent a similar memo to Hull at Quebec as a last-ditch effort to save the joint statement. (No author or date is given, but the joint statement is appended.) Hull MSS., Box 66. Though this move failed, his proposed solution was adopted by the State Department a few months later.

43. Both Roosevelt and Churchill, in their secret wartime correspondence (FDRL), devoted little attention to Nazi atrocities and to the fate of European Jewry. "Jews" as a topic came up twice for discussion in the President's press conferences (FDRL) during 1943; "Palestine", never. The joint statement also never came to the attention of Roosevelt's cabinet. It should be added, in this regard, that at the next Allied conference, in Moscow, the two Western leaders and Stalin released a declaration against German barbarities with no mention of Jewry. *FRUS*, 1943, 1, pp. 768-769.

44. Sir Isiah Berlin interview with author, July 1, 1976. In lieu of a definitive study of Jewish (Zionist and other) activities on both sides of the Atlantic during World War II, various aspects may be examined in Feingold, *Politics of Rescue*; Samuel Halperin, *The Political World of American Zionism* (Detroit, 1961); Yehuda Bauer, *From Diplomacy to Resistance, A History of Jewish Palestine, 1939-1945* (Philadelphia, 1970); J.C. Hurewitz, *The Struggle for Palestine* (New York, 1950). It should be emphasized that postponement of the joint statement was singularly due to American Zionists. Their British and Palestinian counterparts, as minutes of the Jewish Agency Executive in London and Jerusalem indicate, knew the entire story and its significance only after the event. Non- and anti-Zionist organizations in the U.S. and England were not aware of the statement at all. See the archives of the AJC, American Council for Judaism, Jewish Labor Committee and American Joint Distribution Committee (New York), Board of Deputies of British Jews and Anglo-Jewish Association (London). State Department and Foreign Office records do not indicate Arab awareness, either.

45. Welles to Hull, May 17, 1943, 867N.01/1857½, SD; Sumner Welles, *We Need Not Fail* (Boston, 1948), pp. 29-30. Welles' knowledge of Roosevelt's pro-Zionist inclinations (*ibid,*) was circumscribed to his tenure in the State Department. Historians have neglected to note that the Hull-Welles feud was also reflected in their respective positions on the Palestine issue, especially with Hull's support of Hoskins and Welles' of Weizmann. Subsequently, Welles played an important part in securing Zionist objectives after the war.

46. The question of Palestine and its impact on Anglo-American diplomacy during the Roosevelt years still awaits its historian. A preliminary review of some events subsequent to postponement of the statement can be obtained in *FRUS*, 1943, 4, pp. 812-813, 816-821; *FRUS*, 1944, 5, pp. 560ff.; *FRUS*, 1945, 8, pp. 683-687. In a visit to London at the close of 1943, Hoskins

attempted to revive the joint declaration in some form, but the British, burned once and working on their own solution for Palestine, washed their hands of the matter. Stanley to MacMichael, December 10, 1943, FO 371/35042, PRO; Hoskins report, December 13, 1943, Long MSS., Box 199.

47. Stimson diary and papers, and Ickes diary, June-July, 1943; OF 56, FDRL. Strong emphasized, in his August 5 memo to Marshall, that just when 50% of the world's oil reserves, outside the Western Hemisphere, could be found in the Persian Gulf alone, petroleum experts were informing Roosevelt that U.S. reserves were adequate for only fourteen years at the current rate of consumption. See above, note 39. For background on the oil question, see Gabriel Kolko, *The Politics of War, The World and United States Foreign Policy, 1943-1945* (New York, 1968), pp. 294-298.

48. Based on the author's research at the Public Record Office, the Central Zionist and Weizmann Archives. Also see Woodward, *British Foreign Policy;* G. Cohen, *loc. cit.;* and Katzburg, *Palestine Problem in British Policy.* George Kirk's *The Middle East in the War* (London, 1952), given the author's anti-Zionist bias, should be used with caution.

49. Berlin to Malcolm, August 9, 1943, FO 371/35037, PRO. For the Jew as "total outsider," see Saul Friedländer, "The Historical Significance of the Holocaust," *Jerusalem Quarterly* 1 (Fall 1976): 36-59. This fundamental fact is overlooked in recent studies which argue that greater unity in American Jewish organizational ranks would have significantly ameliorated the plight of their European co-religionists during the Holocaust. Saul S. Friedman, *No Haven For the Oppressed* (Detroit, 1973); Selig Adler, "American Jewry and That Explosive Statehood Question, 1933-1945," in Bertram Korn, ed., *A Bicentennial Festschrift for Jacob Rader Marcus* (Waltham, 1976), pp. 5-22. As for Palestine, notwithstanding Jewish internal squabbles, Roosevelt announced before the 1944 elections his support for a Jewish State there, and he attempted to convince Ibn Saud to change his anti-Zionist convictions during their meeting of February, 1945. That failure led the President to revert to his (and Hoskins') earlier views. Robert E. Sherwood, *Roosevelt and Hopkins, An Intimate History* (New York, 1948), p. 872; *FRUS*, 1945, 8, pp. 690-691. On the other hand, even with near-unity among Jews and wide-spread non-Jewish encouragement on the need for a Jewish State in Palestine after the war, the State Department consistently maintained its former position. The same was true for the British Foreign and Colonial Offices. Subsequently, reminiscing on those years and on events since the establishment of the State of Israel, Sir Isaiah Berlin agreed with the conclusion of his late friend, Yaacov Herzog, that the Jews are "'a people that dwells alone.'" Berlin interview with author, July 1, 1976.

50. The one analysis of this subject, while offering no wider perspective on the Holocaust, is also confined to documents at the British Public Record Office and to the published volumes of the U.S. State Department. See Katzburg, *Palestine Problem in British Policy,* Ch. 3; Michael J. Cohen, "American Influence on British Policy in the Middle East During World War Two: First Attempts at Coordinating Allied Policy on Palestine." *American Jewish Historical Quarterly* 57 (September 1977): 50-70, has the same limitations.

51. Celler to author, January 26, 1977; *FRUS*, 1944, 5, pp. 591, 597, 656; Emergency Committee to Save the Jews of Europe and Hebrew Committee of National Liberation records, Jabotinsky Archives, Tel Aviv; Morgenthau Diaries, 1943-1944, and War Refugee Board MSS., FDRL; Yehuda Slutzki, "Palestine Assistance to European Jewry," *Yad VaShem, Jewish Resistance During the Holocaust* (Jerusalem, 1971), p. 417.

The American Christian Palestine Committee

By Carl Hermann Voss

In the annals of support of Zionism by non-Jews, few chronicles are as heartwarming and reassuring as that of the American Christian Palestine Committee, whether of its antecedent groups, the American Palestine Committee originated in 1932 and the Christian Council on Palestine begun in 1942, or the merger of the two organizations into the American Christian Palestine Committee in 1946. The interfaith cooperation, interethnic amity, and interpersonal understanding on the part of the ACPC's staff and members were of a high order; and aided greatly in strengthening Jewish efforts to interpret Zionist aspirations to an American public, then singularly callous and uncaring about the rescue of Jewish refugees from annihilation by Hitler and not at all concerned with the future of a Jewish national home in Palestine.

During the fateful mid and late 1940s the American Christian Palestine Committee played a significant, often strategic role in mobilizing public opinion on behalf of opening Palestine's gates to the remnant of European Jewry spared the Nazis' gas chambers and of helping establish the foundations of the newly proclaimed Jewish state of Israel on May 14, 1948.

The American Palestine Committee,[1] publicly launched at a dinner in Washington, D.C. on January 12, 1932, and attended by members of both Houses of the U.S. Congress and many other dignitaries of the U.S. Government, including Vice-President Charles Curtis, was organized primarily by Dr. Emanuel Neumann, an American member of the World Zionist Executive. Neumann had become deeply concerned in 1931 about the retreat by the British Government from the commitments of the 1917 Balfour declaration and their League of Nations Mandate for Palestine, just as in 1930 he believed the publication of the

Labor Government's White Paper on Palestine presaged disaster for Zionist hopes.

Encouraged and guided by Zionism's "elder statesman" and *"éminence grise,"* U. S Supreme Court Justice Louis D. Brandeis, Neumann gathered for this meeting of non-Jewish sympathizers with Zionist objectives an array of outstanding government officials who, he hoped, would make American influence felt in British governmental circles and perhaps turn the unfavorable tide: Senator Robert M. LaFollette, Jr. of Wisconsin, Senator William H. King of Utah, New York's Congressman Hamilton Fish, Jr., Assistant Secretary of State James Grafton Rogers, and Idaho's doughty Senator William E. Borah (who had another engagement but agreed, at the urging of Rabbi Stephen S. Wise, to serve as honorary chairman). Neumann prevailed on the controversial Felix Frankfurther of Harvard University's Law School faculty to address the dinner, a task he performed with characteristic skill.

A more impressive moment of the evening, however, was the reading of a letter from President Herbert Hoover:

> I am interested to learn that a group of distinguished men and women is to be formed to spread knowledge and appreciation of the rehabilitation which is going forward in Palestine under Jewish auspices, and to add my expression to the sentiment among our people in favor of the realization of the age-old aspirations of the Jewish people for the restoration of their national homeland. I shall appreciate it if you will present my cordial greetings to those attending the dinner in Washington on January 17th to advance this enterprise.

Yet the American president actually said nothing new, for he was merely giving a qualified approbation whereas on several occasions Woodrow Wilson had spoken of his "personal approval of the [Balfour] Declaration" and had written in 1919: "I am . . . persuaded that the Allied Nations, with the fullest concurrence of our Government and people, are agreed that in Palestine shall be laid the foundations of a Jewish commonwealth." President Hoover only echoed what, with perhaps less reflection and comprehension, had been said to Zionist delegations and conventions by his predecessors, Warren G. Harding and Calvin Coolidge, in the 1920s.[2]

Considerable publicity emerged from this initial dinner of the American Palestine Committee; but the APC, so well started, soon lapsed into desuetude because its guiding spirit, Emanuel Neumann, left for Palestine soon afterward to assume duties there in the Zionist Executive, not to return until 1941. By that time, the British White Paper of 1939 on Palestine had been issued; and an end to Jewish immigration to Palestine was a real threat. The pressures of World War Two on British policy seemed to spell doom for any prospects of establishing a Jewish national homeland.

The APC began again, however, in 1941. Dinner meetings in Washington were held once more, primarily to remind non-Jewish leaders in governmental circles that the American government had, by presidential approval through the years and Congressional action on several occasions, given sanction to the 1917 Balfour Declaration. No less important in the eyes of the APC leaders of that time—and subsequent years as well—were the imperatives of the League of Nations Mandate given to Great Britain (and approved by the Congress, despite non-membership of the United States in the League) that the Mandatory Power was to "put into effect the Balfour Declaration," to "facilitate Jewish immigration," to "encourage close settlement by Jews on the land," and to "be responsible for placing the country under such political, administrative and economic conditions as will secure the establishment of the Jewish National Home." These words of 1917 by Balfour and of 1920 by the League's Permanent Mandates Commission had an incalculable effect on the non-Jewish supporters of Zionist aims. They respected the sacredness of the pledged word and believed in the validity of international law, as in the assignment of responsibilities by the Mandates Commission of the League, despite America's rigid isolation and neurotic aloofness from international responsibilities.

By 1942, when the United States was at war with the Axis Powers and firmly yoked to Great Britain as an ally, the British Government sought but failed to impede holding the annual dinner of the American Palestine Committee. On that banquet evening at the Mayflower Hotel in Washington, an international broadcast from Great Britain brought the voice of the famous Lord Josiah Wedgwood across the Atlantic to startle the audience, composed of 55 outstanding Americans—governors, editors, college presidents, and congressmen—as he said, "There is no longer any hope from the British administration. . . . Seek to get your America to act—to press for arms and justice—to accept the Mandate—to build another free land with open doors and open hearts. . . . I have tried to save for my own countrymen the glory of rebuilding Jersualem—of doing justice and creating freedom. . . . It's no use. They won't do it! I can't help. You must turn to America and take on the job yourselves."

As Emanuel Neumann tells the story in his memoirs, Wedgwood spoke directly at (or to) Senator Robert Wagner of New York, partly as a member of the Congress and partly, it appeared, as chairman, along with Senator Charles McNary of Oregon as co-chairman, of the American Palestine Committee; he seemed to cry out across the 3,000 miles of space: "You are as proud of America as I am of England's past. Will you see where lies America's duty? Can you take on the job from our enfeebled hands? . . . The mantle of Elijah has fallen upon Elisha—not only in Palestine. It is your rendezvous with destiny."[3]

Whatever may have been the impact of Wedgwood's extraordinary appeal on the continued reluctance of Britain to fulfill the Mandate in Palestine and on the traditional hesitancy of the United States to assume responsibility, one thing was certain: the issue was now to the fore. American Christians were being urged to demand that their government bethink itself of what it might say and do on the matter.

The American Christian Palestine Committee was still only the American Palestine Committee; not for another four years would it combine its program with that of the soon-to-be-born Christian Council on Palestine. The APC, however, had broadened its constituency; no longer did it number only congressmen and senators, but now it included hundreds of additional public figures: Paul Kellogg, editor of the *Survey* magazine; Johns Hopkins University's William Foxwell Albright; soil expert Walter Clay Lowdermilk; radio commentator Raymond Gram Swing; columnist Edgar Ansel Mowrer of the *Chicago Daily News;* critic and essayist Lewis Mumford; and other molders of public opinion, including many clergymen and teachers of religion.

But there was need for a specific group of ministers, of Christians whose vocations labeled them as such. From that awareness there grew the Christian Council on Palestine in 1942-43. The urgency of the times, when the first reports of Hitler's destruction of European Jewry began to trickle through from Nazi-occupied lands, impelled men like Stephen S. Wise, a leading Zionist and foremost rabbi, to join with his younger colleagues, Rabbis Milton Steinberg and Philip S. Bernstein, to offer aid from the Emergency Committee for Zionist Affairs and enlist the support of such outstanding Protestant leaders as Henry A. Atkinson, secretary-general of the Church Peace Union and the World

Alliance for International Friendship Through the Churches, Daniel
A. Poling, editor of the *Christian Herald,* and Reinhold Niebuhr and
Paul Tillich of Union Theological Seminary.[4]

As chairman *pro tem* and later the elected chairman of the Christian
Council on Palestine, Henry Atkinson convened a meeting at the
Hotel Pennsylvania in New York City and made clear the motivating
conviction: "The destiny of the Jews is a matter of immediate concern
to the Christian conscience, the amelioration of their lot a duty that
rests upon all who profess Christian principles."

A large, genuinely concerned group attended and heard addresses
by Professor S. Ralph Harlow, formerly a missionary in the Middle
East and a convinced pro-Zionist, at this time a well-known faculty
member at Smith College; the widely hailed social liberal, Methodist
Bishop Francis J. McConnell; the world renowned archaelogist,
William Foxwell Albright (who was prevented from attending because
of illness in his family but who sent a message of support); Mrs. Inez
Lowdermilk, wife of Walter Clay Lowdermilk, the world's authority on
Palestine's "absorptive capacity"; the great Stephen S. Wise; and,
outstanding among them all, Reinhold Niebuhr, the preeminent
theologian in Protestantism. On that occasion, as in many earlier
instances and throughout the remaining 29 years of his life, Niebuhr's
word on Zionism, Jewry, and Judaism was forthright and sane.

The previous winter Niebuhr had published two scintillating articles in the *Nation* on "Jews After the War,"[5] in which with logic and
emotional power he had argued for a two-fold emphasis: first, Jews
should be guaranteed the right to migrate to any land upon the face of
the earth, especially since they had been deprived of rights in so many
lands and suffered persecution and expulsion through the centuries;
and secondly, they should be granted a national homeland, preferably
Palestine because of their historic tie to the land and the internationally
assumed obligations in recent decades on behalf of Zionist pleas, made
all the more urgent by the persecution of Jews under the Nazis and the
threat then being carried out to "solve the Jewish problem" by wiping
them from the human race, "a final solution."

With these thoughts, widely publicized by both the *Nation,* then a
magazine of considerable prestige, and a reprint of the articles in the
tens of thousands under the imprint of the American Palestine Committee, Niebuhr built another structure, namely, that of "The Jewish
State and the Arab World." He faced the realistic threat of Arab

hostility by asserting: "It is quite apparent that the formation of a Jewish state in Palestine cannot be achieved by the simple consent of the Arab world," because "no solution acceptable to the Arabs will give such a state any realy integrity." In response to those who accepted the Ichud/Judah Magnes/Martin Buber formula of a bi-national state, he contended that "an Arab-Jewish federation in Palestine would certainly not solve the problem, for it would merely perpetuate animosities into the indefinite future."[6]

He had no illusions about the ease with which the solution was to be achieved:

> Those who believe in the justice of the Jewish claims to Palestine are persuaded primarily by the desperate necessity of the Jews for a homeland and the comparative justice of their claim to Palestine in terms of ancient and historic considerations. With these claims the actual present possession of the disputed territory by the Arabs is in conflict. It is not pretended that there can be a simply "just" solution of such a conflict, when competing claims move on such various levels.

Neibuhr was, however, more practical and, yet at the same time, more prescient than the other speakers, for on that December 14, 1942, he was able to discern the future and foresee what had to be accomplished:

> It is, however, possible in such a circumstance to satisfy the Jewish claims essentially under the compulsion of their great need; and to seek compensation for the Arabs by a total settlement of Near Eastern claims. The Arabs will not have made any substantial contribution to the defeat of the Axis if and when it occurs. It would, however, be a wise statesmanship to allow the Arab world to be federated and to give it this higher unity in compensation for its loss of rights in Palestine.

Anticipating what might ensue in the 1950s, 1960s, and 1970s, Niebuhr went on to say:

> Such a *quid pro quo* would have to involve a genuine disavowal of sovereignty over a sufficient part of Palestine to permit a Jewish state to be established which would have territorial integrity, political independence within the framework of a commonwealth of nations,

and the means of economic survival. It would also demand a genuine improvement of the Arab situation in terms of a greater unity and independence of that world.

He warned, however, that "the settlement would require some rigorous self-abnegation on the part of the Great Powers" and admonished: "They will have to cease the policy of establishing particular zones of influence in this or that Arab state and develop a larger policy of mutual security."

Fully aware of the fact that British power in that region was "embarrassed with the problem of the relation of the Arab to the whole Moslem world, . . . [an] embarrassment for Britain [which] has undoubtedly made the solution of the Palestinian problem more difficult than some of Britain's critics have been willing to admit . . ." and that "French imperial claims [in the area], which have no reality in power or in justice . . . [must undergo an] abridgement of imperial rights wherever they come in conflict with the necessity of an overall settlement of the vexing Jewish-Arab problem and the Jewish-world problem," Niebuhr had a word of advice for his own government:

> There is no reason, however, why America should mold its policy according to such embarrassments or according to French imperial claims. . . . American arms [due to the invasion of North Africa by United Nations forces, primarily American, the previous month] have brought us into a dominant position in that very portion of the world where this issue must be solved. It would be ridiculous ot use our power merely to underwrite the past when we have a chance to underwrite the future and to help in granting justice to a people who have been the first, and most cruelly used, of Hitler's victims.

Although Niebuhr was to be chosen treasurer of the Christian Council on Palestine that very day and began to assume a major role in formulating decisions among Christians of Zionist sympathies, this kind of *Realpolitik* did not become an integral part of the approach the organization was to take in the following years. On the contrary, more simplistic, elementary approaches were characteristic of the CCP and ultimately of the American Christian Palestine Committee, when the APC and CCP united forces, partially in 1944 and fully in 1946. This less complex outlook was reflected in three of the leading Christians committed to Zionist goals but who steered clear of such tortuous, yet rigorously honest and realistic thinking—Henry Atkinson, Walter Clay Lowdermilk, and Eduard Lindeman.

Atkinson, originally a Methodist but ordained a Congregationalist, was a product of the Social Gospel in American Protestantism. He pioneered in the founding in 1910 of the Department of Church and Labor, later to become the Social Service Commission, and the Department of Social Relations of the Congregational churches, and then the Council for Social Action, a model for many other denominations. In 1919, he became secretary-general of the Church Peace Union, a Carnegie-funded interfaith organization bent on world organization and international peace. Atkinson spent much of the year in Geneva, Switzerland, working with the League of Nations Secretariat and the International Labor Office, cooperating with Protestant leaders in the early days of the ecumenical movement, and traveling to many parts of the world. On close terms of friendship with such international leaders as Raymond Fosdick, Sir Eric Drummond, Field Marshal Jan Christiaan Smuts, and Lord Robert Cecil, he firmly believed in the League's intentions with reference to the Balfour Declaration and its assignment of the Palestine Mandate to Great Britain.

Foremost in his makeup was a strong religious belief in the cause of Zionism, so basic that he always said, "I had imbibed my Zionism with my mother's milk, and she fortified it with teachings from the Bible." Thus when Wise, Bernstein, and Steinberg asked him to organize the Christian Council on Palestine, he greeted them as fellow-clergymen and fellow-Zionists, energetically getting the Council under way but naively believing a letter-head organization would swiftly achieve the objective.

When he brought me from my pastorate in Pittsburgh, Pennsylvania in the winter of 1942-3 to serve as executive secretary on a half-time basis, spending the other half of the time at the post of extension secretary of the Church Peace Union and the World Alliance for International Friendship Through the Churches, he advised me, "You'll soon be devoting all your time to the CPU and the World Alliance, for this Palestine stint will be a short term job. As soon as the British see that list of men on our stationery—Niebuhr, Tillich, McConnell, Albright, Sockman, and Poling—they'll open the gates of Palestine and let those Jewish refugees come pouring in. Then we'll disband the committee. It's as simple as that." Shortly before his death in 1960, I reminded him of that prediction; and he ruefully confessed, "How wrong I was, how very wrong."

There was about Atkinson on openness of mind, a heartiness of manner, a down-to-earth quality, all redolent of the open spaces of the

West whence he had come; he was always something of the pioneer, not only in social action and the ecumenical movement, but also in the struggle against fascism, especially, however, in the battle against American isolationism, from the days when Woodrow Wilson went down to defeat at the hands of "a little group of willful men" until the attack on Pearl Harbor, and in the fight against anti-Semitism and in his life-long espousal of a Zionist solution.

The indomitable, crusading spirit emerged dramatically one day in February 1944, when he appeared in Washington before the Committee on Foreign Affairs of the House of Representatives on behalf of a House Resolution supporting a Jewish national home in Palestine. He defined the Christian Council on Palestine, which he represented, as having been founded "for the purpose of bringing to the American people through Christian leadership and membership of churches the conviction that in the post-war settlement Palestine should be made accessible to Jewish refugees from lands of persecution and that the ultimate destiny of the Jews depends upon the reaffirmation and fulfillment of the Balfour Declaration."

He summed up the basic religious conviction of the CCP by asserting:

> We have had our consciences hurt by the recognition that it is only in so-called Christian lands where things like that which happened in Germany could start. Outside of places where there are Christians, the less Christian they are, the more liberty there is for the Jewish people apparently; and we feel the time has come when we ought to face up to the responsibility and recognize that there's hardly a Jewish problem in the world, but there is a very serious Christian problem that we have to face.
>
> We believe that this problem is basically a Christian problem, and thus we appeal on behalf of our members and the people in their churches. We are convinced that the open door of a strongly established and recognized Jewish homeland in Palestine offers the only real hope for most of these suffering men, women, and children, who today linger in misery and ignominy under the heel of Hitler.

In words which visibly moved the members of the House Committee and did not leave untouched anyone present that morning in Washington, he concluded with this plea:

> I firmly believe . . . that Palestine is not only a means of salvation for the Jewish people, but in a larger sense is also a means of safeguarding

our democracy. . . . The attack on the Jews was the entering wedge by which the liberties of all the free people in all the nations were attacked, and the Jew was attacked because he was the most vulnerable in Germany at the time.

Therefore, Mr. Chairman, ladies and gentlemen of the Committee, in the name of humanity and in the name of justice, I strongly urge the passage of these resolutions [Nos. 418, 419—Wright-Compton] in order that we may begin the establishment of a just and durable peace by affirming rather than denouncing and nullifying the Balfour Declaration, the best and most constructive single document that emerged from World War I.[7]

More soft-spoken, yet equally rugged in physique and strong of character, was Walter Clay Lowdermilk, who suddenly sprang into fame in March of 1944 with the publication of a new book, *Palestine: Land of Promise.* A nationwide gathering of the American Palestine Committee and the Christian Council on Palestine, in cooperation with the Free World Association, the Union for Democratic action [later known as Americans for Democratic Action], the American Federation of Labor, the Congress of Industrial Organizations, and several other organizations, met in Washington to unify Christian and other non-Jewish sentiment on behalf of the rescue of Jews from Hitler's Europe and the rebuilding of Palestine as a Jewish national home. On that day a copy of Lowdermilk's *Palestine: Land of Promise* (1944) was given to each of the thousand delegates. The book, a lucid, scientific treatment of Palestine's potential to settle several million people on its once rich but now parched earth, had been long in the making; but now the copious prose had been edited to readable proportions. It presented a message of hope for Jewish pioneers and gave the lie to those who said the "tiny notch of land" (Lord Balfour's words) was "not big enough to swing a cat around in" (Lord Passfield's phrase).

Lowdermilk, a conservation specialist with the Department of Agriculture, had visited Palestine for the first time in 1939 on his return to the United States from China. Fired by what he saw, he declared in speeches and articles that "the Jews of Palestine have done the finest reclamation of old land I have seen on four continents. Theirs is the most successful rehabilitation of land and people in modern times."[8]

When he wanted to tell the story in a longer exposition and perhaps publish it, the British Mandatory officials tried to dissuade him and brought pressure to bear on their American friends to discourage

Lowdermilk from the idea of a book on the subject; the American State Department heeded their British colleagues' entreaties and tried, though unsuccessfully, to head Lowdermilk in other directions. Justice Louis Brandeis, still alive when Lowdermilk began putting his prolix sentences on paper, urged him on; and when, several years after Brandeis's death, the book was published, Lowdermilk traced the basic inspiration to the great jurist. Ultimately it went into fourteen printings and was reissued in paperback editions with translations into six languages.

One of the concepts in *Palestine: Land of Promise* was the National Water Carrier Project of Israel which was later begun by Lowdermilk in 1951. It was carried to completion within five years with such success that the Haifa Technion founded in his honor the Lowdermilk School of Agricultural Engineering, a thriving institution of which he was the first director.

An unfinished project of Lowdermilk's is the Jordan Valley Authority by which he hoped—and his disciples still hope, not without reason—to harness hydroelectric power by the 2400 foot drop between the Mediterranean Sea and the Dead Sea.

When Lowdermilk, aided by his indefatigable wife, Inez, spoke in forums and conferences of the American Palestine Committee and the Christian Council on Palestine, as well as to innumerable Zionist groups, audiences were impressed by their mystic love of the Land of the People and the Land of the Book. Everyone, Jew and non-Jew alike, could not help being stirred by Lowdermilk's oft-repeated statement: "If Moses had foreseen the destruction mankind would bring upon the world, he would have added an Eleventh Commandment dealing with man's responsibility to the Holy Earth." That Eleventh Commandment, engraved on a tablet which graces a wall in the Haifa Technion, reflects Lowdermilk's Christian concern for Israel:

> Thou shalt inherit the Holy Earth as a faithful steward, conserving its productivity and resources from generation to generation. Thou shalt safeguard they fields from soil erosion, thy living waters from drying up, thy forests from desolation, and protect the hills from over-grazing by thy herds, that thy descendants may have abundance forever. If any shall fail in this good stewardship of the earth, thy fruitful fields shall become sterile, stony ground or wasting gullies, and thy descendants shall decrease and live in poverty, or perish from off the face of the earth.[9]

Quite different from Atkinson and Lowdermilk was the celebrated authority on mass psychology and both urban and rural sociology, the widely hailed "father of adult education in America," Eduard Lindeman of the New York School of Social Work. As deeply religious as they, though a humanist/naturalist/non-theist, Lindeman was an immigrant who had endured hardship in his youth and attained his education only in later years. His sympathy with the Jews and the problems of homelessness sprang from his own origins, his fight for identity and survival in earlier decades of a distinguished career. When he spoke at an APC/CCP conference in Philadelphia in the autumn of 1944, he gave as his topic, "Palestine: Test of Democracy," and noted that he was "a fairly recent convert to the idea of a Jewish state, having resisted the appeal of this movement for a great many years."

Lindeman had not "forsaken the idea that democratic strength comes from diversity, not from uniformity," but had "finally come to see that democracy cannot fully succeed unless there is a Jewish state." Then he proceeded in this address, delivered all over America, to list his reasons "why non-Jews should be heartily and thoroughly in favor of building up a strong Jewish state:"

In the first place: there is a moral issue involved — a multi-faceted promise to be kept, . . . an historic promise in the spirit, the hearts, and the minds of Jews, and it will not die; a promise internationally, . . . the Balfour Declaration,. . . . and . . . Mr. Woodrow Wilson assented . . . and a resolution in Congress in 1922, . . . stating we were committed. . . .

Second: . . . I want to bring dignity to all Jews everywhere. I believe that Jews all over the world will walk straighter and that all the furtiveness imposed upon them by their dispersion will disappear once there is a place which will ultimately be not merely an autonomous state but a sovereign state, with all the rights and privileges of sovereignty, brought into existence, managed, and supported by the genius and the labor of Jews . . . They must cease to be the only homeless people on earth.

Third: . . . I believe that the Jewish homeland should be established now, before the War is over, . . . in order to provide a solution for the very large group of Jews among the so-called uprooted people of Europe.

Fourth: A Jewish homeland . . . will help solve the entire problem of minorities. If the Jewish minority can solve its difficulties, then all the other minorities will take hope and learn the methods, devices and

techniques which have helped solve the Jewish question. If the
Jewish question remains unsolved, then the status of all minority
groups will continue to worsen. . . .

Fifth: The minority question is no longer purely European as it was
after the last war. It is now an American disease, too, and we must
help the rest of the world to solve this problem if we wish to avoid in
this country the same kind of trouble which has bedeviled Europe for
the last eighty to ninety years. . . . I feel we can no longer assume that
there cannot be a strong, anti-Jewish movement in this country. It
could be ignited very easily among . . . fifteen million so-called
"Christians." It is therefore for our own sakes as Americans that we
must help to solve the Jewish problem.

Sixth: A Jewish National Homeland will not only bring dignity to
Jews, but remove from non-Jews the stigma of anti-Semitism. Unless
we are rid of that stigma, it seems to me we can become neither
Christian nor democratic.

Seventh: I am in favor of a Jewish Palestine because I believe that only
with its aid can the Near East be developed and enabled to support a
huge population. . . . The energy, skill, and devotion which young
Jews have brought to the building of Palestine demonstrate how the
whole Middle East can be expanded.

Eighth: Palestine is already a going concern. Why should we turn our
backs on something which has been so successful that within the
years of turmoil, when great capitalistic societies like England and
the United States were almost having their death trial and suffering
an unprecedented depression, Jews were building a new economic
society upon new cooperative principles? Palestine is a pragmatic
success, with an investment of a half billion dollars, a growing population, increased health, increased welfare, even for the Arabs, rising
standards of education, culture, art. I do not think it is too much to say
that there is no other example in modern history of a state building
itself, lifting itself by its own bootstraps and building itself out of its
human energy. There is no epic in modern history so magnificent as
this Palestine experiment. . . .

Finally: The Palestine question is the acid test of democracy. . . . the
acid test of the peace. A peace which leaves the Jewish question
unresolved, will leave us who believe in democracy vulnerable to all
the future Hitlers, all the malcontents, who will use this historic
scapegoat to build up their nefarious movements. If we should enter
into such a peace as leaves no room for the solution of the problem of
which Palestine is the symbol, then there will be no peace.[10]

The Niebuhr emphases were not without meaning for the Christian Council on Palestine and its sister organization, the American Palestine Committee; but these organizations' basic *leitmotif* was that of the Atkinson/Lowdermilk/Lindeman view, namely, the Christian conscience which had been touched and was now aroused, the love of the Land and its sacred, responsive soil, and an awareness of what tiny Palestine meant to the democratic world and its democratic ethos, especially in terms of the future of the Jewish people and the awakening of the entire Middle East.

The year 1944 meant a broadening of the program of the APC and the CCP, brought about by the advent of Howard Marion LeSourd who combined the efforts of both groups; he, on a fulltime basis, and I, on a part-time arrangement with the Church Peace Union and the World Alliance, served as co-directors. Seminars and conferences in cities throughout the country were planned. A speakers' bureau, Club Program Service, was organized, thus making it possible for service clubs, church groups, community forums, and university convocations to secure knowledgeable, able speakers such as Helen Gehagan Douglas, Eleanor Roosevelt, Welthy Honsinger Fisher (widow of Gandhi's friend, Bishop Fred Fisher), Lucille LeSourd, George Fielding Eliot, Wendell Phillips, Frank Gervasi, Carl J. Friedrich, Edgar Ansel Mowrer, and Charles Turck.

Literature, especially the publication, *Palestine* (issued by the American Zionist Emergency Council, through which the APC and the CCP were financially supported), and such books as Lowdermilk's *Palestine: Land of Promise*, Frank Gervasi's *To Whom Palestine?*, Ellen Thorbecke's picture-and-text book on *Palestine: Land of Miracles*, Carl Friedrich's *American Foreign Policy and Palestine*, and my own *Answers on the Palestine Question* (issued in continually updated versions) were all widely distributed, especially to the now several thousand members of both organizations and to libraries throughout the land.[11]

LeSourd, a well-known clergyman and educator, was available for the director's post because war-time mobilization had shrunk the graduate student body at Boston University where he had been dean of the Graduate School. He brought both imagination and experience to the position and launched many new projects, not the least of which was an attempt to form a World Committee on Palestine.

Quotations from two letters, one in May 1945, and the other in mid-summer of that year, give some indication of the breadth and depth of the ACPC's program at the time. Immediately after the Allied forces' victory had been achieved in Europe, we joined with Helen Gehagan Douglas, congresswoman from California and national secretary of the ACPC, in sending a letter to every member of the United States Senate and House of Representatives:

> The American Christian Palestine Committee, expressing widespread Christian conviction, believes that every effort must be made now to fulfill the international promises made to the Jews concerning their national homeland in Palestine.
> The Nazi regime in the course of its monstrous campaign of systematic murder and torture has almost annihilated the Jewish communities of Europe; and for millions of Jews, the end of the war in Europe comes too late. Horrible disclosures concerning the Buchenwald, Maidenek, Oswiecim, and other prison and concentration camps have shocked the civilized world. Hitler waged his war against the helpless Jews of Europe with a barbarity and determination which we in this country have only now begun to realize. At this moment we must do all we can to insure justice to the remnant of European Jewry and make impossible a repetition of this tragedy. Therefore we are asking you and the other members of the Senate to sign the enclosed letter addressed to President Truman as a current reiteration of our traditional national policy. The party platforms of both Republicans and Democrats affirm their support of the opening of Palestine to unrestricted Jewish immigration and colonization so that in accordance with the full intent and purpose of the Balfour Declaration, Palestine may be constituted as a free and democratic Jewish Commonwealth.

The results were gratifying, and there emerged a wave of support which was as overwhelming as it was surprising. There is no question about the influence this had on the White House and President Truman's slowly growing interest in and sympathy for the restoration of a Jewish national home.

The other letter, dated July 30, 1945, reflected something of the hope and relief of V-E Day and foreshadowed the dramatic events of the following three years in which the activities, limned in these paragraphs, came to fulfillment; for Howard LeSourd and I had high hopes, many of which eventually achieved reality:

By the time this letter reaches you, we will have traveled to England by plane. Our trip is at the invitation of Sir Wyndham Deedes, chairman of the British Association for a Jewish National Homeland, and Mr. David Ben-Gurion, chairman of the Jewish Agency for Palestine. We have been asked to attend, as observers, the World Zionist Conference in London at the end of July.

Then we outlined our plans for regional conferences in the coming months; told of the Memorial Sunday in May 1945, we had chosen to commemorate the loss of six million Jews at the hands of the Nazis and the hope we expressed that each year there would be some kind of remembrance; described the National Seminar held in early July at the Princeton Inn, with countrywide representation and a roster of resource persons including Carl J. Friedrich, Reinhold Niebuhr, Eduard C. Lindeman, Edgar Ansel Mowrer, and David Ben-Gurion; noted the nationwide radio program we sponsored with the aid of Morton Wishengrad as writer and Paul Muni as star actor; mentioned our sending to President Truman a petition with the signatures of 39 governors gathered at a Mackinac Island conference which asked for "the opening of Palestine to unrestricted Jewish immigration and the land's transformation into a Jewish commonwealth," the resolutions of 33 state legislatures seeking the same objectives, and a letter Senator Robert Wagner brought to President Truman with the signatures of 54 Senators and 256 Representatives (which had indeed been "as overwhelming as it was surprising"); told of a significant meeting held with "leading religious editors [all Protestants but no Roman Catholics], where plans were discussed by which the weekly and monthly magazines reaching the constituency of our Christian churches could be covered more effectively, . . . particularly through a news service with material on Palestine and the present need of the Jewish people"; spoke of the ever growing work of the speakers' bureau, Club Program Service; and then mentioned the most important project of the ACPC:

The prime purpose of our visit to Great Britain is to discuss with Sir Wyndham Deedes the possibility of holding an International Christian Conference in Washington, D.C. next November. There are more than a score of pro-Palestine committees throughout the world—a dozen in the Western Hemisphere, several on the European Continent, and a half dozen in Great Britain and the Dominions, all of which are in basic accord with the principles of the

American Christian Palestine Committee and seek, as do we, to
mobilize Christian opinion on behalf of Jewish aims and hopes in
Palestine. We shall be able to discuss this project more intelligently
and specifically . . . after our return from the British Isles.[12]

From that time on for the next thirty-three and one-half months,
until mid-May of 1948 when Israel was proclaimed an independent
Jewish commonwealth, the activities followed that pattern, all at a
whirlwind pace. The seminars, meetings, petitions, and conferences,
especially the World Conference, held in Washington that November
of 1945 as planned, brought a mounting pressure to bear on Washington and London and on the United Nations at Lake Success.[13]

The 1946 testimony of Reinhold Niebuhr before the Anglo-
American Committee of Inquiry on Palestine served, according to
Richard H. S. Crossman, a British member of the Committee,[14] to
clarify the group's mind and set the members thinking along pro-
Zionist directions. Likewise, the documents presented by the ACPC
to the United Nations Special Committee on Palestine in early 1947
were not without influence, especially because now there was a flood-
tide of protest against Jewish national homelessness and on behalf of
the partition of Palestine as proposed by UNSCOP's findings and as
voted by the General Assembly on November 29, 1947.

Before and after the partition vote by the United Nations, the
American Christian Palestine Committee found itself linked with do-
zens of organizations, Jewish and non-Jewish, pressing for the adoption
of the UNSCOP plan, and then for its swift, effective implementation.
No longer did the ACPC feel itself to be something of a voice crying in
the wilderness. On the contrary, there was now a host of groups,
among which was the influential World Christian Committee for Palestine, speaking out on behalf of what was to become a strong and vibrant
new country, the State of Israel.

The American Christian Palestine Committee continued for another
thirteen years of strong and meaningful programs, interpreting the
new Jewish state to the Christian community, and then dissolving its
status, firm in the knowledge it had known an heroic, unique hour in
the history of the world.

There were, however, grave limitations in the program of the
American Christian Palestine Committee, not the least of which were
the ad hoc nature of the Committee from its very start and the lack of an
informed, concerned constituency on which to draw. Only the griev-

ous crisis of World War Two and the increasingly credible reports of Hitler's annihilation of European Jewry finally galvanized some—all too few—Christians into action. Even when the political stakes became increasingly visible and it was clear that a strong, knowledgeable Christian voice was the necessary ingredient for any kind of solution, a man as courageous and forthright as Henry A. Atkinson insisted on caution, a muted protest, the blunted criticism. During 1946 and 1947, Reinhold Niebuhr frequently expressed anxiety about too harsh an indictment of Great Britain for her failure to administer the Mandate in such a way that Jews might be rescued and the foundations for a Jewish state laid forthwith.

It was difficult to structure a definite, consistent program, except to stir public opinion and carry on as broad and specific an educational project as possible, especially through pamphlets and booklets, radio debates and public forums. We had to rely on letters-to-the-editor and petitions to Congress, protests to the State Department and pressure on the American delegation to the United Nations, especially in the final months from the August 1947 report of the Special Committee on Palestine through the adoption of partition by the General Assembly in late November 1947, on to the incredible reconstitution of the Third Jewish Commonwealth on May 14, 1948. Christians did play a part but not as significantly or as definitively as they should have. They had been conditioned against such action by centuries of deeply ingrained anti-Semitism, conditioning which could not be undone in a few short months or even years.

The American Christian Palestine Committee had all the assets of "a good cause," namely, an urgency and a righteous objective, an elemental justice to secure and a concrete objective to attain, a Christian ethic to hold as its standard and a sensitized conscience to be its guide. But it also had liabilities: a lack of ample funds (although the American Zionist Emergency Council, representing the major Zionist groups among Jews on the American scene, rendered support as generously as possible),[15] a lack of sufficient time in such a crisis to work out a long-term, carefully defined strategy over many years, and an insufficiently "briefed" constituency, for while many Christians "cared," there were not enough of them. Even these few knew precious little of the historical background and even less of the complex circumstances in the Middle East and its power struggles, especially in the latter days of two expiring empires, the British and the French, and the rise to heady power by two imperial giants, the Soviet Union and the United States.

Sudden decisions were often inadequately considered, then ineptly executed. Pronouncements, solemnly, often ardently made in the heat of controversy, appeared later to have been hyper-emotional and ill-conceived. Enthusiastic adherent to the cause turned out in many instances to be fainthearted and, at times, cowardly. Officers of the Committee, working on a voluntary, unpaid, genuinely committed but nevertheless distracted basis, were not always available for consultation and decisions. The organization inevitably suffered from the lag between an urgent need for a statement or an action, on the one hand, and the difficulties, on the other, of formulating carefully reasoned announcements and attaining chosen objectives. This was essentially a propaganda war from beginning to end, a tragic beginning with Hitler's sworn intention to wipe out all the Jews in the world, and a triumphant end, Israel's establishment and the rescue of the remnant of European Jewry.

The greatest problem among Christians lay in their unwillingness, perhaps their inability, to commit themselves to this cause amid so many confused and confusing issues. Indecision and inaction seemed the easiest way out of a dilemma. Most disturbing was the average Christian's willingness to listen to the anti-Zionist diatribes of denominational officials, especially missionaries, who looked askance at Zionism and listened uncritically to Arabists in the U.S. State Department.

Despite the uncertainty and timidity of many Christians, however, there was indeed a Christian voice; and it was expressed, though imperfectly and often ineffectually, by the American Christian Palestine Committee. The founders and the leaders were prophetic—that is, in the ancient meaning of that word, they "spoke for God"—but one is compelled to echo Moses: "Would to God that all His people were prophets"!

FOOTNOTES

1. *Encyclopedia of Zionism and Israel*, 1:34-36; 1155; files on "American Palestine Commit-tee," "Christian Council on Palestine," and "American Christian Palestine Committee" are to be found in the Zionist Archives and Library, New York; also Emanuel Neumann *In the Arena: An Autobiographical Memoir* by (New York, 1976), *passim*.

2. Carl Hermann Voss, *The Palestine Problem Today: Israel and Its Neighbors* (Boston, 1953), p. 11.

3. Neumann, *In the Arena*, pp. 172-73. A full page advertisement in the *New York Times*, Friday, December 31, 1943, lists not only Robert Wagner as chairman and Charles McNary as co-chairman, but also includes an executive committee, consisting of Claude Pepper, U.S. senator from Florida, Eric A. Johnston, president of the U.S. Chamber of Commerce, Arthur H. Vandenberg, U.S. senator from Michigan, Philip Murray, president of the CIO (Congress of Industrial Organizations), William Green, president of the AFL (American Federation of Labor), William H. King, U.S. senator from Utah, Msgr. John Ryan, executive vice-president of the National Catholic Welfare Conference, and Elbert Thomas, U.S. senator from Utah. See also Hertzel Fishman, *American Protestantism and a Jewish State*, (Detroit, 1973), *passim*.

4. Archives of Christian Council on Palestine, Zionist Archives and Library.

5. *Nation* 154 (February 21 and 28, 1942): 214-16, 253-55.

6. Reinhold Niebuhr, "The Jewish State and the Arab World," a paper read on December 14, 1942 at conference of Christian clergy at which the Christian Council on Palestine was founded; available in *précis* in files of American Emergency Committee for Zionist Affairs, Zionist Archives and Library, also in Abba Hillel Silver Archives, Temple Tifereth Israel, Cleveland, Ohio.

7. Atkinson concluded his remarks by saying: "We are horrified by the indescribable brutality of Hitler and his oppressors, and conscious of the tragic plight of millions of Jews in Europe today. We urge that the United States Government help provide appropriate measures to the end that the doors of Palestine be opened for further entry of homeless, stateless Jews of war-torn Europe. We urge that there be full opportunity for colonization in Palestine so that the Jewish people may reconstitute that country as a free and democratic Jewish commonwealth." *Hearings Before the Committee on Foreign Affairs, House of Representatives, Seventy-Eighth Congress, Second Session on H. Res. 418 and H. Res. 419, Resolutions Relative to the Jewish National Home in Palestine, February 8, 9, 15, and 16, 1944, etc.*

8. Quoted in Emma Kimor, "Walter Clay Lowdermilk—Pioneer Environmentalist: A Man Who Cared For the Earth," in *Jerusalem Post*, March 24, 1976.

9. *Ibid.*; also quoted in Inez Lowdermilk, *Modern Israel: Fulfillment of Prophecy—A Christian Speaks Out*, published by the California Christian Committee for Israel [1975 or 1976]. The obstacles Lowdermilk encountered and then overcame in publishing *Palestine: Land of Promise* are described in an 800-page unpublished autobiographical manuscript which is available in the National and University Library of the Hebrew University, Jerusalem, Israel, and the Library of the Haifa Technion in Haifa, Israel.

10. Dr. Eduard C. Lindeman, "Palestine: Test of Democracy," was published by Christian Council on Palestine and American Christian Palestine Committee, 1945.

11. The later (1950-59) publication of the American Christian Palestine Committee, *Land Reborn*, edited by Karl Baehr (from 1947 the extension secretary of the ACPC) and myself, had not yet begun publication. The pamphlet/booklet, *Answers on the Palestine Question*, was thoroughly revised and rewritten in 1953 and published by the Beacon Press of Boston as *The Palestine Problem Today: Israel and Its Neighbors*. Other publications included "Addresses and Messages Delivered at the Second Annual Dinner of the American Palestine Committee" (1942), "Common Purpose of Civilized Mankind: Declaration by 68 Members of the Senate and 194 Members of the House . . . on the Occasion of the 25th Anniversary of the Balfour Declaration" (1942), "Congressional Leaders Petition Pres. Roosevelt For a Jewish Homeland in Palestine" (1943), "Memorandum On Rescue of Jews Submitted to the State Department by Christian Spokesmen" (1944), "United Nations and the Jewish National Home in Palestine" (1942), "Voice of Christian America: Proceedings of the National Conference on Palestine, Washington, D.C., March 9, 1944," "The Jewish Case: The Place of Palestine in the Solution of the Jewish Question" (1945), "Questions and Answers on Palestine" (1945), "To the American People" (1945), "A

Christian Point of View" (Presented to the Anglo-American Committee of Inquiry), 1946, "Benjamin Franklin on Palestine" (1946), "The Truth About Palestine" (1946), "The Arab War Effort" (1947), and "People Speak on Palestine" (1948).

12. Files of American Christian Palestine Committee, Zionist Archives and Library.

13. In his book, *Zionism at the UN: A Diary of the First Days*, (Philadelphia, 1976), Eliahu Elath, director of the Middle East division of the Jewish Agency's Political Department from 1934 to 1945, writes in his entry for June 1, 1945:

> I spent a large part of the evening with Dr. Henry Atkinson, who has returned to San Francisco [from his office at the Church Peace Union in New York City] as an adviser to the American delegation. He gave me a detailed picture of the American Christian Palestine Committee he heads. It was founded at the end of 1942, and is made up of Christians of all denominations. It has a membership of more than two thousand. One of the Committee's first moves was to declare its support for the Biltmore Program [ed. note: in so many words, no; but moving slowly toward this goal]. Atkinson expressed his satisfaction at the fact that among the founders of his committee are some of the most eminent Christian theologians: Reinhold Niebuhr, John Haynes Holmes, Paul Tillich, and Ralph Sockman. Most members are Protestant, but there are also Catholics, some of whom are well known, such as Msgr. John A. Ryan. Dr. Daniel Poling, editor of the *Christian Herald*, one of the most important and widely circulated Protestant periodicals, is an active member of the Committee (p. 234).

14. Richard H. S. Crossman, *Palestine Mission* (New York, 1947).

15. In an otherwise scholarly, readable book, Howard Sachar inexplicably and erroneously writes (*A History of Israel: From the Rise of Zionism to Our Time* [New York, 1976], p. 289) that the American Christian Palestine Committee was "a front group" through which the American Zionist Emergency Council "activated labor leaders, the press, and clergymen, etc., etc." It must be stated categorically the ACPC was anything but a "front." It was a cooperating organization, founded and fostered by leaders within the AZEC, but characterized by independent status and an independent mind which expressed itself in many unique ways. The story is much more complex, interesting, and full of creativity than Sachar allows himself to infer from the ACPC's history or to imply in his handful of words about its programs.

From Neutrality to Involvement: Zionists, non-Zionists and the Struggle for a Jewish State, 1945

by Menahem Kaufman
translated by Sidney Rosenfeld

In the year World War Two ended, important changes occurred in the attitudes of American non-Zionist organizations *vis-à-vis* the problem of the political future of Palestine, the result, in part, of many attempts over the years at a consensus between Zionists and non-Zionists. During the late 1920s, for example, both Dr. Chaim Weizmann, president of the World Zionist Organization, and Louis Marshall, president of the American Jewish Committee (A.J.C.), had tried to bridge the gap between Zionists and non-Zionists, and ultimately succeeded in founding the expanded Jewish Agency in 1929. During the 1930s however, the relationship deteriorated, and only the outbreak of World War Two prevented the formal dissolution of the expanded Jewish Agency. Renewed efforts which Weizmann and David Ben-Gurion made during 1941 and 1942 to arrive at a consensus with the A.J.C. on a minimal program concerning Eretz Yisrael came to nought. Judge Joseph M. Proskauer, elected president of the A.J.C. in 1943, opposed any negotiations in this matter, and when the American Jewish Conference adopted a pro-Zionist statement in 1943, the A.J.C. withdrew. Other "non-Zionist" groups, such as the fraternal order B'nai B'rith and the various organizations of Reform Judaism, stayed in the umbrella Conference, but the estrangement between the Zionist and pro-Zionist groups on the one hand and the non-Zionist groups on the other (especially the A.J.C. and the Jewish Labor Committee) became even deeper until a variety of events led to a closing of American Jewish ranks in 1945.

For many months during 1943 and 1944, the leaders of the A.J.C.

263

claimed that the demand to establish a Jewish Commonwealth immediately would undermine the Allied war effort. As the end of the war neared, however, this argument lost much of its relevance. One signal for the change came from Secretary of War Henry L. Stimson, who removed his objections to a pro-Zionist Congressional resolution in the fall of 1944. Judge Proskauer and his friends then understood that the time was not too distant when they would have to cope with the program of the Zionist movement as a whole, and that the future of Eretz Yisrael would be on that agenda. With the defeat of the Hitler regime, the future of those Jews who survived the Holocaust became a concrete problem for which no one could nor even wanted to avoid finding the best possible solution.

At the beginning of 1945, opinions were still divided. The Zionists kept trying to convince one and all that there was no separating the problems of European Jewry from the future of Palestine. The leaders of the A.J.C. agreed that these were indeed the principal problems, but were as yet unconvinced that these problems constituted one entity, that the solution of the future of the survivors of the Holocaust rested on the political future of Eretz Yisrael. Some of the leaders of the non-Zionist organizations still believed that in the new world order, the importance of national sovereignty as a shaper of a people's destiny would be lessened. It soon became clear, however, that the era of nationalism had not yet passed.

Until the fog which enveloped the Yalta, Potsdam and San Francisco conferences lifted, the leaders of the A.J.C. did not relent in their efforts to secure a legalistic framework in which the uprooted European refugees could be returned to their former homelands and integrated as free citizens in the different national societies of Europe—according to a blueprint which the A.J.C. committee for the Peace Plan had prepared during 1941-1944. From the support Proskauer and his friends gave to the Bill of Human Rights at San Francisco, it is easy to see their goal in this matter. A change took place only after it became apparent that the hopeless situation of the uprooted Jews had not changed; the non-Zionists then had to deal with the reality of a Europe quite different from the model of "Europe After the War" on which the Committee leaders had based their political activities for so long a time.

That change took place in 1945. At the beginning of that year Nahum Goldmann, on behalf of the Jewish Agency, suggested to the leaders of the Joint Distribution Committee that a co-sponsored committee be established in order to coordinate relief work in Europe. The Joint's leaders, however, were not yet ready to respond to this initiative, and rejected the proposal out of hand. Goldmann then suggested the participation of the World Jewish Congress, Higem, Ort, and Ose in addition to the "Joint" and the Jewish Agency in a coordinating committee. He also suggested that such a committee should deal with preparing young people in Europe for emigrating to Eretz Yisrael. He did not propose pooling the financial resources of the participating organizations, and organizational autonomy was assured to all. Committee decisions would not be decided by a majority vote but by general agreement. Goldmann wrote: "The committee, as contemplated, would be purely consultative in nature, and designed to introduce some order into a chaotic situation." Joseph C. Hyman, secretary of the "Joint" answered: "Our consistent policy has been not to associate the J.D.C. formally with any organization or committee of a political character or having political objectives."[1]

The "Joint" still saw "political" activity in training for *aliyah* to Eretz Yisrael, and it view the Jewish Agency as a political organization. It may also be that the heads of the "Joint" were afraid of the reaction of some of their non-Zionist benefactors, and therefore abstained. One should not simply equate the reaction of the leaders of the "Joint" with that of the other non-Zionist bodies, especially the A.J.C.[2] The leaders of the "Joint" certainly were not against any project in Palestine, but in their opinion the exposed political position of their organization obliged them to be extremely cautious regarding contacts with the Jewish Agency. It may also be that Hyman's definite refusal was influenced by the inclusion of the World Jewish Congress as an active partner in the coordinating committee. The relations between the Congress and the "Joint" had been tense for a long time.[3] Probably more important was the fear of a pro-Zionist obligation, and the experience of the American Jewish Conference in 1943, in which the non-Zionists had become an uninfluential minority, also had a negative impact.

In early 1945, Judge Proskauer notified Joseph C. Grew, the Acting Secretary of State, that the A.J.C. had not changed its position *vis-à-vis* the problem of Palestine since it had published its "Statement of Views" on January 31, 1943, in which it said: "Palestine although an important factor, cannot alone furnish and should not be expected to furnish the solution of the problem of post-war Jewish rehabilitation."

The Committee position remained that all who were uprooted in the storm of the war, Jews and non-Jews alike, should be allowed but not forced to return to their homes. As for the displaced persons who refused to resettle in Europe, among them displaced Jews, the A.J.C. suggested the problem could be solved by political means, by treaty and via international immigration authorities. In the opinion of the Committee, the Jewish problem needed special treatment only ". . . so far as necessary to meet their special situation." Palestine did not assume any unique position in the recommendations of the A.J.C. regarding displaced persons. The Committee, Proskauer told Grew, "continues to give the most serious study to the Palestine question in the light of changing conditions as they may develop, and from time to time may make such further recommendations as the Committee deem advisable." Eretz Yisrael still did not appear to the A.J.C. leadership as a preferred goal of emigration.[4]

At the time of the Nazi defeat, America's Jews still remained divided organizationally and without any agreed program of action to offer the Allies. This chaotic condition directly affected the demands which the Jews wanted to present to the United Nations Conference which would convene in San Francisco. In order to qualify for an invitation, Egypt and Syria had declared war on Germany on February 26, 1945; Lebanon had followed suit on February 27 and Saudi Arabia on March 1, the day the list of the nations invited was closed. No Jewish representatives were invited and the Zionist Emergency Council protested this omission on March 8, 1945, but to no avail. Yet the U.N. was to take over the responsibilities of the League of Nations and its authority in the sphere of mandated areas, and would therefore play a very important role in deciding the future of Palestine, then under the British Mandate. The Zionist movement and the pro-Zionist Jewish organizations recognized that any decisions reached by the U.N. on this subject would be crucial to their cause and to Jewish refugees in Europe.

Yet even regarding the importance of the San Francisco Conference for the Jewish people, there was a difference of opinion among the heads of the Jewish organizations. The leaders of the A.J.C. saw it primarily as an important international event and acted accordingly. Within the Executive of the Jewish Agency, different opinions existed, both as to the importance of the Conference and to the political hues of the representatives.[5] The Agency sent Eliahu Elath (then Epstein), Reuven Shiloach (then Zaslany) and the editor of the *Palestine Post*, Gershon Agron (then Agronsky) to San Francisco to add strength to the

Agency representatives in the United States, Nahum Goldmann and Louis Lipsky. Goldmann wanted a combined pro-Zionist group to appear in San Francisco, made up of the Jewish Agency, the World Jewish Congress, and the American Jewish Conference. David Ben-Gurion rejected that suggestion with the argument that "the Jewish Agency is a world institution and should not be in partnership with other bodies." He insisted that the Jewish Agency represented the Jewish People in all that concerned the future of Eretz Yisrael, but recognized that there was no chance that the San Francisco conference would grant formal representation to the Jewish People. In fact, the leaders of the Zionist Movement did not even possess any detailed information on what would take place there. Ben-Gurion and Moshe Sharett guessed correctly, however, that the political fate of Palestine would not be dealt with at San Francisco. Ben-Gurion opposed any discussion of an initiative by the Jewish Agency concerning the future of the British Mandate or the establishment of a trusteeship prior to the San Francisco Conference. He held that the Jewish Agency should plan to discuss only the establishment of an independent Jewish Commonwealth; since Britain and the Allies had not yet formulated their policies, it was better to wait. "If any change will be made which could harm our rights which were promised us in the Mandate," he argued, "we will have to oppose it. Later we will present our own demands."[6]

The delegation of the Jewish Agency appeared at the Conference as a group unto itself. Three other pro-Zionist groups arrived in San Francisco; the American Jewish Conference, the World Jewish Congress and the Board of Deputies of British Jews acted in concert. The American Jewish Conference had rejected the suggestion of Judge Proskauer that it establish a delegation in which the American Jewish Committee would participate; the 1943 walkout of the A.J.C. had not yet been forgotten. The American Jewish Conference, in which the American Zionists had overwhelming influence, assured itself a quasi-official position at San Francisco when the Secretary of State appointed its representatives as consultants to the American delegation, together with the representatives of 41 other organizations.[7] The A.J.C. also found it impossible to establish a united front with other anti-Zionist groups, such as the Jewish Labor Committee and Agudath Israel.

Prior to the San Francisco Conference, Maurice Karpf, who was still officially a member of the Jewish Agency Executive representing the non-Zionists, suggested to the A.J.C. that the time had come to renew the activity of the expanded Jewish Agency. He pointed out, that since the Jewish Agency was an institution which had gained international recognition, it would surely wish to strengthen its position and would need the support of the A.J.C. toward that end. That being the case, it would be a good opportunity for the non-Zionists to regain those privileges in the Jewish Agency which, in his opinion, had been stolen from them. Morris D. Waldman, who had been the executive vice-president of the A.J.C. for many years, also thought that the San Francisco Conference was a good occasion for arriving at a coordinated effort with the other Jewish organizations, but "on our terms".[8]

The position of the A.J.C. was expressed in a detailed memorandum handed to all the participating delegations. The central demand was an international Bill of Human Rights, with means to implement and enforce its provisions. The A.J.C. also demanded the abolition of all anti-Jewish Laws and discrimination against Jews in countries which had been under Nazi rule, the return of confiscated Jewish property and restitution to war victims. On the subject of Palestine, the A.J.C. directed the advocates of peace to the 1943 "Statement of Views," which contained a suggestion to establish an international trusteeship there. The immediate objective of the A.J.C. was the cancellation of the White Paper of 1939 as well as the abolition of limits on immigration which sentenced the Jews of the Yishuv to be a minority forever. As for an independent commonwealth, the American Jewish Committee still opposed the idea, and cited numerous Jewish leaders, including Chaim Weizmann, that a separate political state was unnecessary. Discussions of that subject should be postponed for a long time, perhaps for many years.[9]

Although the heads of the American Jewish Conference knew beforehand that the matter of the future of Palestine would not be discussed at San Francisco, they still submitted a memorandum in full support of the political demands of the Jewish Agency, stressing that the Agency should have full control over immigration into Palestine. In this matter the real difference between the approach of the A.J.C. and the position of the American Jewish Conference and its constituent organizations was revealed. The A.J.C. suggested the cancellation of the White Paper and the creation of possibilities of immigration under the inspection of a "trustee" appointed by the U.N. or the Great Powers. The American Jewish Conference demanded Jewish sovereignty. Together with its allied organizations, it also called for a bill of rights that was much more directed to the problems of anti-Semitism than the A.J.C. statement.[10]

The Jewish Labor Committee which had not arrived at an agreement with the A.J.C., submitted its own document. Regarding Palestine, it demanded unrestricted immigration and the abolition of the land sales laws, but no reference was made to the political future of the country. This omission stemmed from the divergent opinions within the J.L.C., especially from former Bundists. They in particular wanted the establishment of an international agency for the protection of the rights and had endorsed the idea of minority rights for the Jews of eastern Europe in 1919, but did not make such demands in 1945.

What eventually brought about a renewed closeness between the representatives of the Jewish Agency and the heads of non-Zionist organizations was their common interest in the future of the Holocaust survivors, an issue in which the Jewish Agency as a representative world body had a decided advantage over the different local organizations. At the San Francisco Conference, a partial reconciliation took place between the delegates of the Jewish Agency and the delegates of the non-Zionist organizations such as the A.J.C., the J.L.C. and the Agudath Yisrael of America, and new bonds were formed between them.

At the Conference itself two items were discussed which interested the Jewish organizations: the inclusion of the Rights of Man in the charter of the U.N., and the protection of the mandatory rights of the Jews in the *Yishuv*. Nahum Goldmann, in his report on the Conference, noted that: a) it was impossible to raise territorial questions, only to protect Zionist rights according to the Mandate; b) all the efforts of the Arabs to cancel these rights failed; c) the Jewish Agency was supported by all the Jewish organizations, including the A.J.C., with the exception of the Revisionists, who acted on their own; d) the membership of five Arab states in the U.N. made the matter of establishing a Jewish Commonwealth immediately vital.[12]

The fact that discussion on the topic of Palestine was limited prevented the differences of opinion among the various Jewish delegates from becoming public at San Francisco. The contradictions that were noticeable in the various memoranda did not appear on the agenda itself, thus lessening somewhat the damage that had been caused by the appearance of so many Jewish delegations.

The effort to assure the text of the Bill of Human Rights was crowned with only partial success. Proskauer made a concerted effort to win over most of the consultants, and managed to secure, within different paragraphs of the Charter, sentences referring to human rights. But the campaign to include an operative paragraph which would set forth procedures for implementing and enforcing human rights failed. The A.J.C. *Reporter* asked in its July 1945 issue: "Does San Francisco offer us more than words?"[13] The answer was neither clear nor final, but the A.J.C., which saw the struggle for the Bill of Human Rights as central to the success of the U.N., had its reservations. It may well be that this development contributed to the gradual change within the A.J.C. regarding the solution of the problems of the Jews in the European camps. Shortly afterwards, in fact, the heads of the Committee became convinced that the few sentences referring to human rights in the U.N. Charter were not about to solve the Jewish problem. Since the leaders of the A.J.C. remained at all times faithful to their principles to help Jews who were in trouble, they decided to seek alternative solutions. Proskauer's situation was somewhat similar to that of Louis Marshall. A generation earlier, Marshall had succeeded in getting textual assurances at the 1919 Paris Peace Conference guaranteeing the rights of the Jews as a national minority in eastern Europe, but had been disappointed in their implementation. He, too, had turned in other directions, eventually helping establish the expanded Jewish Agency in 1929.

The Arab delegations had tried at the San Francisco Conference to abolish the rights granted the Jewish People by the League of Nations Mandate. The fight against this plan was primarily preventive,[14] but the A.J.C. took an active part in it, despite the fact that there was no unified plan of action among the Jewish delegations. The representatives of the A.J.C. had been especially effective in using their special status as consultants to the American delegation. On May 4, 1945, Proskauer had personally informed Stettinius that the A.J.C. fully agreed with the American Jewish Conference that no action be initiated which would touch on the existing rights of the Jews in Palestine. During the San Francisco Conference, the A.J.C. as well as the J.L.C. had supported all the efforts of the Jewish Agency and the American Jewish Conference to prevent the abolition or limitation of the rights which the Mandate had granted the Jews.[15]

While it is true that Proskauer acted independently at San Francisco, he did meet frequently with the Jewish Agency delegates, and notified the delegates of other nations that the A.J.C. was opposed to the White Paper of 1939. Eliahu Elath reported on the activities of Judge Proskauer as follows: "He was also against any change in the status of the Palestine Mandate and anything included in it. In this question of principle there were no essential differences between the position of the Jewish Agency and that of the A.J.C. This fact is pregnant with great meaning. . . . The position of the A.J.C. demonstrated under those conditions the unity of the important Jewish organizations in the United States and thus added strength and prestige to the Zionist struggle in the eyes of the American delegation at the Conference of the United Nations."[16] It is also possible that Proskauer's stance influenced Harry S. Truman to reevaluate American Jewish public opinion during May and June 1945, since this was the first sign of a cooperative effort without any ideological consensus.

Proskauer, who had previously tried in November 1944 to find ways for cooperation with the Jewish Agency, now hinted to the Agency delegates that he was trying to differentiate between them and the American Zionist leaders, with whom he had serious disagreements. In his first meeting with Elath, he asked him: "Have the Zionists already managed to incite you against me?"[17] Proskauer tried to present the A.J.C. as neutral in political matters because of the heterogeneous make-up of its membership, despite the fact that the A.J.C. frequently put forth its positions couched in subjective and even ideological terms. Proskauer also informed Elath that there were no prospects of getting entry permits for Jewish refugees into the United States, which is why the A.J.C. had demanded the abolition of the British immigration policy.

The awareness that *proclamations* against the White Paper were not sufficient had begun to penetrate the mind of the A.J.C. leader. He had met with British delegates at San Francisco, and when they tried to switch the discussion to the topic of American immigration, he had countered that opening the gates of the United States for refugees was America's business, while opening Palestine was the duty of the government which ruled there, because of the obligations it had assumed under the Balfour Declaration and the Mandate.[18] This was a decided change in Proskauer's style, to direct his tough demands straight at the British delegates. On the other hand, he still demanded that the Zionist leadership not make it difficult for Britain by insisting on the Biltmore Program, which he considered an obstacle in the way of changing Britain's White Paper. Proskauer was still convinced that a Jewish State could not succeed, and continued to have sharp reservations about it in his discussions with the Zionists.

Other non-Zionist organizations were also present at San Francisco, and several underwent similar change of heart shortly after. B'nai B'rith was represented by its president, Henry Monsky, who had strong Zionist sympathies. He was part of the pro-Zionist American Jewish Conference delegation, and brought B'nai B'rith's prestige with him, yet without obligating either himself or the organization to launch any particular political activity.

The Reform organizations did not appear independently at San Francisco, but since they had not left the American Jewish Conference, they formed part of its delegation, while stressing the fact that they did not completely approve of its Palestine resolution. Monsky partly shared this reservation, and proclaimed at a press conference during the San Francisco Conference that several of the organizations linked to the American Jewish Conference did not assume any position on the matter of a Jewish Commonwealth, among them, the Union of American Hebrew Congregations (UAHC); they were, however, cooperating with the Conference in all the other areas of its activity relative to the future of the Jews after the war.[19]

Because of fear of the reaction of its anti-Zionist constituents, the Reform movement and its organizations continued to be neutral in this matter. The fact was made obvious at the 56th Convention of the Central Conference of American Rabbis (C.C.A.R.) at the end of June 1945, in which Abba Hillel Silver was elected president. The problem of Palestine was mentioned in the report of the Committee on Contemporaneous History, which recommended that a demand be made that the White Paper be abolished and that the gates of Palestine be opened to Jewish immigration. Rabbi Julian Morgenstern, a non-Zionist, remarked that there was no sense to send petitions to the British government, and that it would be better if the Convention decided to act together with other Jewish bodies in order to implement this demand. A motion, however, to present a unified program and to act cooperatively at the future conferences of the U. N. was voted down by the plenum.[20]   The outgoing president, Rabbi Solomon B. Freehof, did put a general and non-obligatory statement in his speech: "The rights of Israel in Palestine must not be diminished. They must be expanded and fulfilled." This however was his only reference to the topic of Eretz Yisrael in a speech which lasted over an hour. When he mentioned the struggle and the danger of dissension within the C.C.A.R. during the years 1942 and 1943 he declared: "What happened to our Conference was prophecy, a gloomy prophecy of what was going to happen in American Jewish life." In the fact that the C.C.A.R. had passed the crisis without a split, Rabbi Freehof hoped to see a sign of tendencies toward unity within the entire American Jewish Community. It is doubtful if Abba Hillel Silver, the president-elect of the C.C.A.R., would have been ready at that time to agree to such a sterile neutrality *vis-à-vis* the future of Palestine. However, when Silver served as president of the C.C.A.R., he also agreed to remove his organization from the political struggle, for he had no choice. Moreover, he decided that if the C.C.A.R. could not help in the Zionist political struggle, it was better that it did not harm that struggle.

To the credit of the American Jewish Committee, it did not retreat to a condition of sterile passivity; on the contrary, despite contradictions between its preconceptions and the realities, the A.J.C. continued its search for a solution to the problems of the refugee Jews, while trying to remain faithful to its principles. The heads of the A.J.C. still saw two separate issues in the refugee problem and the Palestine question, but in trying to deal with them on a practical level, they could not avoid a growing awareness that there could be no solution for the Displaced Persons without some solution of the Palestine question. With that awareness came signs of a changed attitude within the non-Zionist organizations, and especially in the A.J.C.

However, in its contacts with President Truman during the summer of 1945, the A.J.C. continued to follow its own political way without any direct contact or coordination with the Jewish Agency and other Zionist organizations. The Committee attempted to maintain the contacts it had formed during the Roosevelt administration and tried to establish similar bonds with Harry S. Truman. Before Truman left for the Potsdam Conference, Joseph Proskauer and Jacob Blaustein asked for an interview, but the meeting had to be postponed until September. In the memorandum which they sent to Truman, however, the many changes made in the draft indicated the changing attitude of the A.J.C. In the first draft prepared by staff members in June 1945, mention was made of the March 20, 1945 meeting between Roosevelt and the heads of the A.J.C. The draft quoted Roosevelt as saying that the time was inappropriate to agitate for a Jewish State, but that Britain should be asked to change her immigration policy. Judge Proskauer erased the remarks Roosevelt had made against the Zionist goals, and wrote to the new president that: "It is our considered judgment that while the population of Palestine remains two-thirds Arab, it is futile to raise this question of statehood, irrespective of its ultimate merits or demerits." In keeping with the political line which the A.J.C. had followed at the San Francisco Conference, President Truman was asked to seek assurances that the Jews of Europe, who had remained after so much suffering, could live in peace with their neighbors there. While Palestine could serve as a haven, the matter should not be confused "with the political aspirations of those who wish to see a Jewish state there created." For those Jews who wish to emigrate to Palestine they ought to be given the opportunity to create "a free and flourishing community within a democratic world." But Proskauer repeated to Truman that he and his Committee continued to opt for an international trusteeship plan.

From all the proposals of immigration which the A.J.C. studied to alleviate the problems of European Jews, the Palestine solution remained the only viable one. The heads of the A.J.C. recognized, after a short time, that "the immigration gates of all countries of the world are practically closed to Jews."[23] The recognition of Palestine as the only practical haven for the Jews was the first step in telescoping the distress of the Jews of Europe and the question of Palestine into a single problem. When the leaders of the A.J.C. finally met with President Truman on September 29, 1945, they suggested a large immigration into Palestine. (Their meeting with Truman took place shortly after he had seen Abba Hillel Silver and Stephen S. Wise, who had demanded the establishment of a Jewish Commonwealth). The Committee wanted Truman to continue his pressure on Britain to give out 100,000 certificates to Jewish immigrants at once, a request which had already been made. However, even in this conversation the leaders of the A.J.C. did not tie this demand with the political future of Palestine, and their emphasis to Truman that a difference should be made between Jewish immigration and a Jewish State as a practical plan was received with adverse criticism by much of American Jewry, of which these remarks in The American Jewish World (October 12, 1945) were typical:

> Immediately following the visit to the White House by Drs. Stephen
> S. Wise and Abba Hillel Silver urging the desperate needs for the

implementation of the Jewish Commonwealth as the only hope for the rehabilitation of broken, decimated Jewry, Joseph M. Proskauer and Jacob Blaustein, of the American Jewish Committee, rushed to the White House to assure President Truman that although they were in favor of Jewish immigration into Palestine they were opposed to Jewish statehood.

Within the A.J.C. different pressures were operating. The anti-Zionists did not give up their efforts to bring the Committee closer to the position of American Council for Judaism. To the anti-Zionists, John Slawson responded that anyone who believed that Jewish life in the United States was only a temporary sojourn, to be ended with the establishment of a Jewish state, did not belong in the A.J.C. At the same time, there was no room in the Committee for anyone who believed that Jews had to completely assimilate in the non-Jewish society. [25] The A.J.C. leaders also made clear to the Council that its support of the Balfour Declaration remained firm, and its opposition to the establishment of a Jewish State was not eternal, but only reflected the reality of present conditions. As to the future, the matter was open to discussion. In such an approach, on the most sensitive and emotional subject for the leaders of the A.J.C., one could discern a return to the approach of Louis Marshall. [26]

While the A.J.C. supported in principle renewed integration of displaced Jews within the countries of Europe, it had already been informed by field representatives that in many cases it could just not be done. By August 1945, the Committee had learned that more than 200,000 Jews would not wish to be reintegrated in the communities from which they had been forced out or exiled. The theory of reintegration which the A.J.C. had preached during the war years did not stand up to the test of reality in 1945.

Moreover, pro-Zionist pressure was being felt in the A.J.C. chapters. Anti-Zionist pressure was exerted by single individuals, the pro-Zionist pressure by the broad Jewish public. Ordinary members from outlying cities demanded that the Committee should not be satisfied with merely an intellectual relationship to the problem of Palestine. They asked Proskauer, Blaustein, and the other leaders what they had done and what they were ready to do in order to bring about the possibility of the refugees emigrating to Palestine. The active A.J.C. members "in the field" warned that if the leadership did not prove that it was working toward the achievement of realistic solutions to the two problems (the D.P.s and Palestine), the gap between the

A.J.C. and the Jewish public would widen and the A.J.C. would find itself completely isolated.[27] The leadership of the A.J.C. was being forced to draw closer to the Zionist solution, but was still wavering between the concept of resettling the surviving remnants in their original countries or their emigration from Europe.

The Committee established field services in Europe in order "to aid in the rehabilitation and settlement of the approximately 100,000 Jews now scattered throughout the Western zones of occupied Germany," but it recognized that "the permanent resettlement of these groups in Palestine or other countries is a complex task." In the final months of 1945, the efforts of the A.J.C. to foster the resettlement of displaced Jews in the East European countries stopped altogether. Blaustein and Slawson informed Secretary of State James Byrnes and his assistant, Dean Acheson, in no uncertain terms that the Jews who had left or had been forced out of these countries did not wish to return there.[28] The Displaced Persons were just not interested in the advice of the A.J.C. on the subject of resettlement in Eastern Europe.

As the winter of 1945-46 was approaching, the heads of the A.J.C. were forced to admit that the matter of highest priority was to bring about a quick solution to the problem of the refugee camp inmates, and the only apparent answer was emigration to Palestine. After the events of the summer, the A.J.C. became convinced that there was no reasonable chance to receive 100,000 immigration permits, even as a humanitarian gesture. Some political solution had to be found to save the last remnants of the Holocaust, and Proskauer eventually concluded that Eretz Yisrael would have to be prepared for self-rule. He continued however, to differ with the methods of the Jewish Agency, which demanded a Jewish state immediately, and which attacked the British government for going back on its promises. The leaders of the Jewish Agency also wanted the Zionist Movement in the United States, by using the so-called "Jewish Vote," to get the United States government to pressure the British into changing the White Paper policy. The A.J.C., true to its tradition, wished to avoid "militancy" of any kind. Proskauer complained that he stretched out his hand to the Zionists in order to achieve a large immigration through cooperative effort, but two obstacles prevented the achievement of that goal: "The constant cry against Great Britain and the demand for the immediate establishment of a Jewish State."[29]

The A.J.C. continued to oppose any sort of "militant" activity in the

United States. Proskauer still thought that the establishment of a trusteeship would bring about a massive immigration and in the future the conditions for self rule would be created. Since he saw in the Jewish Agency a potential partner in political activity, he talked privately with Dr. Weizmann about reestablishing an expanded Jewish Agency, but to no avail.[30]

Other non-Zionist organizations did not work as continuously or as intensively as the A.J.C. but the crisis of the post-Holocaust period, and particularly the critical situation in the refugee camps, forced them to take a stand also.

Even Agudath Yisrael, which had avoided all contact with the Zionist movement for many years, changed its positions under the pressure of post-war conditions, and the possible alignment of Agudath Yisrael with the Jewish Agency, never even considered in the past, became a topic of extensive discussion. In the spring of 1945, the heads of Agudath Yisrael suggested to Dr. Weizmann a cooperative effort in defense of the rights of the Jews in Palestine. The leaders of Agudath in Eretz Yisrael understood that the United States had become an important focus for political activity, and prepared to go to America to participate in negotiations there. In November 1945, Rabbi Jacob Rosenheim, president of the World Agudath Yisrael Organization, contacted President Truman. He explained that the publication of the correspondence between Franklin D. Roosevelt and Ibn-Saud, as well as the negotiations between the United States and England, had led the Agudath Yisrael to believe in a united Jewish front. All Jews now demanded the immediate immigration of the Holocaust survivors to Palestine. Rabbi Rosenheim announced that all of Orthodox Jewry accepted the Balfour Declaration and the Mandate, and demanded the fulfillment of promises and international obligations regarding a National Homeland for the Jews. He suggested that Palestine should be governed by an Anglo-American trusteeship, the White Paper of 1939 and the land sale laws of 1940 should be abolished, and the country opened up for free Jewish immigration, limited only by the economic ability of that country to absorb it.[31] The fact that Agudath Yisrael had turned to the President of the United States testified to the beginning of a broad Jewish front, despite the fact that organizational splits still continued.

The Jewish Labor Committee also made efforts to influence the British government to change its policy, although it too was not yet ready to support the political concepts of Zionism. The J.L.C. proposed that any Jew who wished to emigrate to Palestine should be free to do so, and those camp inmates who wished to return to their former homelands should be assured absolute equality in those countries. On that matter, a great similarity could be found between the socialistic J.L.C. and the *haut bourgeois* A.J.C. To the Bundists in the J.L.C., the return of the Jews to the East European countries also had an ideological dimension; they wanted the returnees to take an active part in building up social democratic states in Eastern Europe, an approach, however, which found few supporters in the D.P. camps in conquered Germany. The J.L.C. also hoped to exploit its contacts with the British Labour Party and in their communications, the heads of the J.L.C. made use of the terminology then current among Socialist Parties. They reminded the Labourites that the working class had lifted up the banner of human morality, and that a workers' government should not be false to that morality. They demanded that Attlee and Bevin act in such a way that the workers of the world could be proud of their action, and not see the solution of the refugee problem as a matter that could be postponed from month to month.[32] The secretary of the Labour Party answered his colleagues in the United States in a diplomatic and vague manner, that the matter of Palestine was being reviewed carefully, and a statement by Clement Attlee, the head of the government, might be expected soon. The announcement of the Labour government made by Ernest Bevin on November 13, 1945, proved very disappointing. Adolf Held, chairman of the J.L.C., appealed directly to Attlee, expressing his pain at the fact that Bevin's declaration in Parliament meant that the White Paper and all the laws stemming from it were not going to be abolished. Held stressed that this declaration did not bring any nearer the realization of a home for the displaced Jews who had already expressed where they wished to go. He demanded that Attlee, head of a free workers' government, open Palestine for immediate immigration and not evade the issue by appointing investigating committees and resorting to other delaying tactics. He wrote:

> We deem it our right as friends and comrades to call this to your attention. We deem it our right to expect that you the leader of the labor government of Great Britain will not pursue the old methods of delay, procrastination and inquiry commissions. We deem it only right that you should act in accordance with your assurances, and in accordance withour own socialist morals.

"It is as brothers and comrades that we approach you," Held concluded, "and it is in this spirit of friendship and fraternity that we hope you will receive our appeal."[33] The J.L.C. thus joined the cooperative Jewish effort to change the British White Paper, but the request fell on deaf ears. Held's turning to Atlee was a cry in the political wilderness.

Within the ranks of the Reform movement as well, many people found themselves influenced by the events of 1945, and moved closer to the proposed Zionist solution. The Reform organizations themselves did not change their positions formally, that is to say, they remained neutral on the political future of Palestine. Within the movement, however, people who shifted their position did not conceal that fact. Thus, Rabbi Julian Morgenstern, the president of Hebrew Union College, announced that he had changed his mind, and that the establishment of a Jewish State in Eretz Yisrael did not frighten him any longer. Rabbi Morgenstern, once a strong anti-Zionist, described himself in the fall of 1945 as a non-Zionist with a sympathetic understanding of Zionism.[34]

The B'nai B'rith Order remained consistently sympathetic toward the Zionist aims, yet still avoided taking a formal stand. B'nai B'rith spokesmen agreed that justice ought to be done to the Jewish People, and believed that most Jews in the United States understood this to mean the establishment of a democratic Jewish commonwealth in Palestine. For other Jews (the minority, in the opinion of B'nai B'rith), "getting justice" meant opening the gates of the Holy Land for immigration and nothing more than that. All Jews, however, were agreed in their demand for a change in the immigration policy. The B'nai B'rith tried, as much as possible, to avoid referring to the Palestine problem as a political struggle, and preferred to present it as an ethical problem. Justice cannot be divided, the fraternal organization maintained, and if justice will not be done to the survivors of the Holocaust and the Jews of Eretz Yisrael, then the "moral core of human relations is involved."[35] All this circumlocution, of course, did not prevent Henry Monsky from taking an active part in the political struggle as chairman of the Executive Committee of the American Jewish Conference.

The Jewish War Veterans did not generally play a significant role in the organized life of the Community, but at the end of World War II it was an important shaper of public opinion. At their fifth Convention in Atlantic City, held in November 1945, the Jewish War Veterans demanded that President Truman exert pressure to open the gates of Palestine, which "shall be constituted a Jewish National State." While it was well known that the Irgun had entré to the Jewish War Veterans, their demand nonetheless testified to the fact that the call for the establishment of a Jewish State was not the bailiwick of a limited group of Zionist politicians and professional workers only.[36]

The growing solidarity of the Jewish community in the United States with their overseas brethren was powerfully demonstrated at a special convention of the United Jewish Appeal in Atlantic City, December 15-17, 1945. The U.J.A., which had passed through serious internal crises, once more became an important focus of identification, particularly for Jews who were not members of Zionist or pro-Zionist Organizations. In Atlantic City the delegates met with representatives of the Holocaust survivors from the D.P. camps, including Joseph Rosenzaft, the leader at Bergen-Belsen. According to Eliezer Kaplan, the importance of the presence of the representatives of the Displaced Persons was not "Vos zei reiden" but "Vos ess redt in zie." Indeed when they spoke to the assembly, they did not use diplomatic or restrained language, but screamed: "We remained alive and it is your duty to help us live. There is one place where we wish to live and that is Eretz Yisrael."[37]

The emotional and aggressive appearance of the refugee spokesmen made a strong impression on the leaders of the "Joint" who had generally abhorred any political interference. Edward Warburg, then chairman of the J.D.C., did not hesitate to say that the hopes of the D.P.s had come to naught. During the Nazi regime they had dreamed of freedom, but were still locked up in camps. Warburg informed the United Jewish Appeal delegates that most of the refugees wished to go only to Palestine, where they would be received by their brethren and where they would be helped to reestablish their ruined lives. Paul Baerwald, who had fought the United Palestine Appeal for years over each percent in apportioning the U.J.A. revenue, joined Warburg and asked that the D.P.s be helped to rebuild their lives anew, and in his opinion the only place where it could be done, was Eretz Yisrael. As Eliezer Kaplan reported, most of the American Zionist leaders were not present at t he U.J.A. Conference at Atlantic City. The participants were, for the most part, "leaders of the local Jewish communities (Federation People), so that this conference was made up largely of sworn and known non-Zionists." One delegate was Adele Levy, the sister of the anti-Zionist Lessing Rosenwald and William Rosenwald, one of the heads of the U.J.A. She had just returned from a trip to

Europe and testified that she was influenced by the fact that she hadn't heard any D.P.s laugh or sing except in the *Hachshara* groups. She asked how anyone could live without laughter or song. "Zionism or non-Zionism, ideology or non-ideology; all this doesn't interest me," she declared. "If Palestine will cause these people to laugh and sing again, these Jews will have to be helped in any way possible." The attitude of Mrs. Levy and others convinced the conference to accept an unprecedented goal of $100,000,000 for 1946, most of it to go to help survivors of the Holocaust.[38]

The U.J.A. served as an indicator of the change in the position of American Jews *vis-à-vis* the fate of the refugees, and the Atlantic City conference reflected some of the internal developments within the U.J.A. itself. More of the J.D.C. money went to finance the immigration of D.P.s to Eretz Yisrael; among others, "Bricha" (Flight and Rescue) received financial aid, although in many cases without the knowledge of the J.D.C. directors in New York.[39]

The very decision at the Atlantic City Conference to triple the U.J.A. budget testifies to changes in values and positions. The change in quantity reflected a change in quality as well. The U.J.A. carried out the job, and collected even more than $100,000,000 in 1946. Many regular contributors increased their donations threefold or even fourfold. Many who had never given a cent to the U.J.A. became regular contributors. A strong connection existed between the 1946 budget of the U.J.A. and the change in attitudes of American non-Zionists concerning the refugee problem. While Henry Montor had originally proposed the $100,000,000 goal, it took the approval of the heads of the "Joint" and the support of the A.J.C. leaders to make it possible. These last had finally come to the conclusion that repatriation to Poland and other European countries was no longer practicable for the survivors of Holocaust. One can also assume that the gap between the objectives of the non-Zionist "Joint" and those of the Zionist United Palestine Appeal within the U.J.A. became narrower; as this happened, the U.J.A. grew stronger until it could influence Jewish public opinion in the United States.

The growing acceptance of the Zionist position among American Jewry was particularly important for those Jews who were afraid of being accused of dual or partial loyalty, if they supported a particularistic Jewish policy. Thus the approval of pro-Zionist resolutions in the American Congress had considerable impact on the Zionist political struggle, and perhaps also had psychological importance for non-Zionist Jews and the heads of their organizations who were afraid of any step that could be interpreted as un-American.

As a final factor, the United States officially joined those searching for a solution to the problem of Jewish Displaced Persons, and tied the Palestine issue to the refugee problem in the appointment of the Anglo-American Investigating Commission, thus giving the last necessary legitimacy to the merging of these two issues into one. Now even those members of non-Zionist organizations who were afraid to do anything that was conceivably not in full agreement with the declared policy of the United States government could, and in good conscience, support the creation of a Jewish state. Indeed, by the end of 1945, the basis had been established for the cooperative effort of American Zionists and non-Zionists to work together in the next two years to help create the State of Israel.

FOOTNOTES

1. Memorandum, Nahum Goldmann to Joseph C. Hyman, January 12, 1945; Hyman to Goldmann, February 13, 1945; Records of Jewish Agency for Palestine-American Section, in Central Zionist Archives (CZA), Jerusalem, Z5/1024.

2. Report of Dr. I. Schwarzbart to Chaim Weizmann on his December 1944 visit to the United States regarding possibility of cooperation with non-Zionist groups. Records of Political Department of World Zionist Organization/Jewish Agency, CZA, S25/1970.

3. Comments of Moshe Shapiro, minutes of meeting of Jewish Agency Executive, February 7, 1945, in CZA.

4. A.J.C., "Statement of Views . . .," *American Jewish Year Book* 45 (1944):690-10; Joseph Proskauer to Joseph C. Grew, February 13, 1945, and enclosure, Records of the United States Department of State, National Archives, Washington, D.C., 867N.2/1345.

5. The Americans and Palestinians differed on this point, with the former giving much more importance to the Conference; see Rose Halprin interview, August 1974, Oral History Collection, Institute of Contemporary Jewry of the Hebrew University, Jerusalem.

6. Minutes of meetings of Jewish Agency Executive, February 25 and March 15, 1945.

7. Louis Lipsky to affiliated organizations of American Jewish Conference, February 27, 1945, and minutes of Conference Executive Committee, April 10, 1945, both in American Section Records, Z5/1076.

8. Maurice Karpf to Joseph Proskauer, April 12, 1945, Karpf Papers, American Jewish Archives, Cincinnati, Ohio, Box 987; Morris Waldman to Proskauer, April 12, 1945, American Jewish Committee Archives, New York, Box II/11.

9. American Jewish Committee, *To the Councellors of Peace, Recommendations* . . . (New York, 1945).

10. *American Jewish Year Book* 47 (1946):490-91.

11. *Ibid.*, p. 491.

12. Jacob Robinson, *Palestine and the United Nations* (Washington, 1947), pp. 2-15; telegram (framed by Goldmann) to Moshe Shertok, May 29, 1945, Political Dept. Records, S25/5334; see also Israel Goldstein interview, January 1, 1974, Oral History Collection, Hebrew University.

13. *The Committee Reporter* 2 (May 2, 1945):2-6.

14. Gershon Agron reported on the San Francisco Conference as follows: "I do not want to say anything regarding success except to mention a Latin proverb which says that the first duty of the doctor is to see to it that the patient's condition doesn't get worse." Minutes of Jewish Agency Executive, July 8, 1945.

15. Proskauer to Secretary of State, May 4, 1945, Karpf Mss., Box 957; *American Jewish Year Book* 48 (1947):496; Goldstein interview.

16. Eliahu Elath, *San Francisco Diary* (in Hebrew, Tel-Aviv, 1971), p. 38.

17. On May 8, 1945, Elath wrote in his diary: "There is little love left between Proskauer and [Stephen S.] Wise; from our point of view, the less that personal animosities among Jewish leadership in this country—Zionist and non-Zionist—bear on our affairs, the better off we will be."

18. *Ibid.*, pp. 145-46.

19. American Jewish Conference, *The Jewish Position in the United Nations Conference* (New York, 1945); Executive Board, Union of American Hebrew Congregations, Annual Report for 1945, pp. 91-94, American Jewish Archives.

20. *C.C.A.R. Yearbook* 55 (1945):59-64.

21. *Ibid.*, pp. 179-92.

22. Draft of memorandum for President Truman, A.J.C. Archives, Box I/3; *American Jewish Year Book* 48 (1947):627-28.

23. John Slawson to Ira M. Younker, September 14, 1945, A.J.C. Archives, Box II/5.

24. A.J.C. Annual Report, *American Jewish Year Book* 48 (1947): 628; Jacob Blaustein to Steering Committee, October 6, 1945, Minute Book, A.J.C. Archives; *J.T.S. Bulletin*, October 1, 1945.

25. Slawson to Younker, cited in n. 23 above; Slawson to Maurice Karpf, July 18, 1945, Karpf Mss., Box 987.

26. Minutes of Administrative Committee, October 9, 1945, A.J.C. Archives.

27. Report of Louis S. Breier to Nathan Weisman, October 24, 1945, *ibid.*, Box II/5.

28. *The Committee Reporter* 2 (October 1945):1, and (December 1945):1,7.

29. Proskauer speech, "Repercussions of the Palestine Situation," to A.J.C. Executive Committee, November 6, 1945, Minute Book, A.J.C. Archives.

30. *The Committee Reporter* 3 (January 1946):4; A.J.C. Minute Book, November 6 and December 4, 1945.

31. Rabbis Levine, Breuer and Blau to Chaim Weizmann, Adar 6, 1945, Political Dept. Records, S25/1466; "Statement Concerning Palestine," November 1945, Harry S. Truman Papers, Truman Library, Independence, Missouri.

32. Interview with Emanuel Muravchik; Adolf Held, David Dubinsky, Joseph Busky and Jacob Pat to British Labour Party, telegram, October 2, 1945. J.L.C. Archives, New York.

33. Morgan Phillips (secretary of Labour Party) to J.L.C. Executive Committee, October 27, 1945; Adolf Held to Clement Attlee, November 30, 1945, *ibid.*

34. *The New Palestine* 35 (September 28, 1945):24.

35. *National Jewish Monthly B'nai B'rith* 60 (November 1945):81ff.

36. "Jewish War Veterans Resolution on Palestine," *The New Palestine* 35 (November 30, 1945):8.

37. Meeting of Jewish Agency Executive, February 10, 1946; Herbert Friedman interview, Oral History Collection, Hebrew University.

38. Text of Warburg's speech and other comments, is in *The New Palestine*, December 31, 1945; meeting of Jewish Agency Executive, February 10, 1946.

39. Yehuda Bauer, *Flight and Rescue: Brichah* (New York, 1970), pp. 128-29; Geraldine Rosenfield, "Overseas Relief and Rehabilitation," *American Jewish Year Book* 48 (1947):206.

Ha Ma'avek: American Zionists, Partition and Recognition, 1947-1948

by Melvin I. Urofsky

The United Nations had not even reached its second birthday when the British dumped the Palestinian hot potato in its lap. Administrative machinery had been established, but only in skeletal form, and there were few precedents to which the world body could refer for guidance in this case. Within the State Department, a general malaise prevailed. For those committed to continued British hegemony in the Middle East, a "wrong" U.N. decision could easily create a power vacuum from which Russia could emerge as the dominant force in the region. Dean Acheson and others believed that the United States would have to assume some leadership, if for no other reason than to secure a "sensible" proposal that the American government and people could accept, since in all likelihood the United States would be asked to finance it.[1]

Yet at the same time, if there was to be any hope for the United Nations to develop into a truly effective and authoritative international body, then neither the United States nor any of the great powers should be able to dictate its policies. As a result, the State Department, which privately favored a partition plan, publicly adopted a neutral position so as not to influence the U.N. member states before they met. Despite repeated requests from Zionist leaders and pro-Zionist congressmen for a clarification of policy. Secretary of State George C. Marshall and chief delegate Warren R. Austin refused to make any statement which, in their opinion, might limit the usefulness of the United Nations.[2]

The special session of the U.N. called to deal with Palestine met on April 27, 1947, and immediately plunged into a debate on the agenda. The Arab states demanded an immediate "termination of the Mandate over Palestine and the Declaration of its Independence," a proposal that received no support from any other nations. A touchier issue involved Jewish representation. The five Arab members would make a full presentation of the Arab case, but who would speak for the Jews? Asaf Ali, the Indian representative, argued that discussing Palestine in the absence of the Jews would be "playing *Hamlet* without the Prince of Denmark." The Jewish Agency had already submitted a formal request to speak for the Jewish people, and after lengthy parliamentary maneuvering, the Agency was recognized as the sole organization to represent the Jewish case before any U.N. body deliberating the Palestine matter.

On May 8, 1947, Abba Hillel Silver, Moshe Shertok, and David Ben-Gurion took their seats between the Cuban and Czechoslovakian delegations to make the first presentation of the Jewish claim to homeland. Each delegation had a small signboard in front of it, denoting the country represented, and now, for the first time in nearly two thousand years, the Jewish people stood again in the family of nations. David Horowitz, an economist and Histadrut official who served on the Agency's U.N. staff, recalled the thrill that shot through the delegation when they saw their own sign: "It was, of course, still only a substitute, a state in the making, and not actual independence; nevertheless, it bore the hallmark of international recognition of Jewry. . . . After hundreds of years of discussion on the nature and national-territorial characteristics of Judaism, the discussion had seemingly been finalized by this modest shingle."[3]

Unable to reach agreement in the committee of the whole, the U.N. appointed an eleven-member Special Committee on Palestine (UNSCOP), consisting of smaller, neutral countries, with the Arab states and the great powers deliberately excluded. The Committee held hearings in Palestine from June 16 to July 24, and then went to Geneva to prepare its report. During its deliberations, the British incredibly managed to create an incident that focused both the Committee's and the entire world's attention on the plight of the Jewish refugees.

A battered Chesapeake Bay ferry, purchased by the Peter Bergson group, had steamed to France where it was refitted to hold some 4500 DP's, and christened "Exodus-1947." As soon as it left French territorial waters, six British destroyers and one cruiser "escorted" the overladen vessel across the Mediterranean. Twelve miles outside of Palestine, the British ships closed for boarding. After several hours of hand-to-hand combat, the British brought up machine guns and gas bombs, and in the ensuing battle killed three Jews and wounded more than a hundred. All the while, a detailed account of the fighting went out on the "Exodus-1947" radio to Palestine, where the Jewish Agency rebroadcast it on a clandestine network for the world to hear. The ship finally surrendered only after the British began ramming it, and stove in one side.

They towed the badly listing ferry into Haifa, where illegal immigrants normally would be transferred to detention camps in Cyprus. But the two facilities on that island were already badly overcrowded, so Ernest Bevin decided to make an example of the refugees by sending them back to Europe. British prison ships carried the DP's to Marseilles, but there, except for a small number of the aged, ill, or pregnant, the refugees refused to leave the boats. The French government offered hospitality, the British officers pleaded with them, all to no avail. The Jewish Agency managed to sneak a correspondent on board, and his description of the inferno beneath the decks did little to enhance British prestige.

After three weeks the French, fearful of epidemics, ordered the ships to depart, and the British Cabinet, meeting in emergency session, decided to take the Jews to Germany. When the ships docked at Hamburg, the refugees again refused to leave, and British troops wielding clubs and rubber hoses literally drove the DP's off the boats and into railroad cars that took them to internment camps. For a month the British tried to register them, but no matter what questions were asked, the refugees had only one answer: "Palestine." A subcommittee of the UNSCOP visited the "Exodus-1947" camps, and in the words of the Yugoslavian member, "it is the best possible evidence we can have." Indeed, the experience of the UNSCOP teams duplicated those of the Anglo-American Committee a year earlier. Although the Arab states wanted the refugee problem disassociated from the Palestine question, the Committee's final report concluded that "if only because of the extraordinary intensity of the feeling displayed in this direction, such a situation must be regarded as at least a component in the problem of Palestine."[4]

Unable to reach unanimous agreement, UNSCOP submitted both a majority and a minority report. The minority proposal, signed by three members, called for the creation of a federal state, composed of two subordinate states, one Jewish and the other Arab, with two legislative bodies, one elected on the basis of population and the other giving both Jews and Arabs an equal vote. The majority called for the partition of Palestine into two states, joined through an economic union, with the city of Jerusalem placed under a special United Nations trusteeship.

The General Council of the World Zionist Organization received the report in Zurich, and immediately rejected the minority plan as "wholly unacceptable." The majority proposal received a qualified endorsement; the Zionists welcomed the creation of an independent Jewish state, but the proposed boundaries left only "a minor part of the territory originally promised to the Jewish people on the basis of its historic rights and does not include areas of the utmost importance." Even Silver and Emanuel Neumann, who had opposed the Agency's partition plan a year earlier, now seemed willing to take half a loaf. But when they returned to New York, Silver reiterated his earlier argument that the Jews "must demand all of Palestine and wait for such an offer on the part of the United Nations Assembly as will prove acceptable." Aware that the majority of American Jews overwhelmingly endorsed the partition plan, the Emergency Council urged caution and moderation on the part of local Zionist leaders and groups. "If the impression is created that the Jewish people regard the majority report as being in their favor," the Council warned, "the efforts of our enemies within the U.N. further to whittle down pro-Jewish recommendations will be greatly facilitated."[5] The final lines had not yet been drawn; if American Jewry appeared too pleased with the UNSCOP report, it would be difficult if not impossible to secure better boundary lines in the U.N. debate.

But despite its shortcomings, the UNSCOP report gave the Zionists their first glimmer that a Jewish state might soon be established. Leaders of the movement began planning how to maintain this momentum, how to counter the anticipated British and Arab opposition. The United States would play an important role in the struggle, and the key to American support lay in the attitudes and efforts of American Jewry. "It will not be worthwhile for the United States to incur Anglo-Arab wrath, or even to offer to cooperate with the British or the U.N. in implementing the committee's proposals, if they are not backed resolutely by the broad mass of the American Jewish Community." The Zionists were therefore delighted when Judge Proskauer, on behalf of the American Jewish Committee, in a public telegram to Secretary of State Marshall, urged the American government to "vigorously and speedily" endorse the UNSCOP majority report.[6]

But while American Jewry welcomed the UNSCOP plan, reactions with the State Department ranged from the incredulous to outright hostility. The Anglophiles and Arabists rejected the plan as undermining the balance of power and British hegemony in the Middle East. The Joint Chiefs of Staff warned that implementation of the plan might require use of American troops, which would surely prejudice American influence and prestige in the Middle East. They urged Truman that no action should be taken that would turn the peoples of the region away from the western powers.[7] Intense opposition came from both military and foreign service officers concerned about access to the area's oil reserves. A special committee, headed by Herbert Feis, had been created in 1943 to study the problem of future oil reserves, and at that time had warned that "unless our ability to derive required supplies from abroad at all times . . . is safeguarded, the United States will be in hazard (a) of having to pay an economic or political toll to secure the oil; or (b) actually fail to secure it." Now led by Secretary of Defense James Forrestal, the "oil" groups in State and Defense put up a vigorous opposition to the UNSCOP plan, fearing that it would so antagonize the Arab nations that American oil supplies would be endangered.[8] As an alternative, they argued that Great Britain had maintained her position in the Middle East by cultivating the Arabs; now that she could no longer do so, the United States had to take over and follow the same formula, otherwise the Arabs would be driven into the arms of the Soviets. As Loy Henderson put it, "Arab friendship is essential if we are to have their cooperation in the carrying out of some of our vital economic programs."[9]

The argument has been made that beneath the veneer of national interest, the real cause of opposition to the creation of a Jewish state was anti-Semitism. Government service, especially in the State Department, had long been an exclusive club, and few Jews held positions of influence there. Undoubtedly during the war years, Breckinridge Long's deep animus against Jews led him to thwart rescue efforts to save a doomed people. After the war, James Forrestal, while not an active bigot, came from a Wall Street firm and family background from which Jews were excluded, and he tended to be indifferent, rather than hostile, to Jewish distress.[10] But the main villain of the drama has usually been identified as Loy W. Henderson. David Niles, Bartley Crum, and Eleanor Roosevelt were contemporary critics, charging

Henderson with being the leading Arabist in the State Department, a man who consistently misrepresented the Jewish case and who worked to thwart presidential directives. Joseph Schechtman, who had impeccable credentials as a Zionist, disagreed. He argued, and I think convincingly, that Henderson was neither anti-Zionist nor anti-Jewish. Rather, he interpreted America's best interests as requiring close ties with the Arab world, and the creation of a Jewish state, insofar as it would drive a wedge between the United States and the Arabs, had to be opposed. "He undoubtedly misjudged the importance of the 'Arab factor' in the global United States policy, but his was a sincere and honest error," wrote Schechtman. "He frankly believed that his stand was in the best interests of America, and he acted accordingly, using his exceptionally wide knowledge of the Middle East and his official position to press unrelentingly for the implementation of the policies he deemed right."[11]

Henderson was a master at bureaucratic infighting, of the art of interpreting directives from superiors so they would be more in tune with the careerists' thinking, but in the fall of 1947 he found the scales tilted too far for him to affect. Secretary of State George Marshall, despite whatever qualms he may have had about the wisdom of partition, believed that the United States had to support the UNSCOP plan as a matter of principle. The President, moreover, saw the UN proposal as the only way to extricate himself from the morass of competing Zionist and British demands. Within the UN delegation, Henderson found Eleanor Roosevelt a strong supporter of partition, while another friend of the Zionists, General John Hilldring (who had been appointed at the suggestion of David Niles), managed to offset the influence of Henderson and his chief aide, George Wadsworth.

The Zionists were also applying pressure, and a mail campaign initiated by the Emergency Council inundated Washington with letters and telegrams. The White House received more than 65,000 pieces of mail supporting partition, while many thousands more found their way to Secretary Marshall's desk. In case Truman had not yet received the message, Clark Clifford reminded him that the Jewish vote would be very important in 1948.[12] At the beginning of October, Truman sent word to the State Department that it should announce the government's approval of partition, and on October 11, Herschel V. Johnson informed the General Assembly that the United States would approved the UNSCOP majority report, although it would suggest geographical revisions. Two days later, to everyone's great surprise, Soviet delegate Semyon K. Tsarapkin declared that Russia would also vote for partition. "Those damned Jews!" one delegate gasped. "They even bring America and Russia together when they want something."

The Soviet decision resulted from months of careful work on the part of the Jewish Agency delegation, especially by Emanuel Neumann, who had made the first contact with the Russians as far back as 1941. When Chaim Weizmann visited the United States that year, Neumann arranged for an interview between the Zionist leader and Soviet ambassador Maxim Litvinoff. The Russian surprised both Weizmann and Neumann when he declared that the Soviet Union did not oppose Zionism. "When Zionism first appeared on the scene it appeared as protegé of Great Britain, and Britain was our enemy, so naturally we were opposed to Zionism, too," Litvinoff explained. "But now we're allies. And we have no Arabs. Britain has Arabs to think about. Why should we be opposed to it. As far as we're concerned it's a matter of indifference."[13]

After the war, Neumann again led the way in contacting the Russians, and the Zionist delegation openly admitted that it sought aid wherever it might be. As David Horowitz noted: "We told the Americans that we were meeting with the Russians, and the Russians of our conferences with the Americans, without holding back anything. . . . We told both the Americans and the Russians that our sole criterion was the Jewish interest."[14] At one point, the United States and Great Britain wanted to have the big four meet with both Jews and Arabs in a final effort to reach agreement. The Russians, suspicious of the maneuver, refused to attend, and Silver insisted that if the Russians did not participate, then the Jewish Agency would also boycott the meeting. In response to the anti-communist arguments of some of the Labor Zionists, Silver lost his temper and declared that hatred for communism could not be allowed to interfere with the creation of a Jewish state.

Finally Neumann and Moshe Shertok (who Hildring had said could sell ice to the Eskimos) went to the Russian embassy to see if the impasse could be broken. Shertok used all of his skill, but Andrei Gromyko insisted that the Russians had made their decision: they would not participate. Suddenly Neumann spoke up. After explaining again the difficulties facing the Zionists, who did not want to forfeit the friendship and good will of either the Americans or the Russians, he offered a suggestion: "You are unwilling to participate in such a discussion. Very well. But couldn't you—by way of protest—attend the meeting without 'participating'?" Gromyko's face broke into a broad grin as he repeated the idea; finally he promised he would let them know early the next day. As the Emergency Council met the following morning, they received a message from the Russian embassy that Gromyko would be at the gathering. Even though nothing came from the meeting, as the Jews had expected, the fine line of communication between the Agency and the superpowers was preserved.[15]

Despite optimism over the backing of both the United States and the Soviet Union, Zionist leaders recognized that many obstacles had yet to be hurdled before the UNSCOP report could be approved. The State Department remained unhappy with the partition plan, and sought out excuses to disparage the *Yishuv* and put the Jewish Agency in a less than favorable light. Intermittent fighting in Palestine, as well as stepped up illegal immigration, the Aliyah Bet, led the Department to call in Zionist officials and warn them that unless the violence in the Holy Land could be brought under control, the United States would be forced to speak out against the Agency. While Dean Rusk delivered this message to Lionel Gelber, the Secretary of State called in Judge Proskauer and warned that if there were any more "Exodus" incidents, the American effort on behalf of partition might be damaged.[16]

Of greater danger was the Department's efforts to appease the Arabs by giving them more territory under the proposed partition plan. The UN Special Committee had recommended that Jaffa be included in the Jewish section for the sake of rationalized borders, despite the fact that it had an almost exclusively Arab population. In the negotiations at the United Nations, Jaffa became part of the Arab state, a more logical arrangement demographically, but one which cut down the already truncated Jewish area. When the State Department proposed detaching much of the Negev (the arid southern section) from the Jews, the Zionists dug in and prepared to fight. The little amount of land already allotted to them was for the most part land they had already developed; for the new state to take in immigrants, there would have to be open land on which to settle them. Moreover, if the Negev fell under Arab control, the Jews would have no water access to Asia. Through Akaba, the Jews could reach the Persian Gulf and establish trade relations with the Far East; without it, they would either be restricted to dealing with Europe and America, or be dependent on the questionable good will of the Arabs for use of the Suez Canal.

American diplomats, however, were less interested in future trade routes for the Jews than in appeasing the Arabs, whom they thought might be placated by getting more land, and they pressed the Jewish Agency representatives to yield the Negev. When the State Department started dropping hints that without this concession by the Jews, the United States would have to reconsider its support of partition, the Emergency Council wired all its local chapters urging them to see that large numbers of telegrams went immediately to the State Department and the White House "by all groups in their respective communities, both Jewish and non-Jewish." And in this moment of crisis, the Zionists turned for help to one man who might possibly influence the president. Chaim Weizmann, ill in a New York hotel suite, was still the master diplomat of the movement, the one person acknowledged even by his opponents as the most persuasive apostle of Zionism to the non-Jewish world.

Truman received Weizmann warmly on the morning of November 19, but after only a few minutes of small talk, the aging Zionist leader plunged into the purpose of his visit. Guided by a memorandum and a map prepared by Eliahu Epstein, he proceeded to give the President of the United States a lesson in political geography, and kept Truman's mind riveted to this one single issue. A fascinated Truman, grasping the force of Weizmann's argument, gave his assent and promised to inform the American UN delegation that the Negev should remain under Jewish control.

The Jewish Agency representatives were scheduled to meet with the Americans at 3:00 that afternoon to give their answer on the Negev question. Weizmann called New York immediately after his interview with Truman to inform Moshe Shertok of the results. Unfortunately Truman, perhaps unaware of the scheduled conference, failed to contact the American contingent with equal speed. At the United Nations, General Hilldring told a confused David Horowitz that, as far as he knew, the Americans were still under instructions to push for cession of the Negev to the Arabs. Horowitz intercepted Shertok outside the building with news of the mix-up, but, unable to evade the Americans, they sat down with Herschel Johnson shortly after three. Johnson, after the usual polite phrases, asked them if they had any news about the Negev decision.

Shertok, in a quandary, could not tell Johnson that Truman had already made a decision in their favor, nor could he accede to the Department's demands. Just then, a messenger came over to inform

Johnson of a telephone call for him; not wishing to interrupt his conversation, Johnson asked Hilldring to take the call. A minute later the general returned and whispered in Johnson's ear that the president was holding at the other end of the line. The chief delegate, in Abba Eban's phrase, "leaped to the telephone booth like a startled and portly reindeer." Twenty minutes later he returned, and stammered out: "What I really want to say to you, Mr. Shertok, was that we have no changes to suggest." The collective sigh that arose from Horowitz and Shertok could be heard across the lounge.[17]

The Negev had been saved, but the partition plan itself still had to be approved, and many of the smaller nations wavered. The British ambassador, Sir Alexander Cadogen, had announced that His Majesty's Government would do nothing to carry out partition, and since it could not be put into effect peaceably, his government would not be a party to implementing it by force. Moreover, the British unilaterally set their own terms for withdrawal in such a manner as to guarantee bloodshed: no gradual transition, no interim councils, and full enforcement of the White Paper until the last moment. If open warfare were to devastate the Holy Land, some delegates suggested, perhaps continued British rule might still be the most preferable option.

In the light of this argument, an enlarged Jewish Agency contingent, directed by Shertok and Silver, labored feverishly at Lake Success, buttonholing delegates and drawing up numerous legal documents in support of their case. Leading American Jews, many of whom were non-Zionists, offered to use their contacts with foreign delegations, and Judge Proskauer, Bernard Baruch, Herbert Bayard Swope, George Backer, Edward M. Warberg, and Henry Morgenthau, Jr., some of whom had bitterly opposed a Jewish state only a short time earlier, now did their best to bring it into being. Tens of thousands of telegrams descended upon the White House and the State Department demanding that the United States not only vote for partition, but use its influence to persuade, indeed to pressure, other nations to do so as well.

Up until almost the last moment, the State Department resisted this pressure. Acting Secretary of State Robert A. Lovett told Loy Henderson that he could inform the Arab ambassadors that the United States would vote for partition, but would not bring pressure on other UN members to follow its lead; Henderson gladly did so, and informed Herschel Johnson at the United Nations of this policy. The White

House also tried to resist the demands of American Jewry. Truman later recalled that: "I do not think I ever had as much pressure and propaganda aimed at the White House as I had in this instance. The persistence of a few of the extreme Zionist leaders—actuated by political motives and engaging in political threats—disturbed and annoyed me."[18] On the day of the scheduled vote, November 27, 1947, Shertok's calculations showed the partition resolution still three to four votes shy of the necessary two-thirds. He decided to filibuster, thus postponing the vote, and thanks to the Thanksgiving recess, gaining another day in which to round up the crucial ballots.

Now the dam broke. Truman, inundated by the mail campaign and besieged by Democratic congressmen and party officials, gave David Niles the go-ahead. Niles immediately phoned Johnson, and on the president's instructions, directed him to lobby actively for partition. Orders went to the State Department: American officials in wavering or opposed countries outside the Moslem world were to exert all pressure possible to get support.[19] The Emergency Council's long cultivation of non-Jewish friends now paid off as well; the tactics they adopted were far from subtle, but too much was at stake. Two justices of the United States Supreme Court wired Philippine president Carlos Rojas that, "the Philippines will isolate millions and millions of American friends and supporters if they continue in their effort to vote against partition." At the same time that the Philippine ambassador to the United States received a "briefing" at the White House, 26 senators called Rojas urging him to change his country's vote from a no to a yes. Harvey Firestone, under threat of a Jewish boycott of his company's products, informed William Tubman, the president of Liberia, that if that country did not change its vote, Firestone would have to reconsider plans to expand their rubber holdings there. The Liberians also were prodded by South Africa's Jan Smuts, one of the fathers of the Balfour Declaration, who acted at Chaim Weizmann's request. Adolph A. Berle, who had once tried to convince Emanuel Neumann to accept Ethiopia in lieu of Palestine, now used his contacts in Latin America to induce Haiti to vote in the affirmative. And Bernard Baruch shocked Alexander Parodi, the French representative to the UN, with a blunt threat to cut off American aid if France went against partition.[20]

Long before the delegates arrived at the converted skating rink that temporarily housed the world organization, the streets of Lake Success were thronged with Jews and their friends waving signs and placards.

Around the nation and in Palestine, people dropped their normal routines to tune in the radio, and with pencil and pad in their laps waited for the debate to end and the tally to begin. Emanuel Neumann, whose observance of traditional Jewish law would have normally prevented him from travelling on Sabbath eve, received a dispensation from a rabbi so that he could attend the crucial session. Shortly after 5:00, Oswaldo Aranha of Brazil, the General Assembly president, gaveled the debate to a close, and reached into a basket to pull out the name of the nation that would lead off the vote.

"Guatemala," he called.

As the Latin American delegate rose amidst the dead silence that gripped the hall, a lone cry rang out from the spectators' gallery.

"*Ana adonay hoshiya!*"—"O Lord, save us!"

One by one, the fifty-six member states rose to announce their votes: 33 for partition, 13 against, 10 abstentions. In New York and London and Tel-Aviv and Jerusalem, wild celebrations broke out. "This was the day the Lord hath made," exulted one rabbi. "Let us rejoice in it and be glad." In Cincinnati, where the Young Zionists convention was in process, hundreds of delegates marched to Fountain Square to see Bernard Marks, captain of the "Exodus 1947" burn a copy of the mandate. In the refugee camps the day of deliverance finally seemed at hand, and more than one observant Jew noted that the United Nations vote almost coincided with Channukah, the feast of lights, which marked the victory of the ancient Maccabees.[21] The next issue of the *New Palestine* carried on its cover the traditional Hebrew prayer of Thanksgiving, the *Shecheyanu* — "Blessed art Thou, O Lord our God, King of the Universe, who has given us life, sustained, and enabled us to reach this season."

Since that historic vote, the argument has been made by both friends and foes of the Jewish state that had it not been for the political pressure exerted by the American Jewish community, both on the American government and on the wavering nations, the necessary two-thirds vote would never have been gathered. David Horowitz wrote enthusiastically that the "one potent factor, which excelled all others operating on our behalf, was the strong action and pressure exerted by American Jewry. This great community, from the Zionists to the American Jewish Committee led by Judge Proskauer of New York, rallied massively to help in the political struggle. . . . American Jewry flung itself into the thick of the fray with an enthusiasm and dedication which had no parallel or standard of comparison in all past experience. The whole of the community, from coast to coast, was aflame with the zeal and ardor of the battle."[22]

Foes of the Jewish state were equally convinced that American Jewry played the decisive role. Edwin M. Wright, a member of the Middle East desk in 1947, charged that "the Zionist propaganda machine was efficient and thorough, blanketing the American political processes in systematic campaigns targeted at the general population, city halls, state houses and on up the ladder to Washington." A study of American periodical coverage of the Palestine debate confirmed that the Zionist viewpoint dominated the medium, with an emphasis on the humanitarian and religious aspects of the movement. Recent studies of Harry Truman's role in the pro-partition decision agree that the Zionist-generated political pressure proved a major factor in the White House over-ruling State Department advice, a conclusion James Forrestal bitterly reached thirty years ago.[23]

Naomi Cohen, while conceding the unremitting Zionist campaign, cautions that ethnic politics was only one determinant of American policy, and that Truman acted for other reasons as well, including his desire to contain Russia.[24] While it is undoubtedly true that many considerations went into the creation of American policy, the fact remains that a sudden and dramatic shift took place in the fall of 1947, with Truman consistently over-riding the State Department, and that the American public overwhelmingly supported partition. Moreover, the capacity to generate the propaganda, to organize mass rallies and telegram campaigns, to secure the help of important personages, both Jew and non-Jew, to touch the various nerve points in the political system—all this did not happen overnight. The success of the Zionist effort in 1947 represented nearly five years of work, of organization, of publicity, of education, and of the careful cultivation of key people in different fields. While the politicians may have reacted to the alleged existence of Jewish bloc-voting in key cities and states, the real power of the American Zionists resulted from their ceaseless and ultimately successful efforts first to win over the Jewish community and then the American public to its side, thus securing the help of influential men and women in the press, the church, the arts, and above all, the government.[25]

But even though the United Nations had voted, much remained to do. Rabbi Abba Hillel Silver, the architect of the American victory, declared that: "November 29 was only the evening and the morning of the first day—the day when light broke through the darkness of our world. Our great community, providentially spared for this hour, must now shoulder the vast economic burdens involved in the setting up of the Jewish State. . . . Our people are fully aware of their new responsibilities and are resolved to meet them. Whatever aid may come from other sources, the primary responsibility is ours."[26] Silver could not yet know that American Zionists would have to wage one more battle with the State Department to save the partition decision. Jews had accepted partition as a necessary price for a Jewish state, but the State Department saw it as a disaster. Despite the American vote in favor of the plan, by mid-December Secretary of State Marshall was privately telling his staff that the government might have made a mistake supporting partition.

Strategists within the bureaucracy began warning that only Russia would benefit from partition. Kermit Roosevelt, who frequently publicized the private views of the careerists, argued that the Soviet Union's pro-partition vote represented only the most recent move in Russia's traditional plan to penetrate the Mediterranean region. Moreover, the recovery of Europe might well depend upon an adequate supply of oil both to the United States and the Marshall plan nations; the United States, in order to protect western democracy, could not antagonize the Arab world. Before the House Armed Services Committee, both Secretary of Defense James Forrestal and Vice-Admiral Robert B. Carney, the Deputy Chief of Naval Operations, sounded dire predictions that Muslim response would endanger the flow of oil. James T. Duce, vice-president of the Arabian-American Oil Company, and other oil executives prophesied evil consequences unless the government did something to win back Arab good will.[27]

The anti-partitionists in the State and Defense Departments recognized that they faced strong popular opposition, since the American people overwhelmingly supported the creation of a Jewish state. But they found and exploited the weak spot in the Zionist armor, the Achilles heel of the pro-partition consensus, the strong reluctance of the public to commit American troops to enforce the United Nations resolution. In mid-1946, when the British had first raised the question of using American troops to keep order in Palestine, 74 percent of the populace opposed the idea. On the eve of the partition vote, only 3 percent of the sample were willing to have American soldiers keep the peace, although 65 percent said they would favor a UN army. In February 1948, with shooting rampant in the Holy Land, only 43 percent now approved of a UN force that would include Americans, while less than one out of ten were willing for the United States to unilaterally send troops to enforce the plan.[28]

General Alfred M. Gruenther, in charge of planning for the Joint Chiefs of Staff, informed the White House in mid-February that from 80,000 to 160,000 troops would be required to impose the partition plan, and that if this were to be a UN force, then Soviet detachments would undoubtedly have to included. Both Secretary of State Marshall and Chief UN Delegate Warren Austin opposed the use of troops, even UN troops. The Security Council, Warren informed its members, "is dedicated to keeping the peace, and not to enforcing partition." The Alsop brothers also joined in the alarm, warning that use of American boys in Palestine could well result in anti-Semitism at home. Even a "serious proposal to send troops," they wrote, "let alone the actual sending of them, would fan the flames of racial hatred in a dangerous and terrible manner." Senators Arthur Vandenberg and Owen Brewster, both of whom the Zionists counted as friends, declared they would not like to see a single American soldier fighting in the Holy Land.[29]

Events in Palestine in the early part of the year only reinforced the misgivings of State and Defense. The Arabs from neighboring states had infiltrated hundreds of irregulars into the country, where they harassed the *Yishuv* in ceaseless guerilla warfare. Although later analysis would show that the Arabs had only inflicted some casualties and had not taken a single settlement away from the Jews, military analysts began issuing jeremiads about the imminent destruction of the *Yishuv*. The Jews labored under a double handicap—the British would not allow them to import arms for defense, and the United States arms embargo prevented them from purchasing weapons here. The embargo, originally proclaimed as a gesture of neutrality, in effect penalized only the Jews, since the Arabs secured all the weapons they wanted from the British. Despite appeals from all sections of American Jewry, including the American Jewish Committee, Truman and the State Department both refused to lift the embargo until after the war of independence.

The Zionists, aware of the growing strength of anti-partition sentiment in the government, reverted to their previously successful tactics of massive mail and telegram campaigns, as well as personal contacts with administration officials. The White House alone received more than 300,000 post cards on the Palestine question during this period, nearly all of them from Jewish groups and individuals urging specific action by the President to sustain the United Nations decision. But the enormous pressure caused an unexpected and dangerous reaction: Harry Truman got his dander up, and absolutely refused to see any Jewish leaders at all, while George Marshall gratefully followed suit. Chaim Weizmann, who had made an uncomfortable mid-winter crossing to America at the Agency Executive's request in order to meet with the American leaders, found all doors barred to him. A personal note to the President, pleading for "a few minutes of your precious time" in the interest of preventing a "catastrophe" in Palestine brought only a brusque official reply that an appointment would be "out of the question." Even the efforts of Democratic political chieftains like Ed Flynn of the Bronx could not budge Truman, who, at the slightest provocation, would rail against the "extreme Zionists" who would not leave him alone.[30]

But the Zionists were not to be put off, and in a desperate end-run, contacted Eddie Jacobson, an old friend of Truman's, who had served with him in the First World War and then had been his partner in an ill-fated haberdashery store. Jacobson, who had open access to the President, managed to shame Truman into agreeing to see Weizmann, but the President insisted that it be a private meeting, with no public announcement and no press coverage. On March 18, an unmarked staff car drove in through the East Gate of the White House, and the ailing Weizmann had his long deferred interview with Truman, in which he pleaded for continued American support for the partition plan. Truman listened sympathetically, and assured Weizmann that the United States would press forward.[31]

Within twenty-four hours, however, Senator Austin proposed that the partition plan be abandoned, and that a special session of the General Assembly convene in order to establish a trusteeship over Palestine. This *volte-face* by the United States set off a storm of protest and confusion. "It took the British twenty-five years to sell out," wailed one Zionist leader, "the Americans have done it in two and a half months." Bernard Baruch demanded that Austin explain "our weather-vaning attitude" on Palestine, in which the United States first asked the world to follow its lead, and then abruptly changed its mind. Clark Clifford reported that every Jew in America considered Truman a "no-good"

who placed greater value on oil than on human lives. The Synagogue
Council of America, an organization that crossed every line of division
in American Jewry, called for a day of prayer "to give expression to the
shocked conscience of America at the inexplicable action of our administration in reversing its Palestine policy and to demand the fulfillment
of the plighted word of this country and of the nations of the world, and
to pray for God's help."[32]

Nor were Jews the only ones outraged by the shift in policy. *Time*
magazine declared that "Harry Truman's comic opera performance
had done little credit to the greatest power in the world." Eleanor
Roosevelt threatened to resign from the American United Nations delegation, while Helen Gehagan Douglas, Leon Henderson, I. F. Stone,
and other liberals condemned the President, with the Republicans, led
by Thomas Dewey, in hot pursuit as well. At the White House, mail
ran 22 to 1 opposing the reversal in policy.[33]

Many observers suggested that the shift represented a loss of control
by the President over foreign policy, and a resurgence of State Department influence. In large part they were right, but they did not
know at the time that the careerists, seizing upon Truman's earlier approval of a contingency plan, had decided to implement that strategy,
despite the fact that the necessary pre-conditions for its adoption did
not exist. Truman had agreed that, if the situation in Palestine deteriorated, the United States might seek some form of trusteeship to hold
things in order until a peaceful solution could be worked out. The Middle East desk, without consulting the President, decided that the
guerilla fighting warranted such a move, and instructed Austin to propose abandonment of partition. Truman, livid with rage, ordered
Samuel Rosenman to New York to explain the situation to Weizmann,
and more importantly, directed Clark Clifford to find out how the
mix-up had occurred in the first place. With the arrival of Clifford,
American policy toward Palestine took on a new tone.

Much of the historiographical debate over Truman's recognition of
Israel, indeed his entire Palestine policy, has concerned the extent to
which domestic political considerations intruded in the realm of
foreign policy. Certainly the Zionists used every weapon in their arse-
nal to bring pressure on the president. Truman, on his part, had shown
through his demand for entry of the 100,000 refugees, that he had been
deeply moved by their plight. Yet time and again he insisted that
domestic politics could not and should not be allowed to dictate the

nation's foreign policy. From the fall of 1947 through the spring of 1948, Truman did his best to resist the demands of Democratic party chieftains for a more pro-Zionist Palestine program. Within the administration, Secretary of State Marshall and Secretary of Defense Forrestal urged Truman not to yield to political expediency.[34] In large measure, the shifts in American policy reflected Truman's ambivalence; with the emergence of Clifford as a key advisor on domestic affairs, political and humanitarian considerations achieved dominance over the oil-centered *realpolitik* of State and Defense strategists.

Clifford made no bones about the fact that Truman, in running for election in 1948, would need Jewish votes, and that he could not get those votes unless he actively supported the creation of a Jewish state. Moreover, as Clifford pointed out, not only the Jews but many segments of the American people wanted to see a Jewish state established, and were confused and angry over American reversals in policy. As for the oil argument, the Arabs could really do very little, other than cut off production completely, a step not likely to be taken since the Arab governments had no other source of revenue. Public support of a humanitarian policy which would reap great political benefit—all this Truman could have, but only if he decided upon a firm policy and stopped vacillating.

Was Truman's Palestine policy, therefore, nothing more than political expediency? In its most simplistic form, the answer is yes, but to look at it only in that light is to miss the complex interaction of foreign affairs and domestic politics in a democratic society. For a foreign policy to be successful, it must have popular support; moreover, the demands of particular segments of society, providing they do not antagonize other groups, must be taken into account. The State Department experts, for all their supposed sophistication about international relations, proved themselves remarkably naive in this area.

On April 23, 1948, the eve of Passover, the holiday of freedom celebrating the Hebrew exodus from Egypt, Truman sent word that he had decided on a policy. As Chaim Weizmann prepared to leave his hotel suite to attend a Seder service, he received an urgent request to come to the Essex House, where Samuel Rosenman lay incapacited by an injured leg. Rosenman, whom many of the Zionists suspected of being unfriendly to their cause, told Weizmann that the president had spoken to him earlier that day, and had begun the conversation by saying that he had "Dr. Weizmann on my conscience." Truman wanted

Rosenman to reassure Weizmann that the United States would not desert the Zionists. A few days earlier, the President had directed that conduct of the Palestine policy be transferred from Loy Henderson to General Hilldring; the new trusteeship proposal would not be pushed in the General Assembly; and most importantly, if the Jewish state were declared, the United States would recognize it immediately. But Truman would deal only with Weizmann, not with the militant Silver, and the substance of the conversation could not be made public.[35]

Much anxiety within Zionist ranks could have been avoided had Weizmann been able to tell his colleagues what he now knew. A meeting of the WZO Actions Committee in Palestine that same day had wrestled with the decision whether or not the *Yishuv* should declare independence on May 15, and finally, agonizingly agreed that no other course was possible.[36] Moreover, American Zionist leaders would have greeted the final State Department campaign with less resentment had they known that the careerists had been outflanked. But they did not know this, and in the final weeks before the mandate expired, they had to resist an enormous amount of pressure from George Marshall on down to delay, if not give up on the idea of a Jewish state.

Military analysts in the government believed that the *Yishuv*, with little more than 650,000 people, could not withstand attacks from an Arab world numbering over fifty millions, and in the early months of 1948 the Haganah seemingly fared poorly at the hands of Arab irregulars. Weizmann, Silver, Neumann, and other Jewish leaders were implored to give up statehood, at least temporarily, in order to avoid the bloodbath that seemed sure to follow British withdrawal. When Jewish leaders resisted this argument, subtle and not so subtle threats crept into the conversations—governmental edicts prohibiting raising money in the United States for foreign arms purchases; the publication of documents detailing American support of Palestinian terrorism; pressures on American Jewry to support their government and not the Zionist leadership; and resort to the Security Council to have it proclaim Palestine a danger to world peace.

At the end of April, Dean Rusk, then an assistant secretary in charge of UN affairs, approached Moshe Shertok and Nahum Goldmann with a new plan, calling for delay of statehood while an emergency conference of Arab states, the Jewish Agency, and the UN committee on Palestine took place, at which an amicable solution could be found. The president's own plane, the *Sacred Cow*, would be available to take the delegates to the meeting. The Zionist leaders were incredulous: Why did Rusk, or anyone else for that matter, think that what had been impossible for thirty years of discussion would now be accomplished in ten days. At a midnight meeting of the American Executive of the Agency on May 3, Silver, Neumann, Rose Halprin, and Rabbi Wolf Gold voted against the proposed delay, while Shertok and Nahum Goldmann voted for it. The following morning, with members of the Political Committee brought in, the American Section was still split, but with a firm majority opposed to any deferment. Shertok wired Rusk that acceptance of the new American procedure, which ignored the United Nations decision, "would involve us in a moral responsibility in respect of those proposals which we cannot possibly accept."[37]

A few days later, Secretary of State Marshall personally invited Shertok to meet with him in Washington, and the Palestinian had little choice but to accept. On May 8, one week before the scheduled end of the Mandate, Shertok, Marshall, and Under-secretary Robert A. Lovett met for an hour and a half. Marshall led Shertok to a map of Palestine. "Here you are surrounded by Arabs," he said, pointing to the Negev, "and here, in the Galilee, you are surrounded by other Arabs. You have Arab states all around you, and your backs are to the sea. How do you expect to withstand this assault?"

"Believe me," Marshall continued, "I am talking about things which I know. You are sitting there in the coastal plains of Palestine while the Arabs hold the mountain ridges. I know you have some arms and your Haganah, but the Arabs have regular armies. They are well trained and they have heavy arms. How can you hope to hold out?"

When Marshall finished, Lovett suggested that if the Jewish Agency refrained from proclaiming a state, and the Arabs did attack, then the United States would have some ground for intervention; it would be helping individuals rather than taking sides in a war between nations. But if the Agency persisted and war followed, the Jews would not be able to look to the United States for aid; they would have to fend for themselves.[38]

Shertok, obviously shaken, tried to remain as noncommittal as possible, but promised to deliver the Secretary's message to his colleagues in Palestine, and was planning to leave for the Holy Land within a few days. But he did push for some clearer understanding of American intent. Did the government actually want a Jewish state, and was trying to remove the difficulties in its way, or did it prefer to abort statehood?

He appreciated Marshall's concern about the military problems, but the Secretary had to realize that the Jewish people now stood on the threshhold of fulfilling a two-thousand-year-old dream. For the Jewish Agency to consent to postponement, without the absolute assurance that statehood would inevitably follow the delay, meant that he and other Jewish leaders would be answerable to Jewish history for that decision, and this they could not do.

Before leaving for Palestine, Shertok returned to New York, where he reported to the American Section's Political Committee, and unburdened himself of his fears. Silver and Neumann, aware that an adverse report by Shertok could sway the *Yishuv's* leaders, called Rose Halprin aside and suggested that she go with Shertok. The Hadassah president knew full well how worried Shertok was about the risks involved, but refused, as she said, "to put myself in the *chutzpadik* position of accompanying Shertok." Instead, she wrote a letter to Ben-Gurion and asked Shertok, who was aware of its contents, to take it. In it she told Ben-Gurion of some of the pressures the American government had exerted to prevent statehood, but declared: "Don't worry about us. The American Jewish community is not to be worried about, and doesn't have to be worried about. You have to make up your mind. Your boys are going to die or not. You know whether you can fight the war, but for goodness sake don't let anybody talk about the pressure that we are under because we're not going to yield to that."[39]

When Shertok arrived in Palestine, Ben-Gurion had him brought to his office immediately, and they went over the situation fully. A few hours later, both men went into a meeting of the national council of the *Yishuv*, the elected body that would ultimately make the decision for or against proclaiming the state. Shertok described the fears in Washington, but nonetheless came out in favor of immediate statehood. Word came from Chaim Weizmann, also urging immediate action. Ben-Gurion, for the first time, revealed what the millions raised by Gold Meir in the United States had wrought—the Haganah had adequate arms, enough to offset the numerical advantage of the larger Arab armies. When Ben-Gurion called for a show of hands, the men and women around the table slowly and gravely agreed that the time had come for a Jewish state to be born.[40]

As the clock drew nearer to the end of the mandate, tensions rose not only in Palestine, but in London, Washington, New York, and in every Jewish community in the world. Only three weeks before, millions of

Jewish families had concluded the Seder service of Passover, the festival of freedom, with the traditional chant *"L'shanah habah b'yerushalayim"*—"Next year in Jerusalem!" Now that dream stood on the edge of realization.

In Washington, Harry Truman summoned his advisors once again to discuss what they should do. At a meeting a few days earlier, Marshall and Lovett had strongly opposed recognition. When Clark Clifford pointed out that the President had already gone on record favoring an independent Jewish state, Marshall's face flushed. "Mr. President," he said, "this is not a matter to be determined on the basis of politics. Unless politics were involved, Mr. Clifford would not even be at this conference. This is a serious matter of foreign policy determination, and the question of politics and political opinion does not enter into it."[41]

But if ever any foreign policy issue was intertwined with domestic politics, Palestine was that issue. Much as the State Department had tried to keep the matter on a "professional" plane, American Jews and their friends had managed to make it the most emotion-laden question of the day. Jacob Arvey, Herbert Lehman, and other leaders of the Democratic Party besieged Truman to recognize the new state immediately. The few pro-Arab voices, like John Badeau, president of the American University at Cairo, were drowned out in an avalanche of letters and telegrams calling for recognition, while the media almost unanimously demanded the same policy.[42] Finally, even Marshall realized that the tide could not be stopped; moreover, the Haganah, in a series of quick victories, had convinced the former chief of staff that the Jews might very well be able to handle the Arabs. So on May 14, he and Lovett informed the President that they no longer objected to recognition; but they did urge caution rather than any precipitate move.

But Clifford and David K. Niles pushed Truman for immediate action. If the new state were to be recognized, let it be done at once. Such a move would not only bolster the position of the new nation, but would also win political support at home. Since it also appeared that the Soviet Union would extend recognition, the United States could steal a march on its cold war opponent. Truman, determined that his pledge to Chaim Weizmann would not be undercut again by the State Department, agreed, and Clifford called up the Jewish Agency's Washington representative, Eliahu Epstein, and told him: "You'd better write a letter asking us for recognition."

At almost the same moment that Epstein sat down to draft his letter,

David Ben-Gurion rose and called to order a meeting in Tel Aviv's municipal museum. There, in front of a protrait of Theodor Herzl, he picked up a parchment scroll, and slowly began to read:

"Eretz-Israel was the birthplace of the Jewish people. Here their spiritual, religious and political identity was shaped. Here they first attained to statehood, created cultural values of national and universal significance and gave to the world the eternal Book of Books. . . ."

At midnight in Jerusalem, 6:00 P.M. in Washington, the British mandate of more than a quarter-century came to an end. The British flag now flew over no buildings in the Holy Land; in its place, in all areas under Jewish control, the blue-and-white star of David rose for the first time over sovereign soil. And eleven minutes later, President Harry Truman announced that the United States, the world's oldest democracy, had extended *de facto* recognition to the world's newest, the State of Israel.

At the United Nations a few minutes later, I. L. "Si" Kenen slipped into the Assembly chamber and handed a slip of yellow paper, torn from the teletype machine with the news of Truman's announcement, to Abba Hillel Silver. The Cleveland rabbi read it, incredulously at first, and then showed it to his colleagues, Rose Halprin, Emanuel Neumann, and Nahum Goldmann, who rose and broke into cheers. The news spread like wildfire, and soon Philip Jessup found himself surrounded by angry and confused delegates demanding to know if it were true. Truman had given the State Department the information in ample time for it to reach the United Nations delegation, but typically, the bureaucratic paperwork prevented its transmission until well after the wire services had picked up the President's announcement.

Jessup charged out of the hall to a telephone, and a few minutes later white-faced and shaken, returned and made his way to the rostrum, where he read Truman's two-sentence statement. In the corridor, Garcia Granados encountered an aide to the American delegation and asked about the news. "That is White House language," came the curt reply, "not State Department." Years later, in his memoirs, Truman allowed himself more than a touch of self-satisfaction when he wrote: "I was told that to some of the career men of the State Department the announcement came as a surprise. It should not have been if these men had faithfully supported my policy."[43]

In Tel-Aviv, a little after midnight, the phone rang in Golda Meyerson's apartment. Expecting the worst, she picked it up to hear a jubilant voice tell her of Truman's announcement. "It was like a miracle," she recalled, "coming at the time of our greatest vulnerability, on the eve of the invasion. I was filled with joy and relief. All Israel rejoiced and gave thanks." Over the furious pleas of Paula Ben-Gurion, Ya'acov Yanai, the Haganah communications chief, pushed his way into the old man's bedroom to ask him to make a radio broadcast to the United States. The sleepy leader pulled on a coat over his pajamas, and had barely begun his statement when the crash of falling bombs rocked the studio. Listen, Ben-Gurion told his audience, those are the sounds of bombs falling on Tel Aviv. Near the Catholic Terra Sancta College in Jerusalem, Farnsworth Fowle, a CBS correspondent, picked up the news on the BBC, and ran to tell Jewish policemen guiding military vehicles. For a few minutes they were all too busy dodging stray bullets, and all the Israelis could say was "Fine—that means we can get arms." When Walter Eytan of the Jewish Agency heard the news, he was skeptical, and in his diary wrote: "How one wished it were true, but surely the man was a babbler."[44]

In the United States people danced the hora in the street, waving small blue and white flags, and shouting *Mazel Tov* over and over again. At 2210 Massachusetts Avenue in Washington, where the Jewish Agency had its office, a group of congressmen, including Emanuel Celler, Jacob Javits, and Sol Bloom gathered with Eliahu Epstein. After a rabbi intoned a prayer, two small children raised the star of David, the old Zionist flag and now the proud emblem of a new nation. When the flag reached the top of the pole, the crowd of hundreds spontaneously burst into *Hatikvah*—"So long as still within the inmost heart a Jewish spirit sings, so long as the eye looks eastward, gazing toward Zion, our hope is not lost—that hope of two thousand years, to be a free people in our own land, the land of Zion and Jerusalem."

FOOTNOTES

1. Dean Acheson, *Present at the Creation: My Years in the State Department* (New York, 1969), p. 180.

2. Joseph B. Schechtman, *The United States and the Jewish State Movement: The Crucial Decade, 1939-1949* (New York, 1966), pp. 210-12; Minutes of the American Zionist Emergency Council, June 4, 1947, in Zionist Archives and Library, New York.

3. David Horowitz, *State in the Making* (New York, 1953), p. 307.

4. Howard M. Sachar, *Europe Leaves the Middle East, 1936-1954* (New York, 1972), pp. 490-91.

5. Schechtman, *U.S. and Jewish State Movement*, pp. 214-17; AZEC Minutes, August 29, 1947; editorial, *The New Palestine* 38 (September 12, 1947): 4.

6. Memorandum by Lionel Gelber, September 3, 1947, in Chaim Weizmann Papers, Yad Chaim Weizmann, Rehovot, Israel; *The New Palestine* 38 (September 26, 1947): 7.

7. Harry S. Truman, *Memoirs* (2 vols., Garden City, 1955-56), 2: 149.

8. Cordell Hull, *The Memoirs of Cordell Hull* (2 vols., New York, 1948), 2: 1517; Sumner Welles, *We Need Not Fail* (Boston, 1948), p. 74.

9. Truman, *Memoirs*, 2: 162; Loy Henderson to George C. Marshall, September 22, 1947, *FRUS, 1947*.

10. Arnold A. Rogow, *James Forrestal: A Study of Personality, Politics and Policy* (New York, 1963), pp. 191-92; James G. McDonald, *My Mission in Israel, 1948-1951* (New York, 1951), p. 13.

11. David K. Niles to Harry S. Truman, July 29, 1947, quoted in David B. Sachar, "David K. Niles and United States Policy toward Palestine," honors thesis (Harvard College, 1959), p. 60; Joseph P. Lash, *Eleanor: The Years Alone* (New York, 1972), pp. 122-23; Schechtman, *U.S. and Jewish State Movement*, p. 412.

12. AZEC Minutes, October 13, 1947; Robert Silverberg, *If I Forget Thee, O Jerusalem* (New York, 1972), pp. 359-60; Gregory William Sand, "Clifford and Truman: A Study in Foreign Policy and National Security, 1945-1949," doctoral dissertation (St. Louis University, 1973), pp. 222-23.

13. Interview with Emanuel Neumann, January 7, 1975; Stalin said basically the same thing to Roosevelt at the Yalta conference.

14. Horowitz, *State in the Making*, p. 274.

15. Emanuel Neumann, *In the Arena: An Autobiographical Memoir* (New York, 1976), pp. 248-49.

16. Chaim Weizmann to Doris May, October 18, 1947, and to Jan Smuts, October 28, 1947, Weizmann MSS; Hadassah National Board Minutes, October 23, 1947, in Hadassah Archives, New York; Lionel Gelber to Jewish Agency Executive, October 31, 1947, Weizmann MSS.

17. Weizmann to Henry Morgenthau, Jr., November 20, 1947, *ibid.*; Chaim Weizmann, *Trial and Error* (New York, 1949), pp. 457-59; Horowitz, *State in the Making*, pp. 269-70; Meyer Weisgal and Joel Carmichael, eds., *Chaim Weizmann: A Biography by Several Hands* (London, 1962), pp. 301-302.

18. Herbert Feis, *The Birth of Israel: The Tousled Diplomatic Bed* (New York, 1969), pp. 45-46; Truman, *Memoirs*, 2: 158.

19. Jacob Arvey to Morton Berman, December 13, 1947, Morton Berman Papers, privately held, Jerusalem, Israel; Welles, *We Need Not Fail*, p. 63; Feis, *Birth of Israel*, pp. 45-46; John Snetsinger, *Truman, the Jewish Vote and the Creation of Israel* (Stanford, 1974), p. 68.

20. L.S. Linton to Jan Smuts, November 27, 1947, Weizmann Mss; Larry Collins and Dominique LaPierre, *O Jerusalem!* (New York, 1972), pp. 29-30; Walter Millis, ed., *The Forrestal Diaries* (New York, 1951), p. 246.

21. *The New York Times*, November 30 and December 1, 1947.

22. Horowitz, *State in the Making*, p. 254.

23. Edwin M. Wright, introduction to Jewish Alternatives to Zionism, *"Pentagon Papers"— 1947: The Origins of Our Problems with "Arab Oil"* (New York, 1973), p. 5; Michael Arthur Dohse, "American Periodicals and the Palestine Triangle, April 1936 to February 1947," doctoral dissertation (Mississippi State University, 1966), p. 230; Snetsinger, *Truman and Creation of Israel, passim; Forrestal Diaries*, p. 361.

24. . Naomi W. Cohen, *American Jews and the Zionist Idea* (New York, 1975), pp. 84-85.

25. Melvin I. Urofsky. *For Jerusalem's Sake* (Garden City, 1978), chs. 1-2.

26. Abba Hillel Silver, *Vision and Victory* (New York, 1949), p. 158.

27. Schechtman, *U.S. and Jewish State Movement*, p. 17; Christopher Sykes, *Crossroads to Israel, 1917-1948* (Bloomington, Ind., 1973 ed.), pp. 344-45; Frank E. Manuel, *The Realities of American-Palestine Relations* (Washington, 1949), pp. 341-42.

28. *Public Opinion Quarterly* 10 (1946): 418, and 12 (1948): 161, 551.

29. Zeev Sharef, *Three Days*, tr. by Julian L. Meltzer (Garden City, 1962), p. 38; *Washington Post*, February 9, 1948; Benjamin Akzin to Israel Goldstein, January 19, 1948, Israel Goldstein Papers, Israel Goldstein Archives, Jerusalem, Israel.

30. Snetsinger, *Truman and Creation of Israel*, pp. 5-6; Truman, *Memoirs*, 2: 160; George Marshall to Felix Frankfurter, March 15, 1948, in Joseph P. Lash, ed., *From the Diaries of Felix Frankfurter* (New York, 1975), p. 350.

31. The Jacobson episode is based upon Jacobson to Josef Cohn, March 30, 1952, published as "Two Presidents and a Haberdasher—1948," *American Jewish Archives* 20 (April 1968): 4-15; Truman, *Memoirs*, 2: 160-61; Maurice Bisgyer, *Challenge and Encounter* (New York, 1967), pp. 190-91; and Frank J. Adler, *Roots in a Moving Stream* (Kansas City, 1972), p. 209.

32. Robert A. Divine, *Foreign Policy and U.S. Presidential Elections* (2 vols., New York, 1974), 2: 187-88; Joseph L. Blau, *Judaism in America: From Curiosity to Third Faith* (Chicago, 1976), p. 88.

33. Alonzo L. Hamby, *Beyond the New Deal: Harry S. Truman and American Liberalism* (New York, 1973), pp. 220-21; Snetsinger, *Truman and Creation of Israel*, pp. 98-99; Lash, *Eleanor: The Years Alone*, p. 130.

34. John Redding, *Inside the Democratic Party* (Indianapolis, 1958), p. 149; Ian J. Bickerton, "President Truman's Recognition of Israel," *American Jewish Historical Quarterly* 58 (December 1968): 173-240, details many of the pressures besetting the president; Snetsinger, *Truman and Creation of Israel*, p. 72; *Forrestal Diaries*, p. 362; Charles E. Bohlen, *Witness to History, 1929-1969* (New York, 1973), pp. 283-84; Patrick Anderson, *The Presidents' Men* (Garden City, 1968), pp. 118-19.

35. Weisgal and Carmichael, *Weizmann*, pp. 309-10; Sharef, *Three Days*, pp. 243-44.

36. Interview with Israel Goldstein, September 12, 1973.

37. Sharef, *Three Days*, p. 80; Neumann, *In the Arena*, pp. 258-59; Moshe Shertok to Dean Rusk, May 4, 1948, in Schechtman, *U.S. and Jewish State Movement*, pp. 294-95. Schechtman, who was a member of the Political Committee, voted against delay.

38. Collins and LaPierre, *O Jerusalem!*, pp. 335-36; Sharef, *Three Days*, pp. 87-88.

39. Interview with Rose Halprin, March 23, 1973; Emanuel Neumann sent a similar message to Ben-Gurion, interview with Neumann, January 7, 1975.

40. Bernard Postal and Henry W. Levy, *And the Hills Shouted for Joy: The Day Israel Was Born* (New York, 1973), p. 189; Collins and LaPierre, *O Jerusalem!*, pp. 378-79; speech by Meyer Weisgal, October 11, 1972, copy in Weizmann MSS; Sharef, *Three Days*, p. 244.

41. "He said it all," Clifford reported, "in a righteous God-damned Baptist tone." Marshall was an Episcopalian. Alexander deConde, "George Catlett Marshall," in Norman A. Graebner, ed., *An Uncertain Tradition: American Secretaries of State in the Twentieth Century* (New York, 1961), p. 257.

42. Jacob M. Arvey to Harry Truman, May 12, 1948, in Berman MSS; Herbert Lehman to Truman, May 13, 1948, in Herbert Henry Lehman Papers, School of International Studies Library, Columbia University, New York; John S. Badeau oral history memoirs, February 25, 1969, in John F. Kennedy Library, Waltham, Massachusetts. The Arabs were convinced that the Jews dominated American media; see William Woodrow Haddad, "Arab Editorial Opinion toward the Palestine Question, 1947-1958," doctoral dissertation (Ohio State University, 1970), p. 34.

43. Postal and Levy, *And the Hills Shouted for Joy*, pp. 274-75; Silverberg, *If I Forget Thee, O Jerusalem*, p. 425; Truman, *Memoirs*, 2: 164.

44. Interview with Golda Meir, June 10, 1975; Collins and LaPierre, *O Jerusalem!*, p. 422; Postal and Levy, *And the Hills Shouted for Joy*, p. 223.

Contributors

HOWARD L. ADELSON is professor of history at the City College of New York and at the Graduate Center of the City University, and is past president of the United Zionist Revisionists of America. He is the author of several books on medieval history, and his numerous articles on Zionism and contemporary Jewish affairs have appeared in a variety of journals.

SELIG ADLER is Samuel P. Capen Distinguished Service Professor of American History at the State University of New York at Buffalo. The author of numerous articles which have appeared in a variety of journals and anthologies, he has also written *The Isolationist Impulse, The Uncertain Giant: American Foreign Policy between the Wars,* and with T. E. Connolly, *From Ararat to Suburbia,* a history of Buffalo's Jewish community.

PHILLIP J. BARAM completed his doctorate at Boston University, and his study of the Department of State's Middle Eastern policy during and after the second world war is to be published shortly. In addition, he has contributed articles to several scholarly journals, and is currently adjunct professor at Boston State College.

NAOMI W. COHEN is professor of history at Hunter College and the Graduate Center of the City University of New York. She is the author of *A Dual Heritage: The Public Career of Oscar S. Straus, Not Free to Desist: A History of the American Jewish Committee, 1906-1966,* and *American Jews and the Zionist Idea.* She has contributed numerous articles and book reviews on American Jewish history to a variety of journals.

MENAHEM KAUFMAN emigrated to Israel with the Youth Aliyah in 1937. He was a member of the Haganah, a founder of Nahal, and an officer in the Israeli Army from 1949 to 1968. He is currently administrative director of the Institute for Contemporary Jewry at the Hebrew University, and working on a study of non-Zionist involvement in the creation of Israel.

JEROME M. KUTNICK is currently completing his dissertation on "Felix M. Warburg and the Jewish Community, 1929-1937" at Brandeis University; he has also done graduate work at the Hebrew University in Jerusalem.

CAROL BOSWORTH KUTSCHER received her doctorate from Brandeis University. She has published poetry, served as contributing editor of the Harvard *Mosaic,* translated Hebrew books and articles, and served as a photographic cataloguer at the Central Zionist Archives in Jerusalem.

DEBORAH E. LIPSTADT is assistant professor of history and comparative religion at the University of Washington in Seattle, and also serves as chair-

310

person of the Jewish Studies Program. Her book, *The Zionist Career of Louis Lipsky,* will be published in the near future.

ISAAC NEUSTADT-NOY recently completed his doctorate at Brandeis University. An Israeli, he is the author of several volumes of children's stories, and served as a news analyst and broadcaster for Kol Yisrael before entering college teaching. He is currently assistant professor of modern Jewish history at Brandeis University.

ESTHER L. PANITZ has written a number of articles and reviews on different aspects of American Jewish history, and has taught courses in this field. Recently, she completed a work dealing with the alienated image of the Jew in English literature. She teaches in a northern New Jersey high school, and holds degrees from Hunter College, the Jewish Theological Seminary and Columbia University.

MONTY N. PENKOWER is associate professor of history and chairman of the department at Touro College in New York. He has written extensively on American culture during the 1930s, and recently published *The Federal Writers' Project: A Study in Government Patronage of the Arts.* He is currently at work on a two-volume examination of Anglo-American relations *vis-à-vis* Palestine from 1939 to 1948.

SARAH SCHMIDT holds a doctorate from the University of Maryland, and has worked extensively in the field of Jewish education; she currently is a lecturer at the University of Maryland. Her articles have appeared in *Jewish Social Studies, American Jewish Historical Quarterly, Judaism, Midstream* and other journals.

DAVID H. SHPIRO has done graduate work at the Hebrew University in Jerusalem and is currently a research associate at the Ben-Gurion Archives.

MELVIN I. UROFSKY is professor of history and chairman of the department at Virginia Commonwealth University in Richmond. He is co-editor of the five-volume *Letters of Louis D. Brandeis* and the author of several books, including *A Mind of One Piece* and *American Zionism from Herzl to the Holocaust.* He recently was a senior fellow of the National Endowment for the Humanities, during which time he completed *For Jerusalem's Sake,* a study of Israel and the American Jewish community.

CARL HERMANN VOSS is professor of religion and philosophy at Edward Waters College. An ordained Protestant clergyman, he was a founder of the Christian Council on Palestine and served as its first executive secretary from 1943 to 1946; he then became chairman of the executive council of the American Christian Palestine Committee. He is the author of several books, including *Rabbi and Minister: The Friendship of Stephen S. Wise and John Haynes Holmes.* He has recently been ecumenical scholar-in-residence at the Ecumenical Institute for Advanced Theological Studies at Tantur, Jerusalem.